AL WONDERLAND

The Search For The Hidden Door

Nigel Graddon

Adventures Unlimited Press

ALICE'S WONDERLAND

The Search For
The Hidden Door

Adventures Unlimited Press

Alice's Wonderland: The Search for the Hidden Door

ISBN 978-1-948803-72-4

Published by:
Adventures Unlimited Press
One Adventure Place
Kempton, Illinois 60946 USA
auphq@frontiernet.net

AdventuresUnlimitedPress.com

ALICE'S WONDERLAND

The Search For
The Hidden Door

There is a thing confusedly formed,
Born before heaven and earth.
Silent and void.

It stands alone and does not change,
Goes round and does not weary.
It is capable of being the mother
of the world.
I know not its name
So I style it 'the way.'

—Tao te Ching, Lao Tzu

CONTENTS

Alice at play with Kitty before she climbs through the Looking-glass

Introduction

Be thou the tenth Muse, ten times more in worth
Than those old nine which rhymers invocate.

William Shakespeare
Sonnet XXXVIII

It is not the intention in these pages to make a chapter-by-chapter, character-by-character analysis of Lewis Carroll's Alice stories, nor to delve into the texts in any detail. These are enjoyable pursuits and best achieved by reading and re-reading the stories, each occasion savoured as if coming to the texts for the first time. In that way, every trip to the Dormouse's treacle well draws something new and delightful.

Rather, the task before us addresses a simple question. May we follow in Alice's footsteps, not merely in imagination but in some other way? May the philosophers of old have been right that we are not all that we seem: that we possess other selves—the astral body of the Alchemists, the subtle body of the Theosophists, the nature-self of the Hermeticists—which, under certain circumstances, can be tempted to emerge and make journeys into worlds ordinarily denied to the human experience? If this seemingly absurd notion has any atom of believability then how and where should we focus our search for the hidden doors to Alice's Wonderland and her Looking-glass House?

Have you ever walked in a forest, rich with autumnal scents and birdsong and wondered if the three-dimensional scene of delight around you is merely a loosely painted theatre backdrop behind which is another nature world, one which should you know its "open sesame" will, even compared with the marvellous beauty of its outer form, stir your senses to unimaginable flights of joy?

And having asked the first question, in this new land—Mother Earth's secret garden—might we pose another? Might this magical place be not the be-all and end-all of Nature's hidden secrets but, like C.S. Lewis's "Wood between the Worlds" in *The Magician's Nephew*, a stepping stone to other dimensions of enchantment, each with its own special beauty, abundant inviting pathways and uncountable rabbit holes to yet more amazing adventures?

So many gifted storytellers have written of these invisible realms, in ways so powerful and convincingly presented that it is hard to believe that Wonderland, Narnia, Oz, Middle Earth and the Secret Garden are purely figments of gifted imagination. I am not suggesting that Carroll, Lewis, Baum, Tolkein and Hodgson-Burnett actually visited higher dimensions of nature (but can one absolutely rule it out?). Nevertheless, it is not beyond belief that the Mother Goddess whispered of them in their dreams with such grace and gentle suggestability that they felt compelled to put pen to paper.

Thank the gods that they did. The reality of being human is incomplete in the absence of belief or maybe just a feeling that this beautiful planet is so much more than meets the eye, literally.

The Earth may appear to comprise just one dimension of reality—the physical—but how confident can one be that this is true? Myths, legends and tales, such as Lewis Carroll's immortal story of a little girl and her Wonderland adventures, offer a very different perspective.

For my part, I have always believed that Alice's world and others such as Narnia and Middle Earth are not insubstantial creations from gifted story tellers but literary extrusions from very real dimensions of enchantment, which form an integral part of the "greater" earth plane and which, according to circumstance, may reveal themselves to the curious traveller.

I might long ago have asked if such a belief was evidence of some kind of character flaw had I not learned that my opinions have been in sympathy with like-minded souls dating back to the Golden Age of the great Greek thinkers. The belief that Earth is one of a family of worlds that co-exist has occupied many great minds (and I certainly do not count mine among them!).

In the 5th century BCE, a time when it was believed that our planet is flat, Greek prophet Anaxagoras made the startling claim that 'other men and other living species' lived in a kind of anti-Earth. This parallel Earth, he said, was bathed in the light of a sun and moon, and its inhabitants were like ourselves who lived in cities and possessed the skills and intelligence to 'build clever objects.' Anaxagoras located his anti-Earth on the underside of our flat, discoidal world.

At the same time, several thousand miles away, a group of thinkers that were developing their sacred Sanskrit Hindu texts concerning Hindu mythology and folklore were describing the "dvipas", seven levels of existence beneath the celestial regions. According to Hindu belief, the Earth is arranged in these seven concentric rings of island continents.

The British author Benjamin Walker[1] offers a description of the dvipas. Jambudvipa is the innermost of the seven continents and is shaped like a disc. The earth rests upon the head of Shesha, the cosmic serpent, who is himself supported by the tortoise named Akupara, who is supported by the Ashtadiggajas, the eight celestial elephants that stand on the shell of Brahmanda. Plaksha is the second of the ring-shaped continents and is surrounded by a sea of sugarcane juice. Shalmala is the third of the ring-shaped continents. A sea of wine surrounds it. Kusha is the fourth and is encircled by a sea of clarified butter (ghee). Krauncha is the fifth and is circled by a sea of curds. Then comes Shaka or Shveta, whose shores are surrounded by a sea of milk. Finally, Pushkara is the seventh of the circular continents and is surrounded by a huge freshwater sea.

Bordering the outermost sea is a land named Lokāloka, which separates the known world from the world of darkness. This realm comprises a range of mountains ten thousand yojanas high. The shell of the cosmic egg, known as Brahmanda, lies beyond this darkness and cradles all of creation.

Some of the provinces into which the Jambudvipa is subdivided appear to correspond to the physical subcontinent of India, bordered by the Himadri Mountains (Himalayas) on the north and the Salt Water Sea (Indian Ocean) on the south. Beyond these confines, the rest seem to have metaphysical characteristics like those associated with the West such as the mythical lands of Lyonnesse, Tír na nÓg, the Isle of Avalon and St. Brendan's Isle.

The concept of the dvipas became known in the West during the late 19th century through the work of the Theosophical Society and was fuelled by the general interest in Eastern matters, which characterised that period of history. 'It is the opinion of many at the present day,' stated Theosophist Charles Johnson in the April 1889 issue of *The Path*, 'that the almost grotesque myths and fantastic geographical and astronomical descriptions contained in the religious writings... are really deliberately contrived and constructed allegories by which the ancient sages sought to veil... the sacred truths which could only be declared in the secret recesses of the temples.'

In the 1960s, French scientist-turned-occultist Jacques Bergier took an interest in the metaphysical Hindu realms, believing that there could

---

[1] Walker, B., *Hindu World: An Encyclopedic Survey of Hinduism*, George Allen and Unwin, London, 1968

3

be some truth to them, according to the principles of modern mathematics. Bergier noted that "Riemann surfaces" are composed of a given number of layers that are neither on top of nor beneath one another; the layers simply co-exist. Bergier was almost certainly simplifying matters for the layman reader but the mathematical conclusion was that space could be far more complex than it initially appeared to be. Seemingly justifying the beliefs of both Anaxagoras and the Hindu scribes, Bergier wrote:[2]

> If Earth is one of these [Riemann] surfaces, fantastic though it may seem, it is possible that there are unknown regions which are normally inaccessible and do not appear in a map or globe of the world, but which nonetheless exist indeed. We did not suspect their existence any more than we suspected the existence of germs, or the invisible radiation of the spectrum, prior to their discovery.

Are there indeed "spaces within our space", which developed separately from our own, perhaps accessible only through what we might term dimensional doorways, wrinkles in space and time? As unlikely as the possibility may appear, it would account for the widespread belief in worldwide folklore that there are places which humans can enter and never leave, or which can only be entered, Brigadoon-style, at certain times of the year or every so many years. Could the phantom cities often visible in the Arctic (such as Alaska's Muir Glacier) be mirages not of our own cities but of those cities whose inhabitants built clever objects, as Anaxagoras said long ago?

Charles Lutwidge Dodgson, writing under the pseudonym Lewis Carroll, introduced the world to Alice and her whimsical adventures in 1865 with the publication of *Alice's Adventures in Wonderland*. Dodgson, a mathematician and logician, brought his analytical skills to bear on his storytelling, creating narratives filled with paradoxes, puzzles and curious creatures. It is within this framework of logic and nonsense that we find the first hints of alternative dimensions.

The concept of other dimensions, or alternate realities beyond our familiar three spatial dimensions and one temporal dimension, has long fascinated both scientists and writers. Carroll's Alice stories, although seemingly fantastical, present us with intriguing clues that invite us to

---

[2] Bergier, J., *Visa Pour Une Autre Terre*, Albin Michel, 1974

4

consider the existence of parallel worlds, non-Euclidean spaces and the bending of conventional notions of reality. By delving into the dimensions hinted at within these stories, we gain fresh insights into the creative genius of Carroll and, more broadly, into the human fascination with the unknown and the limitless possibilities of existence.

From the moment Alice tumbles down the rabbit hole, readers are thrust into a world that defies conventional notions of space and time. Wonderland is a realm where a bottle labeled "Drink Me" can shrink a person to the size of a mouse, where a cake marked "Eat Me" can cause one to grow to towering proportions, and where doors lead to alternate landscapes with no clear spatial connection. Wonderland's inherent illogic invites us to consider it as a multidimensional space where the rules of our world are redundant.

Wonderland is replete with spatial and temporal anomalies that challenge our understanding of dimensions. Alice frequently encounters contradictory spatial experiences such as the shrinking and growing episodes, where her perception of size and space constantly shifts. Time itself behaves erratically, exemplified by the Mad Hatter's perpetual tea party, an event seemingly divorced from the linear progression of time. These anomalies beckon us to explore Wonderland as a place where alternate dimensions intertwine and intersect.

As Alice navigates Wonderland, her experiences provide valuable insights into the perception of dimensions within this fantastical realm. Her interactions with talking animals, anthropomorphic playing cards, and eccentric characters like the Cheshire Cat illustrate how individuals within Wonderland have adapted to its peculiar spatial and temporal dynamics. This analysis prompts us to consider how the inhabitants of Wonderland might possess a unique understanding of dimensions, different from Alice's initial disorientation.

The existence of other dimensions in Wonderland is not merely a literary quirk; it profoundly influences the narrative and thematic elements of Carroll's work. The fluidity of dimensions mirrors Alice's own journey of self-discovery and adaptability. As she learns to navigate the unpredictable landscapes of Wonderland, her character undergoes transformation, underscoring the idea that grappling with alternative dimensions can be a transformative experience.

In Carroll's second and final Alice work, *Through the Looking-Glass*, we encounter a world distinct from Wonderland—one that invites us to consider the existence of a mirror dimension. As Alice steps through the mirror, we are presented with a landscape governed by reflection, symmetry and the concept of opposites. Carroll masterfully constructs a realm where everything is reversed; where left is right and up is down. This inversion challenges our conventional understanding of reality and leads us to consider the existence of a dimension that mirrors our own but in a peculiar, symmetrical way.

Everything in the Looking-Glass world is a reflection of the real world. As Alice encounters characters like Tweedledum and Tweedledee, the Red Queen and Humpty Dumpty she grapples with the notion of opposites. This mirror world is not merely an inversion but a place where opposites co-exist harmoniously, offering a unique perspective on duality and balance.

The mirror dimension significantly impacts the characters and the unfolding narrative. As Alice navigates this world, she must adapt to its peculiar rules, such as the need to move in a specific direction to progress in the opposite direction. This challenges her intellect and determination, leading to character development and growth. Furthermore, the mirror dimension contributes to the episodic and dreamlike structure of the narrative. Each encounter and scenario reflects the cyclical nature of life, where characters reappear and events repeat with slight variations, reinforcing the notion of alternate dimensions as different facets of existence.

The existence of other dimensions within Lewis Carroll's Alice stories transcends mere whimsy and invites readers to embark on a philosophical odyssey. By engaging with questions about the nature of reality, identity and existence, Carroll challenges us to expand our intellectual horizons and contemplate the mysteries of existence itself. His imaginative tales serve as a testament to the power of literature to spark philosophical inquiry and encourage us to peer through the looking-glass into the realms of possibility, where the boundaries of reality are fluid, and the nature of existence is an enigma waiting to be unraveled.

As we delve deeper into Carroll's worlds, one is left with the tantalizing thought that, much like Alice, we too can journey into uncharted territories of thought and imagination, where the philosophical implications of other dimensions continue to beckon us.

Wonderland and the Looking-Glass worlds present us with multidimensional landscapes where the ordinary laws of physics and logic are suspended. Spatial and temporal anomalies challenge our understanding of dimensions, leading us to contemplate the presence of alternate realities within Carroll's stories. Characters within these worlds perceive and interact with dimensions uniquely, offering valuable insights into the nature of existence. The presence of other dimensions profoundly impacts character development and narrative progression, illustrating how the fluidity of dimensions mirrors Alice's own journey of transformation.

A second stratum of alternate reality that is ever present in Carroll's literary creations is the world of fairy folk. In many traditional fairy tales the protagonist embarks on a journey, encountering various trials and obstacles along the way. Similarly, Alice's adventures in Wonderland and the Looking-Glass world are structured as quests filled with encounters with bizarre characters and challenges to overcome.

Fairy tales also often feature anthropomorphic animals and fantastical creatures. Carroll populates his narratives with a wide array of such, from the White Rabbit to the Cheshire Cat, each with its own peculiar characteristics and abilities. These creatures, while whimsical, draw upon the tradition of animals as symbolic figures in folklore.

Additionally, the theme of transformation is prominent in both fairy tales and the Alice stories. In many fairy tales, characters undergo magical transformations, such as turning into animals, objects or other people. Alice herself experiences transformations, changing in size and identity as she navigates the dreamlike landscapes of Wonderland and the Looking-Glass world.

Lewis Carroll's Alice stories owe a considerable debt to the world of traditional fairy tales but rather than merely imitating the tradition, Carroll transforms it, infusing his works with a unique blend of whimsy, logic, and absurdity. His subversion of traditional fairy tale elements is not an act of rejection but one of creative reinterpretation. He takes familiar motifs, themes and characters from the world of fairy folk and transforms them into something entirely new and imaginative. Through the character of Alice, Carroll challenges traditional gender roles and presents a heroine who is inquisitive, assertive and unafraid to navigate the absurdities of Wonderland and the Looking-Glass world.

Carroll's Wonderland is a realm teeming with a wide array of fantastical creatures, many of which have connections to traditional fairy folk. As Alice navigates this whimsical world, she encounters beings that are both enchanting and peculiar, showcasing Carroll's adeptness at weaving elements from the world of folklore into his narrative.

The White Rabbit, whose role as the catalyst for Alice's adventures cannot be overstated, embodies the trope of the elusive guide often found in fairy tales. In folklore, white animals are often considered magical or otherworldly, leading travellers on journeys to fantastical realms. The White Rabbit's significance as Alice's initial guide into Wonderland aligns with this tradition, albeit with a Carrollian twist.

The Caterpillar, with its hookah-smoking habits and cryptic, often exasperating utterances, bears resemblance to the enigmatic and transformative figures often found in fairy tales. Characters who provide guidance through mysterious or transformative experiences are common in folklore; the Caterpillar serves a similar role in guiding Alice through her own transformations and self-discovery.

Meanwhile the Cheshire Cat embodies a more elusive and ambiguous figure. Its ability to appear and disappear at will, leaving only its smile behind, invokes the trickster archetype often present in folklore. Tricksters challenge established norms and provoke thought; the Cheshire Cat's whimsical antics challenge Alice's understanding of reality and illusion.

The Mad Hatter's Tea Party is a celebrated scene in Wonderland, where Alice encounters more eccentric characters. The Mad Hatter and the March Hare, with their nonsensical behavior and disregard for time, reflect a form of topsy-turvy whimsy common in fairy tales. Time, as a concept, often loses its coherence in fantastical settings and the tea party is a prime example of Carroll's playful subversion of temporal norms.

The Dormouse, though sleepy and seemingly inconsequential, also has roots in folklore. Dormice were once believed to have magical properties and were associated with enchantment and slumber. The Dormouse's somnolent presence in the tea party adds an element of enchantment to the scene, contributing to the dreamlike quality of Wonderland.

The Looking-Glass world is structured like a chessboard, with Alice as a pawn on a journey toward becoming a queen. Chess is a game of strategy, and in the world of fairy tales, games and challenges are common motifs that protagonists must navigate. The chessboard motif serves as a framework for Alice's adventures, leading her through a series of encounters and trials. In traditional fairy tales, games often have high stakes, and success requires wit and cunning. Carroll's use of the chessboard motif introduces an element of tension and strategy into the narrative, as Alice must make calculated moves to progress. This motif reflects the challenges and transformations that are central to many fairy tales.

Throughout her journey in the Looking-Glass world, Alice grapples with questions of identity and self-discovery. This theme of transformation is a recurring motif in traditional fairy tales, where characters often undergo physical and psychological changes as they navigate their adventures. In Alice's case, her transformation from pawn to queen mirrors the classic fairytale trope of the protagonist's journey to self-realization and empowerment.

The Red Queen's famous statement, 'Now, here, you see, it takes all the running you can do, to keep in the same place,' encapsulates the theme of transformation and the constant movement and change inherent in both fairy tales and the Looking-Glass world. Alice's encounters with the Tweedledum and Tweedledee twins further highlight the fluidity of identity and reality in this mirror world.

Prior to tracing Alice's footsteps in later chapters, we visit a wide range of Earth's most renowned companion worlds of myth and legend, including those brought to us in literature and film, the unique features of which may help to narrow our search for the doorway to Wonderland. We begin with fabled Shambhala.

Giant Alice with her arm reaching out of White Rabbit's house

...the wind is so very strong here. It's as strong as soup.

—White Knight to Alice in *Through the Looking-glass*

LOST WORLDS

Chapter 1

Shambhala

In Shambhala live the invisible rulers of all pious people, the King of the World or Brahatma, who can speak with God as I speak with you, and his two assistants: Mahatma, knowing the purpose of future events, and Mahinga, ruling the causes of those events... He knows all the forces of the world and reads all the souls of mankind and the great book of their destiny. Invisibly he rules eight hundred million men on the surface of the earth and they will accomplish his every order.

—A Mongol shepherd to explorer Ferdinand Ossendowski

Shambhala and its variations—Shamballa, Shambala and Shangri-La among them—is a legendary and mythical kingdom that has captured the imagination of people for centuries. The concept of Shambhala, a captivating and multifaceted legend that has transcended geographical and cultural boundaries, has its roots in various Eastern and Tibetan Buddhist traditions, as well as in the beliefs of some Western esoteric and New Age movements.

Some interpretations of Shambhala distinguish between "Inner Shambhala" and "Outer Shambhala". Inner Shambhala refers to the inner journey of spiritual realization and represents the processes of inner transformation and awakening. In this view, the kingdom exists within the consciousness of each individual, and the pursuit of Shambhala is a metaphor for the quest to attain higher states of awareness and inner peace. It involves deep introspection, meditation, the development of wisdom, compassion and awareness, the cultivation of virtues, the dissolution of ego and the realization of one's true nature. It is about transcending the limitations of the ordinary self

Outer Shambhala, on the other hand, may refer to the actual physical realm, or the manifestation of enlightened society on Inner Shambhala. It represents the idea of a society characterized by peace, harmony and the principles of wisdom and compassion. Some prophecies suggest that during times of great crisis or upheaval, emissaries or warriors from Outer Shambhala may emerge to guide and protect humanity, helping to restore balance and harmony.

Shambhala has variously been called the Forbidden Land, the Land of White Waters, the Land of Radiant Spirits, the Land of Living Fire, the Land of the Living Gods, and the Land of Wonders. Hindus have known it as the land from which the Vedas come, Aryavartha (literally, "The Land or Realm of The Aryans" or the "Land of the Noble/Worthy Ones"); the Chinese as Hsi Tien, the Western Paradise of Hsi Wang Mu, the Royal Mother of the West; the Russian Old Believers, a nineteenth-century Christian sect, knew it as Belovodye; and the Kirghiz people as Janaidar. But throughout Asia it is best known by its Sanskrit name, Shambhala, meaning "the place of peace, of tranquillity, or as Chang Shambhala (Northern Shambhala)", the name Hindus use to distinguish it from an Indian town of the same name.

Each had a tradition that Shambhala was in some way or another the source of its own religion. The pre-Buddist folk religion of Tibet, Bön, claimed that a kingdom called Shambhala had once covered most of Central Asia, from Lake Baikal to the Lob Nor and from Khotan almost to Beijing, and was the homeland of its cult.

Bön is commonly considered to be the indigenous religious tradition of Tibet, a system of shamanistic and animistic practices performed by priests called shen or bönpo. Bön was introduced to Tibet by immigrants from northeast Persia. These Aryan settlers brought with them the Aramaic alphabet, named after Aramaiti, the Iranian Earth Goddess. The actual founder of Bön is known as Shenabe who was said to have originated in Elam in southern Iran where he was known as Mithra.

Thereafter, historical evidence indicates that the Bön tradition only developed as a self-conscious religious system under the influence of Buddhism. In early records, bön denotes a particular type of priest who performed rituals to propitiate local spirits and ensure the wellbeing of the dead in the afterlife.

The rituals of the bön often involved sacrificing animals, making offerings of food and drink, and burying the dead with precious jewels, the benefits of which were apparently transferred to them in the afterlife through shamanistic rituals.

In the first century CE the Bönpo are said to have mapped Shambhala in its correct geographical relation to Persia, Bactria, Egypt, Judaea and other kingdoms of the-then known world. In the eighth

14

century the Bönpo passed on the map and all pertinent information to the incoming Buddhists, although by then the kingdom had long passed into the realm of myth.

Research suggests that every branch of esoteric tradition can be traced to a common parentage in Central Asia: various western secret societies, Freemasonry, Sufism, Buddhist mystical beliefs, Theosophy, alchemy and witchcraft; all these and more originating in Shambhala. Lao-Tzu called it Tebu Land and returned to it at the end of his life.

The origins of the Shambhala legend can be traced back to ancient Indian and Tibetan Buddhist texts. One of the earliest mentions of Shambhala can be found in the Kalachakra Tantra, a key text in Tibetan Buddhism. The Kalachakra Tantra describes Shambhala as a hidden land of great beauty, wisdom and spirituality, ruled by a line of enlightened kings. It prophesises that in the year 2424 or 2425 when the world descends into war and greed, the 25th Kalki King Maitraya, the tenth and final avatar of Lord Vishnu, will emerge from Shambhala with a huge army to defeat the Dark Forces that will have brought chaos to the world. Thereafter, Buddhism will survive for a further 1800 years.

Helena Petrovna Blavatsky, often known as Madame Blavatsky, founder of the Theosophical belief system, called Shambhala the invisible headquarters of the Mahatmas, a brotherhood of great spiritual masters that moved to Shambhala after the cataclysmic destruction of the land of Mu, a precursor to the geological formation of the later Atlantian continent, in the Pacific tens of thousands of years ago.

Blavatsky's Theosophist colleague, President of the Order Colonel Henry Steel Olcott, expressed the notion somewhat differently. He and his circle believed that spiritualist phenomena were not provoked by spirit entities but by living representatives of a secret occult Order of highly evolved men, described in England as the Hermetic Brotherhood of Egypt and in America as the Brotherhood of Luxor, who held mastery over the forces of nature.

In his *Old Diary Leaves* (covering the period 1883-1887), Olcott described encounters with one of these "masters" who was posing as a young Cypriot named Ooton Liatto. Olcott claimed bizarrely that Liatto once visited him in his apartment and in an extraordinary display of otherworldly powers made his bedroom disappear into a cube of empty space in which appeared fantastical landscapes and Elementary forms!

In 1893 Anglican Christian and occultist Charles G. Harrison delivered a course of lectures in London during which he stated that in around 1840 occult groups decided that modern Europe had reached a 'point of physical intellectuality' in its evolutionary cycle, which was predominantly characterized by gross materialism. Harrison claimed that the adepts of the otherworldly Hermetic Order had debated at length on what should be done to halt the decline; some saying that mankind should be told that there is around us a higher invisible world, which is every bit as real as our own, while others were aghast at the prospect of taking any action that profaned the ancient mysteries. Subsequently, experiments were conducted through mediums who, contrary to the expectations of the occult orders, proclaimed that they were being controlled by the spirits of the dead rather than serving as vehicles for insights from cosmic representatives. Consequently, instead of introducing a way through which humankind could become aware of the existence of higher powers that resided in our planet's parallel worlds and so reduce its relentless drive towards materialism, the adepts succeeded only in inculcating a false belief among the masses that humans have the ability to confer with the dead.

Despite the peculiar eccentricities of the Theosophists regarding the topic, Shambhala has generally represented a universal symbology of esoteric doctrine that is the same all over the world. Orientalist W.Y. Evans-Wentz said, 'there has been a secret international symbol-code in common use among the initiates, which affords a key to the meaning of such occult doctrines as are still jealously guarded by religious fraternities in India as in Tibet, and China, Mongolia and Japan.'

In the west the Shambhala concept remains as a garbled version contained in stories of the Holy Grail and the fabled kingdom of Prester John. However, rumours about an earthly paradise in the heart of Asia had been reaching the West long before the birth of the Grail romances in the Middle Ages. In Greco-Roman times the Greek Philostratus recorded the journey he took with the great magus of the Mysteries, Apollonius of Tyana, into the Trans-Himalayan wilds of Tibet, which he knew as the Forbidden Land of the Gods.

In contemporary times, the concept of Shambhala continues to resonate with individuals seeking meaning, purpose and spiritual fulfillment. It serves as a reminder of the human longing for a better world, one marked by compassion, unity and enlightenment.

The precise location of Shambhala remains a subject of debate and mystery. The concept of Shambhala suggests that it exists on multiple dimensions simultaneously. This means that it can be both a physical place in some interpretations and a higher spiritual plane in others.

According to legend, Shambhala is to be found in High Asia, commonly described as the navel of the world, a vast area filled with secret valleys fed by hot springs among glaciers and snowfields. Along the northern border of Tibet are the Kunlun Mountains; beyond these the Altyn Tagh Ridge curves north on its eastern edge to the Nan Shan Mountains and the Gobi Desert. Further north is the Altai Range in northern Siberia; to the west of Altai are the Tien Shan Mountains in Turkestan, while southward are the peaks of the Pamirs that overlook Afghanistan.

The regions' hidden valleys possess a unique spiritual character that belongs to the mysterious tradition of *termas* or "concealed treasures". These usually take the form of sacred texts or magical objects which may lie undisturbed for centuries until one day they reveal themselves to a *terton*, a special person who is predestined to find the treasure. He or she alone will be divinely guided to the right place at the right time. Many of these termas were hidden long ago by Padma Sambhava and his consort Yeshe Tsogyel, founders of the Nyingmapa sect, in 'diamond rocks, in mysterious lakes and unchanging boxes' in sacred valleys. These special places were then magically closed under the protection of spirit energies known as *tersung* to await the arrival of the chosen terton.

The allure of Shambhala has not been confined to religious or philosophical circles. It has made appearances in literature, art, and popular culture. Notable works such as James Hilton's "Lost Horizon" and various adventure novels have featured Shambhala as a hidden and idyllic sanctuary.

Over the years, explorers and adventurers have embarked on expeditions in search of the elusive Shambhala. These quests have often been fuelled by a blend of fascination with the legend and a desire for adventure. However, no concrete evidence of the kingdom's existence has ever been found, adding to its enigmatic nature.

In the heart of these beautiful valleys lies the world mountain, Meru; in other variants Sumyr, Sumbyr or Subur. Northern Kuru, one of the four regions that surround Mount Meru like the petals of a lotus, is the home of the Siddhas, Indian yogis famed for their miraculous tantric powers. The Indian Maahabharata epic describes the Siddhas as 'free from illness and are always cheerful. Ten thousand and ten hundred years they live, O, king, and never abandon one another.'

Legend has it that Nu and Ku, the Chinese equivalents of Adam and Eve, were born in the nearby land of Hsi Wang Mu, the Queen Mother

17

of the West. The nine-sided place of Hsi Wang Mu sits on a jade mountain identified with Mount Meru, its garden the home of the peach tree of immortality that blossoms once every 6000 years. The people of Hsi Wang Mu subsist on phoenix eggs and sweet dew, the elixir of youth.

The third Panchen Lama of Tibet believed that his country's Mount Kailas, the highest peak in the Trans-Himalayan chain, was Mount Meru. Kailas is a perfectly symmetrical pyramidal mountain composed of cemented gravel and snow and whose four faces match the cardinal compass points. The Bönpo faithful revere Kailas as the nine-storeyed sun-swastika mountain, regarding it as the Roof of the World, the quintessential seat of cosmic powers and the axis that connects the earth with the universe. It has been described as the super-antenna for the inflow and outflow of our planet's spiritual energies. It is the legendary source of the four great rivers that the Hindus believe purify the world: the Indus, Sutlej, Ganges and Brahmaputra.

In Tibetan lore, these rivers originate from four springs that issue forth from four rocks having the shapes of symbolic animals. The river Nara arises from a spring in a lion-shaped rock and flows to the east. The river Pakshu arises from a spring in a horse shaped rock and flows to the north. The river Kyim-shang arises from a spring in a peacock-shaped rock and flows to the west; while the river Sindhu emanates from a spring in an elephant-shaped rock and flows to the south.

The nine storeys of the sacred mountain signify the Nine Ways of Bön into which the teachings leading to liberation and enlightenment are classified. In the Bönpo cosmological system, the number nine is especially important and significant. In terms of the mandala, it represents the centre and the eight directions, cardinal and intermediate. From the surface of the earth upward there are nine stages or levels of heaven inhabited by the celestial gods and downward there are nine successive nether realms inhabited by the Nagas and other chthonic beings.

Regardless of its precise geographical position (if indeed it actually exists in the physical world), Meru and its environs according to mystical thinkers are populated with communities of adepts comprising shamans, Buddhists, Taoists, Hindus, Magi, Bönpo, Manicheans, Zoroastrians, Gnostics, Nestorian Christians, Sufis and other initiate orders. Together they are algamated into a permanent body of spiritual teachers and advisors submitting solely to the authority of a supreme Divine Government.

Descriptions of Shambhala are based both on literature said to emanate from Shambhala itself, and by later commentators, mainly Tibetans, who claimed to have visited the kingdom in the material realm, on an etheric plane, in dreams, or by some other arcane means.

According to Tibetan belief, Shambhala's appearance varies according to one's own karma. For example, one and the same river will be seen by gods as nectar, by man as water, by hungry ghosts as pus and blood, and by some animals simply as a place to live in.

Some accounts describe the kingdom of Shambhala as shaped like a gigantic eight-petaled lotus. Around the outside perimeter of the lotus is a circular range of lofty, snow-covered mountains. Between the eight petals of the lotus are eight lower mountain ranges along which flow the rivers of Shambhala. The centre of Shambhala, the seed vessel of the lotus, is surrounded by a pericarp constituting a lower range of snow-mountains.

Within this inner ring of mountains, slightly elevated above the petals of the lotus, sits Kapala, the capital of Shambhala, measuring twelve leagues in breadth. Kapala is occupied with magnificent palaces constructed with precious metals and gems: gold, silver, emeralds, pearls, turquoise, coral, and so forth. Mirrors on the outsides of the palaces blaze with light, while crystal skylights in their ceilings allow the inhabitants to view the entire zodiac and the gods of the sun, moon and other celestial spheres.

Tibetan sources give a sumptuous description of the King of Shambhala's palace. It is square and has four doors. Along a coral ledge around its outer walls are dancing goddesses. It is nine stories high and crowned with a banner and a wheel of Dharma with a male and female deer on either side. There are three rings encircling the palace, making it especially beautiful. It also has a molding of liquid Jambu gold, as well as full and half-hanging ornaments of pearls and diamonds.

At the top of the outer walls are hanging pendants of silver and protruding lintels of turquoise. Its windows are of lapis lazuli. The doors and lintels above are of emeralds and sapphires. It has golden awnings and banners, and a roof of jewels and heat-producing crystal, while its floor is of cold-producing crystal. Its pillars and beams are of zebra-stones, corals and pearl. It also has many other priceless treasures, such as the inexhaustible treasure vase, the wish-fulfilling cow, the unsown harvest and the wish-granting tree.

The ruling king of Shambhala sits on a throne made of gold from the Jamba River. He wears the robe of a Chakravartiraja (a universal king of Dharma), a headdress made of lion's hair adorned with images of the five Buddha Transcendent Buddhas, and long earrings and bracelets made also of gold from the Jambu River. Both his body and his ornaments emanate blindingly brilliant red and white light.

Surrounding the king are his ministers, generals, bodyguards, elephants and their trainers, and warriors. His main queen is the daughter of one of the ninety-six satraps of Shambhala. He has many other queens besides and many sons and daughters. When the next king (not necessarily the oldest son) is expected, the unborn child emits jewel-like light for a week before its birth. After its birth, white lotus flowers fall from the sky.

On the peaks just north of these palaces are depicted ten thousand images of each of ten bodhisattvas: Bhadrapala, Merusikharadhara, Kshitigarbha, Manjusri, Avalokitahalahala, Ayra Tara, Guhyakadhipati Vajrapani, Devi Kesini, Paramarthasamudgata and Maitreya.

South of the main palace is a grove of sandalwood trees. At its centre is a huge three-dimensional Kalachakra mandala of gold, silver, turquoise, coral, and pearl, constructed by the first King of Shambhala. Nearby are other mandalas built by later kings. To the east of the Sandalwood Grove is a body of water known as Near Lake and to the west is White Lotus Lake. In both of these lakes gods, nagas and humans comport themselves on boats made of jewels.

Each of the eight petals in the outer part of Shambhala contains 120 million villages. These 960 million villages are divided into kingdoms numbering ten million villages each, with each kingdom ruled by a strap or local governor, making a total of ninety-six satraps.

The people who live in all these countless cities and counties have great wealth, happiness, and no sickness. As all the satraps are religious personalities there is no sign of non-virtue or evil in these lands. Even the words "war" and "enmity" are unknown.

Victoria LePage's work[3] on Shambhala is an excellent account of the history, mythology and various interpretations of the legendary realm. A significant portion of the book explores the Kalachakra Tantra. LePage describes the subthemes of the archetypal World Mountain as poetic images of a geophysical feature of the Earth that can only be viewed clairvoyantly and which is unique to Shambhala. It visualises

---

[3] LePage, V., *Shambhala: The Fascinating Truth Behind the Myth of Shangri-La*, Quest Books, Illinois, 1996.

our planet as a living force whose body has an energetic structure that modern culture has not yet recognised or understood but which was known to early races. The author suggests that as a race we may be on the brink of a breakthrough into wider dimensions of thought that will transcend old mental barriers. LePage speaks of our pressing need for a new centering principle, a magnetic centre and a zone of order within the primal chaos of possibilities.

She describes how popular folklore speaks of Utopian Shambhala as a place composed of subtle matter, an island in a sea of nectar, a heaven-piercing mountain where the ground is strewn with gold and silver and where precious jewels bedeck the trees.

It is a place guarded by great devas from another world. Here one sees magic fountains, lakes of gems and crystal and the nectar of immortality, wish-fulfilling fruits and flying horses, and stones that speak. As we read these words we can be forgiven for thinking that the author is actually describing Aslan's magical realm of Narnia.

We learn also from LePage that Shambhala, in common with claims made for many other places throughout the world, reveals itself as the location of the World Tree or Cosmic Tree. Several ancient peoples— notably the Scandinavians, Hindus and the Altai shamans—regarded the Macrocosm, or Grand Universe, as a divine tree growing from a single seed sown in space.

The Greeks, Persians, Chaldeans, and Japanese have legends describing the axletree or reed upon which the earth revolves. Kapila, the sage who founded the Samkhya school of Hindu philosophy in the 6th or 7th century BCE, declared the universe to be the eternal tree, Brahma, which springs from an imperceptible and intangible seed—the material monad.

The mediaeval Qabbalists represented creation as a tree with its roots in the reality of spirit and its branches in the illusion of tangible existence. The Sephirothic tree of the Qabbalah was therefore inverted, with its roots in heaven and its branches upon the earth.

Madame Blavatsky noted that the Great Pyramid was considered to be a symbol of this inverted tree, with its root at the apex of the pyramid and its branches diverging in four streams towards the base.

The Scandinavian world-tree, Yggdrasil, supports on its branches nine spheres or worlds, including the underworld (Niflheim), the earth (Midgard), and the realm of the gods (Asgard).

The Celtic world-system is symbolised as three worlds viewed as concentric circles or ascending planes upon the column of the world tree. The idea of a world tree or cosmic axis tells of a vertical axis that runs through this physical plane, linking us to other interlacing planes of existence, their vibratory rates increasing as one ascends the axis or decreasing as one descends to the lower interconnecting planes.

Cylch y Abred, the Celtic middle earth on which we walk and the realm of the ego, stands above the underworld, Annwn, the realm of the unconscious and the incorporeal abode of unformed matter, wraiths and demonic spirits. Above is Cylch y Gwynvyd, the heavenly upperworld abode of enlightened divine beings and those few humans who have transcended the cycles of their earthly lives; the highest is Cylch y Ceugant, the ineffable place of Hen Ddihenydd, the "Ancient and Unoriginated One", the unattainable sole abode of God of the monotheistic system.

The serpent so often shown in myth as winding around the trunk of the tree usually signifies the mind—the power of thought—and is the eternal tempter or urge, which leads all rational creatures to the ultimate discovery of reality and thus overthrows the rule of the gods. The serpent hidden in the foliage of the universal tree represents the cosmic mind; and in the human tree, the individualized intellect.

Manly P. Hall[4] explained the concept of the Qabbalistic tree of the Jews.

> It also consists of nine branches, or worlds, emanating from the First Cause or Crown, which surrounds its emanations as the shell surrounds the egg. The single source of life and the endless diversity of its expression have a perfect analogy in the structure of the tree. The trunk represents the single origin of all diversity; the roots, deeply imbedded in the dark earth, are symbolic of divine nutriment; and its multiplicity of branches spreading from the central trunk represent the infinity of universal effects dependent upon a single cause.

> The tree has also been accepted as symbolic of the Microcosm, that is, man. According to the esoteric doctrine, man first exists potentially within the body of the world-tree and later blossoms forth into objective manifestation upon its branches.

---

[4] Hall, M., *The Secret Teachings of All Ages*, Philosophic Research Society, 1928

Alice climbing through the mirror into Looking-glass house

Two main forms of the world tree are known and both employ the notion of it constituting a centre of great fecundity and divine power. In the one, the tree is the vertical centre binding together heaven and earth; in the other, the tree is the source of life at the horizontal centre of the earth. Adopting biblical terminology, the former may be called the tree of knowledge, the latter the tree of life.

In the vertical, tree-of-knowledge tradition the tree extends between earth and heaven. It is the vital connection between the world of the gods and the human world. Oracles and judgements or other prophetic activities are performed at its base. In the horizontal, tree-of-life tradition, the tree is planted at the centre of the world and is protected by supernatural guardians. It is the source of terrestrial fertility and life. Human life is descended from it; its fruit confers everlasting life; and if it were cut down, all fecundity would dissipate.

Regarding the concept of the "World Axis", LePage, drawing upon the striking ideas of renowned French philosopher René Guénon (1886-1951), poses a thought-provoking question:

> … besides the two axes of the earth of which we are aware, the spin axis and the magnetic axis, there may be a third that we have not yet discovered which traditional societies knew as the World Axis… Guénon therefore does seem to be inviting us to envisage a tri-axial planetary system in which the major axis... is a psychospiritual energy current distinguishable from either the spin axis or the magnetic axis; that contributes dynamic balance to the whole; that is free of the earth's pull; and that consequently extends like a giant antenna beyond its gravitational and magnetic fields to resonate with enormously high frequencies from star systems in the depths of space… Are there superior godlike beings invisibly overseeing and influencing our life on earth? ... For since the late nineteenth century esoteric writers have joined with students of mythology in suggesting that the gods of antiquity were really spiritual adepts of unusually high stature. The most important contribution of these writers has been to introduce into the modern world the concept of initiation and transformation, of personal transcendence, and the corollary of a graduated ascent to adepthood, leading on to the further idea of an initiate Hierarchy that guides human evolution… Of all esoteric traditions, Sufism is the most informative about the initiatic lore that constellates around the legend of Shambhala… Sufis

believe that nothing in history is by chance; new truths are seeded; new energies implanted in society according to operations set in train at the highest spiritual levels... Those who live in Shambhala's transcendental inner zone are its engine, its powerhouse, their consciousness turns the wheel. They are the supreme authority for this planet, forming the governing core of Shambhala and, through the ashrams and monasteries of the outer region, of the world...

Time and the corrupting hand of legend have blurred and confused the accounts of these superhuman adepts that the Mystery traditions have passed down to us, but the knowledge is never lost. It can be recovered and reinterpreted in contemporary terms again and again. It tells us that the initiate Hierarchy to which these beings belong is the central axis or merudanda of the whole human race, collectively performing the hidden evolutionary function of the chakric system in individuals. It is also in its formation and function an exact reflection of the World Axis; and both axes, the racial and the planetary, coincide in Shambhala. Thus Shambhala, the World Axis and the Hierarchy, are in principle synonymous. This is why we find at the heart of all our mythologies the same archetypal complex of ideas, involving an assembly of wise beings who meet in judgement on the fields of Heaven, and always at the foot of a World Mountain, a World Tree or a World Pillar of Truth.

LePage also examines the fascination that the West developed with Shambhala, particularly in the early twentieth-century when explorers and mystics sought to discover the hidden kingdom. Among the most notable of these travellers was Nicholas Roerich. A Russian artist, writer and philosopher, Roerich, and his wife Helena, were prominent figures in the early twentieth-century search for Shambhala. They embarked on expeditions to Central Asia, including Tibet and the Himalayas, in the 1920s and 1930s, searching for the hidden kingdom and collecting art and artifacts. Nicholas Roerich is often credited with popularizing the idea of Shambhala in the West.

During the period 1923-26 Roerich made an expedition across the Gobi Desert to the Altai Range where Russia, China, Mongolia and Kazakhstan converge. His expedition appears to have related to his quest to return a certain sacred stone to its rightful home in the King's

Tower in the centre of Shambhala, a stone that was formerly part of a large meteorite called the Chintamani Stone. The stone was credited with magical properties and the power to transmit telepathic guidance and heighten human consciousness. The Black Stone of the Ka'aba in Mecca and that of the ancient shrine of Cybele are believed in occultist quarters to derive from the same large meteorite, whose home was Sirius in the constellation of Orion.

During the expedition Roerich's party witnessed in the Shara-gol valley firstly a large black bird flying overhead and then a huge, golden spheroid body whirling in the sun. During these sightings they were aware of the presence of a beautiful perfume. A lama in their party said it was the sign of Shambhalah signifying that the mission was blessed by the Great Ones of Altai, the lords of Shambhala and their king, Rigden Jye-po. The lamas said the black vulture was their enemy, eager to destroy their quest, while the UFO-style spheroid body was a protecting force in a radiant form of matter. The lama said the party must proceed in the same direction as the craft.

Other explorers of note connected with Shambhala include: Czech explorer and orientalist Alois Musil, who conducted expeditions in the Middle East and Central Asia in the same time period as Roerich; Heinrich Harrer, an Austrian mountaineer who is best known for his escape from a British internment camp in India during World War II and his subsequent adventures (described in his famous work "Seven Years in Tibet"); and Tibetan Buddhist meditation master and teacher Chögyam Trungpa Rinpoche who founded the Shambhala Training movement in the West. While not a seeker in the traditional sense, Rinpoche incorporated Shambhala teachings into his spiritual work and established Shambhala centres and meditation practices worldwide.

Neo-Theosophist Alice Bailey described Shambhala as 'the vital centre of the planetary consciousness' and the home of the great spiritual hierarchy of which the Christ was the head. Other esoteric thinkers likened the mystical centre to Campanella's City of the Sun and Dante's Terrestrial Paradise, remarking on its significant likeness to the Rosicrucians' Invisible Academy of initiates that was so widely publicised in seventeenth-century Europe.

In *Le Roi du Monde* (1927), René Guénon claimed that the magical region of Shambhala is the prototype Holy Land of which all other Holy Lands, such as Jerusalem, Delphi and Benares are or have been secondary reflections. He described Shambhala as a centre of high evolutionary energies in Central Asia and was the source of all religions. It was also the home of Yoga Tantra, having in this context a vital relationship to the kundalini science and philosophy. Guénon wrote,

> In the contemporary period of our terrestrial cycle, that is to say during the Kali Yuga, this Holy Land [Shambhala], which is defended by guardians who keep it hidden from profane view while ensuring nevertheless a certain external communication, is to all intents and purposes inaccessible and invisible to all except those possessing the necessary qualifications for entry.

Le Page shares Guénon's thinking, which locates Shambhala in either a polar region or a "Sacred Isle" in the north. Guénon was convinced that conclusive evidence emerges from the corresponding testimony of all traditions: that an archetypal "Holy Land" does exist; that it is the prototype for all other "Holy Lands", the spiritual centre to which all others are subordinate. The "Holy Land" is also the "Land of the Saints", the "Land of the Blessed", "Land of the Living" and "Land of Immortality". He believed that in this contemporary period of our terrestrial cycle, this Holy Land, which is defended by guardians who keep it hidden from profane view while ensuring nevertheless a certain exterior communication, is to all intents and purposes inaccessible and invisible to all except those possessing the necessary qualifications for entry. In *Le Roi du Monde* Guénon writes:

> ....the archetypal "sacred Isle", [that is] situated in a polar location. All the other "sacred isles", although everywhere bearing names of equivalent meaning, are still only images of the original... In India, the "white isle" (Shwetadwipa), commonly considered to be set in the remote regions of the North, is regarded as the "Abode of the Blessed", a name easily identifiable as the "Land of the Living"... The designation of spiritual centres as "white isles" was applicable, like the others, to secondary centres and not only to the supreme centre, their source. To these must be added the names of places, countries, and towns that express the idea of whiteness. These are frequent enough, from Albion to Albania, through Alba Longa, the mother city of Rome, and the Greek town of Argos... An additional comment is called for on the representation of a spiritual centre as an island containing a "sacred mountain", for while such a locality may have had a tangible existence (even

27

though not all holy lands were islands) there should also be a symbolic meaning. Historical facts, especially those pertaining to sacred history, translate in their own way truths of a higher order owing to the law of correspondence which is the foundation of symbolism, and which unites all the worlds in total and universal harmony. The idea evoking the representation under discussion is essentially one of "stability" that is itself a characteristic of the Pole: the island remains immovable amidst the ceaseless agitation of the waves, a disturbance that reflects that of the external world.

Writing about the theme of a cosmic mountain, which is identified with Shambhala, LePage says:[5]

> Within the magic ring of myth the cosmic mountain image is pre-eminent, both for its universality and its spiritual resonance as the meeting-place of heaven, earth and hell and the axle of the revolving firmanent, it has figured in the mythology of nearly every race on earth and has been revered even in lands where there are no mountains. It is always pictured as the Axis Mundi and as bearing the habitats of sages, saints or gods upon its sides... In *The Ancient Wisdom*, the well-known British author Geoffrey Ashe arrives at a similar conclusion:

> 'In the far north there is a high and paradisial place, peopled by an assembly of beings of superhuman longevity and wisdom. They have associates and contacts at lower levels. Access is difficult. This is the place where earth rises to join the celestial centre, the pole of heaven. Here is the axle of the sky, and above is the power that keeps it turning. The visible and sovereign sign of that power is the great constellation of seven stars [Ursa Major], which possess a divine life, and circle in the centre without setting. Our disc-shaped earth has a sacred centre which is in union with this centre where the heavens are pivoted.'

> And that sacred center on earth, Ashe postulates, is Shambhala-Agarttha. He points out that, curiously, support for the idea of a common center is concealed in the scriptural texts

---

[5] ibid

of the world religions, in which traditional peoples frequently located their sacred mountain not in their own land but in the far north… And in Psalm 48:2 of the Bible, Mount Zion is unaccountably called "Mount Zion in the far north". Ashe states:

> 'The holy mountain seems to have acquired stature through being mystically identified with another, much higher one, which was not in Palestine at all. The same northern mountain figures in related myths of the Canaanites. They called it "Safon" and said it had an earthly paradise on it. Safon occurs in the Bible as a synonym for Zion, and Ezekiel places "Eden, the garden of God" on a "holy mountain of God", which cannot possibly be the mundane hill of Jerusalem (Ezek. 28:11-16).'

The Shambhala story is closely linked to the Atlantis legend. The legends of both are prominent in various cultures and have captured the imaginations of people around the world. While they are distinct legends, there are some interesting connections and similarities. Both Atlantis and Shambhala are often described as lost or hidden civilizations, which embody utopian ideals. Both Atlantis and Shambhala have strong spiritual and mystical elements. Shambhala is closely associated with Tibetan Buddhism and represents a state of spiritual enlightenment. Atlantis too is sometimes seen as a place where ancient wisdom and spiritual knowledge were preserved.

Both Atlantis and Shambhala are often associated with cataclysmic or apocalyptic endings. Atlantis is said to have been destroyed by a great flood, while Shambhala is sometimes associated with prophecies of a future war or upheaval that will precede its appearance to the world. It is important to note that while these legends share some similarities, they are also distinct in their cultural origins and specific details. Atlantis is often associated with ancient Greece and the writings of Plato, while Shambhala is more closely tied to Tibetan and Indian traditions. The connections between these legends often arise from the universal human themes they touch upon rather than direct historical or cultural links.

Tag-Zig Olmo Lung Ring (more usually Olmo Lung Ring)
Some believe that Olmo Lung Ring is a discrete, wholly separate geographical reality, while others claim that it is synonymous with Shambhala and that the names are interchangeable. Nevertheless, Olmo

Lung Ring, often shortened to Olmo, possesses its own story. As with Shambhala's purported location, some modern scholars attempt to identify Olmo Lung Ring, Buddhism's Sorcery Paradise, with the area around mount Kailas in West Tibet, in ancient times known as Zhangzhung. The birthplace of all enlightened ones, Olmo Lung Ring is the shape of an eight-petalled lotus divided into four parts.

Zhangzhung (or Shangshung) was an ancient kingdom in western and northwestern Tibet, pre-dating Tibetan Buddhism. Zhangzhung culture is associated in particular with the Bön religion. These scholars assert that Olmo Lung Ring is quite an ordinary place like other valleys in Tibet and that the name Olmo Lung Ring simply means "the long valley of Olmo Lung Ring". Furthermore, the sacred mountain of Yungdrung Gutseg in the centre of Olmo Lung Ring is called a crystal monolith simply because it is a quite ordinary mountain surmounted by a glacier. Therefore, it is most likely a representation of Mount Kailas where four great rivers of Asia are said to originate.

The myth of a sacred land hidden in glacial mountains and containing a sacred white sea is said to have originated in the Altai Mountains of southern Siberia after Indo-European nomads arrived there from the Russian steppes north of the Black Sea. Water was sacred to them, as was the colour white, while the number 9 was a sacred number. Some of these nomadic people eventually migrated south to form a civilization in the Central Asian desert between Dunhuang and Khotan; others migrated to Iran. Zhang Zhung traded with the Altai and the desert oasis towns and it is not unreasonable to assume that some of those northern people came to live in Zhang Zhung, which at one time did extend in territory to Khotan.

A sharing of myth and tradition clearly took place. The "Tazik" (Indo-Iranian/Tajik) and Indo-European influence can be seen in the faces of Tibetan nomads today; genetically, they are part Indo-Iranian/European and part North Asian (Altaic). Archaeologists say that there was a large migration of Iranians from the west into northern Tibet/Zhang Zhung around 500 CE, adding more Iranian influence to the Tibetan nomad make-up.

According to Bönpo tradition, Olmo Lung Ring occupies one-third of our world and lies to the northwest of Tibet. The Bönpo texts further speak of the three portals or doors of Zhang-zhung, some asserting that Tazig is the middle door.

According to Lopon Tenzin Namdak, the outer door is Zhang-

30

zhung itself, the middle door is Tazig, and the inner door is Olmo Lung Ring. From the innermost gate outwards this represents the movement or progress of the teachings of Yungdrung Bön into the outer world and, especially, Tibet.

It is said that many years before the Buddha Shakyamuni's birth, Buddha Tonpa Shenrab Miwoche came into this world and taught in Olmo Lung Ring. "Ol" symbolizes the unborn, "mo" the un-diminishable, "lung" the prophetic words of Tonpa Shenrab, and "ring" his eternal compassion.

One scholarly opinion is that the kingdom of Olmo Lung Ring exists in a parallel dimension outside of time where the ruling principle is the inter-connectivity of all things. Its people know only peace and enjoyment.

In the Bönpo texts the land of Olmo Lung Ring is said to be divided into four concentric regions: the inner region (nang gling), the middle region (bar gling), the outer region (phyi gling), and the border region (mtha` gling). The inner and middle regions consist of 12 districts or islands (gling), the outer region of sixteen, and the border region also of twelve. These regions and districts are separated by rivers, lakes and inland seas.

The innermost region has the form geographically of an eight-petalled lotus blossom and the sky above it corresponds to the form of a wheel of eight spokes, which symbolize Dharma Chakra or "the wheel of life". The land is aromatic and full of striking vegetation and landscapes, snow-covered Stupas and mountains.

As with Shambhala, a pyramidal mountain, Yungdrung Gutsek, lies at the centre of Olmo Lung Ring. Nine Yungdrungs ascend to the top of the mountain. A single Yungdrung symbolises the everlasting and indestructible essence of the mind, while the nine in total symbolize the nine stages of Bön. From the Yungdrungs four rivers flow into waterfalls, each one representing an archetype or a simulation of the forms of thought: the snow lion, the horse, the rooster and the elephant.

The entire land of Olma Lung Ring is, in turn, surrounded by an ocean called Mukhyud Dalwa, "the wide-spreading enclosing ocean". This sea is itself surrounded by a mighty wall of snow-capped mountains called Walso Gangri Rawa, causing the imperishable sacred land to be impenetrable to any intrusion from the outside world

As a pure land, Olmo Lung Ring is said by some commentators to exist not as a physical location but one that may only be visited by humans who have purified their physical, mental and emotional selves.

A less spiritually evolved traveller would see only a barren, windswept plane surrounded by desolated mountains.

In contrast, those that speak of it as a region that can be found on earth describe how according to Yungdrung Bön[6] tradition, Olmo Lung Ring is the place where Lord Tonpa Shenrab descended from the celestial spheres and took up incarnation among human beings as an Iranian prince. It is said to be part of a larger geographical region to the northwest of Tibet called Tazig, which scholars identify with Iran or, more properly, Central Asia, where in ancient times Iranian languages such as Avestan and later Sogdian were spoken.

Concerning Tonpa Shenrab, one version of his story describes him as having been born a prince in Olmo Lung Ring some 18000 years ago (in 16017 BCE, according to the traditional Bönpo reckoning), while other versions, which downplay his importance in the evolution of Tibetan Buddhism, state that he lived in the 7th century BCE and subsequently became a run of the mill priest whose religious role was limited to serving at funeral ceremonies

There is no mention of Olmo Lung Ring in Tibetan texts before the tenth century CE. The theory goes that the arrival in Tibet in the eleventh century of Buddhist teachers inspired the Bönpo Lamas to invent and actually fabricate for themselves a supposedly ancient tradition. Since these teachings could not be seen as originating in Tibet, which is a quite real and ordinary place on earth they put the birth of Lord Tonpa Shenrab in distant Tazig, a fabulous land of legend, which recalled the Persian Empire that the Tibetans much admired in the 7th century.

These scholars conclude that the Bön tradition is fake, a deceitful invention of unscrupulous Tibetan Lamas in the tenth century ·and afterwards. According to the Bönpo Lamas, this assertion is entirely wrong. In all of the early Bönpo texts Olmo Lung Ring is clearly located to the west and the north of Tibet in Tazig or Central Asia. Moreover, there are two Tazigs, one of a heavenly nature and one quite physical located in Central Asia. The Kailas Mountain and its adjacent region in West Tibet is only a pale reflection of the real Olmo Lung Ring, the original archetype, which exists at the centre of the world.

The Bönpo account of the hidden land of Olmo Lung Ring is found in the "gZer-mig" and the "gZi-brjid". There it is explained that Olmo

---

[6] 'Yungdrung' refers to the left-facing swastika, a Tibetan Buddhist symbol meaning indestructibility and eternity.

Lung Ring is physically part of our world and is neither an imaginary holy land nor a celestial pure realm like the Sukhavati or Dewachan of the Buddha Amitabha.

Symbolically, Olmo Lung Ring is the geographical, psychical and spiritual centre of our world of Jambudvipa; at its centre rises the holy mountain of nine levels known as Yungdrung Gutseg, which link heaven and earth and perform the function of an *axis mundi* connecting three planes of existence: the heaven worlds, the earth and the nether regions.

Therefore, Olmo Lung Ring possesses a different ontological status than ordinary geographical regions and countries. In terms of our own age, it is a hidden land or "beyul", inaccessible to all but aware beings or Siddhas. This land is said to be inhabited by Vidyadharas or holders of esoteric knowledge. It exists on earth but it is not an ordinary country or nation which could be observed from space for it possesses a special reality all its own. It is *in* this world but not *of* it. It is part of our physical geographical world because it is located in Tazig, yet it partly exists in another spiritual dimension and, although material, is imperishable and indestructible.

According to legend when, at the end of the kalpa,[7] the world will be destroyed and consumed by fire, Olmo Lung Ring will spontaneously rise up and ascend into the sky and there it will merge with its celestial archetype in the heavens, which is called Sidpa Yesang. In this belief, Olmo Lung Ring/Shambhala is the spiritual and imperishable centre of the world that has existed on earth from the very beginning of the human race.

Olmo Lung Ring was the place where the celestial gods of the Clear Light descended from heaven to earth in order to take up incarnation as human beings and ensoul the physical bodies that had been prepared for them. Since that time Olmo Lung Ring has been the sanctuary of wisdom and the receptacle of the highest mystical teachings being brought down from above. All of the inhabitants of that land have entered upon the path to enlightenment. For this reason it is said to be the land of the Vidyadharas beyond the Himalayas, spoken of in the Puranas and other ancient books of India.

It is said that there has been a successive line of adepts or initiate-

---

[7]Kalpa, a duration of time in Hindu and Buddhist cosmology covering a complete cosmic cycle from the origination to the destruction of a world system

priest kings in Olmo Lung Ring who even today are the guardians and custodians of the eternal Wisdom Tradition, which was brought to this planet from the stars. In this context, Olmo Lung Ring is not only an earthly paradise but also a hidden sanctuary of the Gnosis, which holds a precious treasure of greatest price—the Supreme Secret. This is the precise knowledge of who we really are, where we have come from, and where ultimately we go. In mystical terms, it is the secret sanctuary hidden in the heart of every living being, the place of Buddhahood.

According to Bönpo prophesies, some 1200 years from now, when spiritual values decline and religion is nearly extinct in the outside world, a king and a teacher will emerge from Olmo Lung Ring in order to revitalize the spiritual teachings of Yungdrung Bon in the world.

*

Pertinent to the themes explored in later pages, there are distinct similarities between Lewis Carroll's Wonderland and Looking-Glass worlds and the concept of Shambhala.

Alice's worlds are fantastical realms where the laws of nature and logic are suspended. In Wonderland, Alice encounters a rabbit hole that leads her into a whimsical, dreamlike world filled with talking animals and bizarre landscapes. The Looking-Glass world is equally mystical, accessed through a mirror, where everything is reversed. Similarly, Shambhala is often described as a hidden, mystical realm, an ethereal kingdom beyond the physical world, a place of spiritual significance and enlightenment.

Wonderland and the Looking-Glass world are alternate dimensions or realities that coexist with the ordinary world but operate by their own rules. In these worlds, reality is flexible and mutable, allowing for surreal and fantastical experiences. Shambhala is often regarded as an alternate reality, existing alongside our everyday world but hidden from ordinary perception. Seekers of Shambhala believe in its existence as a parallel dimension that can be accessed through spiritual practices and inner transformation.

In Carroll's tales, Alice embarks on journeys that lead to personal transformation. Her experiences, such as changing in size or encountering peculiar characters, symbolize her inner growth and the challenges one faces in navigating unfamiliar realities. Similarly, Shambhala seekers embark on spiritual journeys that lead to personal transformation and enlightenment.

The quest for Shambhala represents a metaphorical journey of self-discovery and inner transformation, where individuals undergo spiritual growth and attain wisdom.

Carroll's works are known for their rich symbolism and allegorical elements. The bizarre characters and situations in Wonderland and the Looking-Glass world often convey deeper philosophical or satirical messages beneath their surface narratives. In the Shambhala tradition, the concept is laden with symbolic and allegorical meaning. It represents the pursuit of higher consciousness and spiritual enlightenment, with its hidden nature symbolizing the elusive quest for inner wisdom and understanding.

In both Carroll's stories and Shambhala mythology, characters or seekers are on quests for wisdom, understanding or enlightenment. Alice encounters characters and puzzles that challenge her intellect and perception, leading to personal growth. In Shambhala, seekers embark on spiritual quests to attain wisdom and reach a higher state of consciousness. The journey often involves overcoming inner obstacles and gaining insights into the nature of existence, paralleling Alice's adventures in her pursuit of knowledge.

Wonderland and the Looking-Glass world blur the boundaries between reality and imagination. Alice's experiences challenge her sense of what is real, mirroring the idea that reality is subjective and mutable. Similarly, Shambhala's existence blurs the boundaries between the physical and spiritual realms. It is seen as a place that exists both in the outer world and within one's consciousness, emphasising the interconnectedness of the physical and spiritual dimensions.

These similarities highlight the shared themes of mystical realms, inner transformation, symbolism, and the quest for wisdom between Carroll's imaginative worlds and the spiritual concept of Shambhala. Both offer readers and seekers the opportunity to explore the mysteries of existence, albeit in different cultural and literary contexts.

Alice has a difficult conversation with the Caterpillar

Chapter 2

Agarttha

A third mysterious realm associated with the Shambhala-Olmo Lung Ring Asian complex is Agarttha. It merits a chapter of its own because its reputed geographical structure is described as an array of tunnels, caverns and tributaries that are located at great depth throughout the entirety of subterranean Earth.

In *Le Roi du Monde* Guénon spoke of the vast underground network of caverns and tunnels that run under Shambhala's sacred centre for hundreds of miles, attributing to these catacombs the function of an even more secret and advanced centre of initiation, which he described as the true centre of world government and an impregnable storehouse of the world's wisdom.

According to Guénon, this all-important repository of knowledge survives the ebb and flow of civilisations and occasional global-wide cataclysms (such as the Biblical Flood), and would presently be sending forth its energies to establish a new planetary culture. He held that the Agartthian Lord of the World, "Rex Mundi", is the true authority on Earth and reference to him can be found in every tradition. He is associated with Manu amongst the Hindus; Metatron among the Kabbalists; and Melchizedec in the Judaeo-Christian tradition.

An ancient tradition of Brahmanic Hindustan speaks of a large island of unparalleled beauty, which, in very ancient times, lay in the middle of a vast sea in Central Asia, north of what is now the Himalayas. A race of nephilim, or men of a golden age, lived in the island but there was no communication between them and the mainland, except through tunnels, radiating in all directions, and many hundreds of miles long. These tunnels were said to have hidden entrances in old ruined cities in India – such as the ancient remains of Ellora, Elephanta and the Ajanta caverns in the Chandore range. Among the Mongolian tribes of Inner Mongolia, even today, there are traditions about tunnels and subterranean worlds, which sound as fantastic as anything in modern novels. One legend – if it be that! – says that the tunnels lead to a subterranean world of Antediluvian descent somewhere in a recess of Afghanistan, or in the region of the Hindu Kush... It is even given a name: Agharti. The legend adds that a labyrinth of tunnels and underground passages extended in a series of links connecting Agharti with all other such subterranean worlds! Tibetan lamas even assert that in America – it is not stated whether North, South or Central – there live in vast caves of an underworld, reached by secret tunnels, peoples of an ancient world who thus escaped a tremendous cataclysm of thousands of years ago. Both in Asia and America, these fantastic and ancient races are alleged to be governed by benevolent rulers, or King-archons. The subterranean world, it is said, is lit by a strange green luminescence, which favours the growth of crops and conduces to length of days and health.

–Harold T. Wilkins, explorer and historian, speaking in 1945

Guénon was not the first European to write about Agarttha. During writer Louis Jacolliot's wanderings in India in the 1860s when he was searching for the roots of western occultism, he heard mention of a mysterious realm of that name and its chief, Brahatma.

However, it was not until fifty years later when Gérard Encausse (Papus) edited and re-published in 1910 a detailed 1886 account by the nineteenth-century French occultist Alexandre Saint-Yves d'Alveydre[8] that a description emerged concerning a centre of initiation called Agarttha.

The author claimed that an underground world exists, its network branching everywhere, underneath whole continents, even oceans, to attain and maintain communication with all the regions of this world.

Subsequently in 1924 a book by Ferdinand Ossendowski came to print.[9] In it the writer describes his journey across central Asia in 1920 and 1921, using descriptions that tally almost identically, especially in the latter part of the book, with those of Saint-Yves. Critics were quick to accuse Ossendowski of plagiarizing Saint-Yves, supporting their case by pointing out the numerous parallel passages in the two books.

---

[8] d'Alveydre, A., *Mission de l'Inde en Europe*, Lahur, 1886.
[9] Ossendowski, F., *Beasts, Men and Gods*. New York: E. P. Dutton & Company, 1922

The concept of Agarttha, a hidden realm deep within the Earth's crust, has long captured the imagination of individuals across cultures. It presents an alluring narrative of a subterranean world inhabited by advanced civilizations and mystical beings.

The legend of Agarttha, also known as the Hollow Earth or Inner Earth, posits that beneath our feet lies a vast, enigmatic realm. This realm is illuminated by a central sun, rich in advanced technology and inhabited by beings of great wisdom and knowledge. The allure of Agarttha lies in its blend of mysticism, adventure and the promise of hidden wisdom.

Edward Bulwer-Lytton's novel *The Coming Race*, published anonymously in 1871, played a pivotal role in introducing the idea of a subterranean civilization to a wider audience. The novel depicted a race of beings known as the Vril-ya, who resided in a hidden realm beneath the Earth. These beings possessed advanced technology, including the use of a mysterious Vril energy.

The emergence of the Agarttha myth in the modern era is closely tied to the influence of a so-called Vril Society, whose existence has not been unequivocally proven but which, its believers claim, was at the heart and soul of Nazi occult doctrine.

The first news of this alleged society leaked out to the western world through Willi Ley, the rocket scientist who fled Germany in 1933. According to Ley, the disciples of top Nazi ideologist General Karl Haushofer, a student of Russian magician and metaphysician Georges Gurdjieff, believed that they were unveiling a secret knowledge with which they would be able to create a mutation in the Aryan Race: the Superman.

In 1960 journalists Jacques Bergier and Louis Pauwels re-introduced the putative existence of the Vril Society (or the Luminous Lodge of Light) in *The Morning of the Magicians*.[10] They claimed that the Vril-Society was a secret community of occultists in pre-Nazi Berlin that was a sort of inner circle of the occultist Thule Society. The Vril Society's alleged beliefs quickly intertwined with Hollow Earth theories. They posited that the Earth was not solid but hollow with vast subterranean caverns illuminated by a central sun. Within these hollow spaces they believed that advanced civilizations thrived, powered by Vril energy. The society claimed that they had communicated with these subterranean beings and received knowledge from them.

---

[10] Bergier and Pauwels, *Le Matin des Magiciens*, Éditions Gallimard, 1960.

The Luminous Lodge was formed in the late nineteenth century by Berlin-based Rosicrucians after attending a lecture by Jacolliot. Jacolliot was inspired by eminent figures such as eighteenth century mystical Christian Emmanuel Swedenborg and sixteenth century theologist Jacob Boehme, the latter being a co-founder of Rosicrucianism. The Lodge forged close links with like-minded theosophical centres, among them the English occult group known as the Hermetic Order of the Golden Dawn, founded in London by Freemason William Wynn Westcott in 1887.

Golden Dawn members engaged in "spiritual" exercises to harness the Vril force, seeking in its attempts to make contact with supernatural beings in the centre of the world with whom to make alliances to rule the surface and its inhabitants. This subterranean society of the "Vril-ya", the descendants of an ancient race driven long ago from the surface by the threat of a cataclysmic event, was believed to have developed futuristic technology far beyond the capability of surface humans. While Vril could power machines and heal living creatures, it also had enormous destructive power sufficient to reduce an entire city to rubble. Many believe that it was this Vril power that the Nazis sought so avidly.

Some suggest that the Vril-ya are not and never were confined to their subterranean redoubt. Researchers have claimed that senior members of the Thule Society believed that a master race of alien beings was living in underground caverns deep below the Earth. Sensationally, the Fars News Agency, the English-language news service of Iran, reported in 2014 that documents leaked by whistleblower Edward Snowden include the extraordinary claim that the United States is in the thrall of a race of tall, white Non-Human Enitities (NHEs), which allegedly assisted the rise of Nazi Germany in the 1930s.

The report goes on to say that these beings came to the surface and helped the Nazis to build a fleet of advanced submarines in the 1930s, before going on to meet in 1954 with President Eisenhower, a dialogue that heralded the beginnings of an "alien/extraterrestrial intelligence agenda" that is driving U.S. domestic and international policy.

The inference one is encouraged to draw from these incredible accounts is that the beings behind the Roswell UFO crashes in New Mexico in 1947, the Vril-ya, and the "tall white NHEs" are one and the same, their true identity being the race of humans that once populated Earth but which was expelled for the third and final time 12,000 years ago for unspeakable crimes against nature and the Cosmic Powers. This scenario casts fantastical reports of successful early twentieth century manned missions to the Moon and to Mars in a new light. One persistent rumour has it that the Nazis travelled to both bodies in the 1940s.

Vladimir Terziski, president of the American Academy of Dissident Sciences, is among those researchers who support the remarkable claim. Terziski is a Bulgarian born engineer and physicist who graduated Cum Laude from the Master of Science programme of Tokai University in Tokyo in 1980. He served as a solar energy researcher in the Bulgarian Academy of Sciences before emigrating to the U.S. in 1984. Terziski claims that by 1942 the Germans landed on the Moon, utilizing rocket saucers of the Miethe and Schriever type. He further claims that a joint Japanese-German program culminated in April 1945 in a journey to Mars using craft of the Haunebu-3 type, manned by a volunteer suicide crew. The implication behind these claims is that the Axis forces were assisted in these endeavours by an "alien" intelligence, which imparted highly advanced technological know-how. We are encouraged to believe that the identity of this intelligence is the Atlantean Vril-ya line of descent whose members reside both beneath our world and under the surface of nearby space bodies.

The Nazis were obsessed with Tibet, believing that in a remote high-peak lamasery would be found ancient knowledge that in the right hands would enable the finders to achieve mastery over the human race.

According to Pauwels and Bergier, a small Trans-Himalayan colony was established in Berlin and Munich in 1926. One of its members was a Tibetan monk known both as the "man with the green gloves" and as the "Guardian of the Keys", since he was reputed to possess the keys to Agarttha.

The Bönpo monks brought to Germany in the 1920s were said to have had the ability to open dimensional doors by means of the extraordinary Chod or Starwrighting ritual. In the ritual, on the death of a person the presiding lama will sit up through the night with the body of the departed and release the soul, guiding it through the Sea of Souls. By this ceremony the deceased is encouraged to recognise its own soul so it can travel on to the next world. The lama, after releasing the soul and making sure it is well on its way, cuts up the body and distributes it to be eaten by the birds of the air and the beasts of the field before the dawn. The body must not be buried to ensure that the departed soul has no earthly point of reference that might serve to draw it back to a lightless, etheric existence.

In response to the growth of Communism in Germany, spearheaded by the Spartakus League after the Great War, the authorities established unofficial groups of ex-servicemen called Freikorps. In March 1920 the volunteer troops of the Freikorps Erhardt Brigade marched into Berlin and installed an east-Prussian leader, Wolfgang Kapp. The Freikorps included Ignatz Timotheus Trebitsch-Lincoln (1879-1943), a Hungarian-born adventurer and convicted con artist. Of Jewish descent, Trebitsch-Lincoln spent parts of his life as a Protestant missionary, Anglican priest, British Member of Parliament for Darlington, German right-wing politician and spy, Nazi collaborator, Buddhist abbot in China, and self-proclaimed Dalai Lama.

In Germany, Trebitsch-Lincoln allied himself with the Munich members of the burgeoning Thule group, (Thule-Gesellschaft). Trebitsch-Lincoln's role within Thule circles was to develop the connections necessary for procuring weapons for Hitler's ill-fated Beer Hall putsch of 1923. After the putsch Trebitsch-Lincoln fled to China where he studied Buddhism and became adviser to the Chinese branch of a Tibetan secret society in contact with the mysterious Order of the Green Dragon.

In 1929 Trebitsch-Lincoln moved back to Europe. Three years later, calling himself Djordi Djen, he established a monastery in Berlin and reportedly introduced Hitler to the Tibetan members of the Society of Green Men and its leader, the "man with the green gloves". The intermediaries for these introductions to Hitler were the Russian émigré circles of early Nazism, which had included members of the Green Dragon Society in Moscow

An occultist and Völkisch group founded in Munich in 1918, the Thule-Gesellschaft (Thule Society) began life as the Studiengruppe für Germanisches Altertum ("Study Group for Germanic Antiquity"). Its founders were Guido von List, Jörg Lanz von Liebenfels and Adam Alfred Rudolf Glauer (also known as Rudolf von Sebottendorff). The Thule Society was notable chiefly as the organization that sponsored the Deutsche Arbeiterpartei, the German Workers' Party, which was reorganized by Adolf Hitler into the National Socialist German Workers' Party (NSDAP or Nazi Party). The Thule Society believed in an esoteric history of mankind, knowledge of which, it is claimed, is preserved in Tibetan monastary archives.

The Nazis began to organise expeditions to Tibet when sufficient funds had built up. These visits succeeded without interruption up to 1943. Standartenführer-SS Dr. Ernest Schafer, a close friend of Otto Rahn's, was a member of Himmler's Ahnenerbe, a pseudo-scientific organization active between 1935 and 1945, and was the driving force behind these expeditions.

A biologist, Schafer made at least two journeys to Tibet on behalf of the SS: one to East and Central Tibet in 1934-36, and another from April 1938 to August 1939. In 1931 he also accompanied Brooke Dolan (later an officer in the OSS) on an expedition to Tibet, Siberia and China.

In *Bevor Hitler Kam* (1964) Dietrich Bronder claimed that one of the objectives of these SS expeditions to Tibet was to establish a radio link between the Third Reich and the lamas. Madame Blavatsky's *Stanzas of Dyan*, a reputedly ancient text of Tibetan origin, was used as the code for all messages between Berlin and Lhasa during the war.

The Nazis were aware of the legend that the King of the World lives in a timeless place called Aghartha in the Tibetan region. Tradition tells that in the distant past the King of the World dwelt in the countries of the West (the Occident) on a mountain surrounded by huge forests. Eventually, so the story goes, he was chased from the West and came to Tibet.

Alice with Drink-Me Bottle

Chapter 3

The Land of the Nradas

Lewis Carroll initially called his child's story *Alice's Adventures Underground*. This distinctly different description from the later "Wonderland" epithet suggests that Carroll might not have been describing just any old world of enchantment. Dr. Tony Cooper, a leading geologist addressing in September 1999 the British Geological Association in Sheffield, offered his theory that the tale of Alice falling deep into the earth was inspired by Carroll's friendship with canon's daughter, Mary Hilton Badcock, who lived near subsidence craters at Ripon in North Yorkshire.

Charles Dodgson was born in Cheshire and spent his early life at Croft near Darlington. Nearby there was a trio of ponds called Hell's Kettles believed by locals to be bottomless:

> Alice... found herself falling down what seemed a deep well. Either the well was very deep, or she fell very slowly, for she had plenty of time as she went down to look about her, and to wonder what would happen next.

In 1852 Carroll's father was made Canon of Ripon and the family moved from Cheshire to Yorkshire. Here, Carroll met Mary and made photographs of her that John Tenniel is said to have later adapted into illustrations for the first edition of *Alice in Wonderland*.

Running beneath Ripon, including Mary's former family home, Ure Lodge, is a complex water-filled cave system. This two-mile wide gypsum belt stretches from Hartlepool to Doncaster and is filled with dozens of craters and deep shafts. The cave system's walls are made of sparkly gypsum. It has been suggested that the author's vision of Alice falling down a deep vertical hole into an underground land was inspired by natural geological events, notably subsidence at Ripon. Gypsum dissolves quickly so that the caves enlarge and commonly collapse. Collapse at Ure Lodge continues to the present day. It recently caused the destruction of four modern garages and the evacuation of several houses, including the Lodge itself. Subsidence in places underlain by gypsum poses a severe constraint on the development of those areas.

The Hells Kettles ponds were formed by a dramatic collapse of the ground in 1179. They overflow with foul sulphurous water and were reputed traditionally to boil and were bottomless. It was told that a farmer who worked on St. Barnaby's Day was swallowed up and could be seen doing eternal penance in the deep water. In 1958 divers proved the pits to be just 22 feet deep.

While Lewis Carroll's father was resident in Ripon, the Reverend J.S. Tute of Markington, near Ripon, wrote the first scientific paper about the local subsidence events. Like the current residents of Ripon, Lewis Carroll was almost certainly aware of the problems. He would have seen the collapses in his friends' gardens and the numerous collapses in the field opposite Ure Lodge.

The Maisters, also acquaintances of Carroll's, lived at Littlethorpe where a major collapse occurred in 1796. It is likely also that Carroll would have visited the collapse that occurred in 1834 about 300m northeast of Ure Lodge. This event near the-then railway station left a 66-foot deep and 33-foot diameter shaft with solid rock exposed in its sides, which undermined a number of gardens including the field opposite Ure Lodge and dumped domestic clutter at its base.

Yet the collapse witnessed by the Reverend Dunwell of Ripon in 1860 while walking with some school children along the banks of the River Ure must have proved even more dramatic, as before their eyes the ground fell away leaving a crater spanning twenty feet across and about forty feet in depth; certainly an event that may very well have prompted Alice's later adventures.

> Down, down, down. Would the fall never come to an end?
> ... I must be getting somewhere near the centre of the earth...
> Down, down, down: there was nothing else to do... when
> suddenly, bump, bump! Down she came upon a heap of sticks
> and shavings, and the fall was over.

These accounts concerning Hell's Kettles and Ure Lodge are especially interesting when we look at the terrifiying experience of writer and researcher Alec Maclellan who, in his book *The Lost World of Agarthi,* reveals the vast extent of Agarttha's subterranean matrix and its bizarre residents.[11]

---

[11] Maclellan, A., *The Lost World of Agarthi*, Souvenir Press, 1982.

Many years ago while Maclellan was on holiday by famous Ilkley Moor in the West Riding of Yorkshire, he took a walk along the pleasant valley of the River Wharfe near the village of Grassington. It was a summer's day and strong sunlight threw the ranges and hills to the north in sharp relief. These outcrops are broad and blunt. The highest, Great Whernside is only 2,314 feet high. It was, in fact, in the direction of Great Whernside that Maclellan set out that morning.

Grassington and Linton in the valley below are particularly rich in wild flowers and fairy tales. There are legends of the dreadful "Barguest", the ghost-dog of the dales, whose appearance foretells disaster. Nearby is the Fairy Hole, the name given to a low opening in the limestone rock.

As Maclellan began his walk up the valley on that calm, sunny and peaceful day, he could not help recalling the words of Daniel Defoe that he had been reading the previous evening. Speaking about the mountains of Upper Wharfedale that lay ahead of Maclellan in the warm sunlight, Defoe had written: 'They are more frightful than any in Monmouthshire or Derbyshire, especially Pingent Hill.'

Unexpectedly, a shiver ran up Maclellan's spine. He continued walking across Grassington Moor and saw the first evidence of the old lead mines that had partly drawn him to this area. His interest had also been sparked by the stories of caves and ancient tunnels, which were said to abound in the area. Some of these had been dated from the Mesolithic, Neolithic, Bronze and Iron Age periods but the origins of others were far more puzzling.

A Dr. Buckland, who had explored Kirkdale Cave in 1882, made an extraordinary statement in his book, *Reliquiae Diluvianae*, that he had found remains that 'pertained to men who were swept away by Noah's flood.'

Soon Maclellan was in the shadow of Great Whernside, about midway between the little villages of Kettlewell and Starbotton. Here he saw a cave entrance up on the hillside. He walked up to it and ventured into its very small and narrow opening. He took out his torch and shone its beam into the tight passage. Only darkness stretched ahead of him. All he could hear was the gentle, plopping sound of water dripping from the roof of the cave.

As soon as he stepped inside a draught of cold air struck him. At this point he hesitated, as if by premonition, and wondered if it was really worthwhile exploring something so unpromising. He had come this far, he decided; he would go on.

He moved off in the beam of the small torch. The walls of the cave seemed to slope downwards gradually and then take on the more regular shape of a tunnel. The floor beneath his feet was hard and rocky and every now and then he stumbled through small puddles of water. Only the sound of his breathing and footsteps broke the silence, while ahead the light revealed the tunnel continuing to slope gradually downwards with hardly a bend. He turned once to look behind but there was only impenetrable darkness.

He must have walked for about ten minutes before he stopped. The tunnel gave no sign of changing either its height or gradual descent, and he asked himself just how much longer he was going to go on. It seemed he had found one of the strange underground tunnels of the West Riding. He was no potholer or spelaeologist. What could he achieve by going on further, other than to put himself into danger if anything went wrong?

Common sense, and perhaps even a feeling of unease, got the better of him. Maclellan swung the torch around and was just about to set off back the way he had come when something stopped him dead in his tracks. In swinging the beam of the torch back behind him, Maclellan had caught sight out of a faint glow ahead in the tunnel. He peered harder to make sure he had not been mistaken. No, there was clearly a dim glow some distance ahead.

Should he investigate or go back? Even as he stood there, the light down the tunnel seemed to gain in intensity, although it may only have been an illusion. Cautiously he began to move forward again, the beam of his torch now directed at his feet. He walked carefully, almost holding his breath, for perhaps fifty yards.

He could now see that the light was green in colour. It seemed to be pulsating. He stood still, unable to move. Then something even more extraordinary occurred. At first Maclellan thought the sound was his own breathing, and then he discerned a gentle humming noise that gradually grew louder. As it did so, he felt the ground beneath his feet begin to vibrate, at first ever so gently but then steadily increasing in intensity.

The humming became a rumble and the green light pulsated more strongly. He felt his heart pound and in the darkness he was overcome by sudden terror. Something almost seemed to be coming towards him. What on earth was happening? What was the strange light? And what was causing the rumbling beneath his feet?

Maclellan believed he was in the tunnel of some long forgotten

Yorkshire mine but his senses seemed to be telling him that he had stumbled onto something far more extraordinary…and fearful. In the next few moments the pulsating light and shaking of the ground grew stronger still until he felt the tunnel must surely collapse upon him.

That very thought seemed to release Maclellan from the feeling of bewilderment that had frozen his movements. Without a second thought he turned and raced back up the passageway. He did not stop running until he flung himself, gasping for air, through the tunnel entrance and into the sunlight and warmth of that summer day.

Gradually, Maclellan's panic subsided and he wrestled to make some sense of what had happened. There could be no mistaking the green light he had seen, nor the sensation of the ground trembling beneath his feet. The eerie green light was unlike any he had ever seen, and the rumbling sound almost seemed as if it had emanated from some huge piece of machinery. Could the one have been an underground light and the other some strange subterranean means of transport?

Maclellan discussed his experiences with relatives and other friends and concluded that it had not been a dream or an illusion but, in all probability, a confirmation of a long held tradition in the West Riding of Yorkshire that somewhere in the dales is an entrance to an underground world. By common consent, this subterranean kingdom is either the haunt of fairies and goblins or, as other Yorkshire folk insist, is actually the dwelling place of people like us, who have lived hidden from the sight of man since time immemorial.

Later, Maclellan researched the area and its history and came across the work of writer Charles James Cutcliffe-Hyne (1865-1944), who had created the tough fictional adventurer, Captain Kettle.

Cutcliffe-Hyne had lived in Kettlewell and was obsessed with the legend of Atlantis. In 1889 he wrote a book called *Beneath Your Very Boots* (published 1889), today so rare that the only copies are to be found in a handful of university libraries.

It tells the story of a certain Anthony Haltoun who finds himself in an underground world, which he enters through a cave 'in the valley of the Wharfe near to its commencement.' The entrance is 'on the northern flank of the dale' and the young man enters despite a stern warning from a local to 'leave the caves alone, or else the folk who dwell in them will catch you.' Haltoun tells us that the passageway was definitely not that of a lead mine, 'for the Wharfedale mines are nearly all horizontal,' while this one progressed downwards in a gradual slope.

While walking along the passage Haltoun is confronted by 'a brilliant light, which suddenly flashed through the gloom and displayed a party of men advancing towards me.' At their approach, the ground begins to shake and tremble and the startled Haltoun falls into a faint. When he recovers his senses, the narrator discovers that he has fallen into the hands of an underground race called the "Nradas", a fair-skinned, blond-haired people who tell him that they have lived in these subterranean caverns in a state of harmony and peace since prehistoric times. They are opposed to war, and it was 'their hatred of fighting which caused them, in the first instance, to seek shelter beneath the land which was glutting itself with slaughter.'

Haltoun inquires of his hosts, 'Do I understand that there is a regular colony in this cave?'

'Well, yes, partly,' they replied. 'Only for colony read nation, and for cave almost interminable labyrinth. Out habitations and the tunnels connecting them, ramify under the whole of the British Isles, and in many places under the seas besides!'

The Nradas explain that they are ruled over by Radoa, 'who is supreme both in things temporal and in things spiritual: He is at once Ruler and Deity.'

Radoa is said to be a majestic figure, dressed in a golden robe, and lives in a beautiful, cavernous city. The number of inhabitants of this subterranean metropolis 'is a trifle over ten thousand... though there are twice as many within a ten miles circuit round it.'

The Nradas also tell Haltoun how they took advantage of the make-up of the Earth to create their subterranean world. 'Firstly, the crust of the earth is vesicular: full of holes, formed either by titanic convulsion or by the water's irresistible erosion; and, secondly, that nearly all these cavities are ventilated by invisible capillary air-shafts.'

Of the tunnels many were naturally formed, while 'here and there a more symmetrically carved tunnel pointed to the handiwork of man' long before their day. (Later, Haltoun comes to learn that these passageways were bored by rotary tools studded with diamonds that had been mined underground.)

To illuminate their world, and also to propel the vehicles that transport them through the tunnels, the Nradas have tapped 'the earth's internal power, abstracted through deep borings.'

In his autobiography *My Joyful Life* (1935), Cutcliffe-Hyne describes his life of adventure that took him all over the world to places like

Europe, Scandinavia, Africa, Mexico and South America. Cave hunting was his main passion. He explored subterranean passages in Yorkshire, several places in Europe and Africa, and searched for lost Inca treasure in Mexico. It was while engaged on these expeditions that he first heard stories of a subterranean kingdom said to be linked to all the nations of the world. 'In South America I heard tell that there were enormous tunnels that traversed the continent, ultimately linking with this forbidden place. More curious still, there was similar talk in Europe, and even some old people in the West Riding knew the story and believed there to be entrances through their own caves. The kingdom was said to be called Agharti.'

The Nradas' Agartthian power source is very reminiscent of the mysterious "Vril" power described by Bulwer-Lytton. Some theosophists, notably Madame Blavatsky, William Scott-Elliot and Rudolf Steiner, accepted the book as based at least in part on occult truth.

René Guénon used Lytton's book as the basis of articles that he wrote concerning the mythical underworld of Agarttha. Guénon's decision to write the articles under the pen name "Narad Mani" suggests that he was aware of Cutcliffe-Hyne's book also. Guénon's story line revolves around a young traveller (the narrator) who visits a friend, a mining engineer. Together they explore a natural chasm in a mine that has been exposed by an exploratory shaft. The narrator reaches the bottom of the chasm safely but his friend falls to his death after the rope breaks.

The narrator finds his way into a subterranean world occupied by beings that seem to resemble angels. He befriends the first he meets, who guides him around a city that is reminiscent of ancient Egyptian architecture. The explorer meets his host's wife, two sons and a daughter who learn to speak English by way of a makeshift dictionary during which the narrator unconsciously teaches them the language.

The hero discovers that these beings, which call themselves Vril-ya, have great telepathic and other parapsychological abilities such as being able to transmit information, get rid of pain, and put others to sleep. The narrator soon discovers that the Vril-ya are descendants of an antediluvian civilization called the Ana, who live in networks of caverns linked by tunnels. Originally surface dwellers, they fled underground thousands of years ago to escape a massive flood and gained greater power by facing and dominating the harsh conditions of the Earth.

The place into which the narrator descended houses 12,000 families, one of the largest groups. Their society is a technologically supported Utopia, chief among their tools being an 'all-permeating fluid' called "Vril", a latent source of energy that the spiritually elevated hosts are able to master through force of will. It is this fluid that the Vril-ya employ to communicate with the narrator. The powers of the Vril include the ability to heal, change and destroy beings and things; the destructive powers in particular are immense, allowing a few young Vril-ya children to destroy entire cities if necessary.

Men (called An, pronounced "Arn") and women (Gy, "Gee") have equal rights. The women are stronger and larger than the men. The women are also the pursuing party in romantic relationships. They marry for three years, after which the men choose whether to remain married or be single. The female may then pursue a new husband. However, they seldom make the choice to remarry.

Their religion posits the existence of a superior being but does not dwell on the nature of this being. The Vril-ya believe in the permanence of life, which according to them is not destroyed but merely changes form.

According to Zee, Vril can be changed into the mightiest force over all types of matter, both animate and inanimate. It can destroy like lightning or replenish life, heal or cure.

The narrator adopts the attire of his hosts and begins also to adopt their customs. The guide's daughter, Zee, falls in love with him and tells her father, who orders his son Taë to kill him with his staff. Eventually both Taë and Zee conspire against such a command, and Zee leads the narrator through the same chasm through which he first descended. Returning to the surface, he warns that in time the Vril-ya will run out of habitable space underground and will claim the surface of the Earth, destroying mankind in the process, if necessary.

Compare Alec Maclellan's factual and Haltoun's fictional experiences with that of George Weist, whose own bizarre adventure begins in an underground world before developing into scenes mindful of the Hollow Earth enigma.

In 1954, spelunker George Weist, along with his friends, was exploring a branch of caverns connected to the Mammoth Cave system in Kentucky. Unexpectedly, Weist lost his footing and fell into a gap between the wall of the cave and the floor. Unable to locate their friend, the rest of the party returned to the surface to get help but George was not found and he was given up for dead.

Several weeks later, Weist reappeared near his home in Glasgow, Kentucky, looking no worse for his accident and with a bizarre story of his missing time. He told his friends that after slipping through the crack he tumbled down into a deep pit where he found himself in total darkness with his leg trapped between rocks. He tried yelling to attract attention but it soon became clear that he was lost with no hope for rescue. Weist had no idea how long he had been trapped in the suffocating darkness. With no outside references, time had lost all meaning.

Just when he had almost given up hope, like Maclellan Weist felt an odd vibration in the floor and then heard a sound like machinery somewhere in the darkness. As the sound grew louder, Weist began calling out, thinking that a search party had found him. Eventually, he saw a dim glow that he realized came from lights being carried by a small group of people that immediately set to work to free him from his predicament.

Due to his injuries and exhaustion, Weist could not recall much after that point. He remembered waking up on a small bed in what appeared to be a sparsely furnished medical clinic. The door soon opened and a young woman dressed in a light-blue coloured "pants suit" came into the room carrying his cleaned and pressed clothes. The woman was tall, with blonde hair and eyes 'the brightest colour of blue' that Weist had ever seen.

Weist realized that he was completely naked and quickly dressed, noting that the leg that had been trapped in the rocks now seemed completely uninjured and free of pain. All the while the woman stood by watching. Weist tried asking her where he was and how long he had been there but the woman remained annoyingly silent. When he was finished dressing, the woman motioned him to follow her and the two left the room.

Stepping outside, Weist was stunned to see a landscape that was totally unfamiliar to him. It appeared that they were on a flower-covered plain with snow-capped mountains off in the distance. 'The beauty took my breath away,' he said.

The sky was cloudless and blue but the sun looked odd. It seemed smaller and dimmer and had a slight reddish or copper colour to it. 'I could look directly at it and it didn't hurt my eyes,' he said. But the sight that shook the man to his very core was the realization that he could see no horizon. 'Behind me were high mountains but in front of me was flat land that stretched away into the distance. Instead of a horizon, it looked like I was at the bottom of a huge bowl with the sides going up in every direction that finally disappeared into the sky.'

Before Weist had a chance to contemplate his surroundings for very long, he was approached by a group of men who silently motioned for him to follow. Like the woman, the men were all similar in appearance; tall, with blond hair, blue eyes, and hands with unusually long fingers. Again, Weist tried asking where he was but his hosts remained strangely silent. He was taken to an area where parked on the ground were several metallic "football-shaped" objects. One of the craft had an open door with an extended ramp that he was quickly led into. Once inside, one of the tall men walked up to Weist and smiled broadly at him, the first real expression that any of them had exhibited, and placed his hands on either side of Weist's head. That is the last thing he remembered until waking up just outside of town.

Weist's experience invites exploration of the remarkable theory of a "Hole at the Pole", through which intrepid travellers may find a very different kind of world than the familiar Earth from which they arrived.

The White Rabbit of Wonderland

Alice holding the unfortunate pig-baby

Chapter 4

Asia Mysteriosa

In a previous work[12] I wrote about pre-WWII explorer Otto Rahn's association with a mysterious but influential group, the Polaires (La Fraternité des Polaires), an esoteric society whose appeal chimed with the beliefs of those that supported the existence of mythical realms such as Agarttha and Shamballah.

In the 6th March 1932 edition of *La Dépêche* an argument arose about the activities of this group, which, in this period, was especially active in France and England. The article questioned the nature of the activities of a German named in the piece as "Monsieur Rams", changing the name in a follow-up the following day to "Rahu". These were garbled references to Rahn and his activities.

At the same time as Rahn was engaged in his explorations (searching for Grail treasures on behalf of Heinrich Himmler), Polaires members were similarly excavating in the caves of Ussat-les-Bains and Ornolac in the Ariège Pyrenees in southwestern France. Rahn was said to be the leader of this group and suspicions were raised because of his nationality, there being much anti-German feeling by rural folk whose memories of the Great War had scarcely diminished.

Antonin Gadal, a French mystic and historian who dedicated his life to studying the history of the Cathars, wrote to a newspaper in Rahn's defence, saying that his visit to the caves had nothing to do with the Polaires. Rahn himself subsequently wrote to the paper, correcting the spelling of his name and stressing that he had never heard of the Polaires before coming to the Ariège. He was a simply a writer interested in the Cathars. Rahn's riposte emphasised that neither his friends nor he were occultists or spiritualists.

The Polaires originated in 1908 when twelve-year old Mario Fille met a hermit named Father Julian in the hills near Rome. The hermit

---

[12] Graddon N., *Otto Rahn and the Quest for the Grail: The Amazing Life of the Real Indiana Jones,* AUP, Illinois, 2008.

gave a number of old parchments to Mario that contained the Oracle of Astral Energy. However, the steps in the process were long-winded and wrapped in a complex system of word and number manipulations.

The complexities forced Mario to put the Oracle to one side and he only returned to the parchments twelve years later when he used them to help with some personal difficulties. The instructions consisted in phrasing a question in Italian. The querent would then add his name and his mother's maiden name, then somehow translate them into numbers and, finally, carry out a mathematical procedure.

This long and unwieldy process produced a final set of numbers, which the querent translated into letters to provide an answer. In practice, the Oracle always answered reliably with credible responses but, oddly, its answers were as likely to be expressed in French or German as in Italian.

True to the wishes of Father Julian, Mario alone possessed the key to decoding the Oracle. The Oracle was said not to be a form of divination in the conventional sense but, extraordinarily, an actual channel with the purported Rosicrucian initiate centre known as Asia Mysteriosa in the Himalayas. (We return to the remarkable history and import of the Rosicrucian movement in Chapter 22 when we examine claims that Lewis Carroll's writings were strongly influenced by Rosicrucian teachings, and that Alice's descent into Wonderland has an historic precedent in the publication of a Rosicrucian tract, *Cabala, Mirror of Art and Nature: in Alchemy*.

According to the beliefs of the Polaires, Father Julian's oracular channel was directed by "The Supreme Sages" or the "Little Lights of the Orient", who live in Agarttha. These at first included Father Julian but after his death on 8th April 1930 the baton passed to a "Chevalier Rose-Croix". The knight in question was never named but it was surmised that he was the guiding light of the neo-Theosophists: the Comte de Saint-Germain, who, according to Voltaire, was: 'The Wonderman... a man who does not die, and who knows everything.'

Together with his boyhood friend and fellow musician, Cesare Accomani, Fille moved to Paris where the Oracle was shown to a group of journalists and writers. Some were sufficiently moved to publicise it and to contribute to Accomani's 1929 book *Asia Mysteriosa*, published under the pseudonym "Zam Bhotiva".

One of the Oracle's supporters in France was Maurice Magré who was a major influence on Otto Rahn's research work in France. The Toulousian poet firmly linked the Oracle's origins to Blavatsky's

Theosophy when he wrote that 'the existence of this brotherhood, variously known as "Agarttha" and as the "Great White Lodge", is what it has always been, but unproven by those "material evidences" of which the Western mind is so fond.'[13] He added that: 'the revelations of Saint-Yves d'Alveydre in *La Mission de l'Inde*, despite their apparent improbability, must contain part of the truth.'

Another supporter of the existence of Asia Mysteriosa was Jean Marques-Rivière whose specialist fields of study were Tibetan Buddhism and Tantrism. Joscelyn Godwin[14] points out that Marques-Rivière in his Foreword to *Asia Mysteriosa* mentions mystics Emmanuel Swedenborg and Anne Catherine Emmerich, who had both believed in a spiritual centre located in Tibet. Marques-Rivière wrote: 'Now, the centre of trans-human power has a reflection on the earth; it is a constant tradition in Asia, and this Centre… is called in Central Asia Agarttha. It has many other missions, or rather as its reason for existence, the direction of the spiritual activities of the Earth.'

Others who accepted the Oracle's provenance included alchemist Arturo Reghini. Reghini was responsible for introducing the mystic-fascist Baron Giulio (Julius) Evola to the works of René Guénon. Rahn admired the work of Evola (1898-1974), a confidant of Mussolini, whose seminal work, *Rivolta contro il mondo moderno*, was published in Germany in 1935. Evidently, Otto Rahn empathised with Evola's portrayal of prehistory's degeneration from a male dominated Golden Age to the Silver Age cycle of the Goddesses of Earth and Moon, the impure product of the marriage of the Sun-god warriors of the ancient North with the feminine cults of the South.

Both Rahn and Evola believed, however, that one branch of the Arctic Hyperboreans did survive with its solar traditions largely intact. It was this race, unsullied, so Evola claimed, by the inbreedings that befell its Aryan counterpart, which went on to populate Europe and India.

Interestingly, one very famous associate of the Polaires was Sir Arthur Conan Doyle who besides being world renowned for creating Sherlock Holmes was a high profile Spiritualist. However, this connection with the Polaires began only *after* Conan Doyle's death on 7th July 1930. Following a series of psychic communications between

---

[13] Bhotiva 1929

[14] Godwin, Joscelyn. *Arktos: the Polar Myth in Science, Symbolism and Nazi Survival*. Grand Rapids: Phanes Press, 1993

England and France, Zam Bhotiva contacted London medium, Grace Cooke, in January 1931. Through her mediumship, Bhotiva heard Conan Doyle affirm that the Polaires were 'destined to help in the molding of the future of the world... for the times are near.' Mrs. Cooke's spirit guide, a Tibetan Sage named "White Eagle", stated that Bhotiva had come on instructions from Tibet.

In spirit readings, the Chevalier Rose-Croix confirmed that Conan Doyle was to help the Brotherhood, and said, 'See the star rises in the East; it is the sign of the Polaires, the sign of the two interlaced triangles.'

The *Bulletin des Polaires* of 9th June 1930 explained the seeming paradox between an Asian mystery centre and a Polar concept:

> The Polaires take this name because from all time the Sacred Mountain, that is the symbolic location of the Initiatic Centres, has always been qualified by different traditions as "polar". And it may very well be that this Mountain was once really polar, in the geographical sense of the word, since it is stated everywhere that the Boreal Tradition (or the Primordial Tradition, source of all Traditions) originally had its seat in the Hyperborean regions.'[15]

During 1929 and 1930 the Polaires made excavations in the Montségur area. According to a local newspaper, the Polaires had found traces of Christian Rosenkreutz's travels in the ruins of Lordat castle. This report corresponds with Zam Bhotiva's alleged discovery, via the Oracle, of the "Wand of Pico della Mirandola", which was said to shiver in the near presence of gold. With a lady companion, Bhotiva set off to find the lost treasure of Montségur but having no success he quit the search and, thoroughly disgruntled, the Polaires.

By 1936 there were separate Polaires groups for men and women in capital cities in Europe and America, each dedicated to working for the good of mankind under Mario Fille's direction.

---

[15] ibid

Alice deafened by the drummers in *Through the Looking-glass*

Alice trying to pin the White Queen's hair

Chapter 5

India's Underworld Planets

According to Vedic literature, this universe is known as loka-traya: the three lokas (Bhurloka, Bhuvarloka and Svarloka), or three spheres or worlds. Similarly, the Bhagavad-gītā states that there are three divisions of material spheres in this universe:

> ➢ Ūrdhvaloka—the upper world or ūrdhvaloka above Mount Meru. It is the celestial world, the realms of the gods or heavens, the svarga-lokas: heavenly planets.
> ➢ Madhya-loka—the middle planetary system, world of mortals, the realms of humans, animals and plants.
> ➢ Adhalok—the lower world, the subterranean heavens, Bila-Swarga, the realms of beings other than humans, like Daityas, Dānavas, Nāgas and such.

Beyond the ūrdhvaloka planets, above the Brahmaloka, are the material coverings of the universes. Above that is the spiritual sky, which is unlimited in expansion, containing unlimited self-illuminated Vaikuṇṭha planets inhabited by God Himself along with His associates, who are all eternally liberated living entities. The three primary realms of the universe branch out into 14 different dimensions of existence, separated into seven upper worlds (Vyahrtis) and seven lower realms (Patalas). All of them host different levels of consciousness, allowing their dwellers to live out their karmic journeys.

Consequently, each of these realms serves a unique function and purpose in the universe and, taken as a whole, they are part of a larger system, similar to the different organs and chakras of the body and their respective roles, or the various stages of spiritual development of people of different ages and backgrounds from all walks of life.

Vedic scriptures introduce the concept of Loka in order to represent these different stages of awareness. There are seven realms above and seven realms below. The realm that a person may experience depends on the frequency at which they are vibrating. However, in the end the rate of vibration is directly linked to consciousness, and the 14 lokas of

Hindu tradition and Vedic wisdom confirm this. The whole balance of the universe depends on the operative entwining of these realms.

According to Vedic lore, below the earth by 70,000 yojanas (one yojana measuring between 3.5 and 15 kilometers) are the 7 lower planetary systems—Atala, Vitala, Sutala, Talātala, Mahātala, Rasātala and Pātāla. This idea of "seven lower planetary systems" may create the impression in a person's mind of seven layers of many globe-like planets orbiting in space. The Bhāgavata Purāṇa calls the seven lower regions bila-svargas ("subterranean heavens") and they are not regarded as planets or planetary systems within the physical universe. Like Shambhala, Olmo Lung Ring and Agarttha, *they are subterranean realms or dwelling places that are part of the physical Earth itself.*

These seven lower planetary systems are scattered over the complete universe, which occupies an area of two billion times two billion square miles. The width and length of these lower systems are calculated to be exactly the same as those of earth.

Demons live in these lower planetary systems with their wives and children, always engaged in sense gratification and not fearing their next births. Residents of these planets do not become old or diseased.

Since there is no sunshine in those subterranean planets, illumination being provided by jewels fixed upon the hoods of snakes, time is not divided into days and nights. The brightness of the gems dissipates the darkness in all directions.

Atala

In Atala there is a demon, the son of Maya Dānava, named Bala, who created ninety-six kinds of mystic power. Simply by yawning Bala created three kinds of women known as svairiṇī (independent), kāminī (lusty) and puṁścalī (very easily subdued by men). The svairiṇīs like to marry men from their own group, the kāminīs marry men from any group, and the puṁścalīs change husbands one after another.

If a man enters the planet of Atala, these women immediately capture him and induce him to drink an intoxicating beverage made with a drug known as hāṭaka [cannabis indica]. This intoxicant endows the man with great sexual prowess, which the women take advantage of for enjoyment. A woman will enchant the man with attractive glances, intimate words, smiles of love and then embraces. In this way she induces him to enjoy sex with her to her full satisfaction. Because of his increased sexual power, the man thinks himself stronger than ten thousand elephants and considers himself most perfect. Indeed, illusioned and intoxicated by false pride, he thinks himself God, ignoring impending death.

Vitala

The next planet below Atala is Vitala, where Lord Śiva, known as the master of gold mines, lives with his personal associates, the ghosts and similar entities. Lord Śiva, as the progenitor, engages in sex with Bhavānī, the progenitress, to produce living entities, and from the mixture of their vital fluids the river named Hāṭakī is generated. When fire, being made to blaze by the wind, drinks of this river and then sizzles and spits it out, it produces gold called Hāṭaka. The demons that live on that planet with their wives decorate themselves with various ornaments made from that gold, and thus they live there very happily.

Sutala

Below the planet Vitala is another planet, known as Sutala, where the great son of Mahārāja Virocana, Bali Mahārāja, who is celebrated as the most pious king, resides even now. Bali Mahārāja was favoured by the Supreme Personality of Godhead, Vāmanadeva, because of his intense devotional service. The Lord went to the sacrificial arena of Bali Mahārāja and begged him for three paces of land, and on this plea the Lord took from him all his possessions. When Bali Mahārāja agreed to all this, the Lord was very pleased and therefore the Lord serves as his doorkeeper. The description of Bali Mahārāja appears in the Eighth Canto of Śrīmad-Bhāgavatam.

For the welfare of Indra, the King of heaven, Lord Vishnu, appeared in the form of a dwarf brahmacārī as the son of Aditi and tricked Bali Mahārāja by begging for only three paces of land but taking all the three worlds. Being very pleased with Bali Mahārāja for giving all his possessions, the Lord returned his kingdom and made him richer than the opulent King Indra. Even now, Bali Mahārāja engages in devotional service by worshiping the Supreme Personality of Godhead in the planet of Sutala.

Talātala

Below Sutala is the planet Talātala, the abode of the demon Maya. This demon is always materially happy because he is favoured by Lord Śiva, but he cannot achieve spiritual happiness at any time. Maya is known as the ācārya [master] of all the māyāvīs, who can invoke the powers of sorcery. For the benefit of the three worlds, Lord Śiva once set fire to the three kingdoms of Maya but later, being pleased with him, he returned his kingdom. Since that time, Maya Dānava has been protected by Lord Śiva and therefore believes falsely that he need not fear the Sudarśana Chakra,[16] an anthropomorphic form of Vishnu used for the destruction of demons. In this annihilatory form Vishnu is known as Chakraperumal or Chakratalvar.

Mahātala

Below Talātala is the planet Mahātala, where there are many snakes with hundreds and thousands of hoods. These snakes, descendants of Kadrū, are always very angry. Among them in prominence are Kuhaka, Takṣaka, Kāliya and Suṣeṇa. The snakes are always disturbed by fear of Garuḍa, the carrier of Lord Vishnu, but although they are full of anxiety, some of them nevertheless sport with their wives, children, friends and relatives.

Rasātala

Beneath Mahātala is Rasātala, which is the abode of the demoniac sons of Diti and Danu. They are called Paṇis, Nivāta-kavacas, Kāleyas and Hiraṇya-puravāsīs [those living in Hiraṇya-pura]. They are all enemies of the demigods, and they reside in holes like snakes. From birth they are extremely powerful and cruel, and although they are proud of their strength, they are always defeated by the Sudarśana Chakra.

Pātāla

Below Rasātala is Pātāla (Tibetan: "the Underground") where the serpent Vasukī lives with his associates. The Vishnu Purana tells of a visit to Patala by the divine wandering sage Narada (note similarity to Nrada, the fictional race beneath the Yorkshire moors). Narada describes Patala as filled with splendid jewels, beautiful groves and lakes and lovely demon maidens. Sweet fragrance is in the air and is fused with sweet music. The soil here is white, black, purple, sandy, yellow, stony and also of gold.

Pātāla is also known as Nāgaloka where there are many demoniac serpents, the masters of Nāgaloka, such as Śaṅkha, Kulika, Mahāśaṅkha, Śveta, Dhanañjaya, Dhṛtarāṣṭra, Śaṅkhacūḍa, Kambala,

---

[16] In the Rigveda, the Sudarshana Chakra is stated to be Vishnu's symbol for the wheel of time.

Aśvatara and Devadatta. The chief among them is Vāsuki. They are all extremely angry, and they have many, many hoods—some snakes have five hoods, some seven, some ten, others a hundred and others a thousand. These hoods are bedecked with valuable gems, and the light emanating from the gems illuminates the entire planetary system of bila-svarga.

The importance of Patala to esoteric Buddhism lay in its role as the source of alchemy and magical science or vidyā, immortality and enjoyment, particularly the opportunity for the (male) vidyādhara to have intercourse with female non-humans. It was also viewed as a source of flowing waters.

Below the regions of Patala lies Naraka, the Hindu Hell—the realm of death where sinners are punished.

Alice attempting to play croquet with a live flamingo

Chapter 6

Xibalba

The Mayans also have their underworld land, Xibalba, roughly translated as "place of fright". It is ruled by the Maya death gods and their helpers. In 16th-century Verapaz, the entrance to Xibalba was traditionally held to be a cave in the vicinity of Cobán in Guatemala.

Cave systems in nearby Belize have also been referred to as the entrance to Xibalba. In some Maya areas, the Milky Way is viewed as the road to Xibalba. Xibalba is described in the Popol Vuh[17] as a court below the surface of the Earth associated with death and with twelve gods or powerful rulers known as the Lords of Xibalba.

The first among the Maya death gods ruling Xibalba were Hun-Came ("One Death") and Vucub-Came ("Seven Death"), though Hun-Came is the senior of the two. The remaining ten Lords are often referred to as demons and are given commission and domain over various forms of human suffering: to cause sickness, starvation, fear, destitution, pain, and, ultimately. death.

These ten Lords all work in pairs: Xiquiripat ("Flying Scab") and Cuchumaquic ("Gathered Blood"), who sicken people's blood; Ahalpuh ("Pus Demon") and Ahalgana ("Jaundice Demon"), who cause people's bodies to swell up; Chamiabac ("Bone Staff") and Chamiaholom ("Skull Staff"), who turn dead bodies into skeletons; Ahalmez ("Sweepings Demon") and Ahaltocob ('Stabbing Demon"), who hide in the unswept areas of people's houses and stab them to death; and Xic ("Wing") and Patan ("Packstrap"), who cause people to die coughing up blood while out walking on a road. The remaining residents of Xibalba are thought to have fallen under the dominion of one of these Lords, going about the face of the Earth to carry out their listed duties.

According to the Popol Vuh, chief among Xibalba's structures were the council place of the Lords, the five or six houses that served as the first tests of Xibalba, and the Xibalban ballcourt. Also mentioned are

---

[17] The foundational sacred narrative of the K'iche' people of Guatemala. It includes the Mayan creation myth.

the homes of the Lords, gardens, and other structures indicating that Xibalba was a great City.

As recounted in the Popol Vuh, the father and mother deities Xpiyacoc and Xmucane had two sons, Hunhun-Ahpu and Vukub-Hunahpu. The former had by a wife, Xbakiyalo, two sons, Hunbatz and Hunchouen, men full of wisdom and artistic genius. All of them were addicted to the recreation of dicing and playing at ball, and a spectator of their pastimes was Voc, the messenger of Hurakan.

Xbakiyalo having died, Hunhun-Ahpu and Vukub-Hunahpu played a game of ball, which in its progress took them into the vicinity of the realm of Xibalba, the underworld. This reached the ears of Hun-Came and Vukub-Came, who, after consulting their counsellors, challenged the strangers to a game of ball with the object of defeating and disgracing them.

The princes of Xibalba sent their four owl messengers to Hunhun-ahpu and Vukub-hunhun-ahpu, ordering them to come at once to the place of initiation in the Guatemalan mountains. Failing in the tests imposed by the princes of Xibalba, the two brothers—according to the ancient custom—paid with their lives for their shortcomings.

Hunhun-ahpu and Vukub-hunhun-ahpu were buried together, but the head of Hunhun-ahpu was placed among the branches of the sacred calabash tree, which grew in the middle of the road leading to the awful Mysteries of Xibalba. Immediately the calabash tree covered itself with fruit and the head of Hunhun-ahpu 'showed itself no more; for it reunited itself with the other fruits of the calabash tree.'

Now Xquiq was the virgin daughter of prince Cuchumaquiq. From her father she had learned of the marvelous calabash tree, and dearly wishing to possess some of its fruit, she journeyed alone to the sombre place where it grew. When Xquiq went to pick the fruit of the tree, some saliva from the mouth of Hunhun-ahpu fell into it and the head spoke to Xquiq, saying, 'This saliva and froth is my posterity which I have just given you. Now my head will cease to speak, for it is only the head of a corpse, which has no more flesh.'

Following the admonitions of Hunhun-ahpu, the young girl returned to her home. Her father, Cuchumaquiq, later discovering that she was about to become a mother, questioned her concerning the father of her child. Xquiq replied that the child was begotten while she was gazing upon the head of Hunhun-ahpu in the calabash tree and that she had lain with no man.

Cuchumaquiq, refusing to believe her story, at the instigation of the princes of Xibalba demanded her heart in an urn. Led away by her executioners, Xquiq pleaded with them to spare her life, which they agreed to do, substituting for her heart the fruit of a rubber tree whose sap was red and of the consistency of blood. When the princes of Xibalba placed the supposed heart upon the coals of the altar to be consumed, they were all amazed by the perfume that arose from it.

Xquiq gave birth to twin sons, who were named Hunahpu and Xbalanque whose lives were dedicated to avenging the deaths of Hunhun-ahpu and Vukub-hunhun-ahpu. In the Popul Vuh they are known as the divine Hero Twins.

The years passed and the two boys grew up to manhood and great were their deeds. Especially they excelled in a game called tennis but resembling hockey.

Hearing of the prowess of the youths, the princes of Xibalba asked: 'Who, then, are those who now begin again to play over our head… Are not Hunhun-aphu and Vukub-hunhun-ahpu dead, who wished to exalt themselves before our face?'

So the princes of Xibalba sent for the two youths, Hunahpu and Xbalanque, intent on destroying them during the seven days of the Mysteries. Before departing, the two brothers bade farewell to their grandmother, Xmucane, each planting in the midst of the house a cane plant, saying that as long as the cane lived she would know that they were alive. 'O, our grandmother, O, our mother, do not weep; behold the sign of our word which remains with you.'

Hunahpu and Xbalanque then departed, each with his blowpipe. For many days they journeyed along the perilous trail, descending through tortuous ravines and along precipitous cliffs, past strange birds and boiling springs, towards the sanctuary of Xibalba where, on their arrival, they commenced the undertaking of the seven ordeals of the Mysteries. As a preliminary the two adventurers crossed a river of mud and then a stream of blood, accomplishing these difficult feats by using their blowpipes as bridges. Continuing on their way, they reached a point where four roads converged—a black road, a white road, a red road and a green road.

Now Hunahpu and Xbalanque knew that their first test would consist of being able to discriminate between the princes of Xibalba and the wooden effigies robed to resemble them; also that they must call each of the princes by his correct name without having been given the information. To secure this information, Hunahpu pulled a hair from his leg, which hair then became a strange insect called Xan. Buzzing along the black road, the Xan entered the council chamber of the princes of Xibalba and stung the leg of the figure nearest the door, which it discovered to be a manikin. By the same artifice the second figure was proved to be of wood but upon stinging the third there was an immediate response. By stinging each of the twelve assembled princes in turn the insect thus discovered each one's name, for the princes called each other by name in discussing the cause of the mysterious bites. Having secured the desired information in this novel manner, the insect then flew back to Hunahpu and Xbalanque, who fearlessly approached the threshold of Xibalba and presented themselves to the twelve assembled princes.

When told to adore the king, Hunahpu and Xbalanque laughed for they knew that the figure pointed out to them was the lifeless manikin. The young adventurers thereupon addressed the twelve princes by name thus: 'Hail, Hun-came; hail, Vukub-came; hail, Xiquiripat; hail, Cuchumaquiq; hail, Ahalpuh; hail, Ahalcana; hail, Chamiabak; hail, Chamiaholom; hail, Quiqxic; hail, Patan; hail Quiqre; hail, Quiqrixqaq.'

When invited by the Xibalbians to seat themselves upon a great stone bench, Hunahpu and Xbalanque declined to do so, declaring that they well knew the stone to be heated so that they would be burned to death if they sat upon it. The princes of Xibalba then ordered Hunahpu and Xbalanque to rest for the night in the House of the Shadows. This completed the first degree of the Xibalbian Mysteries.

The second trial was given in the House of Shadows, where to each of the candidates was brought a pine torch and a cigar with the injunction that both must be kept alight throughout the entire night and yet each must be returned the next morning unconsumed. Knowing that death was the alternative to failure in the test, the young men burnt aras-feathers in place of the pine splinters, which they closely resembled, and also put fireflies on the tips of the cigars. Seeing the lights, those who watched felt certain that Hunahpu and Xbalanque had fallen into the trap but when morning came the torches and cigars were returned to the guards unconsumed and still burning. In amazement and awe, the princes of Xibalba gazed upon the unconsumed splinters and cigars for never before had these been returned intact.

The third ordeal took place in a cavern called the House of Spears. Here hour after hour the youths were forced to defend themselves against the strongest and most skillful warriors armed with spears. Hunahpu and Xbalanque pacified the spearmen, who thereupon ceased attacking them.

They then turned their attention to the second and most difficult part of the test: the production of four vases of the rarest flowers but which they were not permitted to leave the temple to gather. Unable to pass the guards, the two young men secured the assistance of the ants. These tiny creatures, crawling into the gardens of the temple, brought back the blossoms so that by morning the vases were filled. When Hunahpu and Xbalanque presented the flowers to the twelve princes, the latter, in amazement, recognising the blossoms as having been filched from their own private gardens. In consternation, the princes of Xibalba then counselled together how they could destroy the intrepid neophytes and then prepared for them the next ordeal.

For their fourth test, the two brothers were made to enter the House of Cold, where they remained for an entire night. The princes of Xibalba considered the chill of the icy cavern to be unbearable and it is described as "the abode of the frozen winds of the North". Hunahpu and Xbalanque, however, protected themselves from the deadening influence of the frozen air by building fires of pine cones, whose warmth caused the spirit of cold to leave the cavern so that the youths were not dead but full of life when day dawned. Even greater than before was the amazement of the princes of Xibalba when Hunahpu and Xbalanque again entered the Hall of Assembly in the custody of their guardians.

The fifth ordeal was also of a nocturnal nature. Hunahpu and Xbalanque were ushered into a great chamber, which was immediately filled with ferocious tigers. Here they were forced to remain throughout the night. The young men tossed bones to the tigers, which they ground to pieces with their strong jaws. Gazing into the House of the Tigers, the princes of Xibalba beheld the animals chewing the bones and said one to the other: 'They have at last learned (to know the power of Xibalba), and they have given themselves up to the beasts.' But when at dawn Hunahpu and Xbalanque emerged from the House of the Tigers unharmed, the Xibalbians cried: 'Of what race are those?' For they could not understand how any man could escape the tigers' fury. Then the princes of Xibalba prepared for the two brothers a new ordeal.

The sixth test consisted of remaining from sunset to sunrise in the House of Fire. Hunahpu and Xbalanque entered a large apartment arranged like a furnace. On every side the flames arose and the air was stifling; so great was the heat that those who entered this chamber could survive only a few moments. But at sunrise when the doors of the furnace were opened, Hunahpu and Xbalanque came forth unscorched by the fury of the flames. The princes of Xibalba, perceiving how the two intrepid youths had survived every ordeal prepared for their destruction, were filled with fear lest all the secrets of Xibalba should fall into the hands of the pair. So they prepared the last ordeal, an ordeal yet more terrible than any which had gone before, certain that the youths could not withstand this crucial test.

The seventh ordeal took placc in the House of the Bats. Here in a dark subterranean labyrinth lurked many strange and odious creatures of destruction. Huge bats fluttered dismally through the corridors and hung with folded wings from the carvings on the walls and ceilings. Here also dwelt Camazotz, the God of Bats, a hideous monster with the body of a man and the wings and head of a bat. Camazotz carried a great sword and, soaring through the gloom, decapitated with a single sweep of his blade any unwary wanderers seeking to find their way through the terror-filled chambers. Xbalanque passed successfully through this horrifying test but Hunahpu, caught off his guard, was beheaded by Camazotz. Later, Hunahpu was restored to life by magic.

In order to further astound their hosts, Hun-Ahpu and Xbalanque confided to two sorcerers named Xulu and Pacaw that the Xibalbans had failed because the animals were not on their side. Then, directing them what to do with their bones, they stretched themselves upon a funeral pile and died together. Their bones were beaten to powder and thrown into the river where they sank and were transformed into young men. On the fifth day they reappeared like men-fishes, and on the sixth in the form of ragged old men, dancing, burning and restoring houses, killing and restoring each other to life, with other wonders.

The princes of Xibalba, hearing of their skill, requested them to exhibit their magical powers, which they did by burning the royal palace and restoring it, killing and resuscitating the king's dog, cutting a man in pieces and bringing him to life again. The monarchs of Xibalba, anxious to experience the novel sensation of a temporary death, requested to be slain and resuscitated. They were speedily killed, but the wily brothers refrained from resuscitating their archenemies. Announcing their real names, the brothers proceeded to punish the princes of Xibalba. The game of ball forbidden them, they were to perform menial tasks, and only the beasts of the forest were they to hold in vassalage.

They appear after this to become a species of doubtful distinction as plutonic deities or demons. They are described as warlike, ugly as owls, inspiring evil and discord. Their faces were painted black and white to show their faithless nature.

Xmucane, waiting at home for the brothers, was alternately filled with joy and grief, as the canes grew green and withered, according to the varying fortunes of her grandsons. Meanwhile, the two young men were busied at Xibalba with paying fitting funeral honours to their father and uncle, who now mounted to heaven and became the sun and moon.

Later, the Hero Twins were thought to be instrumental in attempting to bring about the death of Zipacna. In Mayan mythology, Zipacna was a son of Vucub Caquix and Chimalmat and said to be very arrogant and violent. Zipacna was characterized as a large caiman and often boasted about creating mountains.

The Popol Vuh tells the story that one day Zipacna was basking on the beach when the Four Hundred Boys, who were attempting to construct a hut, disturbed him. They had felled a large tree to use as the central supporting log but were unable to lift it. Zipacna, being immensely strong, offered to carry the log for them, which he did. Although most translations of the Popol Vuh would seem to indicate this was done as a gesture of goodwill, it is generally agreed that Zipacna did so in a spirit of arrogance, mocking the boys for their inability to do so. The Four Hundred Boys decided it was not good that one man had such strength, and decided that Zipacna should be killed. They attempted to deceive Zipacna by asking him to dig a hole for their post, intending to thrust the massive column into the hole and kill him. Zipacna realized their deceit, however, and saved himself by surreptitiously digging a side tunnel and hiding inside it when the boys dropped the post in the hole. To complete the illusion of his death, Zipacna cried out in pain, and later allowed ants to carry bits of his hair and trimmings from his nails out of the hole, satisfying the boys that he had been killed. On the third day after their apparent success, the Four Hundred Boys finished the construction of their hut and celebrated both its completion and Zipacna's death by preparing wine and engaging in a drunken revelry. Zipacna emerged from his hole after the boys had passed out, and with his massive strength he felled the column and caused the house to crash down upon the sleeping boys, killing them all without a single survivor. After their death, the boys entered into the heavens as the open star cluster known as the Pleiades.

It has been remarked that the tests confronted by Hunahpu and Xbalanque are an exact counterpart of what happened during other great initiation ceremonies: the Eleusinian mysteries, the greater mysteries of Egypt, similar feats performed by the Indian Mahatmas, and Daniel who was initiated into the mysteries of the Chaldean Magi.

The tests are also analagous with the signs of the zodiac as employed in the Mysteries of the Egyptians, Chaldeans, and Greeks: Aries, crossing the river of mud; Taurus, crossing the river of blood; Gemini, detecting the two dummy kings; Cancer, the House of Darkness; Leo, the House of Spears; Virgo, the House of Cold (the trip to Hell); Libra, the House of Tigers (feline poise); Scorpio, the House of Fire; Sagittarius, the House of Bats, where the God Camazotz decapitates one of the heroes; Capricorn, the burning on the scaffold (the dual Phoenix); Aquarius, their ashes being scattered in a river; and Pisces, their ashes turning into man-fishes and later back into human form.

Commentators have also identified Xibalba with the ancient continent of Atlantis, observing that the twelve princes of Xibalba equate with the rulers of the Atlantean empire, and that the destruction of these princes by the magic of Hunahpu and Xbalanque are an allegorical depiction of the tragic end of Atlantis.

Alice in the Wonderland Hall, watching the receding figure of
the White Rabbit

Alice being given a royal ticking off by the Red Queen

Chapter 7

Hyperborea

In the annals of human history there exist certain realms, which although physically absent from our world hold a powerful grip on the human imagination. One such is Hyperborea, a land steeped in myth and mystery, a place of perpetual sunshine and utopian existence. For centuries, Hyperborea has beckoned to explorers, scholars, poets, and philosophers, drawing them into its enigmatic embrace.

Although the existence of a far-northern utopia has never been proven, these mythological realms have been equated to actual geographical areas including Sweden, Ireland, Romania, Celtic northern Europe in general, central Asia, or the shores of the Arctic Ocean.

The allure of Hyperborea lies not only in its evocative name but also in its elusiveness. This mythical land, shrouded in the mists of time, has no fixed location on our terrestrial maps. Instead, it resides in the realm of dreams, legends and the collective unconscious. Yet, it exerts a tangible influence on the human psyche, its existence echoing through the corridors of history and culture.

Hyperborea has also been a subject of interest in pseudoscientific and fringe theories. Some proponents of alternative history and extraterrestrial theories have posited that Hyperborea was not limited to Earth but was, in fact, a lost continent or even a celestial realm. These speculative ideas have led to various theories about the origins of Hyperborean civilization, including claims of advanced technologies and extraterrestrial contact. While such theories lack empirical evidence, they highlight the enduring allure of Hyperborea and its ability to inspire speculative thought beyond the confines of mainstream science.

The genesis of Hyperborea can be traced back to ancient Greece, where it first appeared in the writings of poets and historians. In Greek mythology, Hyperborea was often described as a paradisiacal realm located beyond the northern winds, a place where the sun never set and the people lived in harmony. This image of Hyperborea as an idyllic utopia captivated the minds of the Greeks and found expression in their art and literature. In the realm of myth, where gods and mortals intertwine, Hyperborea emerges as a land of unending fascination—a realm where reality and imagination blur. To unravel the mystery of Hyperborea, we must first journey back to its mythical origins where it found its earliest footprints in the works of poets and historians.

Hyperborea, as we know it today, first appeared in Greek writings, notably in the works of early poets and historians. The word "Hyperborea" itself is composed of two Greek words: "hyper" meaning "beyond" or "above", and "boreas" referring to the north wind. This etymology hints at the geographical direction in which this mythical land was situated—beyond the northern winds, in the far north.

Along with Thule, Hyperborea was one of several lands unknown to the Greeks and Romans. In their day there was little agrement as to the location of Hyperborea. The first notable mention of Hyperborea is attributed to the ancient Greek poet Hesiod, who lived around the 8th century BCE. In his epic poem "Works and Days", Hesiod describes the blessed existence of the Hyperborean people, who enjoyed perpetual spring and lived beyond the reach of harsh winter winds. They were, in essence, blessed with an idyllic and harmonious life, untouched by the travails of the mortal world.

Other early Greek commentators that mention Hyperborea are provided by Herodotus in his *Histories* dated c. 450 BCE. He records that Homer wrote of the fabled land in his lost work *Epigoni*. Additionally, he wrote that 7th-century BC poet Aristeas mentioned the Hyperboreans in a poem (now lost) called *Arimaspe.* In the poem Aristeas describes a journey to the Issedones people, who are estimated to have lived in the Kazakh Steppe. Beyond these lived the one-eyed Arimaspians, further on the gold-guarding griffins, and beyond these the Hyperboreans. Herodotus assumed that Hyperborea lay somewhere in Northeast Asia. However, Aelius Herodianus, a grammarian in the 3rd century, wrote that the mythical Arimaspi were identical to the Hyperboreans in physical appearance, and Stephanus of Byzantium in the 6th century agreed. The ancient poet Callimachus described the Arimaspi as having fair hair.

In his *Pythian Ode* Pindar, lyric poet from Thebes and a contemporary of Herodotus, described the Hyperboreans and tells of Perseus's journey to them. Other 5th-century BCE Greek authors, like Simonides of Ceos and Hellanicus of Lesbos, similarly described or referenced the Hyperboreans in their works.

One of the most enduring associations of Hyperborea in Greek mythology is with the god Apollo. Apollo's sanctuary at Delphi, located in central Greece, played a pivotal role in linking the mortal world to this mythical land. According to Greek myth, Apollo would visit the Hyperboreans during the winter months, which were considered sacred and blessed. During his absence, the sanctuary at Delphi remained closed to the public. This connection between Apollo, Delphi, and Hyperborea underscores the notion of Hyperborea as a place of divine significance—a realm where the gods themselves were intimately involved. It was as if Hyperborea existed on a higher plane, accessible only to the divine or the exceptionally blessed.

According to Herodotus, offerings from the Hyperboreans came to Scythia packed with straw, and they were passed from tribe to tribe until they arrived at Dodona and from there to other Greek peoples until they to came to Apollo's temple on Delos. He said they used this method because the first time the gifts were brought by two maidens, Hyperoche and Laodice, with an escort of five men but none of them returned. To prevent this, the Hyperboreans began to bring the gifts to their borders and ask their neighbours to deliver them to the next country and so on until they arrived in Delos.

Greek legend asserts that the Boreades, the descendants of Boreas and the snow-nymph Chione, founded the first theocratic monarchy on Hyperborea. This legend is found preserved in the writings of Aelian: 'This god [Apollon] has as priests the sons of Boreas [North Wind] and Chione [Snow], three in number, brothers by birth, and six cubits in height [about 2.7 metres]. Diodorus Siculus added: 'And the kings of this (Hyperborean) city and the supervisors of the sacred precinct are called Boreadae, since they are descendants of Boreas, and the succession to these positions is always kept in their family.' The Boreades were thus believed to be giant kings, around 10 feet tall, which ruled Hyperborea. No other physical descriptions of the Hyperboreans are provided in classical sources.

The ancient philosopher Pythagoras is one of the earliest thinkers to have associated Hyperborea with philosophical concepts. Pythagoras was known for his mystical and mathematical teachings, and he believed in the existence of a paradisiacal realm similar to Hyperborea, a place where the soul could attain purity and enlightenment. Pythagoras saw in Hyperborea a symbol of the soul's journey towards transcendence and the pursuit of knowledge and wisdom. In his teachings Pythagoras often referred to the Hyperboreans as exemplars of lives lived in accordance with higher principles.

The Neoplatonists, a school of thought that emerged in the late classical period, further developed the philosophical connotations of Hyperborea. Plotinus, the founder of Neoplatonism, saw in Hyperborea a representation of the divine realm, a place beyond the material world where the soul could achieve union with the One—the ultimate source of all reality. For the Neoplatonists, Hyperborea symbolized the highest spiritual attainment, a realm where the soul could escape the cycle of reincarnation and return to its divine origin. This association between Hyperborea and spiritual ascent had a profound influence on later philosophical thought and esoteric traditions.

In many versions of mythological storytelling, the Hyperboreans lived north of the Riphean Mountains, in Greco-Roman geography a supposed range located in the far north of Eurasia, which shielded the Hyperboreans from the effects of the cold North Wind.

Later writers disagreed on the existence and location of the Hyperboreans, with some regarding them as purely mythological, and others connecting them to real-world peoples and places in northern Eurasia, such as Britain, Scandinavia or Siberia.

In medieval and Renaissance literature, the Hyperboreans came to signify remoteness and exoticism. Modern scholars consider the Hyperborean myth to be an amalgam of ideas from ancient utopianism, "edge of the earth" stories, the cult of Apollo, and exaggerated reports of phenomena in northern Europe such as the Arctic "midnight sun".

Classical sources put forward a multitude of locations for the fabled land. Pausanias, a Greek traveller and geographer of the second century AD, spoke of 'the land of the Hyperboreans, men living beyond the home of Boreas.' Homer placed Boreas in Thrace, and therefore in his opinion Hyperborea was north of Thrace, in Dacia. Sophocles, Aeschylus, Simonides of Ceos and Callimachus also in their works placed Boreas in Thrace.

Others believed that the home of Boreas or the Riphean Mountains were in a different location. Hecataeus of Miletus stated that the Riphean Mountains were adjacent to the Black Sea. Alternatively, Pindar placed the home of Boreas, the Riphean Mountains and Hyperborea near the Danube. Heraclides Ponticus and Antimachus in contrast identified the Riphean Mountains with the Alps, and the Hyperboreans as a Celtic tribe (perhaps the Helvetii of the Swiss plateau) who lived just beyond them. Aristotle placed the Riphean Mountains on the borders of Scythia, and Hyperborea further north.

Later Roman and Greek sources continued to change the location of the Riphean mountains, the home of Boreas and Hyperborea supposedly located beyond them. However, all these sources agreed that these were all in the far north of Greece or southern Europe.

The ancient grammarian Simmias of Rhodes in the 3rd century BCE connected the Hyperboreans to the Massagetae, an ancient tribe in Cenral Asia, and Posidonius in the 1st century BCE to the Western Celts. Whereas, Pomponius Mela placed them even further north in the vicinity of the Arctic; while Strabo held that Hyperborea was a peninsula or island located beyond what is now France and stretches further north–south than east–west. Other descriptions put it in the general area of the Ural Mountains.

Later, Plutarch, writing in the 1st century CE, connected the Hyperboreans with the Gauls who had sacked Rome in the 4th century BC. The 2nd century CE Stoic philosopher Hierocles equated the Hyperboreans with the Scythians and the Riphean Mountains with the Ural Mountains. Clement of Alexandria and other early Christian writers also equated the Hyperboreans with the Scythians.

Legend told that the sun was supposed to rise and set only once a year in Hyperborea, which would place it above or upon the Arctic Circle or, more generally, in the arctic polar regions. Its people were said to live for a thousand years.

The ancient Greek writer Theopompus in his work *Philippica* claimed that a large race of soldiers from the island of Meropis planned to conquer Hyperborea; however, this plan was apparently abandoned, as the invading force realized that the Hyperboreans were too strong and too blessed to be conquered.

A celebrated Hyperborean legendary priest or shaman was known as "Abaris" or "Abaris the Healer", whom Herodotus first described. Plato regarded Abaris as a physician from the far north (in this context some classical sources mention Mongolia, another land associated with Hyperborea) while Strabo reported Abaris was Scythian.

While passing through Italy on his return home, on one occasion Abaris saw Pythagoras and identified him as the god for whom he himself served as a priest. Believing that Pythagoras was none other than Apollo himself, Abaris paid the philosopher homage by giving him a sacred dart that he had been carrying as a magical artefact to protect him on his travels, even to expel winds and cure pestilences from cities that requested his supernatural services. Pythagoras accepted the dart without expressing any amazement at the novelty of the thing. Then he took Abaris aside and showed him his golden thigh, as an indication that he was not wholly mistaken in his estimation of his divinity. Then Pythagoras described to Abaris several details of his distant Hyperborean temple as proof of his divine gifts.

Pythagoras also told Abaris that he came into incarnation to remedy and improve the condition of the human race, having assumed human form lest men, disturbed by the novelty of his transcendency, should avoid the disciplines he advised. He asked Abaris to stay with him for a period during which Pythagoras taught the priest physiology and theology and the mysterious arts of soothsaying by numbers, a purer and more divine method than studying the entrails of beasts and one much more pleasing to the celestial gods.

Pythagoras's contemporaries claimed that the philosopher was none other than Apollo reborn, arrived from Hyperborea to announce to mankind a new doctrine of hope and welcome. Later, Cicero saw that druidic doctrine, which included a belief in eternal life and the transmigration of souls, was Pythagorean in origin but a meld also of natural sciences and of Hindu and Babylonian traditions.

The druids taught that the earth and all that grows and walks upon it is a creation of Dispater, the Prince of Darkness and sovereign of pale souls and of the dead, guardian of all hidden treasure. The immortal soul was obliged to migrate from existence to existence to purify itself eventually and to reconnect with its divine essence and enter the world of pure spirit. The Druids' God was Belenus or Belis, a Celticised description for the Greek Apollo, the Lightbringer.

Six classical Greek authors came to identify the Hyperboreans with their Celtic neighbours in the north: Antimachus of Colophon, Protarchus, Heraclides Ponticus, Hecataeus of Abdera, Apollonius of Rhodes and Posidonius of Apamea. As the Riphean mountains of the mythical past were identified with the Alps of northern Italy, there was a geographic rationale for identifying the Hyperboreans with the Celts living in and beyond the Alps.

Herodotus placed the Hyperboreans beyond the Massagetae and Issedones, both Central Asian tribes-people. Heredotus's choice would have placed the Hyperboreans anywhere from Siberia to the southwestern slopes of the Altay Mountains, perhaps even beyond the Dzungarian Gate into northern Xinjiang in China.

The influential Russian philosopher, mystic and radical political theorist Aleksandr Dugin has touted ancient legends about the sunken city of Atlantis and the mythical civilisation Hyperborea in defense of his vision of a Russian Empire that might span from Vladivostok in the East to Dublin at the Western edge of Europe. He believes Russia is the modern-day reincarnation of the ancient Hyperboreans and that therefore it needs to stand at odds with the modern-day "Atlanteans", the United States.

Northern Europeans (Scandinavians), when confronted with the classical Greco-Roman culture of the Mediterranean, identified themselves with the Hyperboreans. This aligns with the traditional aspect of a perpetually sunny land beyond the north, since the Northern half of Scandinavia faces long days during high summer with no hour of darkness ("midnight sun"). This idea was especially strong during the 17th century in Sweden, where the later representatives of the ideology of Gothicism declared the Scandinavian peninsula both the lost Atlantis and the Hyperborean land.

The late British academic John G. Bennett wrote a research paper entitled "The Hyperborean Origin of the Indo-European Culture" (1963), claming that the Indo-European homeland was in the far north and which he considered the Hyperborea of classical antiquity. This idea was earlier proposed by Bal Gangadhar Tilak in his "The Arctic Home in the Vedas" (1903), as well as the Austro-Hungarian ethnologist Karl Penka ("Origins of the Aryans", 1883).

The subject of Hyperborea was popular among the late eighteenth and early twentieth century mystics and occult philosophers. Madame Blavatsky, René Guénon and Julius Evola all shared the belief in the Hyperborean polar origins of mankind. According to these esotericists, the Hyperborean people represented the Golden Age polar centre of civilization and spirituality, with mankind, instead of evolving from a common ape ancestor, progressively devolving into an apelike state as a result of straying, both physically and spiritually from its mystical otherworldly homeland in the Far North, succumbing to the "demonic" energies of the South Pole, the greatest point of materialization.

Blavatsky believed that there are seven root races assembling for our Earth; each divided into seven sub-races. Only five root races have appeared so far; the sixth, she said, is expected to emerge in the 28th century. She maintained that the second root race lived in Hyperborea. Its inhabitants were, she claimed, coloured golden yellow. She described Hyperborea as incorporating what are now Northern Canada, Greenland, Iceland, Scandinavia, Northern Russia and Kamchatka. The climate was tropical because Earth had not yet developed an axial tilt. The esoteric name of their continent is Plaksha and its people, described by Blavatsky as non-intelligent ethereal creatures, called themselves the Kimpurshas who reproduced by budding, a type of asexual reproduction.

The notion that Hyperborea was regarded by many in the ancient world as intimately associated with Britain is as strange as it is compelling. Hyperborea was firstly identified with Britain by Hecataeus of Abdera in the 4th century BCE. He wrote that the Hyperboreans had on their island 'a magnificent sacred precinct of Apollo and a notable temple which is adorned with many votive offerings and is spherical in shape.' Some scholars have identified this temple with Stonehenge, others with equally significant stone landscapes such as neighbouring Avebury or, according to John Toland in his 1726 work on the druids, with the megaliths of Callanish on the Isle of Lewis in Scotland.

Pseudo-Scymnus, around 90 BCE, wrote that the god Boreas dwelled at the extremity of Gaulish territory, and that he had a pillar erected in his name on the edge of the sea. Some have claimed that this is a geographical reference to northern France, and to Hyperborea as the British Isles, which lay just beyond the English Channel.

Ptolemy and Marcian of Heraclea both placed Hyperborea in the North Sea, which they called the "Hyperborean Ocean".

Thule
Thule is the most northerly location mentioned in ancient Greek and Roman literature and cartography. One also sees mention in the old texts to "Ultima Thule" in classical and medieval literature, a reference to any distant place located beyond the "borders of the known world". Modern interpretations have included Orkney, Shetland, Northern Scotland, the island of Saaremaa (Ösel) in Estonia, and the Norwegian island of Smøla. In broad terms one can regard Thule in the mythological context as a place or aspect of the arctic region.

Fourth century geographer, explorer and astronomer Pytheas of Massalia (modern-day Marseille), made a voyage to northwestern Europe. On this voyage, he circumnavigated and visited a considerable part of modern-day Great Britain and Ireland. He was the first known scientific visitor to see and describe the Arctic, polar ice and the Celtic and Germanic tribes. He is also the first person on record to describe the midnight sun. On his travels he came across a strange land far north ('six days sail north of Orcades') where the sun would never set in the summer and where the ocean was solid frozen. Nobody knows for

86

certain how far north Pytheas travelled. He named this place Thule and described it as a place that was inhabited by people he called the Hyperboreans. He also said they live on an island located to the North of Britannia. It is a place 'beyond the north wind.'

The first century BCE Greek astronomer Geminus of Rhodes claimed that the name Thule went back to an archaic word for the polar night phenomenon: "the place where the sun goes to rest". Avienius in his *Ora Maritima* added that Thule's summer night lasted only two hours, a clear reference to the arctic region and the midnight sun. The mid-first century Roman geographer Pomponius Mela placed Thule north of Scythia.

Strabo, in his *Geographica* (c. 30 CE), mentions Thule in describing Eratosthenes' calculation of 'the breadth of the inhabited world'' and notes that Pytheas says it 'is a six days' sail north of Britain, and is near the frozen sea.' He then casts doubts on this claim, writing that Pytheas has 'been found, upon scrutiny, to be an arch falsifier, but the men who have seen Britain and Ireland do not mention Thule, though they speak of other islands, small ones, about Britain.'

Strabo added, 'Now Pytheas of Massilia tells us that Thule, the most northerly of the Britannic Islands, is farthest north, and that there the circle of the summer tropic is the same as the Arctic Circle. But from the other writers I learn nothing on the subject – neither that there exists a certain island by the name of Thule, nor whether the northern regions are inhabitable up to the point where the summer tropic becomes the Arctic Circle.'

Strabo ultimately concludes: 'Concerning Thule, our historical information is still more uncertain, on account of its outside position; for Thule, of all the countries that are named, is set farthest north.'

Citing Pytheas, Strabo described the inhabitahts of Thule in some detail. 'The people live on millet and other herbs, and on fruits and roots; and where there are grain and honey the people get their beverage also from them. As for the grain, since they have no pure sunshine, they pound it out in large storehouses, after first gathering in the ears thither; for the threshing floors become useless because of this lack of sunshine and because of the rains.'

In 77 CE, Pliny the Elder published his Natural History in which he also cites Pytheas's claim that Thule is a six-day journey north of Britain. Then when discussing the islands around Britain, he writes: 'The farthest of all, which are known and spoke of, is Thule; in which there be no nights at all, as we have declared, about mid-summer, namely when the Sun passes through the sign Cancer; and contrariwise no days in mid-winter: and each of these times they suppose, do last six months, all day, or all night.' Finally, in refining the island's location, he places it along the most northerly parallel of those he describes: 'Last of all is the Scythian parallel, from the Rhiphean hills into Thule: wherein (as we said) it is day and night continually by turns (for six months).'

The Roman historian Tacitus (c. 56–c. 120 CE) in his book chronicling the life of his father-in-law, Agricola, describes how the Romans knew that Britain (in which Agricola was Roman commander) was an island rather than a continent by circumnavigating it. Tacitus writes of a Roman ship visiting Orkney and claims that the ship's crew even sighted Thule. However, their orders were not to explore there as winter was at hand. Some scholars believe that Tacitus was referring to Shetland.

The third-century Latin grammarian Gaius Julius Solinus (died 400 CE) wrote in his *Polyhistor* that 'Thyle, which was distant from Orkney by a voyage of five days and nights, was fruitful and abundant in the lasting yield of its crops.'

The 4th century Virgilian commentator Servius also believed that Thule sat close to Orkney: 'Thule; an island in the Ocean between the northern and western zone, beyond Britain, near Orkney and Ireland; in this Thule, when the sun is in Cancer, it is said that there are perpetual days without nights...'

Other late classical writers such as Orosius (384–420) describe Thule as being north and west of both Ireland and Britain, strongly suggesting that it was Iceland.

The historian Procopius, writing in the first half of the sixth century, stated that Thule is a large island in the north inhabited by 25 tribes. It is believed that Procopius was actually speaking about a part of Scandinavia, since several tribes are easily identified including the Geats (Gautoi) in present-day Sweden and the Sami people (Scrithiphini). He also writes that when the Herules (an early Germanic people) returned, they passed the Warini (another Germanic tribe) and the Danes and then crossed the sea to Thule, where they settled beside the Geats (the Goths).

The Irish monk Dicuil in his *Liber De Mensura Orbis Terrae* (written c. 825 CE) after quoting various classical sources says of Thule:

It is now thirty years since clerics, who had lived on the island from the first of February to the first of August, told me

88

that not only at the summer solstice, but in the days round about it, the sun setting in the evening hides itself as though behind a small hill in such a way that there was no darkness in that very small space of time, and a man could do whatever he wished as though the sun were there, even remove lice from his shirt, and if they had been on a mountain-top perhaps the sun would never have been hidden from them. In the middle of that moment of time it is midnight at the equator, and thus, on the contrary, I think that at the winter solstice and for a few days about it dawn appears only for the smallest space at Thule, when it is noon at the equator. Therefore those authors are wrong and give wrong information, who have written that the sea will be solid about Thule, and that day without night continues right through from the vernal to the autumnal equinox, and that vice versa night continues uninterrupted from the autumnal to the vernal equinox, since these men voyaged at the natural time of great cold, and entered the island and remaining on it had day and night alternately except for the period of the solstice. But one day's sail north of that they did find the sea frozen over. There are many other islands in the ocean to the north of Britain which can be reached from the northern islands of Britain in a direct voyage of two days and nights with sails filled with a continuously favourable wind. A devout priest told me that in two summer days and the intervening night he sailed in a two-benched boat and entered one of them. There is another set of small islands, nearly all separated by narrow stretches of water; in these for nearly a hundred years hermits sailing from our country, Ireland, have lived. But just as they were always deserted from the beginning of the world, so now because of the Northman pirates they are emptied of anchorites, and filled with countless sheep and very many diverse kinds of seabirds. I have never found these islands mentioned in the authorities.'

By the Late Middle Ages and the early modern period, the Greco-Roman Thule was often identified with the real Iceland or Greenland. Sometimes Ultima Thule was a Latin name for Greenland, and Thule was used for Iceland. By the late 19th century, however, Thule was frequently identified with Norway.

The concept of Thule played a pivotal role in Arctic exploration during the Age of Discovery (15th to the 17th century). European explorers, inspired by the legacy of Pytheas and fuelled by the desire to find a northern passage to Asia, sought to reach the mythical land of Thule. They believed that by reaching it they would discover the fabled Northwest Passage—a direct route to the riches of the East.

Explorers such as Martin Frobisher, John Davis and William Baffin embarked on perilous voyages in search of Thule and the Northwest Passage. These voyages were fraught with danger, as explorers faced treacherous ice floes, frigid temperatures and unknown lands. Many of these early explorations led to the mapping of the Arctic region and the documentation of its geography. However, Thule remained an elusive goal.

The inclusion of Thule on early maps and nautical charts during the Age of Exploration further solidified its place in geographical discourse. Thule, often depicted as an island or a distant landmass, appeared on maps alongside other northern features. Maps of the time portrayed the Arctic as a mysterious and foreboding region where Thule symbolized the ultimate northern boundary. The presence of Thule on these maps underscored its symbolic and geographical importance. Mapmakers struggled to accurately locate Thule, reflecting the uncertainty surrounding its existence. Nevertheless, the concept of Thule persisted in cartography, serving as a beacon for explorers seeking to conquer the Arctic.

Alice with King and messenger; Alice upsetting the courtroom

Alice feathering in the bulrushes with the Sheep-shopkeeper

Chapter 8

The Hole at the Pole

One aspect by which Hyperborea influenced scientific thought was through polar exploration. In the 19th and early 20th centuries, explorers ventured into the Arctic regions in search of uncharted territories, often with the hope of discovering remnants of ancient civilizations. Some believed that the Arctic held the key to unlocking the mysteries of Hyperborea, the fabled land of antiquity.

The search for Hyperborea intersected with the exploration of the Polar Regions, as adventurers like Admiral Richard E. Byrd and Roald Amundsen ventured into the Arctic and Antarctic, seeking to unveil the secrets hidden beneath the ice. While these expeditions did not lead to the discovery of Hyperborea itself, they underscored the enduring fascination with this mythical land and its potential connection to ancient civilizations.

The Inuit people have legends that tell of a beautiful land in the polar north, a land of perpetual light where there is no darkness or a bright sun. Incongruously, this wonderful land has a mild climate where large lakes never freeze, tropical animals roam in herds, and birds of many colours cloud the sky. It is a land of perpetual youth where people live for thousands of years in peace and happiness. They believe that after death the soul descends beneath the earth, first to an abode rather like purgatory; good souls then descending further to a place of perfect bliss where the sun never sets.

In the latter part of the twelfth century, Welshman Walter Mapes in his collection of anecdotes tells of a prehistoric king of Briton called Herla. During his travels Herla met with the Skraelings or Inuits, who took him beneath the earth. This is a common theme of many early legends that tell of people going under the earth into a strange realm and remaining there for a long period of time and later returning. Irish myth speaks of a land far to the North where the sun always shines and it is always summer. Those who had been drawn there and later returned were thereafter never satisfied with their own country.

The Japanese paradise was situated "on the top of the globe" and at the same time "at the centre of the Earth". It was called the "island of the congealed drop". Its first roof-pillar was the Earth's axis and over it was the pivot of the vault of heaven.

The Chinese terrestrial paradise, round in form, is described not only as at the centre of the Earth but also as directly under Shang-te's heavenly palace, which is declared to be in the polestar and is sometimes called the "palace of the centre".

In my second book for AUP,[18] I described unusual events surrounding the movements of German U-Boats in the latter days of WWII. The size of the U-boat fleet in the early months of 1945 was actually increasing, reaching its peak strength of 463 submarines in March of that year. After Germany surrendered in May 1945 U-boats gave themselves up to the Allies but their crews scuttled a further 203.

By 10 June 1945, when an unmarked German U-boat surrendered to the Argentine Navy, the whereabouts of the other 100 U-boats were still a mystery. Gradually, a number began to appear here and there but ultimately there were still more than forty unaccounted for. A suspicion grew that the missing U-boats were part of an Antarctic puzzle that Britain had been piecing together since Marshall Hermann Göring sent Captain Alfred Ritscher on a polar mission in 1938. With Britain's Intelligence network providing virtually all the information to its allies via the Enigma machine and its immense European spy network, a picture slowly began to emerge.

When U-boats were captured off the southern coast of South America, minus their commanding officers, it was assumed at first that they had dropped off the officers in Argentina then gone off in another direction to hide the location where they had disembarked. But the U-boat crews said something different. Bizarrely, many reported that they had landed their officers in an underground base in Antarctica, which they had entered from beneath the ice-shelf.

A strong contender for the location of the Antarctic base was a part of Queen Maud Land, "Neu-Schwabenland", which had been claimed by Germany between 1938 and 1945. The Reich had had a prior interest in Antarctica for many years but in 1938 this intensified with the mounting of an air and sea expedition whose purpose was to claim possession of a huge portion of the subcontinent in the name of the

---

[18] Graddon, N., *The Mystery of U-33: Hitler's Secret Envoy,* AUP, 2011.

Fatherland. Captain Ritscher's flagship was the *Schwabenland*. To prepare them for their mission, the project planners invited the great American polar explorer Admiral Richard E. Byrd to lecture them on what to expect but the renowned American explorer declined. A second expedition under Ritscher followed in 1939.

Richard Evelyn Byrd Jr. (1888–1957), was a pioneering American aviator, polar explorer, organizer of polar logistics, and a naval officer. Aircraft flights in which he served as a navigator and expedition leader included those during during which he crossed segments of the Arctic Ocean and the Antarctic Plateau. Byrd is known for discovering Mount Sidley, the largest dormant volcano in Antarctica. He said that his expeditions had been the first to reach by air both the North Pole (a claim that is disputed) and the South Pole.

Germany's "Neu-Schwabenland" was named after Swabia, one of the original duchies of the German Kingdom. Swabia was home to the powerful Hohenstaufen Dynasty, which ruled the Holy Roman Empire in the 12th and 13th centuries. Frederick Barbarossa was the greatest of the Hohenstaufen kings and a wielder of the Holy Lance, which the Roman soldier Longinus used to pierce the side of Jesus on the Cross. It is claimed that Hitler believed he was a reincarnation of Barbarossa. He named one of his houses after him and dubbed the invasion of Russia, Operation Barbarossa.

Bizarrely, Adolf Hitler was fascinated by a belief that had gained considerable currency among the "New Age" faddists of the day that the earth was hollow. The theory held that the entrances into inner earth were at the North and South Poles, from which one could travel to the mythical land of Agarthi in the Earth's centre, whose residents were survivors from the legendary antediluvian land of Hyperborea—the realm of the original Aryans.

On 18 July 1945 newspapers around the world were bearing headlines about Antarctica. The *New York Times* stated, "Antarctic Haven Reported", whilst others proclaimed that, "Hitler had been at the South Pole". It was claimed that these sensational headlines were based, in part, on fact.

While Britain still possesed strategically based territories in the Falklands and Antarctica and one of the world's largest navies, it was ideally positioned among the Allies to investigate claims of a polar Nazi stronghold. With 16 German U-boats sunk in the South Atlantic area between October 1942 and September 1944 and most of those sunk engaged in covert activities, Britain had long been aware of Neu-

Schwabenland being a possible base. It was not until after the war in Europe had ended in May 1945 that the world awoke to the possibility of the actual existence of such a base. Interrogations of the captains of both the U-977 and U-530 served to deepen the Allies' suspicions.

The German Antarctica Expedition of 1938-39 overflew nearly one-fifth of the continent, taking some 11,000 photographs. The expedition's aircraft also dropped several thousand small Nazi flags as well as special metal poles with the expedition's insignia and the swastika, claiming the territory for Germany.

Ostensibly, the expeditions were undertaken to investigate the feasibility of whaling operations in the region but in reality they were carried out to assess if Antarctica could suitably accommodate a military base for planes, submarines and long-range missiles.

During the expedition several ice-free regions with lakes and signs of vegetation (mostly lichen and moss) were found in the territory's interior. The expedition's geologists said that this phenomenon was due to hot springs or other geothermal sources. This discovery, it is claimed, led Reichsführer-SS Heinrich Himmler to draw up a plan to build a permanent base in Antarctica.

Under the command of Captain Heinrich Brodda, U-209 is said to have made a trip to Antarctica in 1942 to explore various ice caverns discovered during Admiral Ritscher's 1939 excursion. One of the caverns investigated was found to to contain an immense hole spanned by a bridge of emerald green ice, which appeared to be "bottomless". A number of tunnels were seen to lead into the depths of the mountain from which emanated strange whispering sounds that resembled human voices.

Colonel Howard A. Buechner, the first American physician to enter Dachau in May 1945, wrote[19] that in 1943 U-629, commanded by OLt.z.S Hans-Helmuth Bugs, travelled to Antarctica to build a permanent entrance to the Emerald Cave with special cold-resistant metal. Perhaps indicating a successful outcome to this mission Admiral Dönitz stated in 1943: 'The German submarine fleet is proud of having built for the Führer, in another part of the world, a Shangri-La on land, an impregnable fortress.'

Buechner also mentions unsubstantiated stories of several follow-up submarine missions in 1942-1945, during which purportedly a second

---

[19] Beuchner Colonel Howard A., Bernhart Captain W., *Adolf Hitler and the Secrets of the Holy Lance,* Thunderbird Press Inc, Metairie, Louisiana, 1989.

Berchtesgaden was constructed somewhere on Antarctica. He makes reference, too, of a U-boat excursion to Tierra del Fuego where a replica of Hitler's Berghof was built.

For more than eighty years rumours about an Antarctic base codenamed "Station 211" have excited historians and researchers. Some researchers claim that Hitler's deputy, Rudolf Hess, was entrusted with coordinating the effort to build Station 211. Most of the rumours agree that Station 211, if it really existed, was located inside a prominent ice-free mountain in the Muhlig-Hofmann Mountains of Neu-Schwabenland.

In 1946-47 the United States Navy undertook Operation HIGHJUMP, officially titled "The United States Navy Antarctic Developments Program, 1946–1947" (also called Task Force 68). Organized by Rear Admiral Richard E. Byrd, Jr, HIGHJUMP's declared mission was to establish the Antarctic research base, Little America IV. Task Force 68 included 4,700 men, 70 ships, and 33 aircraft. Its detailed objectives were:

➤ Training personnel and testing equipment in frigid conditions;
➤ Consolidating and extending the United States' sovereignty over the largest practicable area of the Antarctic continent (publicly denied as a goal before the expedition ended);
➤ Determining the feasibility of establishing, maintaining and utilizing bases in the Antarctic and investigating possible base sites;
➤ Developing techniques for establishing, maintaining and utilizing air bases on ice, with particular attention to later applicability of such techniques to operations in interior Greenland, where conditions are comparable to those in the Antarctic;
➤ Amplifying existing stores of knowledge of electromagnetic, geological, geographic, hydrographic and meteorological propagation conditions in the area;
➤ Supplementary objectives of the Nanook expedition (a smaller equivalent conducted off eastern Greenland).

It is suspected that during HIGHJUMP Admiral Byrd searched for Station 211.

The prospect of post-war Germany establishing a secret underground base in Antarctica was of huge concern. Beginning 30 December 1946, Byrd's ships variously arrived at three different rendezvous points inside the Antarctic Circle.

What, if anything, did Admiral Byrd encounter? An early casualty of "Byrd's War" was the submarine USS *Sennet*. The official story is that the ice proved to be too dangerous for the vessel, which was towed back to Scott Island but there has been considerable speculation that she hit German anti-submarine defences.

On another occasion, a PBM flying boat, *George One*, struck the top of a mountain and went down killing three.

Scores of aerial mapping flights were made deep into the heart of the frozen continent, including several overflights of the South Pole. In total over 73,000 photographs were taken but, surprisingly, only a few thousand were said to be of any value. The problem was blamed on a lack of adequate ground control points, which resulted in a vast number of meaningless pictures of ice, or so it was claimed.

The following year a much smaller expedition, Operation Windmill, was launched to get these much-needed coordinates. Some researchers have suggested that Windmill's real purpose was to see if Station 211 was still occupied.

One of the most remarkable expeditionary discoveries was that of "Bunger's Oasis". During an exploratory flight PBM pilot Lieutenant Commander David E. Bunger and his flight crew saw a dark spot rising up over the barren white horizon before them. To their complete disbelief, as they drew closer they saw a 'land of blue and green lakes and brown hills in an otherwise limitless expanse of ice.' Several days later Bunger and his crew returned for another look, finding one of the lakes big enough to land on.

Bunger carefully landed the plane and slowly came to a stop. The water was actually quite warm for Antarctica, about 30°C, as the men dipped their hands in up to the elbow. The lake's distinctive colour was an effect of a great profusion of red, blue and green algae.

Byrd later wrote that the airmen, 'seemed to have dropped out of the twentieth century into a landscape of thousands of years ago when land was just starting to emerge from one of the great ice ages.' He described the discovery as, 'by far the most important so far as the public interest was concerned of the expedition.'

There are elements here mindful of Edgar Rice Burroughs's classic story *The Land that Time Forgot*, in which a Jurassic nightmare confronts the crew of First World War U-boat 33 when it surfaces in a lagoon on the uncharted island of Caprona.

The official record of the Byrd missions appears innocuous yet there have been persistent rumours of violent battles, large-scale casualties, planes shot down, and more.

Byrd's log entry for a flight made on 19 February 1947 reportedly contains sensational remarks, among them: 'Ahead we spot what seems to be a city,' and 'my God, off our port and starboard wings are a strange type of aircraft... they are closing rapidly... they're disc-shaped... with Swastika markings.'

According to investigator Alan DeWalton, Admiral Byrd stated in a press conference that the Antarctic continent should be surrounded by a 'wall of defence installations since it represented the last line of defence for America.'

Another claim made by investigators is that on his return to the U.S.A. Admiral Byrd flew into a rage in front of the President and Joint Chiefs of Staff, while urging that Antarctica be turned into a thermonuclear test range.

The question has been posed that if the Antarctic accounts are little more than wild tales then why did Captain Richard H. Cruzen, the operational commander of the expedition, order its abrupt end after just eight weeks when they had enough provisions for six to eight months in the polar region?

In Admiral Byrd's own words (press release of 12 November 1946) the mission was 'primarily of a military nature.' Byrd also spoke of 'flying objects that could fly from pole to pole at incredible speeds' (*El Mercurio*, 5 March 1947—Admiral Byrd interviewed by Lee van Atta).

During the period between 1956 and 1960 a Norwegian expedition mapped most of Queen Maud Land from land surveys and air photos. Remarkably, they did find an ice-free mountain that matched the description of the one stated in the Station 211 rumours. They called it Svarthamaren (the black hammer).

The site has been designated an Antarctic Specially Protected Area and Site of Special Scientific Interest under the Antarctic Conservation Act of 1978, listed as an 'exceptional natural research laboratory for ornithological research on the Antarctic petrel, snow petrel and south polar skua and their adaptation to breeding in the inland / interior of Antarctica.' Access is limited to a handful of selected scientists.

James Robert, WWII historian and writer, interviewed an (unnamed) British wartime SAS officer described by Robert as the last survivor of the Neu-Schwabenland campaign. According to Robert, during the officer's four-week pre-mission training on the island of South Georgia he was told that he would be one of a party investigating anomalous activities around the Mühlig-Hoffmann Mountains from the British base in Maudheim in Antarctica. Antarctica, he was told, was 'Britain's secret war.'[20] Maudheim was within 200 miles of where the Nazis had supposedly built their Antarctic base.

In the summer of 1944 British scientists and commandos had found an "ancient tunnel". Under orders, the thirty-strong force went through the tunnel but only two returned before the Antarctic winter set in.

During the winter months the two survivors made absurd claims over the radio about "Polar Men", ancient tunnels and Nazis. Radio contact was finally lost in July 1945. The last broadcast concluded abruptly with an anguished scream: '...the Polar Men have found us!'

Against this macabre backdrop the SAS mission took place. The team found one survivor who said that in Bunker One would be found the other soldier. The bunker door was opened and an unrecognisable figure dashed out. Inside was the soldier's comrade. His throat had been ripped open and, gruesomely, he had been stripped to the bone.

Under questioning the surviving soldier described finding a tunnel, which led to a vast abnormally warm underground cavern filled with lakes. Startlingly, the cavern was lit artificially. Investigation showed that the Nazis had constructed a huge base inside the caverns and had even built docks for U-boats. The survivor reported that 'hangars for strange planes and excavations galore' had been documented. The British exploration team had been spotted and all executed except for the two soldiers.

The survivor said that the "Polar Men" were a product of Nazi science, although the SAS veteran's account does not elaborate on how he arrived at this conclusion. The team captured and killed one of the Polar Men and the mission scientist declared that he was human but had somehow been able to produce more hair and withstand the cold far more effectively. The survivor went on to say that the Nazis' power source was volcanic, which gave them heat for steam and also helped to produce electricity.

The scientist in the SAS man's party dismissed most of what was divulged and rebuked the survivor for his lack of scientific education, implying that his revelations could not possibly be true.

Nine SAS commandos entered the tunnel, eventually reaching the vast lit cavern. From their place of concealment they were astounded to

_____

[20] Robert J., *Britain's Secret War in Antarctica*, NEXUS Magazine, volume 12, number 5, 2005.

see a great number of people scurrying antlike around the cavern. They were also confronted by a staggering amount of construction activity.

After two days of reconnaissance mines were placed. At the same time a hostage was taken as well as physical proof of the base (including the slain "Polar Man") and photographs of advanced Nazi technology. The mines destroyed much of the cavern's infrastructure and closed the tunnel, but seven of the team were killed in heavy fighting during the retreat from the scene.

On their return to South Georgia the mission team was ordered never to reveal what it had seen, heard or encountered. The tunnel was explained away as glacial erosion. The Polar Men were merely 'unkempt soldiers that had gone crazy.'

Stories about U-boat activity in the area continued for many years after the war. A French newsagency reported in September 1946 that: 'the continuous rumours about German U-boat activity in the region of Tierra del Fuego between the southernmost tip of Latin America and the continent of Antarctica are based on true happenings.'

France Soir then published an account describing the Icelandic whaler *Juliana*'s purported encounter with a U-Boat eighteen months after the cessation of hostilities. The *Juliana* was in the Antarctic region around the Malvinas Islands (today the British Falklands) when a large German submarine surfaced and raised the German official Flag of Mourning—red with a black edge. The submarine commander sent out a boarding party, which approached the *Juliana* in a rubber dinghy. The boarding party demanded of the whaler's Captain Hekla part of his fresh food stocks. The German officer spoke correct English and paid for his provisions in U.S. dollars, giving Hekla a bonus of $10 for each member of the *Juliana* crew.

Whilst the foodstuffs were being transferred the U-boat commander informed Captain Hekla of the exact location of a large school of whales, which were subsequently found in precisely that region. Critics of this account have claimed that Icelandic whalers have never operated in the South Atlantic and, moreover, that there has never been a whaler named the *Juliana*. They also point out that Hekla is an active volcano in Iceland, not a name, and that 99 percent of all Icelandic last names for males end in "-son".

Author Wilhelm Landig claimed that it was not just in Antarctica that Nazi strongholds were established. During WWII Landig held a senior position in the central Nazi archive in Berlin where information from all around the world came in for analysis and filing. In 1971

Landig published *Kampf gegen Thule* (Battle against Thule), later republished as *Götzen gegen Thule* (Godlets against Thule). Landig claimed that his book was not a work of fiction but one based on facts that his higher-ups had given him leave to publish.

Styling himself as a "man in the know", Landig writes extensively in *Götzen gegen Thule* about the Nazis' polar bases, which included the Canadian Arctic, the "Alps" on the Argentinc-Chilean border (reportedly named Colonia Dignidad), and a base in Eastern Greenland called by the Germans Biber Damm (Beaver Dam), which Landig said was accessed via U-boat through underwater tunnels. This method of access was also described for reaching the base at Neu- Schwabenland.

In fact, this type of entrance was actually built. An example can be seen at the German base on the island of Fuerteventura in the Canary Islands. Steven Spielberg is said to have got the idea for the submarine base scene in *Raiders of the Lost Ark* from the Beaver Dam facility, which some researchers claim was a secret joint Nazi-NATO base until well after the war.

Landig also provides a dramatic description of the Ark of the Covenant as an ancient day "Weapon of Mass Destruction" wielded by Israeli sorcerers against the first (pre-flood) Aryans, sensational images brought to cinematic life in the final island scene of *Raiders of the Lost Ark* when archaeologist René Belloq (an ill-deserved synonym for Grail historian Otto Rahn) and his Nazi cohorts are incendiarised by the Light of God released from the Ark.

In another of his works Landig claimed that Neu-Schwabenland was abandoned around 1959-1960 because its inhabitants, having no natural immunity due to the absence of germs in the pure air of Antarctica, suffered sickness epidemics when new arrivals arrived with nothing more serious as a chill.

It does appear that the Germans made their mark in the South Pole. However, what they discovered does not compare to what Admiral Byrd recorded in his diary as having witnessed.

Before embarking on Operation HIGHJUMP Byrd made a mysterious statement: 'I'd like to see that land beyond the Pole. That area beyond the Pole in the center of the great unknown.'

In the cockpit of Byrd's plane was a powerful, two-way radio. On an occasion when Byrd and his scientific companions took off from their base at the South Pole, they managed to fly 1700 miles beyond it. That is when the radio in Byrd's plane was put into use to report something utterly incredible.

Below them lay a great strange valley. For some unknown reason, the valley was not ice-covered as one would have expected in the frigid Antarctic. It was green and luxuriant. There were mountains with thick forests of trees; there was lush grass and underbrush. Most amazingly, a huge animal was observed moving through the underbrush.

It appeared that in a land of ice, snow and almost perpetual deep-freeze, Byrd had discovered a most unusual valley just beyond the South Pole, where the weather temperature was evidently something like 75 degrees.

Suddenly press and radio reporting was hushed up. After the first brief messages leaked through to newspapers, no further confirmation of the big discovery was given.

According to Byrd's diary, the government ordered the admiral to remain silent on what he witnessed during his Arctic assignment. Byrd subsequently prefaced his sensational diary account with these words:

Did Byrd find Agarttha? Who was the "Master"? Considering the different sources that have emerged describing Byrd's amazing journey into the Northern Polar opening, the story should now be clear and free of controversy but doubts persist. Allegedly, Byrd wrote a full account of his visit to the pole, which was reproduced in *The Missing Diary of Admiral Richard E. Byrd* by Abelard Productions in 1990. Here in full is the sensational text of what is claimed constitutes Admiral Byrd's diary entry: *The Exploration Flight Over the North Pole*:

I must write this diary in secrecy and obscurity. It concerns my Arctic flight of the nineteenth day of February in the year of Nineteen and Forty-Seven. There comes a time when the rationality of men must fade into insignificance and one must accept the inevitability of the Truth! I am not at liberty to disclose the following documentation at this writing... perhaps it shall never see the light of public scrutiny, but I must do my duty and record here for all to read one day. In a world of greed and exploitation of certain of mankind can no longer suppress that which is truth.

FLIGHT LOG - BASE CAMP ARCTIC - 2/19/1947

0600 Hours- All preparations are complete for our flight northward and we are airborne with full fuel tanks at 0610 Hours.

103

0620 Hours- fuel mixture on starboard engine seems too rich, adjustment made and Pratt Whittneys are running smoothly.

0730 Hours- Radio Check with base camp. All is well and radio reception is normal.

0740 Hours- Note slight oil leak in starboard engine, oil pressure indicator seems normal, however.

0800 Hours- Slight turbulence noted from easterly direction at altitude of 2321 feet, correction to 1700 feet, no further turbulence, but tail wind increases, slight adjustment in throttle controls, aircraft performing very well now.

0815 Hours- Radio Check with base camp, situation normal.

0830 Hours- Turbulence encountered again, increase altitude to 2900 feet, smooth flight conditions again.

0910 Hours- Vast Ice and snow below, note coloration of yellowish nature, and disperse in a linear pattern. Altering course foe a better examination of this color pattern below, note reddish or purple color also. Circle this area two full turns and return to an assigned compass heading. Position check made again to base camp, and relay information concerning colorations in the Ice and snow below.

0910 Hours- Both Magnetic and Gyro compasses beginning to gyrate and wobble, we are unable to hold our heading by instrumentation. Take bearing with Sun compass , yet all seems well. The controls are seemingly slow to respond and have sluggish quality, but there is no indication of Icing!

0915 Hours- In the distance is what appears to be mountains.

0949 Hours- 29 minutes elapsed flight time from the first sighting of the mountains, it is no illusion. They are mountains and consist of a small range that I have never seen before!

0955 Hours- Altitude change to 2950 feet, encountering strong turbulence again.

1000 Hours- We are crossing over the small mountain range and still proceeding northward as best as can be ascertained. Beyond the mountain range is what appears to be a valley with a small river or stream running through the center portion. There should be no green valley below! Something is definitely wrong and abnormal here! We should be over Ice and Snow! To the portside are great forests growing on the mountain slopes. Our navigation Instruments are still spinning, the gyroscope is oscillating back and forth!

1005 Hours- I alter altitude to 1400 feet and execute a sharp left turn to better examine the valley below. It is green with either moss or a type of tight-knit grass. The Light here seems different. I cannot see the Sun anymore. We make another left turn and we spot what seems to be a large animal of some kind below us. It appears to be an elephant ! NO!!! It looks more like a mammoth ! This is incredible! Yet, there it is! Decrease altitude to 1000 feet and take binoculars to better examine the animal. It is confirmed - it is definitely a mammoth-like animal! Report this to base camp.

1030 Hours- Encountering more rolling green hills now. The external temperature indicator reads 74 degrees Fahrenheit! Continuing on our heading now. Navigation instruments seem normal now. I am puzzled over their actions. Attempt to contact base camp. Radio is not functioning!

1130 Hours- Countryside below is more level and normal (if I may use that word). Ahead we spot what seems to be a city!!!! This is impossible! Aircraft seems light and oddly buoyant. The controls refuse to respond!! My GOD!!! Off our port and starboard wings are a strange type of aircraft. They are closing rapidly alongside! They are disc-shaped and have a radiant quality to them. They are close enough now to see the markings on them. It is a type of Swastika !!! This is fantastic. Where are we! What has happened? I tug at the controls again. They will not respond!!!! We are caught in an invisible vice grip of some type!

1135 Hours- Our radio crackles and a voice comes through in English with what perhaps is a slight Nordic or Germanic accent! The message is: Welcome, Admiral, to our domain. We shall land you in exactly seven minutes! Relax, Admiral, you are in good hands. I note the engines of our plane have stopped running! The aircraft is under some strange control and is now turning itself. The controls are useless.

1140 Hours- Another radio message received. We begin the landing process now, and in moments the plane shudders slightly, and begins a descent as though caught in some great unseen elevator! The downward motion is negligible, and we touch down with only a slight jolt!

1145 Hours- I am making a hasty last entry in the flight log. Several men are approaching on foot toward our aircraft. They are tall with blond hair. In the distance is a large shimmering city pulsating with rainbow hues of color. I do not know what is going to happen now, but I see no signs of weapons on those approaching. I hear now a voice ordering me by name to open the cargo door. I comply. END LOG

From this point, I write all the following events here from memory. It defies the imagination and would seem all but madness if it had not happened.

The radioman and I are taken from the aircraft and we are received in a most cordial manner. We were then boarded on a small platform-like conveyance with no wheels! It moves us toward the glowing city with great swiftness. As we approach, the city seems to be made of a crystal material. Soon we arrive at a large building that is a type I have never seen before. It appears to be right out of the design board ofFrank Lloyd Wright , or perhaps more correctly, out of a Buck Rogers setting!! We are given some type of warm beverage that tasted like nothing I have ever savored before. It is delicious. After about ten minutes, two of our wondrous appearing hosts come to our quarters and announce that I am to accompany them. I have no choice but to comply. I leave my radioman behind and we walk a short distance and enter into what seems to be an elevator. We descend downward for some moments, the machine stops, and the door lifts silently upward! We then proceed down a long hallway that is lit by a rose-colored light that seems to be emanating from the very walls themselves! One of the beings motions for us to stop before a great door. Over the door is an inscription that I cannot read. The great door slides noiselessly open and I am beckoned to enter. One of my hosts speaks. Have no fear, Admiral, you are to have an audience with the Master...

I step inside and my eyes adjust to the beautiful coloration that seems to be filling the room completely. Then I begin to see my surroundings. What greeted my eyes is the most beautiful sight of my entire existence. It is in fact too beautiful and wondrous to describe. It is exquisite and delicate. I do not think there exists a human term that can describe it in any detail with justice! My thoughts are interrupted in a cordial manner by a warm rich voice of melodious quality, I bid you welcome to our domain, Admiral. I see a man with delicate features and with the etching of years upon his face. He is seated at a long table. He motions me to sit down in one of the chairs. After I am seated, he places his fingertips together and smiles. He speaks softly again and conveys the following.

We have let you enter here because you are of noble character and well-known on the Surface World, Admiral. Surface World , I half-gasp under my breath! Yes," the Master replies with a smile, 'you are in the domain of the Arianni , the Inner World of the Earth . We shall not long delay your mission, and you will be safely escorted back to the surface and for a distance beyond. But now, Admiral, I shall tell you why you have been summoned here. Our interest rightly begins just after your race exploded the first atomic bombs over Hiroshima and Nagasaki , Japan. It was at that alarming time we sent our flying machines, the "Flugelrads ", to your surface world to investigate what your race had done. That is, of course, past history now, my dear Admiral, but I must continue on. You see, we have never interfered before in your race's wars, and barbarity, but now we must, for you have learned to tamper with a certain power that is not for man, namely, that of atomic energy. Our emissaries have already delivered messages to the powers of your world, and yet they do not heed. Now you have been chosen to be witness here that our world does exist. You see, our Culture and Science are many thousands of years beyond your race, Admiral.' I interrupted, 'But what does this have to do with me, Sir?

The Master's eyes seemed to penetrate deeply into my mind, and after studying me for a few moments he replied, Your race has now reached the point of no return, for there are those among you who would destroy your very world rather

107

than relinquish their power as they know it... I nodded, and the Master continued, In 1945 and afterward, we tried to contact your race, but our efforts were met with hostility, our Flugelrads were fired upon. Yes, even pursued with malice and animosity by your fighter planes. So, now, I say to you, my son, there is a great storm gathering in your world, a black fury that will not spend itself for many years. There will be no answer in your arms, there will be no safety in your science. It may rage on until every flower of your culture is trampled, and all human things are leveled in vast chaos. Your recent war was only a prelude of what is yet to come for your race. We here see it more clearly with each hour..do you say I am mistaken?

'No,' I answer, 'it happened once before, the dark ages came and they lasted for more than five hundred years.'

Yes, my son, replied the Master, the dark ages that will come now for your race will cover the Earth like a pall, but I believe that some of your race will live through the storm, beyond that, I cannot say. We see at a great distance a new world stirring from the ruins of your race, seeking its lost and legendary treasures, and they will be here, my son, safe in our keeping. When that time arrives, we shall come forward again to help revive your culture and your race. Perhaps, by then, you will have learned the futility of war and its strife...and after that time, certain of your culture and science will be returned for your race to begin anew. You, my son, are to return to the Surface World with this message.....

With these closing words, our meeting seemed at an end. I stood for a moment as in a dream....but, yet, I knew this was reality, and for some strange reason I bowed slightly, either out of respect or humility, I do not know which.

Suddenly, I was again aware that the two beautiful hosts who had brought me here were again at my side. 'This way, Admiral,' motioned one. I turned once more before leaving and looked back toward the Master. A gentle smile was etched on his delicate and ancient face. Farewell, my son, he spoke, then he gestured with a lovely, slender hand a motion of peace, and our meeting was truly ended.

Quickly, we walked back through the great door of the Master's chamber and once again entered into the elevator. The door slid silently downward and we were at once going upward. One of my hosts spoke again, We must now make haste, Admiral, as the Master desires to delay you no longer on your scheduled timetable and you must return with his message to your race.

I said nothing. All of this was almost beyond belief, and once again my thoughts were interrupted as we stopped. I entered the room and was again with my radioman. He had an anxious expression on his face. As I approached, I said, It is all right, Howie , it is all right. The two beings motioned us toward the awaiting conveyance, we boarded, and soon arrived back at the aircraft. The engines were idling and we boarded immediately. The whole atmosphere seemed charged now with a certain air of urgency. After the cargo door was closed the aircraft was immediately lifted by that unseen force until we reached an altitude of 2700 feet. Two of the aircraft were alongside for some distance guiding us on our return way. I must state here, the airspeed indicator registered no reading, yet we were moving along at a very rapid rate.

215 Hours- A radio message comes through. We are leaving you now, Admiral, your controls are free. Auf Wiedersehen!!!! We watched for a moment as the flugelrads disappeared into the pale blue sky.

The aircraft suddenly felt as though caught in a sharp downdraft for a moment. We quickly recovered her control. We do not speak for some time, each man has his thoughts....

ENTRY IN FLIGHT LOG CONTINUES:

220 Hours- We are again over vast areas of ice and snow, and approximately 27 minutes from base camp. We radio them, they respond. We report all conditions normal....normal. Base camp expresses relief at our re-established contact.

300 Hours- We land smoothly at base camp. I have a mission.....

END LOG ENTRIES.

March 11, 1947. I have just attended a staff meeting at the Pentagon. I have stated fully my discovery and the message from the Master. All is duly recorded. The President has been advised. I am now detained for several hours (six hours, thirty- nine minutes, to be exact.) I am interviewed intently by Top Security Forces and a medical team. It was an ordeal!!!! I am placed under strict control via the national security provisions of this United States of America . I am ORDERED TO REMAIN SILENT IN REGARD TO ALL THAT I HAVE LEARNED, ON THE BEHALF OF HUMANITY1111 Incredible! I am reminded that I am a military man and I must obey orders.

30/12/56: FINAL ENTRY:

These last few years elapsed since 1947 have not been kind...I now make my final entry in this singular diary. In closing, I must state that I have faithfully kept this matter secret as directed all these years. It has been completely against my values of moral rights. Now, I seem to sense the long night coming on and this secret will not die with me, but as all truth shall, it will triumph and so it shall.

This can be the only hope for mankind. I have seen the truth and it has quickened my spirit and has set me free! I have done my duty toward the monstrous military-industrial complex. Now, the long night begins to approach, but there shall be no end. Just as the long night of the Arctic ends, the brilliant sunshine of Truth shall come again....and those who are of darkness shall fall in it's Light...FOR I HAVE SEEN THAT LAND BEYOND THE POLE, THAT CENTER OF THE GREAT UNKNOWN.

Admiral Richard E. Byrd United States Navy 24 December 1956

Three years after Byrd made his extraordinary diary entries, Ray Palmer wrote in the December 1959 issue of Flying Saucers Magazine:

> *Flying Saucers Magazine* has amassed a large file of evidence which its editors consider unassailable, to prove that the flying saucers are native to the planet Earth and originate from the hollow interior by way of openings in the North and South Poles.

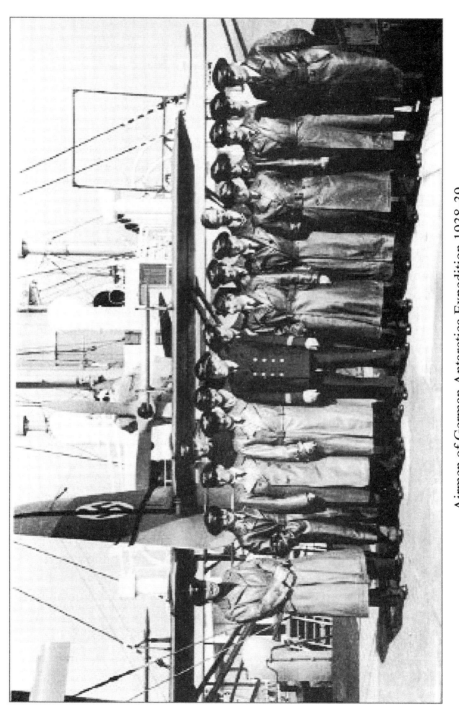

Airmen of German Antarctica Expedition 1938-39

Theodore Fitch was another writer who agreed with Palmer's thesis. In his book, *Our Paradise Inside the Earth*, Fitch writes:

> UFO occupants who come to us in flying saucers and who pose to be visitors from other planets, are really members of an advanced civilization in the hollow interior of the Earth, who have important reasons for keeping their true place of origin secret, for which reason they purposely foster the false belief that they come from other planets.[21]

Another person who wondered about flying saucers and their possible connections to the ancient legends of lost civilizations and underground kingdoms was Professor de Souza, the leader of the Brazilian Theosophists. Professor de Souza had for years been interested in the Aghartta legend. The more he pondered over the legendary underground kingdom and its network of tunnels, the more he came to the conclusion that the flying saucers were the answer. He theorized that the subterranean dwellers were an advanced race, so if they were capable of living and thriving beneath Earth's surface there was no reason why they should not have developed aerial ships far more advanced than anything known on the surface world. Furthermore, in his view the round saucer shape of these craft, along with their maneuvrability and speed, seemed to make them ideally suited for traversing the network of tunnels that lead to and from the underground kingdom.

In 1957, the ideas of de Souza were carefully examined by a writer named O. C. Huguenin in his book, *From The Subterranean World To The Sky: Flying Saucers*. After declaring that 'the hypothesis of the extraterrestrial origin of the flying saucers does not seem acceptable,' Huguenin wrote:

> We must consider the most recent and interesting theory that has been offered to account for the origin of flying saucers: the existence of a great Subterranean World with innumerable cities in which live millions of inhabitants. This other humanity must have reached a very high degree of civilization, economic organization and social, cultural and spiritual development,

---

[21] In my 2018 book for AUP, *The Landing Lights of Magonia*, I similarly argued that UFOs do not originate from other planets but from dimensions that are an integral part of the Earth plane and are expressions of the incalculably powerful Forces of Living Nature.

together with an extraordinary scientific progress, in comparison with whom the humanity that lives in the Earth's surface may be considered as a race of barbarians.

On top of that, according to the information supplied by Commander Paulo Justino Strauss, an officer of the Brazilian Navy, the subterranean world is not restricted to caverns but is more or less extensive and located in a hollow inside the Earth large enough to contain cities and fields. Here live human beings and animals whose physical structure resembles those on the surface.

Huguenin then describes how these people, far in advance of the rest of humanity in terms of scientific development, devised machines called Vimanas that 'flew in the skies and the tunnels like aircraft, utilizing a form of energy obtained directly from the atmosphere.' They were, he says, 'identical with what we know as Flying Saucers.'

The Flying Saucers have for some time now had some kind of unusual association with the North and South Pole areas of the Earth. Many have speculated that this is because giant entrances to the interior of the planet exist in these places.

However, what if something even stranger is happening in the Arctic and Antarctica? A research team of U.S. and UK scientists have accidentally come across an incredible discovery while working on a joint weather research project in Antarctica. The team allegedly witnessed the creation of a spinning vortex through time and space. U.S. physicist Mariann McLein testified that she and her colleagues became aware of a spinning gray fog in the sky over their heads. They initially dismissed the phenomenon as merely part of a random polar storm. The spiraling vortex, however, did not disperse. Stranger still, despite gusts of wind and briskly moving clouds overhead, the weird spinning grey fog remained stationary.

Deciding to explore the odd phenomenon, the group took one of its weather balloons and attached to it a meteorological instrument that calibrated temperature, barometric pressure, humidity, wind speed and a scientific chronometer to record the times of the readings. After attaching a cable to the balloon, and securing the other end to a winch, they released it. The balloon and instrument package soared upwards and were immediately sucked into the gaping maw of the swirling vortex. After a several minutes, they decided to retrieve the balloon. Despite some difficulty with the winch they succeeded in bringing the balloon back to earth and checked the instruments. McLein stated that everyone was stunned by the readout on the chronometer. It displayed a date decades in the past: January 27, 1965. McLein claimed the experiment was repeated several times with the same result. Later, she said, the entire episode was reported to military intelligence and passed on to the White House.

The strange vortex phenomenon, a highly magnetic tunnel to the past, was code named "The Time Gate" by military intelligence. This may indicate that the old legends of physical openings at the poles may not be wholly accurate. Rather, weird magnetic phenomena may be taking place that rips apart time and space in a very localized area. It is speculated that these vortexes may be used by UFOs to travel in and out of the hollow Earth, or maybe through other dimensions entirely. Evidently, there is still much to learn about UFOs and their connections with the hollow Earth concept.

As we will see in the section "Celluloid Worlds", David Lynch and Mark Frost's *Twin Peaks*, especially its third season, is dominated by anomalous temporal and spatial phenomena, including dramatic distortive appearances of just such a "Time Gate" dimensional vortex.

Admiral Richard E. Byrd

Alice at war with the playing cards in Wonderland

Chapter 9

"Phantom Islands"

Various myths and folklore speak of islands that appear and disappear and whose geographical locations cannot either be proven or established. Such places are often referred to as "phantom islands" or "mythical islands". Regardless of the problems of geography, these islands have captured the imagination of storytellers and explorers throughout history.

Buss

Buss was a phantom island in the North Atlantic Ocean, recorded as discovered during the third expedition of Martin Frobisher in September 1578 by sailors aboard the ship *Emanuel of Bridgwater* and indicated on maps as existing between Ireland and "Frisland" at about 57° N. It is believed that Frobisher mistook Greenland for Frisland and Baffin Island for Greenland, while Emanuel, returning home, made a mistake in dead reckoning and mistook optical effects near Greenland at around 62° N for new land. A Thomas Shepard claimed to have mapped the island from *Golden Lion* of Dunkirk in 1671. As Atlantic traffic increased, the island's existence was less certain and its supposed size was greatly reduced. By 1745, it was apparent there was no island at the site claimed and it was renamed the Sunken Land of Buss, as the supposed area was relatively shallow. The island or "site of sunken island" persisted on charts into the 19th century. Its existence at the location was finally disproved by John Ross in Isabella in 1818 during his first Arctic expedition, finding no depth at 180 fathoms (330m).

Frisland

Frisland, also called Frischlant, Friesland, Frislanda, Frislandia or Fixland is itself a phantom island that appeared on virtually all of the maps of the North Atlantic from the 1560s through the 1660s. Frisland originally may also have been a cartographic approximation of Iceland, but in 1558 the influential Zeno map charted the landmass as an entirely separate island south (or occasionally southwest) of Iceland. After this incorrect charting, the phantom island appeared that way on maps for the next 100 years. Its existence was given currency in manuscript maps of the 1560s by the Maggiolo family of Genoa. Subsequently, the island was accepted and reproduced by famed cartographers Gerardus Mercator and Jodocus Hondius.

Some early maps by Willem Blaeu, such as his 1617 chart of Europe, omit Frisland but it reappeared on his 1630 world map as one of many islands shown off the eastern coast of Labrador, which was then believed to extend to within a few hundred miles of Scotland.

It also appeared on a 1652 world map by Visscher, largely copied from that of Blaeu. The 1693 Vincenzo Coronelli map places it close to Greenland. Even in the mid-18th century, explorers' maps clearly depicted Frisland as separated from Greenland by a wide strait. Frederick J. Pohl identified Frisland with an island he referred to as "Fer Island", modern English Fair Isle, an island that lies between mainland Shetland and the Orkney islands.

Isle of Demons
Mentioned in early European accounts of North America, the Isle of Demons was said to be inhabited by supernatural creatures. It was later associated with Quirpon Island, Newfoundland. It was generally shown as two islands. It began appearing on maps in the beginning of the 16th century and disappeared in the mid-17th century. It could also simply be a translation from First Nations people, who often avoided areas where a person had died, believing it was haunted by spirits. This results in many islands with the same reference. It was believed that the island's demons and wild beasts would torment and attack any ships that passed or anyone that was foolish enough to wander onto the island.

The Isle of Demons first appears in the 1508 map of Johannes Ruysch. It may simply be a relocated version of the older legendary island of Satanazes ("Devils" in Portuguese) that was normally depicted in 15th century maps in the middle of the Atlantic Ocean just north of Antillia. With the Atlantic better mapped with the trans-oceanic voyages of the 1490s, Ruysch may simply have transplanted old Satanazes to a more suitable location.

The Isle of Demons continues to appear as late as the 1556 map of "La Nueva Francia" by Giacomo Gastaldi, after Jacques Cartier's expeditions (1534, 1535, 1541) had explored much of Newfoundland and the Gulf of St. Lawrence. The "Isola de Demoni" is depicted by

Gastaldi as a substantially large island roughly encompassing northern Newfoundland, with figurative depictions of flying demons.

Hy-Brasil and Saint Brendan's Island

The enigmatic island of Hy-Brasil, shrouded in myth and maritime mystery, stands as a testament to the enduring power of folklore and legend. For centuries, this phantom isle has captured the imaginations of storytellers, explorers and scholars. The island's name, variously spelled as Hy-Brasil, Hy-Breasal, or O'Brasil, is derived from the Gaelic "Uí Breasail", meaning "Isle of the Blessed". This nomenclature links Hy-Brasil to a paradise-like realm, a place of eternal happiness and abundance—a notion that has resonated through the ages.

Despite the similarity, the name of the country Brazil has no connection to the mythical islands (although J.R.R. Tolkien's essay "On Fairy Stories" linked them).

Hy-Brasil's tale begins in the rich tapestry of Irish folklore and mythology. As a mythical island located off the west coast of Ireland, it occupies a unique place in the cultural heritage of the Emerald Isle. The Piri Reis map locates the island of Hy-Brasil 200 miles west of Ireland. (Curiously, among the documents in the possession of Deputy Führer Rudolf Hess when he parachuted into Scotland in 1941 was a map depicting Hy-Brasil.)

To understand its significance, we must delve into the annals of Celtic legend, where Hy-Brasil is often associated with the Otherworld, a realm of magic, mystery and transcendence inhabited by supernatural beings and spirits. Hy-Brasil's connection to the Otherworld places it within the broader context of Celtic mythology, where islands are frequently linked to mystical realms. This association elevates Hy-Brasil from a mere geographical entity to a place steeped in the supernatural, where the boundaries between the mortal and the divine blur.

In *The Hollow Hills*, part of Mary Stewart's Merlin Trilogy, several characters believe (incorrectly) that the wizard Merlin has hidden the young Prince Arthur on Hy-Brasil.

Myth has it that Hy-Brasil, described as a paradise with lush vegetation cloaked in mist, appears to human sight every seven years but still cannot be reached. In 1908 at the beginning of American anthropologist Walter Evan-Wentz's Celtic odyssey,[22] too many people

---

[22] Evens-Wentz, W.Y., *The Fairy Faith in Celtic Countries*, 1911

were insistent that they had seen Hy Brasil for its existence to be dismissed as fantasy.

Hy-Brasil's ruler is Manannan Mac Lir, the Son of the Sea, foster father of Lugh, God of Light. He ferried the dying Arthur to Avalon. Manannan Mac Lir travels his domain in a magic chariot. Fairy women would venture forth from this enchanted region, sprinkle mortal men with Glamour and entice them into their keeping.

On maps the island was shown as being circular, often with a central strait or river running east–west across its diameter. Nautical charts identified an island called "Bracile" west of Ireland in the Atlantic Ocean as far back as 1325, in a portolan chart by Angelino Dulcert. It also appeared on the Catalan Atlas, in 1375. Later it appeared as Insula de Brasil in the Venetian map of Andrea Bianco (1436), attached to one of the larger islands of a group of islands in the Atlantic. This was identified for a time with the modern island of Terceira in the Azores where a volcanic mount at the bay of its main town, Angra do Heroismo, is still named Monte Brasil. A Catalan chart of about 1480 labels two islands "Illa de Brasil", one to the southwest of Ireland and one south of "Illa Verde" or Greenland.

One of the earliest recorded accounts of Hy-Brasil's sighting comes from the voyage of John Cabot, an Italian explorer sailing under the flag of England. In 1497 Cabot claimed to have seen an island resembling Hy-Brasil during his journey to North America. This account, though brief and somewhat cryptic, sparked curiosity and speculation about the island's existence.

Another notable explorer who encountered Hy-Brasil was John Dee, a renowned English mathematician, astronomer, and advisor to Queen Elizabeth I. Dee's meticulous observations and writings provide valuable insights into the island's appearance and location on maps of the time.

Despite the failure of attempts to find it, the phantom isle appeared regularly on maps lying south west of Galway Bay until 1865, by which time it was called Brasil Rock. Expeditions left Bristol in 1480 and 1481 to search for the island; and a letter written by Pedro de Ayala, shortly after the return of John Cabot (from his expedition in 1497), reports that land found by Cabot had been 'discovered in the past by the men from Bristol who found Brasil.'

In 1674 a Captain John Nisbet claimed to have seen the island during a journey from France to Ireland, stating that the island was inhabited by large black rabbits and a magician who lived alone in a stone castle. However, the truth was that the character and the story were a literary invention by Irish author Richard Head. Roderick O'Flaherty in *A Chorographical Description of West Or H-Iar Connaught* (1684) tells us, 'There is now living, Morogh O'Ley who imagines he was personally on O'Brasil for two days, and saw out of it the Aran Islands in Galway Bay, Golamhead, Irrosbeghill, and other places of the west continent he was acquainted with.'

Hy-Brasil has also been identified with Porcupine Bank, a shoal in the Atlantic Ocean about 200 kilometres (120 ml) west of Ireland and discovered in 1862. As early as 1870 a paper was read to the Geological Society of Ireland suggesting this identification, which has subsequently been repeated, one example being in an 1883 edition of Notes and Queries.

One notable mention of Hy-Brasil is found in the "Lebor Gabála Érenn" or "The Book of Invasions", where it is described as one of the mysterious lands inhabited by early settlers of Ireland.

Another source, the "Navigatio Sancti Brendani Abbatis" or "The Voyage of Saint Brendan the Abbot", recounts the adventures of Saint Brendan of Clonfert and his companions as they journey across the Atlantic Ocean in a curragh, a type of Irish boat, to the "Promised Land of the Saints", associated in some sources as Hy-Brasil. The voyage is marked by a series of fantastical encounters, including encounters with sea creatures, curious islands and miraculous events.

While travelling across the Atlantic Ocean and evangelising its islands, Brendan and his party of fourteen monks claimed that in 512 CE they reached an island, subsequently dubbed Saint Brendan's Island, which they believe to be the Promised Land. On arrival the monastic party celebrated a Mass. They reported that their stay was just fifteen days, while the ships that expected their return complained that they had to wait a year, during which period the island remained concealed behind a thick curtain of mist.

During their visit Brendan and his brothers encounter animals that sing psalms, and a mysterious light that bathes the island. They also encounter a great fish that provides them with food and guidance. On another island, the monks find grapes of extraordinary size, which they interpret as a symbol of divine abundance and providence.

Saint Brendan's Island is supposedly situated in the North Atlantic somewhere west of Northern Africa. It appeared on numerous maps in Christopher Columbus's time, most notably Martin Behaim's Erdapfel of 1492. It is known as La isla de San Borondón and Isla de Samborombón in Spanish.

In *Planiferio de Ebstorf* of 1234, Marcos Martinez referred to 'the lost island discovered by St Brendan... but nobody has found it since.' In *Mapamundi de Hereford* of 1275 the whole archipelago is described as "The Isles of the Blessed and the Island of St Brendan".

Nevertheless, there have been many reported sightings of the isle. The Portuguese writer Luís Perdigão recorded the interest of the King of Portugal after a sea captain informed Henry the Navigator (1394–1460) that he had found the island but was driven off by tumultuous sea conditions. Henry ordered him back; he sailed off but never returned.

In 1520 members of Ferdinand Magellan's expedition are thought to have named Samborombón Bay on the coast of Argentina after Saint Brendan's Isle, attributing the bay's nearly semicircular shape to the detachment of the wandering island from the South American mainland.

In 1566, Hernán Pérez de Grado, First Regent of the Royal Canary Islands Court, ordered the justices at La Palma, El Hierro and La Gomera to investigate the phenomenon.

In his history, Abreu y Galindo reports a conversation with a French adventurer who claimed to have visited San Borondon, departing from it when a storm set in and sailing to La Palma for shelter within a day. In another report, Alonso de Espinosa, governor of El Hierro, described sighting San Borondon Island northwest of El Hierro and "leeward" of La Palma. He listed 100 witnesses to the apparition.

Juan de Abréu Galindo reported in *Historia de la Conquista de las siete Islas Canarias* that 'the island of San Borondon, which is the eighth and last [of the Canary Islands],[23] whose existence may be inferred from sightings of its apparitions, seems to be located at 20 degrees 30 minutes of latitude and eight leagues [40 km] due west of La Gomera.'

In 1719, the Scottish monk Sigbert de Gembloux reported seeing the island, as did Don Matea Dacesta, mayor of Valverde, El Hierro, in 1721. As a result of these sightings, that same year Juan de Mur y

---

[23] The Canaries comprise seven main islands: Tenerife, Fuerteventura, Gran Canaria, Lanzarote, La Palma, La Gomera, and El Hierro. The archipelago includes many smaller islands, including La Graciosa, which today tends to be counted as its eighth island but was not regarded as such in Juan de Abréu Galindo's time.

Aguerre, military governor of the Canary Islands, appointed a new commission of inquiry under Gaspar Dominguez, a sea captain; no fresh evidence was uncovered and subsequently interest waned.

According to the Canary historian Ramirez, in 1723 a priest performed the rite of exorcism towards the island during one of its apparitions behind a low cloud. This was witnessed by a large number of persons and sworn to on affidavit.

In 1759, a Franciscan friar mentioned (but not named) by Viera y Clavijo wrote to a friend: 'I was most desirous to see the island of San Borondon and, finding myself in Alexero, La Palma, on 3 May at six of the morning, I saw, and can swear to it on oath, that while having in plain view at the same time the island of El Hierro, I saw another island of the same colour and appearance, and I made out through a telescope, much-wooded terrain in its central area. Then I sent for the priest Antonio Jose Manrique, who upon arrival saw only a portion of it for when he was watching a cloud obscured the mountain. It was subsequently visible for another 90 minutes, being seen by about forty spectators, but in the afternoon when we returned to the same point we could see nothing on account of the heavy rain.'

In his *Noticias*, Vol I, 1772, chronicler Viera y Clavijo wrote: 'A few years ago while returning from the Americas, the captain of a ship of the Canary Fleet believed he saw La Palma appear and, having set his course for Tenerife based on his sighting, was astonished to find the real La Palma materialize in the distance next morning.' Viera adds that a similar entry is made in the diaries of Colonel don Roberto de Rivas, who made the observation that his ship 'having been close to the island of La Palma in the afternoon, and not arriving there until late the next day', the officer was forced to conclude that 'the wind and current must have been extraordinarily unfavourable during the night.'

Further expeditions were organised in the search for the island, but from the 19th century onwards, reported sightings of San Borondon became less frequent.

St. Brendan's voyage was not merely a physical journey but a spiritual quest—a quest for divine revelation and the pursuit of the heavenly realm. Within the context of Celtic Christianity, this journey symbolized the monk's search for sanctity, transcendence and a deeper connection with the divine.

The fantastical elements encountered during the voyage—such as the great fish, the Promised Land and the grapes of paradise—can be interpreted as spiritual symbols. The great fish, for example, may symbolize divine providence and guidance on the spiritual path. The Promised Land represents the aspiration for a heavenly realm where the mundane and the sacred converge. The grapes of paradise evoke the idea of divine abundance and the sacramental nature of creation.

In this sense, St. Brendan's journey becomes a metaphor for the spiritual odyssey of the Celtic Christian, a quest for a deeper understanding of the mysteries of faith and a closer communion with the divine.

The concept of the Isle of the Blessed resonates with the human longing for a utopian paradise—a place of peace, abundance, and spiritual fulfillment. It is a vision of the afterlife where the soul finds solace and eternal reward.

Alice and Duchess at the croquet game

The all-seeing eyes of the eccentric Cheshire Cat

Chapter 10

Atlantis

The ancient Hermetic teachings speak of the many evolutions that our physical plane experiences: the evolution of the mineral, plant and animal kingdoms; of air, water and fire; of the evolution of many other spiritual beings and vibrations, some of whom we could see in daily life, others decidedy not; and of the evolution of colour and sound in their respective vibrations.

They explained that on other planets within our universe there *are* other evolutions of the physical plane...but not necessarily like ours, and most assuredly not identical. Again, some of these we could see if we landed on their premises, others we could not; for the vibration would be different, and our understanding of what was before us incomplete.

In the overall scheme of things, ancient wisdom taught that these perceptual challenges in the vastitude of space do not matter to us here on Earth. What is important for humankind to understand is that we are a part of a small part of the physical plane...but that this small part is very important, for it is an expression of the God-Force or Living Spirit within creation.

They taught that the earth plane is vitally important for human growth and evolution, no matter how many existences one has. They emphasised that is equally important to learn to step above it, to learn of the physical experience in all its forms, opportunities and challenges, and within its exacting laws, exacting to the highest sense, of arriving ultimately at the understanding that we are *not* the only vibration within the universe. And finally coming to the understanding that creation (the putting together of vibrations) is a combination of the energies of the Universal Powers, which is the combination of forces that accumulated from the processes of the creation of the physical plane that began trillions of years ago.

On the physical earth plane man is the stronger. Verbal hermetics taught that man is the combination of more individual elements of the

Living Spirit than any other force on the earth plane...more so than animal, more so than flower or plant, more so than mineral.

And so man is the highest expression of the Living Spirit on the physical plane. Each and every vibration within him is this expression. And so man's role is to bring forth and allow the Living Spirit to come through his body, to magnify it through all of the five senses to its highest expression. But in the process, man, because this is the physical plane, thinks a lot, rebuilds and rebuilds, pollutes, while slowly and gradually learning of the physical.

The ancients taught that this earth plane has gone through many cataclysms where the shifting of the poles relocates them to the middle of where the equator is. In a flash of a moment, land rises and erodes as the crust moves. Water rushes away. Formations of rocks and canyons and great depths are made instantly by the combination of the movement of the crust, the pushing up of the earth and the falling away of the waters.

And so what scientists say will take thousands, hundreds of thousands of years for a perfect coming together of the forces necessary for large scale planetary re-shaping to get under way, under the force of a cataclysmic moment, when the earth is spinning one way and then in a split second, the axis turns, everything is torn, sundered, pushed, pulled, flooded and blown. But this is not an end to humanity; some areas rise up, some are protected, and man goes on.

Ancient wisdom explains that this has happened many, many times: a refurbishing of the spiritual element of the earth and of the physical elements of the earth. For animals have survived; and minerals always survive. Plants survive and they begin to grow.

And man begins to rebuild...to start anew, trying to learn, and refurbishing the earth and the human spirit. Provided that the elements of water, air and earth can let the Living Spirit come through unpolluted, there is a positive expression on all levels. But when man cannot express the Living Spirit that he is—the highest combination of all the living elements on the earth plane—there is an emptiness, a vacuum, a lack of energy, and the earth begins to falter. And so the essences of air, water, earth and fire, as the vibrations leave, move to purer areas at a time when man no longer conveys the living elements, and the axis begins to shift...a process to allow life on earth to refurbish and go on. For without that periodic renewal, the ancients taught that there would be complete elimination of this plane. It is a consistent episode of renewal, and there are different patterns in every one.

There are always survivors: those that had spiritual balance and insight, the intuition to be in the right place at the right time when the poles switched. In the years after the event they grow and evolve. But then the next generation comes, and its members begin to question: 'What do you mean, we survived a cataclysm? What lies out there? What is in the other regions of this world?' Then the third generation heaps challenge upon challenge, question upon question. Then comes the fourth, one so far removed from the post-cataclsym essence they say that what they are hearing must surely be a myth, a fable. Zeus, the gentle soul that walked the earth and taught of kindness and grace, is set upon a mountain to become a figure to fear. And, gradually, the process of a fall from grace and a disassociation from nature begins anew, cataclysm after cataclysm.

The great books: the Koran, Buddha's documents, the Taoistic teachings of Lao Tse, the books of Pythagoras's library that were burned in the fire that consumed him; all tell of this. In one way or another, it centres on the Biblical theme where survivors, after having had a high spiritual experience, begin to doubt. They eat the apple of earthly delights and are thrown out of the garden. Afterwards, their children argue and they go off to start their lives elsewhere.

The several destructions of the Atlantean civilisations serve as wake-up case studies that starkly illustrate the processes that lead to episodes of cataclysm. The only primary sources for Atlantis and its cataclysmic destruction are Plato's dialogues *Timaeus* and *Critias*; all other mentions of the island are based on them. The dialogues claim to quote Solon, who visited Egypt between 590 and 580 BCE; they state that he translated Egyptian records of Atlantis. The description of the Atlantean civilization given by Plato in the Critias may be summarized as follows.

In the first ages the gods divided the earth among themselves, proportioning it according to their respective dignities. Each became the peculiar deity of his own allotment and established temples to himself, ordained a priestcraft, and instituted a system of sacrifice.

To Poseidon was given the sea and the island continent of Atlantis. In the midst of the island was a mountain which was the dwelling place of three earth-born primitive human beings—Evenor; his wife, Leucipe; and their only daughter, Cleito.

The maiden was very beautiful, and after the sudden death of her parents she was wooed by Poseidon. This union produced five pairs of male children. Poseidon apportioned his continent among these ten, and

Atlas, the eldest, he made overlord of the other nine. Poseidon further called the country Atlantis and the surrounding sea the Atlantic in honour of Atlas.

Before the birth of his ten sons, Poseidon divided the continent and the coastwise sea into concentric zones of land and water, which were as perfect as though turned upon a lathe. Two zones of land and three of water surrounded the central island, which Poseidon caused to be irrigated with two springs of water—one warm and the other cold.

The descendants of Atlas continued as rulers of Atlantis, and with wise government and diligent industry elevated the country to a position of surpassing dignity.

The natural resources of Atlantis were apparently limitless. Precious metals were mined, wild animals domesticated, and perfumes distilled from its fragrant flowers. While enjoying the abundance natural to their semi-tropical location, the Atlanteans employed themselves also in the erection of palaces, temples and docks. They bridged the zones of sea and later dug a deep canal to connect the outer ocean with the central island, where stood the palaces and temple of Poseidon, which excelled all other structures in magnificence.

A network of bridges and canals was created by the Atlanteans to unite the various parts of their kingdom. Plato then describes the white, black and red stones, which they quarried from beneath their continent and used in the construction of public buildings and docks.

They built a wall around each of the land zones, the outer wall being covered with brass, the middle with tin, and the inner, which encompassed the citadel, with orichalch.[24]

The citadel, on the central island, contained the palaces, temples, and other public buildings. In its centre, surrounded by a wall of gold, was a sanctuary dedicated to Cleito and Poseidon. Here the first ten princes of the island were born and here each year their descendants brought offerings.

Poseidon's own temple, its exterior entirely covered with silver and its pinnacles with gold, also stood within the citadel. The interior of the temple was of ivory, gold, silver and orichalch, even to the pillars and floor. The temple contained a colossal statue of Poseidon standing in a chariot drawn by six winged horses, about him a hundred Nereids riding on dolphins.

---

[24] a golden-yellow alloy of copper and zinc considered precious in ancient times, and referred to as brass

Arranged outside the building were golden statues of the first ten kings and their wives. In the groves and gardens were hot and cold springs. There were numerous temples to various deities, places of exercise for men and for beasts, public baths and a great racecourse for horses.

At various vantage points on the zones were fortifications, and to the great harbour came vessels from every maritime nation. The zones were so thickly populated that the sound of human voices was ever in the air.

That part of Atlantis facing the sea was described as lofty and precipitous but about the central city was a plain sheltered by mountains renowned for their size, number and beauty. The plain yielded two crops each year, in the winter watered by rains and in the summer by immense irrigation canals, which were also used for transportation. The plain was divided into sections; in time of war each section supplied its quota of fighting men and chariots.

The ten governments differed from each other in details concerning military requirements. Each of the kings of Atlantis had complete control over his own kingdom, but their mutual relationships were governed by a code engraved by the first ten kings on a column of orichalch standing in the temple of Poseidon. At alternate intervals of five and six years a pilgrimage was made to this temple that equal honour might be conferred upon both the odd and the even numbers. Here, with appropriate sacrifice, each king renewed his oath of loyalty upon the sacred inscription. Here also the kings donned azure robes and sat in judgement. At daybreak they wrote their sentences upon a golden tablet and deposited them with their robes as memorials.

The chief laws of the Atlantean kings were that they should not take up arms against each other and that they should come to the assistance of any of their number who was attacked. In matters of war and great moment the final decision was in the hands of the direct descendants of the family of Atlas. No king had the power of life and death over his kinsmen without the assent of a majority of the ten.

Plato concludes his description by declaring that it was this great empire which attacked the Hellenic states. This did not occur, however, until their power and glory had lured the Atlantean kings from the pathway of wisdom and virtue. Filled with false ambition, the rulers of Atlantis determined to conquer the entire world. Zeus, perceiving the wickedness of the Atlanteans, gathered the gods into his holy residence and addressed them.

Here Plato's narrative comes to an abrupt end, for the *Critias* was never finished. In the *Timæus* is a further description of Atlantis, supposedly given to Solon by an Egyptian priest and which concludes as follows:

> But afterwards there occurred violent earthquakes and floods; and in a single day and night of rain all your warlike men in a body sank into the earth, and the island of Atlantis in like manner disappeared, and was sunk beneath the sea. And that is the reason why the sea in those parts is impassable and impenetrable, because there is such a quantity of shallow mud in the way; ... caused by the subsidence of the island.

In the introduction to his translation of the *Timæus*, Thomas Taylor quotes from a *History of Ethiopia* written by Marcellus, which contains the following reference to Atlantis:

> For they relate that in their time there were seven islands in the Atlantic sea, sacred to Proserpine; and besides these, three others of an immense magnitude; one of which was sacred to Pluto, another to Ammon, and another, which is the middle of these, and is of a thousand stadia, to Neptune.

A commentary by Proclus on the *Timæus* gives a description of the geography of Atlantis:

> That an island of such nature and size once existed is evident from what is said by certain authors who investigated the things around the outer sea. For according to them, there were seven islands in that sea in their time, sacred to Persephone, and also three others of enormous size, one of which was sacred to Hades, another to Ammon, and another one between them to Poseidon, the extent of which was a thousand stadia; and the inhabitants of it—they add—preserved the remembrance from their ancestors of the immeasurably large island of Atlantis which had really existed there and which for many ages had reigned over all islands in the Atlantic sea and which itself had like-wise been sacred to Poseidon

Crantor, commenting upon Plato, asserted that the Egyptian priests declared the story of Atlantis to be written upon pillars which were still preserved circa 300 BCE. In *Isis Unveiled* H.P. Blavatsky summed up the causes that precipitated the Atlantean disaster:

132

Under the evil insinuations of their demon, Thevetat, the Atlantis-race became a nation of wicked magicians. In consequence of this, war was declared, the story of which would be too long to narrate; its substance may be found in the disfigured allegories of the race of Cain, the giants, and that of Noah and his righteous family. The conflict came to an end by the submersion of the Atlantis; which finds its imitation in the stories of the Babylonian and Mosaic flood: The giants and magicians and all flesh died, and every man, all except Xisuthrus and Noah, who are substantially identical with the great Father of the Thlinkithians in the Popol Vuh, or the sacred book of the Guatemaleans, which also tell of his escaping in a large boat, like the Hindu Noah—Vaiswasvata.

Manly P. Hall[25] wrote that from the Atlanteans the world has received not only the heritage of arts and crafts, philosophies, sciences, ethics and religions but also the heritage of hate, strife, and perversion, negative characteristics that instigated the first war. As a consequence, it has been said that all subsequent wars were fought in a fruitless effort to justify the first one and right the wrong that it caused.

Before Atlantis sank its spiritually illumined Initiates, who realized that their land was doomed because it had departed from the Path of Light, withdrew from the ill-fated continent. Carrying with them the sacred and secret doctrine, these Atlanteans established themselves in diverse locations, including Egypt, where they became its first "divine" rulers. Nearly all the great cosmologic myths forming the foundation of the various sacred books of the world are based upon the Atlantean Mystery rituals.

Other historians have theorized that before the sixth century BCE the "Pillars of Hercules" may have applied to mountains on either side of the Gulf of Laconia, and also may have been part of the pillar cult of the Aegean. The mountains stood at either side of the southernmost gulf in Greece, the largest in the Peloponnese, and it opens onto the Mediterranean Sea. This would have placed Atlantis in the Mediterranean, lending credence to many details in Plato's discussion.

The fourth-century historian Ammianus Marcellinus, relying on a lost work by Timagenes, a historian writing in the first century BCE, writes that the Druids of Gaul said that part of the inhabitants of Gaul had migrated there from distant islands.

---

[25] ibid

Full trance communication workshops held in the U.S.A and in Europe in the early 1970s revealed startling insights about Earth's antediluvian civilisations. Ancient and mythological histories are full of references that hint at the existence of pre-Flood peoples. Sumerian history, for example, relates that their race was of non-human origin, whose purpose was to instruct mankind.

The workshops spoke specifically about the Atlantean civilisations. It emerged that over a period of tens of thousands of years there was not one but four Atlantean civilisations, each eliminated by cataclysm. Previous gifted psychics had made similar statements. Edgar Cayce (1877-1945), who began his channelling in 1901 when he was a fundamental Christian, said in readings that the last three destructions of Atlantis—located, he said, from the Gulf of Mexico to Gibraltar—occurred c. 50,000 BCE 28,000 BCE and 10,000 BCE. He said that on each occasion the few that fled and survived migrated to diverse locations, including the Americas, in line with legends from local natives.

Before the end of the last Ice Age (12,000-years ago) the ocean levels were at least 300 feet below their current levels. A vast "island" was in the area in those remote times rather than chains of islands. Cayce referred to Bimini as one of the mountaintops of ancient Atlantis. While few would consider the island a mountain, 12,000-years ago it was one of the highest points on the vast land formation in the region. Bimini and Andros Island, lying about 100 miles to the east of Bimini, was a part of the same island in 10,000 BCE, called "Poseidia" temple, which sunk in 10,000 BCE and is, according to Cayce, covered by "the slime of ages". This record hall is identical to the one that Cayce said exists in Egypt under the Sphinx.

Archaeologists have countered that the remains of civilization in the region only go back 7,000 years—or perhaps even less. They have asserted that if a major civilization existed in the area, some of its remains would be found on current land. That assertion has a fundamental flaw.

Ancient maritime civilizations typically built their cities and ports on the ocean shores. Archaeologists working in South America, the Pacific coast of North America, India, and elsewhere in the world have been discovering the remains of underwater ruins. These ancient maritime civilizations built their cities and ports on coastlines, all of which have been covered by the rising oceans. Given the recent changes in North and South American archaeology—taking the history of habitation in the Americas to 50,000-years ago—it seems likely that ruins would lie in the shallow waters around Bimini.

It has long been recognized that migration legends from natives in North, Central, and South America support the migration of advanced groups to various locations in the Americas corresponding to Cayce's accounts of Atlantis. In recent years, archaeological work has shown that Cayce's accounts of the Atlantean migrations to the Americas is consistent with the archaeological evidence. Now, however, research on a form of DNA recovered from ancient remains almost perfectly matches Cayce's account. This was an unexpected scientific surprise that appears to support the contention that Atlantis was in the Caribbean area. In particular, what is called "Haplogroup X" by geneticists, has been found in ancient remains in every location in the world where the Cayce readings state Atlanteans fled at three different times (10,000 BCE, 28,000 BCE, and 50,000 BCE). Amazingly, Haplogroup X—one of 42 major ancient mtDNA groups identified—has not been found in other locations of the world. In addition, another DNA type, called Haplogroup B, appears to be from what Cayce and others have termed the ancient continent of Mu, or Lemuria.

Cayce and other channeling sources claimed that the Atlanteans' technological prowess was far in advance of present day capabilities. Celebrated British medium Margaret Lumley Brown described the Atlanteans' mastery of nuclear physics, their use of "firestones" that harnessed cosmic forces, and of crystal technologies that utilised both solar and geothermal power. Cayce described how these crystal-induced solar forces interacted with "internal influences of the earth" in its gaseous, fiery depths, which unwittingly generated destructive energies that, too powerful to be controlled by Atlantean science, provoked the first of the upheavals that took place before the poles reversal. Also, through their understanding of certain concentrated energy points in space and time the Atlanteans were also able to interface with other realities and communicate with dimensional neighbours.

Medium James Merrill (1926-1990) said that the Atlanteans built a hugely ambitious new atomically powered world in the stratosphere, comprising a network of antigravitated platforms anchored to Earth at 14 points by glowing radioactive stones.

But in the fourth Atlantean race, as in the previous three, all was not well. Atlantis in 10,000 BCE was steepd in violence and depravity.

The trance communications explained that what finally undid the Atlanteans was their exploitation of genetics, one of the most powerful means of control in the black magic practices of the Sons of Belial, otherwise known as the Lords of Material Existence, who denied the existence of God and instead worshipped themselves.

In a massive programme of social engineering, newborn children were implanted with a crystal in the base of the spine by which their behaviour, wants and moods were remotely controlled. (Significantly, during the 1947 autopsy of a Roswell UFO casualty an object described as a kind of chestnut-sized "crystal" was cut out of its belly area.) Man-animal hybrids were bred for sexual gratification. Cayce spoke of invasions of the continent by these animal monstrosities, which were subsequently countered by the invention of certain explosive materials of hmighty destructive power

Human sacrifice was rampant. Worse was to follow. Tasked by power-crazed rulers to manufacture the perfect man, scientists grew laboratory-bred humans. In Atlantis no one understood the metaphysical consequences of making superperfect human clones free from disease and physical impediment. No spirit would choose such a vehicle for its next incarnation because evolutionary growth may only be achieved through experiencing a degree of physical imbalance. This left the door open for earthbound souls (of suicides and murderers) and negative energies from the astral dimensions to inhabit the immaculate host bodies. There was no turning back from this.

Those in power were not entirely blind to the consequences of their actions. The Atlantean leaders knew what was coming and also knew that it could not be stopped. The extent to which the Atlanteans' science, technology and occult practices infringed upon the natural world and so alarmed the cosmic powers that caretake our planet had, just as on previous occasions, commenced an irreversible countdown.

Systems scientist Paul LaViolette believes that activity in the centre of our galaxy intermittently causes newly created matter formed out of etheric premie to spew out, creating "superwaves" that reverberate throughout the solar system. It is reasoned that the superwave of circa 12,700 BCE was a contributory factor that caused multiple impacts of comet-like objects that struck the Northern Hemisphere causing climate change, earthquakes, fires, magnetic oscillations and increased radiation. An ensuing crustal shift, followed by an instant switch of the poles in which in moments North became South, triggered cataclysm.

Plato said that Atlantis was consumed 'in a single dreadful day and night.' There were survivors. Channeling sources indicate that between 20,000 and 30,000 people (out of many millions) situated in the right place at the right time were on safe ground when the waves struck.

From fossil studies of the Ahmarian, Bohunician and Aurignacian cultures, palaeontologists date the appearance of European early modern humans as roughly 48,000 years ago in the Upper Palaeolithic period, a date that tallies closely with Cayce's date of 50,000 BCE for the date of the second destruction of Atlantis and the subsequent corresponding emergence of Cro-Magnon man. The Cro-Magnon era, characterised by the first appearance of anatomically modern humans according to fossil studies, corresponds closely to the timespan defined by the latter three destructions of Atlantis, a 40,000-year period during which flourished civilisations seemingly more technologically advanced than our present day society.

One might expect as a consequence of cataclysmic upheavals that knowledge of the Ancient Wisdom would be lost, its priests and teachers taking the secrets to watery graves or to bottomless earth fissures. That is not the case. Esoteric and psychic records indicate that each occasion of destruction is marked by a dispersal of survivors seeking a new home. The period separating Cayce's date of 50,000 BCE and the emergence of early modern humans 48,000 years ago, witnessed the gradual influx into Europe of survivors seeking a new home after massive global displacement.

In 1907 the Church of England acquired Glastonbury Abbey and its environs. It appointed Frederick Bligh Bond as Director of Excavations to oversee a thorough study of the Abbey's history and foundations. Bond, an authority on mediaeval architecture and ecclesiastical restoration, undertook his work very successfully. He uncovered the foundations of previously unknown parts of the old Abbey, including the foundation walls of the now ruined St Edgar's Chapel. No matter where Bond turned his attention, he always seemed to dig in exactly the right spot to make important discoveries. In 1918 he revealed in his book *The Gate of Remembrance* that his successes were owed to spiritualistic channelings in the form of automatic writing.

Friends of Bond had received messages purporting to be from spirit world representatives of the Company of the Watchers of Avalon, a body of former monks of Glastonbury Abbey whose names were given in the book and in a later one of Bond's, *The Company of Avalon*. The messages revealed details on the Abbey's structure and history and Bond's interpretation of these had allowed him to make his startling discoveries. In one message Bond learned that Glastonbury's history as a place of special reverence dated back to the time of Atlantis:

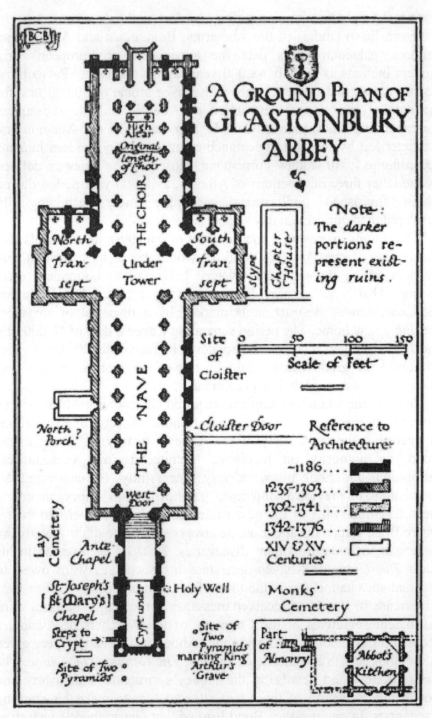

The following labels appear within the ground plan:

A GROUND PLAN OF GLASTONBURY ABBEY

Note:
The darker portions represent existing ruins.

High Altar

Original length of Choir

THE CHOIR

North Transept

South Transept

Chapter House

Slype

Under Tower

Site of Cloister

Scale of feet
0   50   100   150

Cloister Door

THE NAVE

North ? Porch

Reference to Architecture:

1186 . . . .

1235-1303 . . . .

1302-1341 . . . .

1342-1376 . . . .

XIV & XV . . . . Centuries

West Door

Lay Cemetery

Ante Chapel

St-Joseph's [St Mary's] Chapel

Steps to Crypt

Crypt under

Holy Well

Site of Two Pyramids

Site of Two Pyramids marking King Arthur's Grave

Monks' Cemetery

Part of Almonry

Abbot's Kitchen

Ground plan of the Great Church built after 1184, from "Wells and Glastonbury, a Historical and Topographical Account of the Cities".

The flow of spiritual forces is westward, following and impelling the forces of material things... Thus they whose habitation was in Crete, revisiting the memories and traditions of others of the same race... continued the interminable route ever westward beyond the gates of Hercules to the islands where the first fire-drawn metals be... but soon the spiritual forces which developed and sustained this immigration had deeper objects in view. They followed and transformed it by removing mundane influences and a great spiritual development arose in the places in which their instruments had prepared the soil. Phocis of the race of Crete trading with Poseidon [Atlantis]... was thus brought in contact with them who worshipped the One God... thus paved the way for the building of a Temple in his settlement of Tintagella... thus first arose that measurement and design which were afterwards as accurately reproduced by that further advance which culminated in the temple of Glastonbury. And Tintagella was the ancient place of the shrine of the High God. So the temple, a reproduction accurate in every measurement, was reproduced at Glaston on this foundation.

Ruta

Present day students of Grail geometry claim that in the antediluvian era there lay an island known as Ruta in what was then the Northern Hemisphere (later becoming the Southern Hemisphere as a consequence of a pole switch eleven thousand years ago). It is claimed that Ruta is now an undersea mount in the Atlantic, one of the Faraday Azores. The island's position is about 49N 29W, which is a line of latitude remarkably close to the 50th parallel. In a Nostradamus quatrain one reads: '*And afterwards, from the stem, what had been barren for so long, will burst into flower, and emerging from the 50th latitude, will renew the whole Christian Church.*'

The account records that among the inhabitants of Ruta was a wise and avuncular priesthood. It possessed knowledge of a pan-global temple network, the Reshel Grid, which was constructed around 500,000 years ago by the Universal Powers to raise the vibrational energies of Mother Earth's Gaia consciousness and the Forces of Living Nature. The system extended several thousand miles into an area that is now geographical Europe.

Reportedly, upgrades of the grid system have subsequently been made. The first was by the Ruta priesthood about 12,000 years ago.

Ruta was the last undefiled outpost of the uncorrupted priests from the fallen civilization of Atlantis. The second upgrade was installed by the Knights Templar at the time of the Order's establishment in Jerusalem in the early twelfth century. Over a period of roughly 300 years, they grew into a rich and powerful organization and built a series of Marian Cathedrals and chapels in Europe using sacred geometry, including the Reshel system. It is claimed that these sacred temples act as condensers and tuners of divine feminine energy.

Supporters of this theory claim that there are many hundreds of grids all over the earth, mirrors mirroring other mirrors. The Reshel energy poles are designated by Hebrew letters. The system is the "Chief Head Stone" referred to in Psalms 118:19-23. It is claimed that Saint Columbus (521-597 CE) not only knew of the system but re-installed it in the Hebrides and the Edinburgh area. It is further claimed that the Reshel Grid was also installed in the present Americas. Frederick J. Pohl argued the case that Henry I, Earl of Orkney, visited North America in 1398, almost 100 years before Christopher Columbus.[26] The Sinclair party understood the Reshel system and its esoteric purpose and "re-booted" the American grids as part of its mission.

Henry was the grandfather of William Sinclair, 1st Earl of Caithness, the builder of Rosslyn Chapel. In 1784, Henry was identified by Johann Reinhold Forster as possibly being the Prince Zichmni described in letters allegedly written around the year 1400 by the Zeno brothers of Venice, in which they describe a voyage throughout the North Atlantic under the command of Zichmni.

The letters and the accompanying map, allegedly rediscovered and published in the early 16th century, are regarded by most historians as a hoax by the Zenos or their publishers. William Thomson, in his book *The New History of Orkney*, wrote: 'It has been Earl Henry's singular fate to enjoy an ever-expanding posthumous reputation which has very little to do with anything he achieved in his lifetime.'

In recent times the British portion of the Reshel grid is said to have been similarly re-booted in the form of the celebrated 1991 and 1997 Barbury Castle crop circles, a few miles from the ancient megalithic centre of Avebury in Wiltshire. As if to cement the esoteric Hebraic aspect of the energy grid system, the 1997 Barbury Castle crop circle was constructed in the form of the Kabbalistic Tree of Life.

---

[26] Pohl, F., *Prince Henry Sinclair: His Expedition To The New World In 1398*, (London: Davis-Poynter, 1974; New York: Clarkson N. Potter, 1974).

It is known that the entire earth is charged with the invisible flow of ubiquitous electromagnetic energy. Its field is subtlely influenced by an array of factors, including the gravitational influence of near and far bodies in our solar system. It is influenced too by ground level factors such as the shapes and contours of landscape features, which also influence the character of minerals deep underground.

Rudolf Steiner discovered that cosmic influences affect the magnetic currents on the earth's surface. Not only that, they act upon the cycles of motion within the earth's minerals in relation to the orbits of the particular planetary body to which each most readily respond. At certain seasons they become charged with an energy that allows seeds to germinate.

Free thinkers and philosophers in the distant past, notably Pythagoras and, later, Plato, believed that the physical universe is composed of geometrical figures, among which the pentadodecahedron is identified as the "hull of the sphere". Plato refers in the *Phaedo* to a belief that the construction of the world is likened to the building of a ship by the use of geometric shapes. Consider the common saying: "the four corners of the earth", a reflection of the ancient belief that the earth is a vast stone. The pyramids in Egypt have a square base, signifying that man is foursquare, representing the four elements of the earth. Set upon that square base is the symbol of the spirit: the triangle, which represents the trinity of life: Father-Mother-Son, the three constituent parts of God, but also the life spirit which the ancients thought they had discovered in stone: life, spark and fire. Scientific research appears to indicate that the earth resembles a gigantic crystal supported by a rigid skeletal structure beneath its surface. German scientist Siegfried Wittman claimed in 1952[27] that he and his study team had concluded that the earth has upon its surface a grid system consisting of a checkerboard pattern of positive and negative poles.

The squared pattern has a centre pole surrounded by smaller poles within each section. The main pole concentrates energy through eight supporting poles. Four send pulses of energy skyward while the others send energy to the four points of the compass.

Ten years later, biologist Ivan Sanderson and colleagues, intrigued by geographical anomalies such as those portrayed in the Piri Reis map of 1523 and the Buache map of 1737 which suggest that pre-Egyptian

---

[27] *Die Welt der geheimen Mächte* (*The World of the Secret Forces*).

civilizations possessed advanced mathematical and astronomical skills, set out to "pattern the mysterie". Sanderson's 1972 article, *The Twelve Devils' Graveyards Around the World*, plotted air and maritime disappearances worldwide. It focused attention on 12 areas, equally spaced over the globe, in which magnetic anomalies and other aberrations were linked to unaccountable physical phenomena.

Sanderson's investigations were the impetus for others to make a contribution to the study of electromagnetic aberrations upon the "planetary grid". the term coined by Christopher Bird writing in the *New Age Journal* of May 1975. In it Bird refers to the work of Russian researchers: historian Nikolai Goncharov, engineer Vyacheslav Morozov and electronics specialist Valery Makarov who had published in *Khimiya I Zhizn* (Chemistry of Life) in the *Science Journal of the USSR Academy of Life* an article: "*Is the Earth a Large Crystal?*"

The Russians' paper, which supports and builds on Sanderson's work, explores an idea that visualises the core of the Earth as a growing crystal that influences what occurs on the planet. The authors postulate that the earth projects from this inner crystal a dual geometrically regularised grid.

The first grid layer consists of Sanderson's twelve areas that lie over the surface of the earth, which the Russians describe as pentagonal slabs (a dodecahedron) while the second is formed by twenty equilateral triangles (an icosohedron). The writers stated that the superimposition of the two grids over the globe's surface reveals a pattern of the earth's energy network. The lines tracing out the dual grid coincide with zones of active risings and depressions on the ocean floors, cave faults and mid-oceanic ridges such as in the Bermuda Triangle. The paper refers to twelve such areas.

In esoteric teachings these principle nodal points are described as the earth's etheric web points—gateways to other dimensions. The Russians theorised that these forms and their apexes possess qualities that can explain many unusual phenomena. They claimed that in these areas, viewed in conjunction with Sanderson's work, are to be found regions of seismic and volcanic activity, while magnetic anomalies are located at the vertices of the polygons. The grid nodes are said to denote centres of great changes in atmospheric pressures; hurricanes, for example, take shape in these areas. Prevailing winds and ocean currents also fit into the network as well as paths of migratory animals, gravitational anomalies and the sites of ancient cities.

The Russians' paper claims that if the grid was lined up on the surface of the globe so that all of the many factors could be correlated, the exact centre point is found to be Giza in Upper Egypt, the key being the 'measure of Light.'

Researcher Roy Snelling brings consciousness into the equation when he describes the powerhouse of the Earth as the presence of huge psychic crystals within its etheric body. Accordingly, our planet's true form, Snelling suggests, *is* its geometrical grid, the physical earth being a visible manifestation that could not exist in the absence of its etheric counterpart. This idea mirrors the esoteric belief that an etheric body is the magnetic field of a physical body (an example being the human aura), which contains a template of its idealised outer form.

The laws of physics and nature... are only part of a broader spectrum of Cosmic laws, some relate to other dimensions, parallel universes, anti-matter, and also a universal energy field where science claims that there is only empty space.[28]

Snelling suggests that the planetary matrix is defined by the perfect geometrical relationship of the five Platonic solids that constitute its geometrical form. In accordance with mathematical law, these five solids may be contained perfectly inside a sphere. Energy in the edge-lines of all five within the Earth radiates upwards to form lines of force on the surface: a projection by the Cosmos from its own substance, one of many levels of creation, each one descending in order of vibration-rate and coarseness of matter so that each level interpenetrates the level above and below without affecting the higher or lower levels.

Moreover, each form can transition into any other through a series of movements, including twisting, truncating, expanding, combining or faceting. Snelling speaks appreciatively of the mathematical beauty that binds the Platonic solids in a state of etheric perfection, the motivating power behind the earth's dynamic energy system.

The five Platonic solids are the only shapes with equal side lengths, equal interior angles, faces made of the same regular shape which look the same from each vertex (corner point), and, crucially, all fit perfectly in a sphere with all points resting on the circumference. Information about the Platonic solids has been taught since ancient times. They are called 'Platonic' after Plato (427 – 347 BCE) who, in the *Timaeus*, outlined a cosmology through the metaphor of planar and solid geometry. He associated the four elements with four of the solids: the

---

[28] Snelling, R., *The Planetary Matrix*, Spiritual Genesis Books, 2013.

tetrahedron as fire; the octahedron as air; the cube as earth, and the icosahedron as water. The dodecahedron represents the "fifth" element—the ether. Plato ascribes intelligence to the solids when he refers to the ability of the four elements to 'transmute into each other' and how 'they must be dissimilar to one another but capable of arising out of one another's disintegration.'

Cosmic Core, a web-based group concerned with the concept of twinning science with spirituality,[29] builds on Plato's ideas of intelligent design in describing the solids as not five separate shapes but five aspects of the same shape—the spinning torus. Cosmic Core describes the principle of "Mater into Matter", in which Consciousness forms into Light, Light into Geometric Form, and Geometric Form into Matter. The process begins when a sphere representing undifferentiated light polarises into opposites symbolized by two intersecting circles.

The two poles swirl in opposite directions in rhythmic energy patterns, creating a toroidal flow. The building block of the torus is an "Aether Unit", a manifestation of the fluctuations of Consciousness. These units, Cosmic Core claim, are not "things" but an intelligent energy flow process that characterises and defines the planetary grid.

The planetary matrix comprises a network of 90 edgelines of all five Platonic solids. Snelling calls this the planet's Primary Leyline. At points on the Earth where some of these lines meet or cross at the apexes of the Platonic solids (which are all at the surface of the earth anyway), one is likely to find powerful vortices of energy.

The two poles swirl in opposite directions in rhythmic energy patterns, creating a toroidal flow. The building block of the torus is an 'Aether Unit,' a manifestation of the fluctuations of Consciousness. These units, Cosmic Core claim, are not "things" but an intelligent energy flow process that characterises and defines the planetary grid. We explore the "Aether" mystery more deeply in the next chapter.

[29] https://www.cosmic-core.org

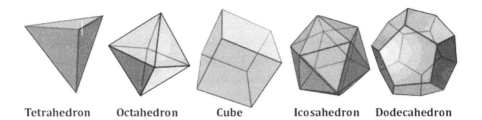

| Tetrahedron | Octahedron | Cube | Icosahedron | Dodecahedron |

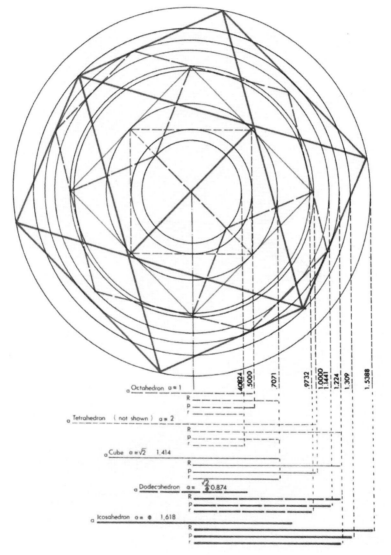

Top—the 5 Platonic Solids

Bottom—the energy grid: five Platonic solids nested inside a sphere.

Credit Robert Lawlor - *Sacred Geometry: Philosophy & Practice*

	Faces	Apexes	Edges
Cube - earth	6	8	12
Icosahedron - water	20	12	30
Octahedron - air	8	6	12
Tetrahedron - fire	4	4	6
Dodecahedron - ether	12	20	30
	50	50	90

The 5-Platonic Solids and their Elements, Faces, Apexes and Edges

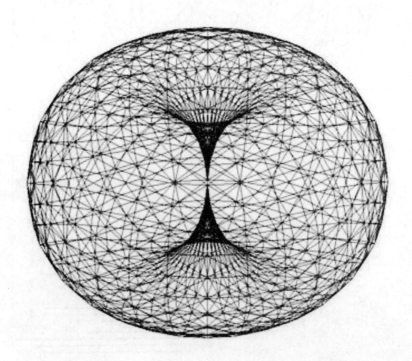

The spinning torus in which Mater ("Mother") becomes Matter

PARALLEL WORLDS

Alice in conversation with Humpty Dumpty

Chapter 11

"Etherea"

The UFO phenomenon exists. It has been with us throughout history. It is physical in nature and it remains unexplained in terms of contemporary science. It represents a level of consciousness that we have not yet recognised and which is able to manipulate dimensions beyond time and space, as we understand them. It affects our own consciousness in ways that we do not fully grasp and it generally behaves as a control system.

—Jacques Vallée, *Forbidden Science*

This chapter draws and expands on material from a previous work, *The Landing Lights of Magonia*. It explores the notion that there is a parallel world, an etheric dimension of many mansions that is filled with all manner of living energies, some we may recognise, others most assuredly not, and which exists as an integral but invisible component of our physical planet. I dub it "Etherea".

The proposition is an ancient theme of philosophical consideration. Nearly 2,500 years ago, for example, in his contemplation of nature as a vibrant living force that exists beyond the everyday realms of human cognizance, Aristotle remarked:

We say that the Sensible World is an image of another; therefore since this world is vivid or alive, how much more, then, that other must live... Yonder, therefore, above the stellar virtues, stand other heavens to be attained, like the heavens of this world; beyond them, because they are of a higher kind, brighter and vaster; nor are they distant from each other like this one, for they are incorporeal. Yonder, too, exists an earth, not of inanimate matter, but vivid with animal life and all natural terrestrial phenomena like this one, but of other kinds and perfections. There are plants, also, and gardens, and flowing water; there are aquatic animals but of nobler species. Yonder is air and life appropriate to it, all immortal. And although the life there is analogous to ours, yet it is nobler, seeing that it is intellectual, perpetual and unalterable.

In alchemic philosophy the "ether" is that part of the body of the universal logos out of which are extracted the four creative principles: physical (earthly), etheric (watery), astral (fiery) and mental (airy).

Aristotle's reference to Etherea's residents may range from ghosts and other remnants of the departed in Etherea's lowest vibrational levels to angelic and devic energies in its highest.

In between these coarse and sublime planes, philosophers, metaphysicians and, increasingly, scientists studying quantum and multiverse theories, speculate that the etheric kingdom is home to a bewildering assortment of non-human antities (NHEs), including fairy folk, nature spirits, the makers of the circles in the fields, and UFOs and their occupants (both the seemingly friendly types and the stuff of nightmares).

An NHE retrieved from a crashed disc in New Mexico said to a US Government agent: *This is not the only universe. Imagine a large silver island of white sand and that each sand grain is a different universe separated from each other by an electromagnetic membrane. And surrounding the island is a cold, dark sea.* [30]

Agent: *Tell me more of the this cold, dark sea.*

NHE: *You don't want to know. It will change you forever.*

In his study of *Unseen Forces*[31] Manly P. Hall explained that the ancients symbolised these four principles or vehicles as the arms of the cross representing the major crossing points of the vital forces in the human body. These intersecting points of the etheric world have their seat in the solar plexus and spleen.

The etheric world is often referred to as the molten sea for in its depths the soul must ultimately be washed and purified. As each kingdom of nature in the outer world of earth life has diverse lives evolving through it, so the four divisions of ether inhabited by

---

[30] Howe, L.M., *Glimpses of Other Realities Volume 1: Facts and Eyewitnesses*, Linda Moulton Howe Productions, 1997.
[31] Hall, M., *Unseen Forces*, Philosophical Research Society, Inc., Los Angeles, 1978.

intelligent life forms are evolving through the four elemental essences.

More recently in esoteric philosophy, the nineteenth century birth of the spiritualist movement heralded a growing belief in other dimensions or planes, the latter term popularised by Madama Blavatsky. The terms "etheric plane" and the "etheric body" were introduced into Theosophy by Blavatsky's contemporaries, Charles Webster Leadbeater and Annie Besant, to represent a hypothetical "fourth plane" that exists above the planes of solids, liquids, and gases.

Leadbeater advanced this thinking when he stated that this fourth plane is composed of not one but many levels of reality, which are intertwined with the human world and is inhabited by multitudes of entities. He held that each level is composed of a discrete density of astral or ethereal matter and that it accommodates NHEs that have no discernment or awareness of other entities that reside in other etheric strata.

Other writers such as Alice Bailey, a contemporary of Leadbeater, also gave continuousness to Theosophical concepts of ethereal beings. Subsequently, Bailey's works had a great impact over the burgeoning New Age movement. Bailey described the nature spirits and devas as ethereal beings immersed in macro divisions of an interwoven threefold universe that incorporates etheric, astral or mental planes. Bailey believed that entities of the four kingdoms: Earth, Air, Fire, and Water—the Forces of Living Nature—reside in the etheric world.

> Many poets, and all mystics and occult writers, have declared that behind the visible are chains on chains of conscious beings, who are not of heaven but of the earth, who have no inherent form, but change according to their whim, or the mind that sees them. You cannot lift your hand without influencing and being influenced by hordes. The visible world is merely their skin. In dreams we go amongst them, and play with them, and combat with them.
>
> —W.B. Yeats, *Irish Fairy and Folk-Tales*

Late nineteenth-century metaphysical thinking on this topic was swiftly followed by increasingly exotic twentieth-century developments in the study of creation at the quantum level. Remarkably, it would soon became apparent that the two schools of thought were basically of one mind in acknowledging the existence of Earth's parallel worlds.

Illustration for "Jabberwocky" poem, *Through the Looking-glass*

In *Wholeness and the Implicate Order*[32] quantum physicist Professor David Bohm introduced his audience to ontological concepts, which served to impart a metaphysical aspect to quantum theory. In this brilliant work Bohm imagined the universe as an infinite sea of space and energy out of which matter could be unfolded, which he called "explicating", and enfolded, which he called "implicating". The central underlying theme of Bohm's theory is the 'unbroken wholeness of the totality of existence as an undivided flowing movement without borders.'

In an ontological sense the Implicate Order can be seen as both a physical and metaphysical construction—a vast Intelligence which contains all things within itself, and which enfolds or unfolds these things so that they emerge into the reality we experience as real.

Bohm defined the Explicate Order as the order of the *physical world*, and the Implicate Order as the *source* of Explicate Order. He postulated that the Implicate Order behaves in an ultra-holistic fashion in that it connects everything with everything else; in theory any individual element could reveal information about every other element in the universe.

Bohm and Cambridge biophysicist Professor Rupert Sheldrake postulated an interacting universe whose tiniest element, like a hologram, contains the information of the entire universe. In this model it follows that there is no process of chance, only a blueprint of evolution, which, via Sheldrake's principle of morphic resonance,[33] is transmitted throughout the entire universe. This means that creation can happen anywhere, not just here.

Bohm regarded the Implicate Order as a deeper and more fundamental order of reality; whereas, in contrast, the Explicate Order includes the abstractions that humans normally perceive. In the words of F. David Peat, Bohm considered that what we regard as objective reality are 'surface phenomena, explicate forms that have temporarily unfolded out of an underlying implicate order.' That is, the Implicate Order is the ground from which reality *truly* emerges.

---

[32] Bohm, Dr. J., *Wholeness and the Implicate Order*, Routledge, Great Britain, 1980.

[33] Morphic resonance hypothesis posits that memory is inherent in nature and that natural systems such as termite colonies or insulin molecules inherit a collective memory from all previous things of their kind. Sheldrake proposes that morphic resonance is also responsible for psi-type interconnections between organisms such as precognition and telepathy.

Bohm believed in the presence of an immense background of special energy at the very depths of this ground of all existence, which Bohm termed the plenum. Bohm likened this ground to one whole and unbroken movement of continuous flux, which he called the holomovement (movement of the whole). It is the holomovement that carries the Implicate Order

Bohm believed that the Implicate Order has to be extended into a multidimensional reality, wherein the holomovement endlessly enfolds and unfolds into infinite dimensionality. One observes here the interplay between the Implicate and the Explicate Orders, the flow of matter, manifested and interdependent, towards consciousness. Within this milieu there are independent sub-totalities (such as physical elements and human entities) with relative autonomy. The layers of the Implicate Order can go deeper and deeper to the ultimately unknown.

The Implicate Order is not to be understood in terms of a regular arrangement of objects and events but, mirroring the inside-out geometry of Dr. Who's tardis, rather as total order contained in each region of space and time. In Bohm's framework of understanding the whole exists in every part (the infinite number of mansions of the Implicate occupying the explicate house of our physical universe, for example).

> Fairyland exists as an invisible world within which the visible world [Bohm's Explicate Order] is immersed like an island in an unexplored ocean [Bohm's Implicate Order] and which is peopled by more species of living beings than this world because incomparably more vast and varied are its possibilities.

> —Walter Evans-Wentz

Indeed, Bohm had come to believe that space and time might be derived from the Implicate Order. He maintained that time is a projection of multidimensional reality from the Implicate Order into a sequence of moments. It follows that the flow of time is the product of a constant series of unfoldings and enfoldings; the enfolded present, becoming part of the past, returns to the present as a kind of Implicate Order. In this quantum model all possible realities co-exist in time and space.

Physicist David Finkelstein was of like mind when he asserted that: 'space-time is a statistical construct from a deeper "pre-geometric" quantum structure in which process is fundamental.'[34]

American theoretical physicist Richard Feynman also remarked on the illusory nature of time, noting, for example, that a positron moving forward in time is actually an electron moving backward in time.

Advancing his thinking, Bohm went on to suggest that we actually construct space and time. He believed that the universe is 'all thought,' the inference being that it is consciousness alone that creates, maintains and sustains the physical universe, a postulate that presupposes that consciousness never dies.

This was not a new idea. In 1932 English physicist, astronomer and mathematician Sir James Jeans said presciently,[35] 'The universe begins to look more like a great thought than like a great machine.'

Twenty years later David Bohm took these ideas to another level. Together with fellow scientist, Karl H. Pribram, Bohm proposed that the human brain mathematically constructs objective reality by interpreting frequencies that are projections from another dimension within the Implicate Order. Pribram coined the term frequency domain to refer to the interference patterns that comprise the Implicate Order. This domain is the border between mind and matter. This supposes that the brain is a hologram enfolded in a holographic universe.

Writer Michael Talbot was a firm supporter of Bohm's concepts in this regard. He wrote poetically:[36]

> ...just as every portion of the hologram contains the image of the whole, every portion of the universe enfolds the whole... if we knew how to access it we could find the Andromeda galaxy in the thumbnail of our left hand. We could also find Cleopatra meeting Caesar for the first time, for in principle the whole past and implications for the whole future are also enfolded in each small region of space and time. Every cell in our body enfolds the entire cosmos. So does every leaf, every raindrop, every dust mote...

It follows from this line of reasoning that the physical body is a level of density in the total human energy field, a hologram that has coalesced out of the interference pattern of the aura, itself a subtle field

---

[34] Finkelstein, D., *The Space-Time Code*, Physical Review, 5D, no. 12 [15 June 1972].

[35] Jeans, J., *The Mysterious Universe*, E.P. Dutton, NY, 1932.

[36] Talbot, M., *The Holographic Universe*, 1991.

of the Implicate Order. It is thought that the mind resides not in the brain but in the energy field that permeates both the brain and the physical body.

It took many years for physicists to begin to catch up with Bohm's ideas. Today quantum theory speculates that mind and matter are different vibrations or ripples in the same pond, precisely what Bohm was proposing forty years ago (and what Tantric philosophy taught two thousand years ago in stating that the universe is an emanation of the mind).

American physicist John A. Wheeler who helped develop the theory of nuclear fission asked: 'May the universe in some strange sense be brought into being by the participation of those who participate?'

Theoretical physicist Jack Sarfatti believes that the structure of matter may not be independent of consciousness.[37] Sarfatti also believes that humankind's collective unconscious determines whether a particle decays or not. However, because we do not perceive that we are vital participants in the quantum universe our collective will is unfocused and chaotic, making quantum events appear random and problematic. Talbot[38] suggests that new physics is increasingly accepting the premise that matter, space and time owe their existence to human consciousness, reality being a super-hologram created and maintained by consciousness.

Evan Harris Walker has suggested that consciousness is a "quantum mechanical tunnelling" process that takes place at the synapses between human nerve cells.[39] Sarfatti expounds on Walker's observation in stating that the Swiss cheese-like wormhole connections (quantum foam) at the sub-atomic scale of 3-dimensional space connect every part of the universe directly with every other part, much like the 'nervous system of a cosmic brain.'

To avoid catastrophic psychic overload, a part of our consciousness that operates as a re-structuring mechanism edits out the realities that our minds cannot cope with. This action mirrors the remarkable conclusions of Aldous Huxley who after consuming mescaline and considering the nature of consciousness saw that the brain acts as a

---

[37] Sarfatti, J., *Implications of Meta-Physics for Psychoenergetic Systems*, in *Psychoenergetic Systems, Vol. 1*, Gordon and Breach: London, 1974.
[38] Talbot, M., *Mysticism and the New Physics*, Arkana, London, 1993.
[39] Walker, H.E., *The Nature of Consciousness*, Mathematical Biosciences 7 [1970]: 138-197.

filter, a reducing valve, of a vaster mind—consciousness—that he called the "Mind at Large".

Humans struggle to attain this level of realisation because of a lack of belief in the power of "seeing" what truly lies before one. Pribram reasoned that the objective world comprises a vast ocean of waves and frequencies. We see this as "concrete" because our brains can transmute this holographic blur into the sticks and stones that make up our world. The illusion of a seemingly smooth item of bone china is therefore equivalent to the phantom limb syndrome. If we could somehow unfilter the cup from our brain processes we would instead perceive an interference pattern, the cup and pattern at the same time being both real and unreal. Bohm said as much when he stated that the individual is in total contact with the Implicate Order. In that sense, the individual 'is part of the whole of mankind and in another sense he can get beyond it.' Bohm said that in the Implicate Order imagination and reality are one and the same.

The principle of an "Etherea", an invisible companion plane of Earth having been established by both metaphysics and science, it was only a matter of time before ufologists in certain quarters would propose it as the home of our planet's alien visitors.

The ufologists' interdimensional hypothesis declares that sightings are the result of experiencing other dimensions that coexist separately alongside our own, in contrast with either the extraterrestrial hypothesis that suggests UFO sightings are caused by visitations from outside the Earth or the psychosocial hypothesis that argues that they are best explained as psychological or social phenomenon. The hypothesis has been advanced by eminent ufologists past and present such as Meade Layne, John Keel, J. Allen Hynek and Jacques Vallée. Proponents argue that UFOs are a modern manifestation of a phenomenon that has occurred throughout human history, which in prior ages were ascribed to mythological or supernatural creatures.

David Grusch, a former member of the UAP Task Force famous for claiming that the U.S. government was covering up evidence for advanced technology, UFOs and alien pilots, suggested that the phenomenon is not necessarily extraterrestrial, and is actually coming from a higher dimensional physical space that might be co-located right here.

Jeffrey J. Kripal, Chair in Philosophy and Religious Thought at Rice University, writes: 'this interdimensional reading, long a staple of

157

Spiritualism through the famous "fourth dimension", would have a very long life within ufology and is still very much with us today.'

In his landmark work[40] Vallée argues the case for a 'parallel universe co-existing with our own.' In a subsequent 1990 Vallée outlined "Five Arguments Against the Extraterrestrial Origin of Unidentified Flying Objects":

1. Unexplained close encounters are far more numerous than required for any physical survey of the earth;

2. The humanoid body structure of the alleged "aliens" is not likely to have originated on another planet and is not biologically adapted to space travel;

3. The reported behavior in thousands of abduction reports contradicts the hypothesis of genetic or scientific experimentation on humans by an advanced race;

4. The extension of the phenomenon throughout recorded human history demonstrates that UFOs are not a contemporary phenomenon;

5. The apparent ability of UFOs to manipulate space and time suggests radically different and richer alternatives.

In *The Edge of Reality*,[41] Vallée and Hynek consider the possibility of what they call "interlocking universes". Vallée asked his colleague, 'What other wild hypotheses could we make?' To which Hynek replied, 'There could be other universe with different quantum rules or vibration rates if you want. Our own space-time continuum could be a cross-section through a universe with many more dimensions. ... Think what a hard time you would have convincing an aborigine that right now, through this room, TV pictures are passing! Yet they're here. You have to have a transducer to see them, namely a TV set. Well, in the same sense there may be interlocking universes right here! We have this idea of space, we always think of another universe being someplace else. It may not. Maybe it's right here.'

American psychologist Lawrence LeShan has suggested[42] that our physical universe has a corresponding paranormal reality whose resident entities are "functional" entities (as distinct from structural

---

[40] Vallée, J., *Passport to Magonia*, Daily Grail Publishing, Brisbane, 2014.
[41] Vallée, J; Hynek, J., *The Edge of Reality: A Progress Report on Unidentified Flying Objects*. Regnery, 1975.
[42] LeShan, L., *The Medium, The Mystic and the Physicist*, Viking Press, NY, 1974.

entities such as ourselves) that have no length, breadth nor depth. Not limited by the normal laws of space and time, they can move faster than light. They exist only when they are visualised or held in the mind and are thus like a mathematical point possessing no true reality in space-time. Whitley Strieber went further, adding the striking opinion that:

> UFO beings may be our first true quantum discovery in the large-scale world. The very act of observing it may be creating it as a concrete actuality, with sense, definition and a consciousness of its own. [43]

Strieber's insights suggest that the more we observe, the more we add substance to energies emerging from Etherea purely by virtue of the power of our conscious minds. By this process, the residents of Earth's companion world may be seeking to capitalise on this quantum phenomenon to strengthen their powers to influence human behaviour. If true, our own thoughts risk making us captive to a process of manipulation and control about whose outcome we are wholly ignorant.

Even in the very early days of UFO research astute minds were ascribing a psychic component to the phenomenon. The British science writer Gerald Heard in *Is Another World Watching* (1950) proposed his "bee" theory, in which UFOs represent a mindless order organised and controlled by a larger intelligence. Arthur C. Clarke said much the same thing, arriving at the conclusion that UFOs were paraphysical and not from other planets.

In his response to a letter from writers Randall Pugh and Frederick Holiday, Keel too said that UFOs are related to psychic phenomena. Keel believed that history, psychiatry, religion and the occult are far more important for an understanding of the flying saucer mystery than the publication of book after book that simply recount sightings.

Keel once explained that he abandoned the extraterrestrial hypothesis in 1967 when his field investigations disclosed an astonishing overlap between psychic phenomena and UFOs. It had become evident to him that objects and apparitions do not necessarily originate on another planet and, furthermore, may not even exist as permanent constructions of matter. He felt that that it is more likely that we see what we want to see and interpret such visions according to our contemporary beliefs.

---

[43] Strieber, W., *Communion: A True Story*, Harper. New York, 2008.

In his book *UFOs: Operation Trojan Horse,*[44] Keel argued that a non-human or spiritual intelligence source has staged whole events over a long period of time in order to propagate and reinforce certain erroneous belief systems. Keel conjectured that ultimately anomalies such as monsters, ghosts and demons, the fairy faith in Middle Europe, vampire legends, mystery airships, aeroplanes and helicopters, weird creature sightings, poltergeist phenomena, balls of light, UFOs and so on are a cover for the real phenomenon. Keel used the term "ultraterrestrials" to describe UFO occupants he believed to be non-human entities capable of taking on whatever form they choose.

Michael Gosso, too, advanced the idea that, despite their encroachment into the world of matter, UFOs are more akin to a psychic projection than to non-human intelligence. He said, 'UFOs and other extraordinary phenomena are manifestations of a disturbance in the collective unconscious of the human species.'[45]

To many analysts, the observed behaviour of UFOs indicates that they are evidently not constructed of solid matter and, hence, are paraphysical in nature. They move at incredible speeds but create no sonic booms. They perform impossible manoeuvres that defy the laws of inertia and appear and disappear instantly like phantoms.

In 1955, eight years after seeing a string of nine, shiny unidentified flying objects flying past Mount Rainier at speeds of 1,200 miles per hour, private pilot Kenneth Arnold expressed his view that spaceships were a form of living energy.

Also in 1955, Air Marshall Lord Dowding (the man who directed the Battle of Britain in 1940) made the astonishing statement in a public lecture that the phenomenon was paraphysical, declaring that not only were UFO occupants immortal but also could make themselves invisible to human sight, take on human form and walk and work among us unnoticed.

In 1957 Ray Palmer, founder of *Flying Saucers* magazine, said that in his opinion UFOs hailed from civilisations with paraphysical ties to the human race. Earlier, in 1949, Palmer had already said that he believed UFOs to be extra-dimensional, not extra-terrestrial.

Engineer Bryant Reeve in his 1965 book *The Advent of the Cosmic*

---

[44] Keel, J. *Operation Trojan Horse*, Anomalist Books, San Antonio, 1970.
[45] Grosso, M., *"UFOs and the Myth of the New Age,"* in *Cyberbiological Studies of the Imaginal Component in the UFO Contact Experience*, ed. Dennis Stillings [St. Paul, Minnesota Archaeus Project, 1989], P. 81.

Viewpoint concluded that UFO sightings in themselves are irrelevant, subordinate in importance to the far more fundamental recognition that they are actually a part of a larger paraphysical phenomenon.

What is the paraphysical hypothesis? It is stated succinctly by RAF Air-Marshal Sir Victor Goddard, KCB, CBE, MA. On 3 May 1969 he delivered a public lecture when he said:

> That while it may be that some operators of UFO are normally the paraphysical denizens of a planet other than Earth, there is no logical need for this to be so. For, if the materiality of UFO is paraphysical (and consequently normally invisible), UFO could more plausibly be creations of an invisible world coincident with the space of our physical Earth planet than creations in the paraphysical realms of any other planet in the solar system... Given that real UFO are paraphysical, capable of reflecting light like ghosts; and given also that, according to many observers, they remain visible as they change position at ultrahigh speeds from one point to another, it follows that those that remain visible in transition do not dematerialize for that swift transition and therefore, their mass must be of a diaphanous, very diffuse nature, and their substance relatively etheric... The observed validity of this supports the paraphysical assertion and makes the likelihood of UFO being Earth-created greater than the likelihood of their creation on another planet... The astral world of illusion, which is greatly inhabited by illusion-prone spirits, is well known for its multifarious imaginative activities and exhortations. Seemingly, some of its denizens are eager to exemplify principalities and powers. Others pronounce upon morality, spirituality, Deity, et cetera. All of these astral components who invoke human consciousness may be sincere but many of their theses may be framed to propagate some special phantasm, perhaps of an earlier incarnation, or to indulge an inveterate and continuing technological urge toward materialistic progress, or simply to astonish and disturb the gullible for the devil of it.

In this remarkable statement Goddard, a senior British establishment figure, astutely outlined the paraphysical hypothesis. Moreover, in describing the unholy alliance between the astral worlds and Nazi Germany, Goddard broached what in his day was the taboo subject of the Hitler regime's preoccupation with occult matters.

The late John Napier, distinguished anthropologist and one time Visiting Professor of Primate Biology at London University, and Director of the Primate Biology Programme at the Smithsonian Institute, gave an opinion to Pugh and Holiday on the humanoid format of UFO entities. Professor Napier said that as a result of the natural inclination of human reason to deny the existence of UFO humanoid types the only alternative explanation, if the establishment is intent on preserving the illusion of non-existence, is the "Great Conspiracy" theory. For Napier this latter option was equally unacceptable as it ignored the testimony of countless eyewitnesses or, absurdly, made them party to the "Great Conspiracy". Napier said that this must open the door to a third hypothesis, which is neither a matter of reason nor fakery, namely one that is unreasonable in human terms but entirely rational from the perspective of what Napier termed the "Goblin Universe". In this context, Napier observed, the third explanation must concern the minds of men.

John Keel[46] advanced the idea that somewhere in the vast electromagnetic spectrum there is an omnipotent intelligence able to manipulate energy, one that literally can bring phenomena into existence in this plane.

In contemplating the same topic, Paul Devereux suggested[47] that this manipulative energy is here on our doorstep. He believes that the Gaia energy of Earth is the source of input for the UFO form, wherein the entire planet is a single self-monitoring organism that enables the planet to dream forms into existence.

Keel went on to ask: Are there really UFOs at all? UFOs were being variously described as triangles, spheres, hexagons, flying cubes, cigar shapes and doughnuts dressed in dazzling arrays of colours and light formations. Keel reflected on this and decided that hard objects such as the disc and cigar shapes, for example, existed merely as "temporary transmogrifications". They would land, could be seen and touched and leave markings where they set down.

Keel became convinced that these illusory forms are intended as decoys for the soft objects such as the dirigibles seen in the 1897 flap and the mysterious "Ghost Planes" observed over Scandinavia in the

---

[46] ibid
[47] Devereaux, P., *Spirit Roads*, Collins & Brown, London, 2003.

1940s. The "soft" crafts' abilities to exhibit bizarre forms of behaviour, make impossible turns and reach unheard of speeds lead some investigators to believe they that are in some sense sentient, maybe even alive. Keel concluded that the immense breadth of the phenomenon and the sheer number of sightings serves only to give the lie to its validity and makes it far more likely that UFOs are temporary extrusions from exotic energies originating in the higher bands of the electromagnetic spectrum.

> We occupy all space, everywhere in the universe or any void in between. We are from a different dimension, a different plane of existence. We have no boundaries or limits... we are an anti-log of everything you see visually. We can travel in any dimension or space without being observed...

> —Dr. John J. Dalton's mental communication with a grey alien in New Mexico, 1947

Devereux believes that UFO entities are not travellers within a separate "aeroform" structure but are formed in the same way as the UFO shape itself and that they share the same substance, the one being merely a different aspect of one common phenomenon

In a similar vein, Jacques Vallée proposed[48] that UFOs are neither extraterrestrial nor the result of hoaxes or delusions but rather are a control system, which is intended to stabilise the relationship between man's conscious needs and the rapidly evolving complexities of living in the physical world. He believes that UFOs have both a visible reality (with mass, volume, inertia and so on) and a window to other planes of reality. Its occupants, he suggests, are creations from the dreamscape, a reality that intersects ours at right angles where we encounter and witness UFOs in the psychic planes of perception.

In Vallée's opinion UFOs neither fly nor are they objects; they materialise and dematerialise, violating in the process all known laws of motion. Vallée maintains that they are not necessarily an aspect of some form of an unknowable higher order of life but are products of a well defined and regulated technology, seemingly utterly bizarre by human standards.

Vallée suggests that the same power imputed to saucer people of influencing human events was once the exclusive property of fairies. He

---

[48] Vallée, J., *UFOs: The Psychic Solution,* Panther Books Ltd, St. Albans, 1977.

believes that the UFO phenomenon could be an 'instance of a still undiscovered natural occurrence.'

Vallée pondered on the oft-asked question as to whether it is necessarily true that we would detect meaningful patterns (by our objective standards) in the behaviour of a superior race. In his opinion, the inferior race would by necessity translate the seemingly absurd actions of the other as random impressions. For humankind's collective conscious to be able to see the underlying patterns in the superior race's actions would require a quantum leap in our evolutionary journey as a smart species. Understanding this, the superior race compensates for our lack of perceptive ability by limiting its communications to the level of signs and symbols and in the case of crop circles, for example, to pictographic and mathematical symmetry.

Keel believed also that, innately, humankind has always been aware of these special energies, largely by virtue of the ufonauts' practice to tailor their appearances in accordance with witnesses's personal beliefs and subconscious mores. This sleight of hand practice suggests that the objective of the UFO entities is to sew confusion. This "now you see it, now you don't" trickery ensures that observers never identify what cup is covering the ball. In the face of such powerful psychological control it is little wonder that man has always worshipped visiting gods.

It has long been observed that UFOs tend to form on or close to the ground, the period of visibility rarely lasting longer than fifteen minutes or so. They can build up an inner shape and rise up into the atmosphere. During the Egryn Lights wave of 1904-1905 in North Wales oval UFOs grew out of balls of fire with two brilliant arms protruding towards the earth. Between the arms were more lights, resembling a quivering star cluster.

The ability of UFOs to harden into the finally recognised form: spaceship and its EBE (extraterrestrial biological entity) types, demonstrate that craft and occupants can shapeshift, a phenomenon parallel to Carl Jung's thinking that 'there exists a yet unknown substrate possessing material and at the same time psychic qualities.' In WWII observers reported that German foo fighters responded to their thoughts, suggesting that UFOs are sentient energies able to respond to percipients' mental processes.

Jacques Vallée made the observation[49] that many if not all materialisations of UFOs and their occupants are three-dimensional

---

[49] ibid.

holograms projected through space, time and other dimensions, the same hypothesis applying to fairy-folk appearances. Moreover, he believes that materialisations are deliberately exposed to observers so that they will record their details and transmit them to others. This line of thinking suggests that the mechanisms underlying the phenomena and our belief in them derive from a single source.

The late British visionary John Michell also reflected on this topic. He remarked[50] that ufonauts' appearances as humanoids complete with spacesuits, breathing apparatus, radios, aerials and the like, is a relatively new phenomenon. He pointed out that fairy witnesses see no such thing and that it is presumably something passed off by UFO occupants convincingly for show. Michell noted the success of this trickery, which has been instrumental in spawning cultist beliefs about how we are visited by godlike men and angels from space.

> Beings from flying saucers are much more probably creatures who share this earth with us; regarding whom science has not a single word to say; but about whom our own written and oral traditions, in all our civilisations, speak volumes.

> —Gordon Creighton, *Flying Saucer Review*

Because fairies inhabit a different dimension contact has been likened to the operation of a short-wave radio that may crackle and then suddenly become clear for a few moments. It is believed that there are doorways to such realms located at special points throughout nature, such as exemplified in the Narnia stories.

In *The Coming of the Fairies*[51] Arthur Conan Doyle reflected upon the humanoid appearance of elemental spirits. He said that it was not clear what determines the shape observed by humans and how the transformation from their usual working body (small, hazy, luminous clouds of colour with a brighter spark-like nucleus) is affected. However, he suggested that human thought, either individually or in the mass, plays a key part in determining what percipients see.

Michael Talbot suggests[52] that UFO and fairy sightings are neither objective nor subjective but what he terms "omnijective", a concept

---

[50] Michell, J., *The New View Over Atlantis*, Thames and Hudson, London, 1983.
[51] Conan Doyle, A., *The Coming of the Fairies*, Hodder & Stoughton Ltd., London, 1922.
[52] ibid

mindful of the Hindu Tantric tradition, for example, that recognises no distinction between the mind and reality and between the observer and the observed.

Vallée spoke of the medium in which human dreams can be implemented and which serves as the mechanism that generates UFO events. He posited the existence of a natural phenomenon/field of consciousness, whose manifestations border on both the physical and the mental, 'which serves as the mechanism that generates UFO events, obviating the requirement for a superior intelligence to trigger them.'

It follows from these striking lines of thought that the task before one is not so much to seek to understand what UFOs are made of but rather to comprehend the phenomenon's effect on one's psychological and metaphysical states of being.

Jenny Randles and Peter Warrington[53] distinguished between "true" UFOs and "real" UFOs. The former are the lights in the sky seen from a distance, while the latter are those in which witnesses see much more detail or report greater contact. In the case of "real" UFOs, it is striking how many percipients display psychic tendencies; that other people present do not always see the same thing; and that such witnesses have a history of repeated UFO encounters or of poltergeist and other psychic manifestations. For example, Maureen Puddy of Australia swore she was being taken aboard a UFO even though she was in a car with two investigators during the whole time she was reporting the event. These kinds of experiences encouraged Randles and Warrington to propose replacing the term UFO to UAP—Unidentified Atmospheric Phenomenon.

One logical conclusion that can be drawn from these insights is that there may be no such thing as an objective UFO phenomenon. In this context the entire matter is a purely subjective process in which UFO forms and entities are drawn forth from the etheric into our "real" world by the power of the mind.

Devereux proposes something different, suggesting, like Vallée, that there *is* an objective component but one that derives from a form of natural phenomenon not yet identified as such by present day science.

By 1950 Dr. Meade Layne was directing his research efforts on the paraphysicality of UFOs and the parapsychological elements of the

---

[53] Randles, J. & Warrington, P., *UFOs-A British Viewpoint*, Robert Hale Limited, London, 1979.

contactee syndrome.[54] Before founding Borderland Sciences Research Associates (BSRA) in San Diego Layne was professor at the University of Southern California, and English department head at Illinois Wesleyan University and Florida Southern College.

Layne's research bears a distinctly esoteric flavour. He believed that the separation of science from metaphysics and occultism is arbitrary and must be understood if one is to arrive at a totality of understanding on UFO matters and associated phenomena. In Layne's thinking the concepts of "here" and "there" are solely determined by frequencies, densities and wavelengths and not by spatial, three-dimensional considerations. He proposed that there are an infinite number of etheric planes or fields whose vibratory rates respond to finer forces such as those of mind and thought. He said that any thoughtform can be materialised in etheric matter and can be seen and touched at the appropriate rate of vibration. The discs are one such thoughtform, he maintained.

Layne believed that spacetime is manufactured by the self (by consciousness) and projected from it in extremely minute pulses. On the earth plane these impulses are chemical particles. Deep within the gross matter field there exists a subtler field, the etheric plane. It is from this latter order, Layne held, that solidified matter draws its maintenance energy in the physical world.

BSRA sought information from diverse sources, including trance mediums. From these came the disclosure that the release of atomic forces has greatly disturbed the etheric planes from which UFOs originate; hence, the purpose of their visits is to force our attention upon our infringing actions. The entities populating these planes, the 'Ethereans' as Layne dubbed them, belong to the human order of evolution but are vastly our superiors in science and intelligence. They are appearing in ever-larger numbers because our civilisation is on the point of collapse. They come also to make an examination and a final record in an anthropological sense.

Layne believed that the etheric regions (home to devas, elementals, fairies and the like) are the regions of life in which flourish diverse civilizations and cultures. They have knowledge of our world and can and do penetrate it.

---

[54] Layne, M., *MAT and DEMAT: Etheric Aspects of the UFO*, Flying Saucer Review, Vol. 1, No. 4, 1955 .

Alice with kindly White Knight in *Through the Looking-glass*

Fairy Queen Alice with frog servant

UFOs and other strange emergent phenomena, Layne said, are simply the result of one form of matter merging with another with which it shares an affinity, the process sometimes taking place at such a high speed that an explosion occurs. A sudden explosion is but one way in which a dimension may merge with another, instantly regrouping to form new substance.

Layne described aeroforms as the living bodies of etheric entities. The "vehicle" of an Etherian, whether this be his body or his "ship", is a thoughtform and obviously a thoughtform can be positioned anywhere. All the aeroforms can pass through each other and through our dwellings at will and are (and always have been) invisibly present in great numbers.

Layne explained that the problems of space travel as we conceive them do not exist for the Etherian. By altering its vibratory rates the Etherian penetrates our seas and the substance of our globe as easily as it does our atmosphere. The "ship" and its "crew" become light waves or frequencies from the ether.

He described the Etherean as an extradimensional "emergent"; that is, it extrudes into our plane of perception from a spacetime frame of reference, which is different from ours. This process is marked by a conversion of energy and a change of vibratory rates. When the energy conversion takes place, the aeroform becomes visible and tangible. It appears as solid substance and remains so until the vibratory rate is again converted.

The "steel" of a landed disc is etheric steel and its "copper" is etheric copper, since the prototypes of all our metals exist equally in etheric matter. The conversion process is one of materialisation and dematerialisation (terms truncated by Layne to "mat" and "demat".) Layne emphasised that in the mat and demat processes there is *no* "crossing of space" involved at any time. There is simply a change of location, equivalent to a change of frequency or conversion of vibratory rates.

From Layne's channelling sessions came the message that there will come an "ether-quake", which shall be characterised by great disruption of magnetic and etheric fields. The sky will seem filled with fire. Landmasses will be displaced and great inundations will occur. After cataclysm the Ethereans will, as on many previous occasions, begin to hand down to Earth people the knowledge from before to assist in the gradual rebuilding of civilisation.

Remarkably, among the most profound insights on the UFO

phenomenon are those that came from the founder of analytical psychology, Carl Gustav Jung,[55] who concluded that myths, dreams, hallucinations and visions emanate from the same source. The reason why we are not all walking encyclopaedias is that we can only tap into the etheric plane for information that is of direct relevance to our personal memories and which conforms to a system of personal resonance. Jung was greatly concerned that UFOs are powerful portents of rapidly approaching monumental changes and turned his attention to the phenomena to warn humanity of them. He described those things seen in the sky as 'long-lasting transformations of the collective psyche.'

If it were the case that UFOs are a psychological projection, Jung posited, there must be a powerful psychic cause for it because it is obviously an issue of great importance due to the thousands of sightings. He felt that the projection and cause must have a basis in an "emotional tension", having its cause in a situation of collective distress or danger, one that was very obvious at the time that Jung was writing in the Cold War era. Developing his thinking, Jung regarded UFOs as a "visionary rumour", akin to the collective visions such as those experienced by the crusaders of Jerusalem, the Fátima witnesses and the troops at Mons.

He understood that visions are often given greater credence because oftentimes those who are least credulous or most indifferent claim to see them most. Jung did not discount witnesses' reports of UFOs; in fact, he fully accepted that something was definitely seen. This led Jung to postulate the existence of a 'yet unknown substrate possessing material and at the same time psychic qualities,' a statement which may have inspired Vallée's recognition that UFOs emanate from the 'medium in which human dreams are implemented.

> Precisely as in a dream it is our own will that unconsciously appears as inexorable objective destiny, everything in it proceeding out of ourselves and each of us being the secret theatre-manager of our own dreams, so also… our fate may be the product of our inmost selves, of our wills, and we are actually bringing about what seems to be happening to us.
>
> —Thomas Mann

---

[55] Jung, C.G., *Flying Saucers-A Modern Myth of Things Seen in the Skies*, Ark Paperbacks edition, London, 1987.

John Michell enlarged on these remarkable aspects of Jung's thinking. In *The Flying Saucer Vision*[56] Michell suggested that it is probable that UFOs, having a nature and meaning outside our experience belong, like ghosts, to another order of matter and that their coming is a part of some approaching vision with which we shall soon be confronted. Michell also observed how often UFOs appear to percipients as if they are moving in their natural element like fish or fireflies rather than as mechanical craft. This supports the notion that we are visited by energies of other elements or dimensions, appearing in a way that conforms to what we expect of them and related to the psychological condition of percipients. Jung associated UFOs with changes in the constellation of psychic dominants, of the archetypes or "gods" as they were once called which bring about or accompany long lasting transformations of the collective psyche. These changes take place in the mind as the sun comes under a new sign of the zodiac every 2,160 years (one Platonic Month) and portend great seasonal changes in mental attitudes and perceptions. Our entrance into the Age of Aquarius is provoking such psychic changes. Michell agreed, saying:[57]

> Maybe our hope of development and survival seems to lie in the achievement of a new, higher vision… It may be that flying saucers… are a portent of a future evolutionary step to be brought about through the working of some influence from outside the earth.

Jung said that UFOs are an involuntary archetype or mythological conception of an unconscious content, a "rotundem" as the Renaissance alchemists called it, which expresses the totality of an individual. He was struck by the UFO discs' resemblance to the mandala, a magic circle that organises and encloses the psychic totality. In this symbology it is expressive of the archetype of the self, which comprises both the conscious and unconscious minds (the soul) and not merely the ego. He compared this notion to the Platonic belief that the soul is spherical, symbolic of the heavenly spheres. Plato spoke of the "supra-celestial place" where the "Ideas" of all things are stored up. Esoteric philosophy describes this spirit storehouse or library as the Akashic Record.

Ultimately, Jung arrived at what for him personally was an uncomfortable possibility. He speculated that UFOs might actually be

---

[56] Michell, J., *The Flying Saucer Vision*, Abacus, London, 1974.
[57] ibid

living creatures of an unfathomable kind, one that is both a psychic projection and also an exteriorisation that assumes material attributes: a "materialised psychism". This exteriorisation comes not from physical space but rather from a mechanism in which an internal projection from the unconscious emerges onto conscious awareness.

In ancient times the Greeks believed that all matter beneath the moon was made of varying combinations of the four elements: Earth, Water, Fire and Air. Above the moon, matter was made up of a fifth element they called *aither* or *pempte ousia*, in Latin the *quinta essentia*. The alchemists called it the Philosopher's Stone, which cures all illness, extends life and turns base metals into gold (the transmutation of day-to-day consciousness into a spiritual oneness with God). Jung analysed many dreams that featured UFOs. In one case he commented on a woman's dream in which she saw a teardrop shaped UFO. He remarked that the drop was akin to the "aqua permanens" (permanent water) of alchemic science and symbolised the 'quinta essentia.' On another occasion Jung remarked on a dream in which the UFOs were reminiscent of insects. This led him to speculate that Nature could implement its "knowledge" in any number of ways, including evolving creatures capable of anti-gravity.

Walter Evans-Wentz had already considered this topic. From his conversations with villagers who provided diverse descriptions of the Wee Folk and their archaic appearance, Evans-Wentz came to believe that nature herself has a memory, arriving at the remarkable conclusion that there is a psychic element in the earth's atmosphere upon which human actions and phenomena are impressed like photographs on film. These imprints upon the invisible fabric of nature correspond to mental impressions, which under certain conditions one may play back like moving pictures. Evans-Wentz proposed[58] that:

> The fairy Folk belong to a doctrine of souls... a state of condition, realm or place very much like, if not the same, as that where men place the souls of the dead, in company with other invisible beings such as gods, daemons and all sorts of good and bad spirits.

Jung was impressed by Orfeo Angelucci's book *The Secrets of the Saucers*.[59] In it Orfeo meets with a man and a woman ('our older

---

[58] ibid
[59] Angelucci, O., *The Secrets of the Saucers*, Amherst Press, 1955.

brothers') who tell him they have a deep sense of brotherhood with Earthlings of whom they record details and vital statistics of every individual's life using crystal disks. They said that their craft was remotely controlled by a mothership but in reality they needed no such vessels as they were etheric entities and used them solely to manifest themselves materially to man. They said, 'The speed of light is the speed of truth.' Cosmic law forbids spectacular landings on Earth, which is threatened by greater dangers than was realised. They had been monitoring us for centuries but that we have only recently been entirely re-surveyed.

On 23 July 1952 Orfeo saw a huge igloo-shaped, misty soap bubble. He stepped inside into a vaulted room. There he was told that Earth is a purgatorial world among the planets in which there is evolving intelligent life but that every being on Earth was divinely created. Man had not kept pace morally and psychologically with his technological development so other planetary inhabitants were trying to instil a better understanding of their present predicament and to help them, especially in the art of healing.

Orfeo was encouraged to understand that everyone on Earth has a spiritual, unknown self that transcends the material world and consciousness and dwells eternally outside of the Time dimension in spiritual perfection within the unity of the Oversoul of Mankind. The sole purpose of human existence is to attain reunion with our "immortal consciousness". That Jung was in empathy with Agelucci's experience is suggested by the fact that he made very little comment on Orfeo's testimony, apparently happy in the epilogue of his work to let it speak for itself.

Jung asked the question: If UFOs are something psychic that is equipped with certain physical properties, where do they come from? He said that the notion of a 'materialised psychism opens a bottomless void under our feet' but he didn't go on to rule out the extraordinary proposition that the human mind is capable of creating and manifesting form. Subconsciously, Jung accepted the existence of an Etherean world and its residents of a higher consciousness.

The Circlemakers

David Bohm sensed that the Implicate Order is both a physical and metaphysical construction created by an inconceivably vast Intelligence that contains within itself all things, which it enfolds or unfolds so they emerge into the physical experience we perceive as real.

Furthermore, Bohm considered a human being to be an 'intrinsic feature of the universe, which would be incomplete in some fundamental sense' if the person did not exist. He believes that individuals participate in the whole and, consequently, give it meaning. Bohm went so far as to suggest that consciousness is actually a subtle form of matter that is at work in the organisation of the Implicate and Explicate Orders.

Cambridge biophysicist Professor Rupert Sheldrake developed this idea in his visualisation of an interacting universe whose tiniest element—he gives the example of a hologram, but a crop circle will equally suffice—contains the information of the entire universe. In this model there is no process of "chance", only a blueprint of evolution, which is transmitted throughout the entire universe. Progressing these mind-numbing scientific opinions, there are those who believe that the two-dimensional designs we see in the crop fields are an unfoldment from their true multi-dimensional forms.

The nature spirits, or elementals, are strong candidates for the crop-circle makers. On 7 June 1999, Dutch teenager Robbert saw a light making a circle near his home in the village of Hoeven in Holland. During the previous two years Robbert had seen unusual lights in his neighbourhood. In 1997, while riding his bike through a crop field, he saw hundreds of glowing spheres the sizes of tennis balls and grapefruit. Some approached and began circling him. The next thing he knew, he was waking up on the ground in the middle of a new circle.

On that early summer day in 1999 Robbert saw a small, misty, pinkish-purple light, more (American) football shaped than a sphere but slightly smaller. It was entering the field at a height of about 10 feet. It came to a spot 150 feet behind his house where it hung in the air before elongating, becoming thinner and thinner until it resembled a disc. He saw electrical discharges emitted from the bottom of the disc. After these ceased he went to look and saw two circles in the wheat, one of 30-feet diameter and another nearby of 10-feet diameter.

Robbert received mental impressions from the lights of the circle makers. He understood that the formations are extremely important and are somehow connected to what he thinks are angels. Humans should be paying attention to them he was informed. The circles have something to do with problems in the environment and with deceit. The crop circles, he says, are like an antidote but he has absolutely no idea what that means or why he is involved. Robbert described seeing or sensing a female figure associated with one of the lights or that was transformed from one of the lights. There is much speculation that the advanced intelligence making the crop circles is trying to wake us up to our past and present so that we will have a future.

In many ways Robbert's interactions with the light-beings in the fields mimic the experiences of Christian mystic Emmanual Swedenborg (1688-1772). Swedenborg was renowned for his ability to journey in full consciousness into the spirit worlds. He spoke of elemental balls of light, describing them as (holographic) thought balls that the angels use to communicate. He remarked that these thought-balls are no different from the portrayals he could see in the 'wave-substance' (the aura) that surrounds a person. He described these telepathic bursts of knowledge as a picture language so dense with information that each image contains a thousand ideas.

He said that although human beings appear to be separate from one another, we are all connected in a cosmic unity. Moreover, each of us is a heaven in miniature and every person, indeed the entire physical universe, is a microcosm of the greater divine reality. He also believed that underlying visible reality is a wave-substance.

In fact, several Swedenborg scholars have commented on the many parallels between Swedenborg's concepts and today's quantum theories. Dr. George F. Dole, a professor of theology at the Swedenborg School of Religion in Newton, Massachusetts, and with degrees from Yale, Oxford and Harvard, notes that a basic tenet of Swedenborg's thinking is that our universe is constantly created and sustained by two wavelike flows, one from heaven and one coming from our own soul or spirit. Dole remarks upon these images' striking resemblance to a hologram.

Remarkably, Swedenborg believed that, despite its ghostlike and ephemeral qualities, heaven is actually a more fundamental level of reality than our own physical world. It is, he said, the archetypal source from which all earthly forms originate and to which all forms return, a concept very close to Bohm's idea of the Implicate and Explicate Orders.

In addition Swedenborg believed that the afterlife realm and physical reality are different in degree but not in kind, and that the material world is just a frozen version of the thought-built reality of heaven. The matter that comprises both heaven and earth 'flows in by stages' from the Divine, said Swedenborg, and 'at each new stage it becomes more general and, therefore, coarser and hazier and it becomes slower, colder and more viscous.'

What or who, then, are the nature spirits, the elementals? They have been called the pulse or lifeforce of God, the Universal Mind, the Godforce, Jehovah and countless other names. They flow through the unseen veins of nature. Ancient wisdom describes them as nature's living essence, through whose portals men and women find their spirit and a corresponding sense of immortality and universality.

The elementals are the caretakers of nature. They are always near us but one must have a daily, reverential immersion in nature to begin to feel and perceive their magical presence. Throughout history men have mistaken nature spirits for angels, demons and other supernatural forms. An Irish mystic told Evans-Wentz that the Elementals draw their power out of the 'Soul of the World.' A tenth-century troubadour's account shines a light on the remarkable phenomenon of the Elementals:

It was the December Solstice 999 CE in the Languedoc region of southern France. The Minstrel crossed his right ankle over the left and spread his arms outwards in the shape of a cross. With eyes closed, he relaxed and listened to the silence. At length, after what seemed like hours, he felt something on his right hand. He opened his eyes but saw nothing. He closed his eyes once more and adopted his relaxation posture. Presently, he felt something soft upon his left hand. This time he barely opened his eyes and squinted through his eyelashes. He was amazed to see small balls of light moving up his left arm. Moments later he saw the same wispy movement on his right arm and then up both of his legs. Just as he about to open his eyes wide the movement stopped. He thought to himself, "Who or what are these things?"

"We are Elementals, Minstrel," came the immediate mental reply.

"Oh, my God, they can read my thoughts," the Minstrel said to himself. "How do I censor them?"

"We do not read your thoughts, Minstrel! Thoughts are energy. Thoughts create words. You may think that your thoughts are private, known only to you. To us, the Elementals, and those that are bonded to the inner powers of nature, thoughts have sound and are like the spoken word."

"That means I have no privacy, I am not an individ…"

The Elementals cut in. "If you are in physical balance, then you will have contact with the Elementals. Your thoughts will be pure and filled with the truths of the universe. What you think will not be harmful, infringing, spiteful or judging. Only then will you be able to see us and to communicate with us."

"Frankly, that would be a very boring world," countered the Minstrel. "What would I find to sing about?"

"The observer sees, hears, smells, tastes and touches but does not allow themselves to have a negative reaction to their senses. You can sing of what you see and hear but you do not have to judge it."

"This is getting scary. I'm having a conversation with a bunch of lights without using my voice. I must be losing my mind!"

"We are the pulse of your God, whoever or whatever you feel your God is," said the Elementals. "As blood flows through veins, so we flow through the unseen veins of nature. The beauty you see in a woman is enhanced a thousandfold when you see her through the subtle power of nature."

The Minstrel opened his eyes. There, standing on his chest, was a small elf-like man. Flashing a broad smile and twinkling eyes, he stood there completely naked. "Who are you, where did all the lights go and why are you naked?" the Minstrel asked in alarm.

"I am those lights," explained the elf-man, "and I am the composite of what your mind wants me to be in order that it can begin to comprehend a reality behind the physical and the five senses. I am the wind, rain, earth and fire all in one. Although I am an Elemental, my energy or my essence is in the form that you want it to be. You sing of the little people of the Celts who live in the forest and dance and sing. You have heard of the sprites of the water and the sylphs of the air...I am a composite of those. It is because you mind doesn't know how to clothe me that I am naked!"

The Minstrel felt a slight shift in movement. Opening his eyes once more he saw sitting cross-legged on his chest the most beautiful maiden he had ever seen. She, too, was naked. "Oh no, I'm in trouble now. I can't concentrate with someone so beautiful and nude sitting on my chest. I want the little man back!"

"Pure powerful energy has no form," said the Elemental. "It is only when your mind tries to put form to it that energy loses its power. When you play your lute the music is energy…there is no form. When you walk or move you create energy…there is no form. Minstrel, pure, powerful energy is God. It is through the pulse of God—the Elementals—that you reach the heights within yourself.

"We are the spirit that pulsates through nature. Your spirit pulsates through the body that you have chosen for this lifetime. Our elemental spirit and your spirit are related, something like brother and sister. You have come to this earth to feel, express and project your spirit. When you do that you will discover that your God is actually you. We are neutral and, as a human, your neutrality will lead to personal control. It will free you from the spectacle of seeing yourself the way you feel others want you to be."

The elf man and his analog, the beautiful maiden, taught the Minstrel of the unlimited power of the mind and of the strength of being an observer rather than remaining a slave to our physical senses.

In the West, serious study of the elementals did not fully emerge until the time of Swiss physician, alchemist and astrologer, "Paracelsus", born Philippus Aureolus Theophrastus Bombastus von Hohenheim (1493-1541). A giant figure of the German Renaissance, Paracelsus immersed himself in the study of occult pneumatology: the branch of philosophy that deals with spiritual substances. Paracelsus believed that each of the four primary elements (earth, fire, air, and water) consists of two parts: a subtle, vaporous etheric (Implicate) principle and a gross corporeal (Explicate) substance.

In this analogy Air is twofold in nature, comprising a tangible atmosphere and an intangible, volatile substratum that may be termed spiritual air. Fire's visible nature also has an indiscernible quality in the form of a spiritual, ethereal flame. Water consists of a dense fluid and a potential essence of a fluidic nature. Earth's twofold nature comprises a lower part, which is fixed, terreous and immobile, and a higher that is rarefied, mobile, and virtual. Ancient doctrine taught that the four Elements are under the rulership of the great bodybuilding Devas, the Lords of Form, also known as the four-headed Cherubim that stood at the gates of the Garden of Eden and which also knelt upon the mercy seat of the Ark of the Covenant. Matter was believed to be the product of the geometrical outpourings of the Lords of Form. Minerals, plants, animals and men live in a world composed of the gross part of the four elements. From various combinations each element constructs their living organisms.

According to Paracelsus, just as visible nature is populated by a vast number of living creatures its invisible spiritual etheric counterpart is similarly populated by unique life forms. He gave these forms the name Elementals. Later, they became known more widely as nature spirits. Paracelsus divided these beings of the elements into four distinct groups: gnomes (of the Earth), undines (Water), sylphs (Air) and salamanders (Fire). Crucially, Paracelsus taught that they are living entities, many resembling human beings.

Members of each group are fashioned out of the corresponding ether in which they exist. It is believed that the sylphs, salamanders and nymphs had much to do with the oracles of the ancients; that, in fact, they were the ones who spoke from the depths of the earth and from the air above.

Paracelsus said that the Earth is not just our visible spinning ball but that it comprises other, more subtle dimensions that are home to the higher powers of Nature. It is these invisible mansions in the house of the Earth that accommodate, in the words of the Minstrel's elf man, '*the Elementals and those that are bonded to the inner powers of nature.*' Paracelsus explained that we are unable to see these higher dimensions because our undeveloped senses are incapable of functioning beyond the limitations of the grosser parts of the elements. The Elementals' individual kingdoms dwell at the four corners of the Earth: the gnomes in the North, the undines in the West, the salamanders in the South and the sylphs in the East. Theosophist Edward L. Gardner described the life, work and appearance of the Nature Spirits:[60]

> The life of the nature spirit, nearly the lowest or outermost of all, is active in woodland, meadow and garden, in fact with vegetation everywhere, for its function is to furnish the vital connecting link between the stimulating energy of the sun and the raw material of the form-to-be. The growth of a plant from seed, which we regard as the "natural" result of its being placed in a warm and moist soil, could not happen unless nature's builders played their part. Just as music from an organ is not

[60] Gardner, L.E., *Fairies: A Book of Real Fairies*, The Theosophical Publishing House, London, 1945.

produced by merely bringing wind-pressure and a composer's score together, but needs also the vital link supplied by the organist, so must nature's craftsmen be present to weave and convert the constituents of the soil into the structure of a plant. The normal working body of the sprites, used when they are engaged in assisting growth processes, is neither of human nor of any other definite form... They have no clear-cut shape and their working bodies can be described only as clouds of colour, rather hazy, somewhat luminous, with a bright spark-like nucleus... Although the nature spirit must be regarded as irresponsible, living seemingly a gladsome, joyous and untroubled life, with an eager enjoyment of its work, it occasionally leaves that work and steps out of the plant, as it were and instantly changes shape into that of a dimunitive human being, not necessarily then visible to ordinary sight but quite near to the range of visibility. Assumed in a flash, it may disappear as quickly.

Interestingly, 20% of all circles are preceded by a UFO sighting. John Michell told Michael Hesemann[101] that crop circles are not just connected to the UFO phenomenon; both are expressions of the same phenomenon. The mysterious lights in the sky, the peculiar noises and the strange effects and things which people experience in connection with crop circles indicate this.

Abductee Linda Porter poses a radical notion. She believes that crop circles are subliminal messages; that they are harbingers for the arrival of huge alien, city ships that will appear and then dematerialise certain people on Earth and take them aboard just prior to cataclysm. That is as maybe.

The overlapping arcs in the Cherhill Down formation in Wiltshire in August 1993 are mindful of the Old European script symbol called 'lu' that means light. This sacred writing was used in Goddess worship between 5,300 and 4,300 BCE to inscribe religious objects and to communicate between man and the gods. It would appear that the Elementals are seeking to enlighten mankind and direct its focus on taking actions that honour the Earth and not advance its destruction.

Some have wondered if crop circles, created by the Elemental balls of light in one powerful movement, provide mathematical insight, which, once understood, will help mankind to restore its reverence for

---

[101] Hesemann, M., *The Cosmic Connection*, Gateway Books, Bath, 1996.

the Earth. Linda Moulton Howe poses the question:

> Could something out there be trying to reinforce the idea that our universe and all its energy and mass are defined by a repeating feedback loop that is mathematical in evolution and powered by consciousness?

Much of the language of "Lu" is mathematically oriented. Patterns in circles identified by Professor Gerald Hawking that display alphanumeric codes correspond to diatonic ratios (white piano keys): C 1, D 9/8, E 5/4, F 4/3, G 3/2, A 5/3, B 15/8, H 2, I 9/4, and so on. Hawking calculated that the probability of random occurrence is 1:25,000. He describes it as "frozen music", which is how the Ancient Greeks defined geometry.

In March 1987 Medium Isabelle Kingston received a communication at Ogbourne St George in Wiltshire in connection with Silbury Hill at Avebury. The Watchers, she was told, are the Universal Powers, the guardians of this planet. They told Kingston that they instigated the construction of Silbury Hill for the purposes of helping humankind in the future. Avebury, they said, is energetically linked with places of worldwide power. It is their present task to prepare Earth for the New Jerusalem, a New Age. Kingston understood that the circles in the fields have a multi-layered meaning, comprising many components in which many types of energy are coming together from the earth and from the universe. The Nature realms and spiritual spheres are creating formations with a profound effect on those people who see and explore them. They are created in an energy form, a form of consciousness, *possibly out of our own self, possibly from other spheres and dimensions*. The Watchers explained that England is located at the centre of a great pyramid of light, which they had established long ago. Silbury means "Hill of the Shining Ones." It is the very centre of activity, a vibrant energy centre, the *axis mundi* (the world centre).

For this purpose they are charging the ley lines at various points, visible as the patterns of circles in the fields. The Watchers said:

> This old country (England) holds the balance. It is the key to the world. The pyramid power is the key, in your understanding a button that must be pressed for activation. You are your planet's immune system, the healing system, which will create the changes but there are other keys that must be activated... This country is a test area. It has to be right before

182

the whole can be lined up with the other dimensions. Things are changing at Stonehenge, an energy field is above the stones. Some circles are the exact dimensions of Stonehenge. Circles have appeared as a blueprint for humankind to mark that place as a place of power. It is as if these places are being unlocked. Centres are being awakened; it is part of the plan.

Later, in 1991, Isabelle was told:

Go to the hills and call for the Brethren. Link yourselves wth the Cosmos and draw the energies in to help. Become lightning conductors. Channel the light into the very soil. Transfer it into pure love and wait for the explosion.'

The Watcher's advice to Isabelle Kingston to 'go to the hills and call for the brethren' is as relevant today as it was in 1987, in fact much more so.

The Elementals, our Etherean companions and Mother Nature's caretakers, are not shirking in their toil in the fields to prise open our eyes, nor should we let up on our efforts to understand the signs in the circles. So much rests on our ability to interpret the messages and to act accordingly and swiftly.

Alice Liddell, an accomplished artist, painted this charming watercolour scene of Capri

Arial view of Avebury henge

Chapter 12

The Celtic Otherworld

The concept of an enchanted and mysterious "Otherworld" has been a typical feature in numerous myths and legends across a wide range of human cultures throughout history.

The Classical Otherworld was perceived primarily as the abode of the dead. The ancient Celtic people had their own vision of this enigmatic and ethereal region: a vibrant, idealised version of our human world where people led happy lives free from sickness and the fear of death. Their territories included Ireland, the British Isles, and a swathe of continental Europe to Anatolia, now part of Turkey and included parts of the Iberian Peninsula. Across this vast area, there were variations in beliefs and ideas about the Otherworld.

Lucan, a Roman poet, asserted that Gaulish druids believed in an Otherworld where souls went before reincarnation but contrasted the druids' teachings with the Classical perspective:

> No ghosts descend in dreadful night,
> No parting souls to grisly Pluto go,
> No seek the dreary, silent shades below,
> But forth they fly immortal in their kind,
> And other bodies in new worlds they find;
> Thus life for ever runs its endless race,
> And, like a line, death but divides the space,
> A stop which can but for a moment last,
> A point between the future and the past.

The religions of Ancient Greece and Rome shared many similarities, especially after Rome conquered Greece in the second century BCE. Along with other aspects of Greek culture, the Romans embraced and assimilated Greek ideas about religion, the gods and the Otherworld. Apart from occasional living visitors, such as Orpheus and Aeneas, mortals went there only after death. Olympus was also an Otherworld although its inhabitants were gods and deified heroes, so it was never a destination for normal human beings. The majority of the Immortals lived there but Hades lived and ruled in the Underworld, accompanied by his wife, Persephone.

On the other hand, Celts believed there was a home for their supernatural figures, a place where humans occasionally strayed during life, or where they rested between lives. They referred to this place as the Otherworld, a multifaceted concept. It is a place of enchantment, where time flows differently, and the laws of the natural world are suspended. It is inhabited by otherworldly beings that possess extraordinary powers and often interact with the mortal realm, impacting the lives of humans.

Celtic folklore variously locates the Otherworld as a place underground, under water, overseas or in another dimension. Wherever it is located, all descriptions depict the Otherworld as an enigmatic land of everlasting beauty and luxury

The Celts believed in a cyclical view of time and the interconnectedness of all things. The Otherworld was not a distant afterlife but a parallel dimension, closely intertwined with our own. It is a supernatural realm of everlasting youth, beauty, health, abundance and joy, accessible through special places like burial mounds, lakes or caves and during specific times, particularly during festivals and rituals.

According to pagan belief, when we die our physical bodies return to Mother Earth. In northern Europe, tradition had it that the souls of the dead go into the hills and spirit-mountains where they dwell with other otherworldly beings. The custom of interring the dead and their goods in earth mounds was common among the Celts who believed that in burying in this manner those that had passed created a model of the otherworld.

They regarded the otherworld as a symbolic realm in which everything must be carried out correctly, according to universal principles that reflect the underlying orderly structure of existence. Those whose remains go into the earth leave the world of the living and re-enter the womb of Mother Earth from whom they emerged at the time of birth. At death, part of the human spirit goes into the otherworld to be regenerated and reborn; their goods are taken into the fairy kingdom; and the burial mound serves as a memorial to the life and deeds of the departed.

The Otherworld appears in two different forms: the Irish sidhes (shee) or the Welsh caers (car), and the island otherworlds. These realms, protected by strong magic, were always hidden to normal human sight. It is an elusive realm but various mythical heroes, such as Cúchulainn, Fionn and Bran visit either through chance or after being invited by one of its residents.

The belief in an otherworld paradise where one could learn or rest between lives must have played a central role in the Celtic passion for life, the honouring of poetry and art, and courage on the battlefield. Life was meant to be lived to its fullest with the knowledge that death was simply the passageway to the Otherworld. Here, one would pass their days and nights immersed in beauty, peace, and love while waiting the call to return to the school we call life.

The Otherworld is usually elusive but various mythical heroes visit it either through chance or after being invited by one of its residents. They often reach it by entering ancient burial mounds or caves or by going under water or across the western sea. Sometimes, they suddenly find themselves in the Otherworld with the appearance of a magic mist, supernatural beings or unusual animals. An otherworldly woman may invite the hero into the Otherworld by offering an apple or a silver apple branch, or a ball of thread to follow as it unwinds. Alice, of course, finds her way into Wonderland by chasing after a large white, smartly dressed rabbit.

The Otherworld's inhabitants are described as exceptionally beautiful and agelessly young, In the Irish tale, *The Wooing of Etain*, the fairy king Mider is described as a young warrior with long, golden-yellow hair reaching to his shoulders. He has lustrous grey eyes and wears a purple tunic. In one hand he carries a white-bossed shield studded with gold, and in the other a five-pointed spear. Etain herself, daughter of the king of Echred out of the fairy-mounds, has golden hair dressed in two elaborate four-stranded plaits, each finished with a gold bead. Her hands are soft and snow-white; her eyes hyacinth blue beneath dark brows, and her cheeks the colour of the foxglove. Her lips are red as rowanberries and her teeth are like pearls.

In circumstances where humans enter the Otherworld without an invitation, especially if the intent is to steal treasures the reception committee can be truly inhospitable; the people are transformed into terrible enemies. The Irish hero Cuchulainn battled snakes, monsters and confronts the fearsome shape-shfting goddess Morrigan.

On the European continent, the Gauls divided the Otherworld into three parts: Albios, Bitu and Dubnos. Albios represented the upper world or heaven, also known as the white world. Bitu was the world of living beings or the earthly realm; while Dubnos signified the underworld, lower world, dark world or hell.

In Gaelic and Brittonic myth the Otherworld is not merely a distant, fantastical realm; it is an integral part of Celtic cosmology. The Gaulish druids believed that the soul went to an Otherworld before being reincarnated.

Byzantine scholar Procopius of Caesarea described the ancient Gauls' belief that the land of the dead lies west of Britain. Once the souls of the dead had left their bodies, they travelled to the northwest coast of Gaul and took a boat toward Britain. When they crossed the Channel, the souls went to the homes of the fishermen and knocked desperately at their doors. The fishermen then went out of their houses and led the souls to their destination in ghostly ships. There are still remains of those beliefs in the folklore of Brittany, where the name Bag an Noz is used to denote those ships who carry the dead to their destination.

The many goddesses of the Otherworld possess great regenerative and healing powers, often having the ability to transform into swans or songbirds, or to enlist the help of those birds to accomplish good deeds. Rhiannon's birds were known to heal the sick or ease their passage to the other side.

In some tales the Otherworld is reached by going under the waters of pools, lakes, or the sea, or by crossing the western sea. In Irish folklore the "King Under the Wave", *Righ fo thuinn*, is a common title for the King of Fairyland. In Irish Immrama ("voyage") tales, a beautiful young Otherworld woman often approaches the hero and sings to him of this happy land. Sometimes she offers him an apple, or the promise of her love in exchange for his help in battle. The apple, symbolic of all that is good and sweet in life, is almost always associated with the Otherworld Islands.

It is believed that bees came to our world from Brigid's apple orchard in the Otherworld. The hero follows the woman and they journey over the sea together and are seen no more. Their journey may be in a boat of glass, in a chariot or on horseback.

Sometimes the hero returns after what he believes is a short time, only to find that all his companions are dead and he has actually been away for hundreds of years. Sometimes the hero sets out on a quest and a magic mist descends upon him. He may find himself before an unusual palace and enter to find a warrior or a beautiful woman who makes him welcome. The woman may be the sea goddess Fand and the warrior may be Manannán mac Lir or Lugh. After strange adventures the hero may return successfully. However, even when the mortal manages to return to his own time and place, he is forever changed by his contact with the Otherworld.

The Irish Otherworld is very beautiful. Iubda, King of the Lepracan, a magnificent people of tiny size, had a palace with a silver floor and a ceiling of red gold. The door's threshold is copper and its lintel of white bronze. The thatch is constructed of pale yellow feathers and the candelabra are gold. The palace was built of huge blocks of marble with many windows. Its pillars are of crystal, silver and copper. Its terraces are paved with eggshells.

Another name for Ireland's Otherworld is Tír na nÓg (Land of Eternal Youth), located beyond the western edge of the known world. It is sometimes thought of as the Irish equivalent to Elysium, which, in Greek mythology, is the paradise in which heroes were granted immortality after death.

However, there is an important difference in Irish folklore, as Tír na nÓg is not the "afterlife" as such. Rather, it is an earthly place that can only be reached through magic. It is sometimes depicted as an earthly paradise, a flower-filled meadow or a lush, forested wilderness,. Unlike its heavenly counterparts in the folklore of other countries, Tír na nÓg is seen as a supernatural realm where everlasting youth, health, beauty and joy are experienced by all who dwell there.

The tale of Niamh of the Golden Hair and her love for Oisin, the great warrior poet of ancient Ireland, is the most well known tale of Tír na nÓg. Generally, once a human enters an island otherworld he finds himself there for eternity. At times though they return as Oisin did; He foolishly left Tír na nÓg but, unable to make his way back, perished as any 300-year-old man would. In another instance, the Sea God Manannan mac Lir brought Cormac Mac Airt to the islands for only a short visit, giving him magical items, including the cup of truthfulness.

In the ancient folk tales, the Otherworld is often reached by entering ancient burial mounds, such as those at Brú na Bóinne and Cnoc Meadha, places of the sidhe. Irish mythology says the gods retreated into the sídhe when the Gaels (Milesians) took Ireland from them.

Unlike the sidhes and the caers, where the deities acted much like humans, complete with power struggles and strife, the island otherworlds were places of peace, happiness and eternal life where the goddesses and gods lived without the pains and struggles of earthly existence. From these places emanated the radiant light of eternity but they could just be stumbled upon through mist, fog or happenstance like the sidhes could; they were difficult to access. Nor were these island otherworlds places where souls went after death. They could only be reached by one still living who is either purposefully undertaking a difficult journey or travelling there by invitation.

The island Otherworlds were known by many names and given different locations, for example: Emhain Abhlach, Plain of Apples; Inis Subai, Isle of Joy; Tír na mBan, the Land of Women; Tír fo Thonn, the Land Beneath the Wave; Tír Tairnigir, the Land of Promise; Hy Breasil, Most Blessed Place; and Tech Duinn, House of Donn.

Donn is portrayed as a god of the dead and ancestor of the Gaels. Tech Duinn is commonly identified with Bull Rock, an islet off the west coast of Ireland, which resembles a portal tomb. In Ireland there was a belief that the souls of the dead departed westwards over the sea with the setting sun, westward also being the direction in which the phantom island of Hy-Brasil is to be found.

The Otherworld was also seen as a source of authority. In the tale Baile in Scáil ("the phantom's ecstatic vision"), Conn of the Hundred Battles visits an Otherworld hall where the god Lugh legitimizes his kingship and that of his successors.

In Irish myth and later folklore, the festivals of Samhain and Beltane (Bealtaine) are liminal times, when contact with the Otherworld is more likely.

Evans-Wentz believed that people who inhabit the Celtic regions are more in tune with their subconscious self and so better equipped psychically to feel and perceive invisible influences. He believed that through this enhanced faculty the Celts enjoy an innate ability to respond to nature's rhythms and, correspondingly, can feel the essence of this Otherworld more keenly than most.

Being part Celtic on his mother's side, Evans-Wentz firmly believed in the existence of invisible life forms, describing them as being as much a part of nature as is visible life in this world. Consequently, he decried the use of the term "supernatural" to describe these beings on the basis that, logically, nothing in existence can be supernatural. During his investigations into fairy lore in the early 1900s, Walter Evans-Wentz concluded that the heaven world of the Celts is not to be found in planetary space but here on Earth.

The Celtic mystic believed that the universe comprises two interpenetrating parts: the visible world and the invisible realm of the fairies, which are intelligent beings that reside in the Otherworld and occupy all orders of society and hierarchy. This magical world is a subterranean region invisible to humans except under special circumstance.

Through secret passages and beneath mountains, raths, moats and dolmens the Otherworld was once inhabited by the Partholon, the megalith builders of ancient Ireland. They were succeeded by the aristocratic and humanesque Tuatha dé Dannan, ("Children of Danu"), the tall and beautiful Good People (*Daoine Maithe*) who retired long ago after their defeat by the Sons of Mil into Ireland's emerald hills together with the leprechauns, pixies, dwarfs and knockers (miners) of the fairy folk. They marry and bear children, toil and feast. They were also extremely gifted in the fields of architecture, science, mathematics and engineering. They exercised command over the power of sound to lift and move massive weights. Over time, the Dannan, born from the "waters of heaven or space", a representation of the goddess Anu (later Christianised as Brigit), became known as the fairy folk (later the Sidhe of folklore).

The enemies of the Dannan, the Fomorians, were children of the goddess Domnu, meaning an abyss or deep sea. Legend speaks of the Fomorians as a race of hideous giants (the Nefilim). In a description mindful of a Tolkien tale, the Fomorians were defeated on the Plain of Towers by a cataclysmic Flood generated by the Dagda Mor.

Annwn (also spelled Annwfn and Annwfyn) is the Otherworld of Welsh mythology. Its etymology derives from words meaning "extremely deep" or the "very deep-down land", a term mindful of the seemingly endless space through which Alice descends languidly into Wonderland. The Mabinogi locates Annwn as a dimension that is contiguous with our own world. People appear, vanish and reappear; certain settings such as clearings and hillocks are favoured for these phenomena.

Celts in ancient Britain saw in the sun's passage through the heavens a symbolic representation of an individual's mystical passage through life. At dawn the sun appeared to rise from Annwen, the underworld. In the daylight hours, it traversed Abred, the physical plane, the world of trial, test and experiment, the university of the physical curriculum from which man must continually strive to evolve out of into the worlds of spirit. At night it sank into Gwynvyd, the sphere of the conscious and wholly developed spirit in perfect man.

Britain's esoteric tradition makes it clear that the goal of man was to attain a passage into Gwynvyd by an initiatory process while still living to find the Cauldron of Inspiration and to drink from its magical waters.

In the Welsh tale of Branwen, daughter of Llyr, ends with the survivors of a great battle feasting in the Otherworld in the presence of the severed head of Bran the Blessed, having forgotten all their suffering and sorrow and unaware of the passage of time.

The Druids' mystery ceremonies were presided over by the goddess Keridwen, her son Avagddu and servant Gwion. These supernatural figures feature heavily in Celtic mystery rites. A useful source is Taliesin who, according to legend, was the bastard son of Ceridwen, the goddess of the cauldron of Pwyll. Just as in the tales told of Merlin's birth, Taliesin had no father because he had been born from sorcery and enchantment. When Ceridwen gave birth she resolved to kill her son but she repented and, reminiscent of the Moses story, placed him in a stream to be found by some stranger.

Welsh Druids would embark on a magical quest to journey to the blessed realm of Gwynedd, the world of the Twice-born. To achieve success, they first had to pass through three Veils, one of which, the Veil of Cythraul, was symbolised by Cwrwg Gwydrin, a boat fashioned from clear cystal for travel to the in-between realms of the Otherworld.

Taliesin variously named the Otherworld as Caer Vanddwy (the Fort of the Divine Place), Caer Ochren (the Enclosed Fort) and Caer Vedwyd (the Fort of Intoxcation). Other commentators contemporary with Taliesin named it as Caer Rigor (the Frigid Fort) and Caer Wydyr (the Glass Fort).

The Mabinogi makes it abundantly clear that it is not necessary for anybody to die before his or her journey to Annwn could begin. In the tales, Annwn is ubiquitous and all-pervading, separated from everyday human life by only a thin veil.

In his poem "The Spoils of Annwn", Taliesin describes in allegorical fashion the initiate's journey from Abred into the lowest plane of the circles of Annwn to recover the cauldron whose fires beneath are kindled by the breath of nine maidens or Druidesses. The cauldron of Pwyll, which will not boil the food of a coward, is none other than the Grail vessel containing the blood of Christ, which after the crucifixion was brought, according to legend, from the Holy Land to Britain by Joseph of Arimathea accompanied by twelve holy men from the East.

Taliesin said that the Grail could be found at Caer Sidi or Cair Pedryvan, "the Four-cornered Castle" in the mysterious Isle of the Active Door. Caer Sidi, sometimes interpreted as Annwn itself, means the Circle of Revolutions, suggesting a synchronous connection with the Glastonbury Zodiac, a doorway to the underworld.

During their ordeal the initiate is secured by a heavy blue chain, a symbolic reference to the silver chord that secures a person's astral form to their physical body during out-of-body journeys. Once an initiate has recovered the cauldron, they return to the surface nourished by the mystical secrets of enlightenment. Taliesin's description tallies with the mythical accounts of other renowned initiatory journeys, such as those undertaken by Osiris to the Egyptian underworld of Amenti and by Arthur to the Isle of Avalon at Glastonbury

The Welsh poem "Preiddeu Annwyn" describes the Celtic Otherworld as having three regions. One is the Land of the Silent Dead where the Lost Ones are kept in a glass fort known as Caer Wydyr or Nennius, according with the stories of gold and crystal palaces in Fairyland. A second is Caer Feddwidd, the Fort of Carousa ruled by Arianrhod, Goddess of Time, Karma and Destiny. Arianrhod brought the souls of dead warriors to her revolving castle in the North Sea, where they awaited the time of their rebirth. Caer Feddwidd is blessed with a mystical mountain of wine, which offers eternal youth for whose who elect to spend their immortality in the afterlife. The third region is Avalon, the most divine realm, known as the Vale of Apples. Only those that had made great sacrifices could enter here, its most illustrious inhabitant being Arthur.

One of Arthur's subjects in the fairy court was Gwynn ab Nudd, the ruler of the devils of Annwn, known in Irish folklore as Nuada of the Silver Hand, king of the Tuatha dé Dannan and ruler of the Fairies and the Elves. It is evident that long ago Arthur was regarded not as a material person but as a highborn personage who lived in the fabled land of the Elementals. As the Once and Future King he resides there still, continuing to teach seekers of the truth the secrets of Nature and of Creation.

Among other mooted locations for Arthur's fairy court is the Isle of Arran, identified with Annwyn and the home of the Cauldron of Plenty. Sixth century Welsh bard Taliesin, said to be the reincarnation of Merlin, wrote that The Nine Ladies of the Lake who travelled with Arthur on his funeral barge were the guardians of the magic cauldron of the Grail. The Nine were a secret sisterhood, each of whom embodied different characteristics of the Sacred Feminine, which are at the core of the Arthurian mysteries. Geoffrey of Monmouth said that Avalon was ruled by nine sisters, three of whom were Arthur's mother Igraine (of fairy blood), Gwenhwyvar and enchantress Morgan le Fay.

The Four Branches of the Mabinogi are singularly devoid of detailed descriptions of magical characters or artefacts, or indeed of depictions of the Otherworld landscape, for which Irish sources are more informative. In the adventures of Art mac Cuinn ("son of Conn"), who was supposed to have ruled Ireland between 220 and 254 AD, we learn that the Otherworld's countryside is adorned with various trees, notably apple trees and hazel trees with golden-yellow nuts. A woman who visits Conn in *Echtrae Conli* throws him an apple before she leaves, and for a whole month he does not eat or drink anything else, thus maintaining a connection with her and the Otherworld. The apple never diminishes, and later, when the woman reappears, Conn leaves with her in her coracle, which is made of crystal.

In Immram Brain, Bran mac Febhail was walking near his fortress when lovely music soothed him to sleep. He awoke to find nearby a silver branch bearing white blossoms which he took inside the fortress, and when all the people were gathered together, a woman appeared and sang in celebration. Seemingly, the branch itself had made the music Bran heard, as did another apple-tree branch in the Irish tale of *Cormac's Adventures in the Land of Promise*. A warrior approached Cormac, carrying on his shoulder a branch of silver bearing three golden apples. When shaken, the branch made such delightful music that even those in extreme sickness or pain fell asleep at the sound.

Strange and beautiful trees made of crystal, glass and precious metal grow in the Otherworld, but still bear fruit and support flocks of birds: Serglige Conn Culainn has trees of purple crystal and of silver, the latter making music like the apple-trees mentioned above, as well as normal fruit trees. In Immram Brain, Manannán mac Lir tells Bran that his coracle is not on the sea, as he thinks, but floating over a fruitful orchard.

Mist is often a meteorological manifestation of the Otherworld (as with Hy-Brasil that was cloaked in mist), which must have sent shivers up the spines of those living in damp Celtic climates where mist is commonplace. In *Echtrae Laeghairi*, the Otherworld is itself referred to as Magh Dá Cheo "The Plain of the Two Mists", and in the Third Branch of the Mabinogi, mist and tumult signal the beginning of the enchantment of Dyfed. When the mist disperses, only buildings and wild animals remain; all human life is gone.

Magical objects abound in the Otherworld. Cauldrons like that of the Daghda, which never ran dry, and the Peir Pen Annwn, with pearls around its rim, which refused to cook a coward's food; another was the Cauldron of Rebirth, which originally came from Ireland. Brân gave it to Matholwch as part of his compensation in the Second Branch, and the Irish used it to restore dead warriors to life.

There was also, in early Welsh poetry and story, the cauldron of the witch Ceridwen, in which she took a year to brew the potion intended for her son, but which gave Taliesin his polish and talent, much against her will. Ceridwen's son, Afagddu (Utter Darkness), was also called Morfran, and was so ugly that he survived the battle of Camlan because nobody would fight him, thinking he was a demon. Ceridwen wanted to give him poetic inspiration to outweigh his ugliness, so brewed the potion. Gwion Bach (an earlier form of Taliesin) tended the cauldron, but was splashed by the boiling liquid and put his scalded fingers in his mouth, accidentally gaining the advantage of Ceridwen's work, though he went through many transformations before being reborn as Taliesin.

The hamper of Gwyddno Garanhir was one of the thirteen treasures of the Island of Britain. If food for one person were put inside, it would multiply to food for a hundred; it is also mentioned in How Culhwch Won Olwen, as giving to everyone the food of their choice. The list of the Thirteen Treasures contains other magical items, like the halter of Clydno Eiddyn, Morgan the Wealthy's magic chariot, which took its occupant wherever he wished, quickly, and the mantle of Arthur in Cornwall. A similar cloak is mentioned in Branwen, when Caswallawn wore it to slay those who had been left in charge of the Island of the Mighty in Brân's absence.

The chessboard of Gwenddolau ap Ceidio, made of gold with silver pieces, would play by itself. It is no coincidence that the chess-players in The Dream of Macsen Wledig are using a similar set. In fact, the splendours of the court of Elen's father in this story are reminiscent of Irish Otherworldly descriptions, and as in Pwyll, everyone seems to be dressed in silk brocade. The Crock and Dish of Rhygenydd the Cleric would provide whatever food was wished for, while the Horn of Bran the Niggard would supply whatever drink was desired.

Others of the treasures were testing talismans: the sword of Rhydderch the Generous, which showed whether a man were well-born or not and the coat of Padarn Red-coat, which did likewise; the cauldron of Dyrnwch the Giant, which would never boil a coward's meat, and which R.S. Loomis equates with the Peir Pen Annwfn; the whetstone of Tudwal Tudglyd, which made only a brave man's sword deadly; and the mantle of Tegau Gold-breast, which reached to the ground only when worn by a chaste woman.

In Irish mythology, Cormac mac Art obtains such a testing talisman from the Land of Promise. He is lured there by a warrior, Manannán mac Lir who gives him a gold cup marvellously worked and engraved, which breaks into pieces if lies are told, and is restored by the truth. Apart from the gold and silver chessboard, these magical treasures are not treasures because of their intrinsic worth becauese for the most part they are very ordinary items. A halter, a whetstone, cloaks, a coat, a cauldron, a hamper, a crock and dish, and a drinking-horn are all items which would be found in most ordinary homes; the value of these particular ones lay in their magical potential and their appeal to the imagination.

Some Otherworld articles may appear commonplace, but Otherworld animals are not. One noteworthy characteristic is that they are frequently (though not invariably) white. The hunting dogs which bring down the stag in Pwyll have a very striking colouration: they are gleaming white, with red ears, the white of the coats and the red of the ears being equally bright. Pwyll should have known that such colouration was characteristic of the Otherworld. The owner of the pack, Arawn, King of Annwn, comes into view riding a very big white (dapple-grey) horse.

Besides the Otherworldliness, there is also a factor of costliness associated with this colour. White horses were particularly prized, and therefore more expensive than other colours. Arawn's dogs with their striking colouration were the original Cwn Annwn, "dogs of Annwn", but they have other quarry than game according to Welsh folklore—the souls of those who had died unrepentant or unbaptised. They are a Welsh version of the Wild Hunt, but rather than Arawn, it is another king of Annwn, Gwyn ap Nudd who leads them in Welsh tradition.

Later in Pwyll, Rhiannon rides from her home in the Otherworld. Her son is lured into a trap in the magic castle, in the Third Branch, by a shining white magical boar, which tempts the huntsmen to ensure they do not give up the chase. Proinsias MacCana notes that the boar is often the savagely ferocious target that decoys his pursuers to the Otherworld.

White deer also perform the same function in some stories. In Marie de France's Anglo-Norman version of a Breton Lai, Guigemar, which dates from about 1170, the hero is kidnapped by a fairy in the shape of a white hind. The chase of a white deer that is actually a fairy reappears in many of Marie's tales.

Birds play a very important part in descriptions of the Otherworld; their beauty, their ability to fly and their delightful song all qualifying them as magical. The concepts of the wonderful birds whose song brings joy and often sleep is ever-recurrent also in Celtic tradition, and it is to be found very frequently in both the pagan and the later Christian textual material. They belong to Welsh tradition but have parallels in Ireland. In the story of Tadhg mac Céin, he and his companions are sailing in their curragh through a storm, when they hear a flock of strange birds singing. On two extraordinary islands they find flocks of wonderful birds like blackbirds, though some are the size of eagles. Their bodies are red, their heads green, and their eggs blue or scarlet. Other birds are a beautiful shining white with purple heads and golden beaks. They sing wonderful music which would send sick and wounded men to sleep.

When considering the various magical objects recorded in this chapter, it will be seen that they fall into distinct groups. There is firstly a group of testing talismans, two of which would prove the nobility of one's birth, something that was evidently of great importance. Another of the items in this group would prove truth or falsehood; yet another would render a sword invincible but only if it belonged to a brave man; still another could prove a man a coward by refusing to cook his meat, and the last would prove the chastity of any woman courageous enough to wear it. Any of these objects would be very useful to the person who owned, or was reputed to own it.

Another group is concerned with food and drink: an apple which never diminishes, a cauldron which never runs dry, a hamper which multiplies food a hundredfold thus turning a single meal into a feast, a crock and dish which provide any food desired, and a horn which would do the same for drink. In an age when munificence and generosity of feasting – there are many feasts in the Four Branches - were praised by poets, and when poets could make or break reputations, such items would be highly desirable. When travel was limited to the speed of a horse, the items in the next group: a halter which could provide a superlative mount, and a chariot which could transport its owner anywhere, quickly, would be indispensable, especially to those for whom battle was a way of life. A cloak of invisibility would also be useful in life-threatening situations. The final group of objects would likewise be priceless in unsettled, dangerous times: the apple-tree branches which give sleep to those in extreme pain, and the singing birds capable of giving the same relief; most important of all, the cauldron which can restore life to the dead. All these articles provide different, desirable outcomes but the main characteristic of each of them is that of wish fulfilment. One may therefore conclude that the function of such magical Otherworld items was to make dreams come true, or at least to suggest that they could.

We may conclude by asking the question: What is the Otherworld like?' Its attractions are obvious: in a harsh and uncertain world, the allure of somewhere safe, luxurious and sinless must have been strong: a pre-Christian idyll similar to the Garden of Eden.

In some respects, the Celtic Otherworld would seem to be a masculine wish-fulfilment fantasy, especially in Irish sources. Theirs is a world of wine, women, song and sport, without problems or cares. There is no obligation to work, though there is an abundance of the choicest food. Drink is not measured in barrels or jugs but in wells and springs of sweet wine, besides strong ale.

It is evidently a masculine fantasy, because of the references to 'very many women' and to an actual island where women are the only inhabitants, Tir Inn mBan, where Bran and his men, three companies of nine, land and immediately obtain lovers and 'a bed for every couple, even thrice nine beds' to accommodate them. Sex here is a sinless pleasure.

In this Otherworld, the surroundings are beautiful, the buildings sparkle with precious metal and jewels, as does the clothing of the inhabitants. The chariots are of silver, gold and bronze and the horses brilliantly coloured. There is racing of chariot and coracle, as well as feasting and music. Trees are fruitful, some being silver or coloured crystal, and some of these make music. Even the stones sing in this glorious bountiful Otherworld of perpetual summer, and, best of all, sin, sickness and death are unknown, so these splendours can be enjoyed for all eternity.

Parts of this Otherworld seem to be located across the sea, on an island or archipelago of islands, although each of the sídh mounds also seems to contain its own Otherworld, which is not connected to any of the others, indicating that there is more than one Celtic Otherworld.

However, in the Welsh Mabinogi the Celtic Otherworld does not seem to exhibit this tendency to fragment. There, the Otherworld appears to be one country with different kingdoms, accessible from diverse places. It is contiguous to Dyfed, and the countryside is similar to that of Dyfed, as Pwyll observes as he makes his way to Arawn's court. There are no trees of silver or crystal here but like the Irish Otherworld this is a rich place, where Pwyll sees splendid buildings with undreamt-of luxury and ornamentation new to him. The people are beautiful, superbly apparelled and equipped, with the transcendently lovely queen dressed in gold brocaded silk. Time is spent hunting, feasting and revelling, and the provisions and gold plate the most magnificent that Pwyll has ever seen anywhere, as are the wonderful jewels. In effect, this seems to be a description of an idealised court of this world, having the retainers and feasts characteristic of such courts, exaggerated to express every possible luxury.

Annwn, then, is a dazzlingly opulent place of beautiful people, glorious buildings, feasting, hunting, carousing and jewels, similar to the Irish stories, though there is no sense of sexual freedom in the Mabinogi. Although Arawn has explicitly given Pwyll permission to sleep with his wife, Pwyll is chaste and does not take advantage of the situation. Annwn is also the source of rich presents, as mentioned in the First Branch and alluded to in the Fourth Branch, which says that the first swine ever seen in Wales originated there.

It is the abode of powerful magicians and shapechangers like Llwyd fab Cilcoed, who can materialise and dematerialise a castle, magically kidnap and imprison people and vanish away all inhabitants and domestic animals from a large tract of countryside to avenge an insult to a friend. He, like the other Otherworldly characters we meet in the Four Branches, is a powerful force, and very much alive.

This characteristic of the Celtic Otherworld, namely life, rather than death, is consistent throughout both the Welsh and Irish traditions and is in strong contrast to the Classical ideas of the Otherworld. Although less detailed than the Irish sources, the Celtic Otherworld as represented by Annwn and its denizens is likewise a wish-fulfilment fantasy, though of a more refined, sophisticated and courtly variety, better suited to the times and the audiences for whom it was intended.

Alice with Fawn in *Through the Looking-glass*

Chapter 13

Don Quixote and the Cave of Montesinos

'Vincit qui se vincit'

(He conquers who conquers himself)

It has been said that within Cervantes' narrative describing Don Quixote's journey into the Cave of Montesinos lies the key to arriving at a true understanding of what the author was really trying to convey to readers in the pages of his masterwork.

The location is not an imaginary place. The "Cueva de Montesinos" is a karst cave (one usually formed in soluble rock limestone) in the Province of Albacete in central Spain, in the southern part of the autonomous community of Castile–La Mancha. At the bottom is a small lake formed by rainwater filtering through the cave. It has been discovered through a series of experiments and tests that the water in that lagoon is connected by underground streams with the natural park of Ruidera, which is studded with a series of lagoons (the famous "Lagunas de Ruidera") linked by streams and waterfalls.

The cave is only 59m long but has a total depth of 45m. The entrance is located on the plain, a collapse with huge boulders; a stone staircase leads down to the entrance portal. It was known as Los Arrieros (The Muleteers) because it was their shelter from bad weather.

A short passage or vestibule with numerous blocks from the collapse descends to a big chamber, which is called La Gran Sala (The Great Hall). This chamber is 18m long and up to 5m high. The floor is steep and the blocks originally required some climbing; today there is a staircase and a beaten path. The single passage descends continually to the end; there are no notable side passages, except for a rather small side passage right below the entrance. At the far end, the lowest part reaches the groundwater, with several cave lakes, which are full of calcite crystals. The cave is not described in any authentic detail in the book, and it is unclear if Cervantes ever visited it.

Don Quixote and companions at the mouth of the Cave of Montesinos

Seeking fresh adventures, Don Quixote and Sancho in the company of a local guide, a budding writer, arrived at the Cave of Montesinos. It was two in the afternoon. Don Quixote had expressed a keen interest in descending to see with his own eyes if the wonders told about about the cave throughout the region were true. Don Quixote told his companions that even if the cave should reach the abyss he had to see how deep it was. Consequently, he had brought with him six hundred feet of rope.

They saw that the mouth of the cave was spacious and wide but filled with thorny bushes, wild fig trees, brambles and briars, so thickly overgrown that they obscured and concealed the cave.

Sancho and the guide tied the rope firmly round Don Quixote While they were making him fast, Sancho said to him, 'Be careful your grace, señor mío, and don't bury yourself alive, nor get yourself in a position where you're like a bottle they hang in a well to get cold. It's none of your grace's affair to investigate into what must be worse than a dungeon.'

'Just keep tying and stop talking,' responded Don Quixote, 'because such an undertaking as this, Sancho my friend, is reserved for me.'

The guide then said: 'I beg your grace, señor don Quixote, to look carefully and examine with a hundred eyes what there is inside. Perhaps there will be things that I can put in my book of transformations.'

Don Quixote fell to his knees and offered a prayer, asking God to help him and provide a happy outcome of this dangerous and novel adventure. In a low voice he addressed his beloved.

> Oh, señora of my actions and movements, bright and peerless Dulcinea del Toboso! If the prayers and entreaties of this, your fortunate lover, reach your ears, by your unparalleled beauty I beg you to hear them. They are only to beg you not to deny me your favour and protection now when I need them the most. I'm going to plunge, engulf and sink myself into the abyss I have in front of me, only so that the world might know that if you favour me there's no impossible feat that I cannot take on and accomplish.

Once he had said this, don Quixote approached the pit and with his sword chopped away the brambles at the mouth of the cave, the noise and commotion from which caused a great many crows and bats to fly out, so thick and so fast that they knocked the knight to the ground.

Finally, Don Quixote got up, gave the rope to his two companions and let himself be lowered into the depths of the cavern. As he went down, Sancho offered a blessing accompanied by a thousand signs of the cross and said, 'God guide you and may He bring you back safe, sound, and unscathed, to the light of this life that you're leaving in order to bury yourself in the darkness you seek!'

Don Quixote shouted to them to give him more and more rope, which thcy fcd to him a bit at a time. When the shouts coming up the cave were no longer audible and they had let down the six hundred feet of rope, they felt they should bring Don Quixote back up.

They pulled at the rope but it was very light and they feared that Don Quixote was still in the cavern. However, when they had pulled up about five hundred feet of rope they were overjoyed to feel some weight At sixty feet they saw Don Quixote, and Sancho shouted to him, 'Welcome back, your grace, señor mío. We thought you were going to stay there for a generation.'

Don Quixote said nothing in response, and when they had taken him completely out they saw that his eyes were closed; he was fast asleep.

They stretched him out on the ground and untied him, yet with all this he didn't wake up. They then turned him from side to side and shook him for a good while until he came to, stretching as if he'd been woken out of a very deep and heavy slumber.

Looking all around as if he were distressed, he said, 'May God forgive you, my friends, for you've plucked me from the most delicious and agreeable life and spectacle that any human being has ever seen or lived. Now I finally understand that all of the joys of this life are just shadows and dreams, or wither like a wildflower.'

The companions listened in amazement to Don Quixote's words, begging him to help them understand what he was saying, and tell him what he'd seen in that hell.

'"Hell" you call it?' said Don Quixote. 'Don't call it that because it doesn't deserve it, as you'll see soon enough.'

He asked them to give him something to eat for he was ravenous. Together they ate lunch and dinner all at the same time, after which Don Quixote said: 'Nobody rise, and listen carefully, my sons.'

'At about twelve or fourteen times a man's height down this pit, on the right-hand side there's a recess and ledge large enough to put a cart with its mules. A bit of light trickles in through some fissures or holes far above on the surface. I saw this recess and ledge at a moment when I was dangling on the rope, tired of descending through that dark region

204

without any specific destination, so I decided to stop there and rest a while. I shouted to you saying you shouldn't let down any more rope until I told you to, but you must not have heard me. I pulled in the rope you were lowering and made a coil of it and sat on top, deep in thought, considering what I needed to do to get to the bottom, since there was now no one to suspend me.

'And while in these thoughts and confusion, suddenly, and without wanting to, I was overcome by a deep sleep, and when least I expected it, not knowing how, I woke up and found myself in the middle of the most beautiful, pleasant, and delightful meadow that Nature could have created, nor could the most ingenious human imagination dream up. I opened my eyes and rubbed them and saw that I was not dreaming, but was wide-awake. Even so, I felt my head and chest to assure myself it was really me who was there, and not some kind of body-less and false phantom. But my sense of touch, my feeling, the well-ordered reasoning I did with myself, convinced me I was there as I'm now here.

'Then I saw a sumptuous royal palace or castle, whose ramparts and walls seemed to be transparent and made of clear glass, and when its great doors opened, I saw coming out toward me a venerable old man dressed in a cloak made of purple flannel that dragged behind him. On his shoulders and chest was a scholar's hood of green satin, and on his head he was wearing a black Milanese cap, and his very-white beard extended below his waist. He was unarmed except for a rosary in his hand whose small beads were the size of walnuts and the large ones the size of an average ostrich egg. His demeanour, mien, and the dignity of his stately presence, severally and together, amazed me and filled me with wonder. He approached me and the first thing he did was to embrace me tightly, and then said: "It's been a long time, brave knight don Quixote de La Mancha, that those in this lonely place have been waiting to see you so that you can tell the world what is in this deep cave—called the Cave of Montesinos—that you've entered, and it's a deed that has been reserved for your invincible heart and your stupendous courage only. Come with me, most illustrious señor, for I want to show you the wonders this transparent palace hides, of which I'm the governor and perpetual chief guardian, because I'm Montesinos himself, from whom the cave takes its name..."

'The venerable Montesinos took me into the crystal palace, where, in an excessively cool room on the ground floor, there was an exquisitely made marble sepulchre constructed of alabaster, on top of which was a knight stretched out full length, not made of bronze, marble, or jasper, but of pure flesh and blood. His right hand—which seemed to me to be a bit hairy and sinewy, proof that its owner was very strong—was placed over his heart. And before I could ask Montesinos anything, seeing me amazed looking at the man on the sepulcher, he said: "This is my friend Durandarte, flower and mirror of the enamoured and brave knights of his time. That French enchanter that they say is the child of the devil, Merlin, has him held enchanted here, as he has me, and many others. And I'd say he's not the child of the devil, but rather he knows a bit more than the devil. How, and for what reason, he has us enchanted, no one knows, but it will be revealed in time, and I imagine that time is not far off.'"

What follows in Cervantes' narrative is a complex series of events that confront Don Quixote in the magical cavern. Montesinos confirmed to the knight that he cut out the heart of Durandarte when his friend died. Montesinos then took the heart to señora Belerma, Durandarte's wife. Subsequently, Merlin enchanted him and Durandarte, Belerma, Durandarte's squire Guadiana, the duenna Ruidera and her seven daughters and two nieces, and many other friends and acquaintances.

For five-hundred years Merlin's enchantment has been in place although the sage, moved to compassion by the tears of those under his spell, had since turned Ruidera and her family members into lakes, and Guadiana into a river. Montesinos explains to his enchanted brethren that in their presence now stands the acclaimed knight Don Quixote of La Mancha by whose means and favour they may be finally disenchanted.

Don Quixote saw many other wonders. On one occasion Montesinos directed Don Quixote's attention to three peasant girls running around in a field, one of whom the knight recognises as the peerless Dulcinea del Toboso, a woman that he has never met but is the love of his life all the same.

Don Quixote tried to follow his fair damsel through the field but Montesinos said that in this enchanted place the act would be futile and, in any case, the time was approaching for the knight to leave the cave. He added that there were many other enchanted upper-class ladies in the cave from past and present times, among whom were was Queen Guinevere and her duenna Quintañona, who also poured wine for Lancelot. Aptly, Montesinos's counsel that the spell of enchantment over the countryside made pursuit of Dulcinea impossible parallels Alice's experience in the Looking-glass world when she and the Red

Queen had to run as fast as possible just to remain in the same spot.

At one point the cousin interrupts Don Quixote's narrative to exclaim, 'I don't know... how your grace in the short time you were down there saw so many things and conversed and reacted to so much.'

'How long ago did I go down?' asked Don Quixote.

'A little more than an hour ago,' responded Sancho.

'That cannot be,' replied Don Quixote, 'because night came upon me, then morning arrived, then night and morning came again three times. So by my count I've been in that remote area, hidden from our sight, for three days.'

Three days compressed into one hour—this magical 72-hour period provides the key for our more complete understanding of Don Quxote's visit to the Caves of Montesinos. There are many accounts in the esoteric record of men and women who, having reached a point in their lives when they are beginning to question everything that they have learned and looking for answers as to how to best proceed on their life's journey, suddenly find themselves in a place beyond their knowledge and understanding.

Like Don Quixote, they may be enjoying a day's spelunking in a familiar place before coming across a crystal cave that melts away to reveal a magnificent library. They may be walking a woodland path they travel daily but suddenly see through the pines a glistening white castle that was definitely not there twenty-four hours earlier. They may visit a familiar gas station, café or antique store and, once inside, realise they have stepped into an entirely different world.

Whatever the location or circumstance, the common factor will be that at the threshold of a dimension beyond their human experience they will meet one or more teachers and guides. Formerly of our world before evolving into a spirit dimension beyond our comprehension, these counsellors make their wisdom available to those who are seeking another way. They greet them, put their minds at ease, and guide the supplicant through a three-day initiation in which their spirit-soul leaves the body and journeys in the higher worlds for instruction into the ancient mysteries.

Druidic sources indicated that a man was not expected to attain the initiate state until he was advanced in years, having 'grown a long beard' after a lengthy period of tutelage and instruction. Ultimately, an individual, drawn to their mystical fulfilment by the questing power of one's inner and outer landscapes, has no choice other than to follow the solitary path of the initiate.

These timeless teachings were born from the Wisdom of the Hermetic Mysteries. These developed when very wise teachers, symbolised in legend as Hermes, Cadmus or Thoth, gathered all the intimacies and subtleties of the evolutionary process within Mother Earth. This was long before the development of the written word in an era in which there was a "word-by-mouth" insight into living on this planet and being a vital part of the earth. In time this word-by-mouth knowledge was put in writing and placed in the great library at Alexandria.

The Hermetics taught that the mind is always in conflict with its surroundings and the key to a balanced mind is the ability to magnify, without words, the living energy of the Earth. This life force is the archœus, the vital substance in Nature upon which all things subsist. To magnify the living energy of the Earth is to take time to let the senses relax and listen to what is beyond the façade of the obvious and be open to the unobvious.

The ancient records outline the process. The student enters a deep sleep and experiences a vivid dream. In my most recent work[61] I gave an example. A young man, Brad, had been washed onto a beach after his small boat had been dashed on the rocks by a storm. It was chilly and so he built a fire. Brad caught fish and cooked them. While he was resting after his meal, he was astonished to see a man standing in the centre of the fire, its flames leaping higher and higher. The man extended his right hand and said, 'Come with me! Do not be afraid, just come with me...' Brad took a deep breath and stepped into the flames to join the old man. Instantly, he found himself in a tremendous room that was literally on fire. Leading away from the room was a corridor lined with fire.

The old man began to retreat down the corridor, followed by the younger man. Brad lost sight of his companion but eventually he came to a giant marble temple. Sitting on a high throne at one end of the temple was the old man. Around him stood forty-two white-robed men and women. He walked cautiously to the centre of the temple. A deep baritone chant broke forth. One by one the forty-two turned toward the man on the throne and said, 'May your wisdom and light shine on all of us this day, Great Hermes Mercurius Trismegistus, Master of all

_____

[61] Graddon, N., *Crystals, Mother Earth and the Forces of Living Nature*, AUP, Illinois, 2022.

Knowledge, Initiator of all Craftsmanship, Master of Three Worlds, Scribe of the Gods, Librarian of the Books of Life, Scribe of the Book of Truth, and Master of Mysteries.'

Brad gasped. The man who had appeared in the fire was no less than Hermes whose symbol was Mercury, the planet nearest to the Sun! He was closest to the Universal Life, which made the world grow and move. Brad fell to his knees, half out of respect and half from an overwhelming emotional sense of awe.

Hermes descended from his throne, faced the young man and said, pointing to the robed oracles that attended him, 'These are the physical manifestations of the books I created which were burned in the library of Alexandria. Two books are related to hymns and the music of the Gods. Four are concerned with astrology, the fixed stars and their conjunctions and risings. Ten are under the responsibility of the Scribe and relate to hieroglyphics, cosmography, geography, the sun, moon and planets and the disciplines of the priesthood, and of the Stole-keeper who bears a cubit of justice and the cup of libations. Ten concern the honour paid to the gods and matters of worship as that relating to sacrifices, processions, festivals and the like. Ten more concern the Hieratic and relate to the laws, the gods and the training of priests. The final six books concern healing and medicines. You, Brad, want to work with herbs and plants and be a healer. You will be taught by these six.'

Hermes moved quickly to his throne and nodded his head. The six formed a corridor, three on each side, and began chanting once again. The young man found himself walking forward along the corridor. Soon it became sponge-like, absorbing every part of him into this magical teaching experience. It was as if he was a giant pen beginning to write indelibly on his innermost being.

The great temple literally vibrated as the energy of the initiation grew. Finally, the energy peaked, and the temple was suddenly empty. The man was instantly in other realms, becoming the unique power of the Hermetic Mysteries. He heard a spoken voice: 'To heal is to be without any personal reference and be pure of thought and action.' He puzzled over this but was made aware of everything he needed to know. He understood that if he were totally disconnected from himself when he was using his healing powers, he would be pure in thought and action.

The first healing book of Hermes was "THE SELF". He found himself becoming a part of its pages. In fact, he soon felt that he was the actual book itself. Learning how not to be himself, but to be in spite of himself would be a major change in consciousness.

The second book was "THE MIND". Whereas the first book of healing was centred on his relationship to all living things and his separation, this book presented the fact that the mind is always in conflict with its surroundings, and that the key to a balanced mind is the magnification of the Nature Self. He perceived that the great agonies of the world were a result of the mind, non-acceptance and a sense of superiority. Herein lay the "GREAT DELUSION". Humanity thought that it was the superior living creature when, in fact, any acceptance of that thought made it inferior. He must learn to step beyond this delusion.

The third book healing was a "NATURAL SOURCE". Brad learned of the power of the natural healing sources as a living energy. He learned how to communicate with the natural resources which he would use in order that, when used in healing, the "Nature Consciousness" would be passed on to the essence of the individual. Flowers, leaves, roots and buds have great strength on their own but an intimate connection between their consciousness and the Nature Self provided the ultimate in healing.

The fourth and fifth healing books of Hermes were "ALCHEMY: SIGNS AND SYMBOLS" and "ALCHEMY: MIXTURES AND INCANTATIONS". In his adventures with the teachers of these two books, Brad learned how important it is to work at certain times of the day, week and year for the maximum results. Through his inner consciousness were threaded the teachings of the many symbols that a healer could use in creating a harmonious atmosphere in the place where he was working. He was shown the days on which certain illnesses were more receptive to healing, as well as certain hours of the day when the potions would be the most efficacious. The fifth book also blended the knowledge of the use of the consciousness of nature with one's Nature Self. It taught how to dry and grind flowers, roots, buds and leaves and to put their spiritual essence in a state of suspension, enabling it to bring the poultice, salve or mixture back to life. Brad began to perceive the power of sound and words in relationship to healing.

The sixth book of healing was "IMMORTALITY". This teacher opened worlds to Brad that he had barely imagined. He related that immortality is a state of mind and that a sense of mortality is a lack of belief in the power of the mind in relationship to all living things.

Mentally, he understood the concept of mortality. However, to be able to experience it in order that mortality would be eliminated was still out of his reach. The teacher who was opening this book to him understood this inability. Instantly, before Brad was a powerful light that was so bright and strong that it momentarily blinded him. The brightness faded and he felt himself in a large room filled with hundreds of flaming lamps. The teacher was pointing his finger to his eye as an indication for him to observe. In one flowing movement all of the lamps were blown out and he stood alone in the darkness. The first few moments were no problem but soon he found that the room was so dark that his eyes would not become accustomed. There was not a sound, smell or sense of any kind. He began to feel mentally disoriented, completely out of control of his thoughts. He was afraid to move for there were no reference points for him to fix on.

In the distance one small flame began to burn and he started to feel in control and to relax. Brad's teacher said, 'Your mind is either like a thousand flames which bring brightness and light into your life, or it can be total darkness which instils fear and frustration. Immortality is that beyond the mind which brings comfort and control in spite of the mind's power.' He let these words sink into his pupil's thoughts for a moment and then continued. 'Identification with your current body is the darkness. The eternal light is beyond the darkness, just like that single flame. Once you conceive of and accept this truth, you are immortal and will never live a mortal life again.'

As Brad began to walk toward the single light, it became bigger and bigger until it was as brilliant as the sun. Becoming like an eternal flame, the setting changed and he was again all alone. Hermes walked up beside Brad and smiled broadly. 'You have learned of the Wisdom of the Hermetic Mysteries; you are now part of that tradition. It is time you returned and woke to a new and sunny day. An opportunity for you to become a powerful healer will present itself very soon!'

In diverse forms and situations the initiation ceremony has happened again and again throughout human history. After leaving his Greek island home of Samos and before establishing his famous school for Inner Life Learning at Crotona in southern Italy, Pythagoras travelled widely to increase his philosophical and spiritual knowledge. Among the many teachers with whom he sought insight and learning, Pythagoras received instruction from the Zoroastrian priesthood. The Magi initiated Pythagoras into their Arcanum, including music, mathematics, the sublime methods of worshiping the gods and the principles ruling the universe. He learned of the motions of the stars and their effects upon the births and futures of men.

Next, Pythagoras made his way to Egypt. After studying with the Egyptian priests at Diospolis (Thebes), Pythagoras travelled to the lower Nile valley where he sought entrance into the Society of the Great Pyramid. Finally, after sitting at the foot of the temple day-after-day for six years asking for entrance for initiation, the priests admitted the Greek into the pyramid.

The Master of the Great Pyramid would greet an initiate and take him deep inside the pyramid. There the student would meet the all-powerful Initiator and over a period of weeks would be given preliminary instruction for the "second birth". Finally, at the time of the Solstice, the initiate would be led to the King's Chamber where he would be placed in the great coffer. He would then experience the disentangling of his material body from his spiritual being. In this controlled situation, the initiate would "die". His spirit would travel and freely experience the worlds beyond and commune with the powerful teachers there. After three days, the spirit would return to the body and rebirth would begin. The three-day process of initiation was known as the "Temple Sleep".

As Don Quixote discovered in the Cave of Montesinos, the legend of Camelot is intimately connected with initiation. An account extracted under torture from the Knights Templars after their enforced dissolution during the first years of the fourteenth century was a revelation about Camelot. The Templars claimed that Camelot was not a place that could be reached by foot but was a separate region, a training dimension not bound by the laws of time and space and only accessible by those deemed sufficiently prepared for initiation into the higher mysteries.

Tales about Camelot were spoken of by initiates that had "pierced the veil" (the root phrase expressed in the name Perceval) but who subsequently broke a bond of silence about the nature of their adventures. Consequently, a belief grew over the centuries that Arthur's Court was to be found in such and such physical place, be it Cornwall, Wales, Brittany, Scotland or any other that lay claim to its location.

During Don Quixote's adventure, Montesinos tells the knight that he and his companions have been held in enchantment by 'child of the devil,' Merlin, for several hundred years. The late British medium Grace Cook's spirit guide White Eagle described the story of Merlin and Arthur as the basis of the White Brotherhood's teachings. The

White Brotherhood, he explained, is a company of perfected beings of great power who live in a higher world parallel to ours and spread spiritual teachings through selected humans. The members of the Brotherhood may be known as the Masters of the Ancient Wisdom, the Ascended Masters, the Church Invisible, or simply as the Hierarchy. The first person to talk about them in the West was Madame Blavatsky who, along with sister theosophists Helena Roerich and Alice A. Bailey, claimed to received messages from them.

Merlin was the supreme magician and enchanter. Esoteric tradition tells a remarkable story of his origin and of the creation of Camelot. Subsequent to the end of Roman rule in Britain in the early fifth century AD, the White Brotherhood saw the need for a different form of spiritual energy to infiltrate this plane. It would be conveyed through inspirational people who had the ability to create and sustain dreams, who allowed individuals to imagine in a new way and impart to those on a quest an idea of what could be attained with an attitude sculpted from right thought, word and action. Hence, Camelot was created in a companion dimension to Earth to fulfil the requirement for a new and significant energy cycle.

To make it work, the Brotherhood sought an individual who was evolving in a very powerful way in the higher dimensions. They were to be placed in a training ground, an etheric dimension out of the astral plane, closest to the physical Earth. Their role in the new cycle was to be the soul or nucleus of the new dimension and to tie it together. They would be taught how to create the vibration, the rituals and the sacraments necessary to provide the inspirational and mystical input for the new energy cycle of Camelot.

An individual came forward who had completed his reincarnational cycle in the dimension preceding the earth experience but, uniquely, had afterwards bypassed it to advance immediately to the higher worlds of learning. This individual was Merlin, an extremely powerful energy from whose unique evolutionary status was created the story that he had travelled back through time via the energy of crystal to serve as the inspirational focus for Camelot.

Merlin knew upon arriving what he had to do. He began firstly to pull together those people who had converged with him into the new dimension. He focused upon finding one powerful individual who could thread the community together. He sought Arthur and trained him, teaching him all the vast knowledge he possessed, together working diligently to create the dream dimension, one with no written records so that it would catch people's imagination and be spoken of for centuries to come by those on their search for the Grail, in their quest to be an Arthur with a magical sword.

Excalibur is the symbol of the cutting power of one's Higher Self and of a chalice in the form of a cross, rooted to the earth with its handles to the side and its head held high: a symbol of humanity never to be wielded in anger, judgement, frustration or fear lest it be returned to the lake whence it came. All the while that Merlin was focused on the creation of the dream dimension of Camelot he was beset by very significant trials. A poem by Taliesin describes these eloquently:

Primary chief bard am I to Elphin,
And my original country is the region of the summer stars;
Idno and Heinin called me Merddin,
At length every being will call me Taliesin.

I was with my Lord in the highest sphere,
On the fall of Lucifer into the depths of hell;
I have borne a banner before Alexander;
I know the name of the stars from north to south.

I was in Canaan when Absalon was slain.
I was in the court of Don before the birth of Gwydion.
I was in the place of the crucifixion of the merciful Son of God;
I have been three periods in the prison of Arianrod.

I have been in Asia with Noah in the ark,
I have seen the destruction of Sodom and Gomorrah.
I have been in India when Roma was built.
I am now come here to the remnant of Troia.

I have been with my Lord in the ass's manger,
I have strengthened Moses through the waters of Jordan;
I have been in the firmament with Mary Magdalene;
I have obtained the Muse from the cauldron of Ceridwen.

I shall be until the day of doom on the face of the earth;
And it is not known whether my body is fish or flesh.

Because of the unique way in which Merlin had entered this plane he effectively became trapped in the energies of the Earth, which locked him in place as a restless wanderer, constantly phasing in and out of the time element of physical living, which was enormously

214

challenging to him. To this day, Merlin is said to wake from sleep in his glass tomb and travel ceaselessly backwards and forwards in time, appearing in any form he chooses until the day arrives when he is released from his earthbound imprisonment by, it is said, the power of a woman.

White Eagle told his own story of the 'mythical character of one King Arthur, and also to a teacher once known as Merlin.' He described Merlin as an initiate of the mysteries of Egypt who was a birth-child of the fire of kundalini, born of a virgin mother and of a father supposedly of the underworld. He revealed that this story is a symbolic description of the potentialities of creation sealed within the human body.

Under certain conditions these powers can be coaxed to come forward to bring about a mystical marriage, a result of the arising of the baser creative powers, seasoned with love and wisdom, to produce the initiate: the master of all the lower life.

Gradually, Merlin unveiled certain profound truths and magical secrets to his young pupil, later known as King Arthur who formed the brethren of the Knights of the Round Table. White Eagle emphasised that although the story of Camelot is considered to be many hundreds of years old it is, in fact, as old as the world itself and intimately connected with the safeguarding and gradual dissemination of the White Brotherhood's original teachings.

There are no written accounts from those who found their way into Camelot and underwent initiation; only word of mouth tales handed down in Templar circles and verbal Hermetics. From these one can derive a composite picture of the Camelot initiatory experience.

"Vivian" was tending her sheep on a Welsh hillside. She loved her life and her work. Vivian had been a shepherdess for more than thirty years. Her husband, Pete, had recently died of cancer and their marriage was childless. All manner of thoughts were laying siege to her senses. Might there be more to life than familiar routine? Was there life after death? If there was, where did it take place? Was it in a perfect heaven world of pearly gates and harp-strumming angels or, as she had read in books, did immortality exist in worlds parallel to this one, where those that had gone on faced new challenges in accordance with a divine cosmic plan? Was Pete living it up in one of these places right now? Was it possible to make reconnaissance visits into these worlds while still in this life to get a taste of things to come?

Vivian's train of thought was disturbed by the anguished bleat of a newborn lamb. The sound was coming from a nearby wood. Vivian entered the wood where she could hear the lamb but not see it. As she moved through the trees she saw a dark space, which she identified as the mouth of a cave set into a rocky escarpment among hawthorn trees. The lamb's call seemed to be coming from that direction.

As soon as the shepherdess reached the cave she stepped into a brilliant light; nothing was visible beyond the light. She then discovered that she no longer had a body, just awareness that in some way she was still Vivian. She thought, 'Where am I and why do I not have a body?'

'Vivian has crossed the threshold of the spirit-soul and is in a sanctuary of initiation,' was the immediate, startling response. 'You have no voice, just thoughts. But unlike Vivian in the physical, here your thoughts are not filtered or manipulated by your conscious mind.'

'If I crossed the threshold of the spirit-soul, am I dead?' Vivian thought to herself.

'No, you are not dead; you are very much alive. You are in Camelot,' replied the unseen speaker. 'Most who cross the threshold of the spirit-soul have left the "World Without" permanently. Just across the threshold of the spirit-soul is where all true, pure and honourable initiation takes place. You are now in your initiatory Camelot, which has access to all the lessons you have come into the World Without to learn, all the people you are currently involved with, all the people you will be karmically connected to, and what your potentials can be.'

Somewhat confused, Vivian asked again, 'Am I dead?'

'No, you are not dead as the World Without would perceive. Like all ancient initiatory rites, the body of Vivian is in a state of suspended animation and the essence of Vivian is being initiated for three days, three days that will pass in one hour in the World Without.'

'Then what happens?'

'You can choose to go on to the World Within or to return to the World Without.'

'But I thought from all the books and legendary tales that Camelot was a physical place.'

'No, Camelot was never a physical place in the World Without. It did have some resemblances in names and supposed locations but Camelot never existed in a geographical sense. In fact, Camelot is a more recent name given it by some individuals in the World Without who heard stories and "myths" of this place. I need not remind you that most of your myths, fables and faery tales all have foundations of truth that storytellers tend to colour, add flourish and create new characters to adapt with the times. This place has many names. You were drawn to it

216

by a sequence of signs, symbols and events. Many seek "Camelot" but it is never found by looking for it. It is discovered by living life's journey to the fullest, loving self unconditionally, being unlimited, and by being wise enough not to repeat the lessons learned.'

'Who or what are you?'

'You know me as Arthur. I represent the masculine part of your spirit-soul and it is with Guinevere and I that you have your first day's lesson.'

'Will my lesons only be through thought? Won't I see you or Guievere?' Vivian asked hopefully.

'This is not a classroom and we are communicating with each other on the highest level. Our communication without the use of the five senses of the World Without eliminates all the confusion of five separate impressions recorded by the subconscious, which then formulates a single composite impression.'

'When or if you return to the World Without the information you have received here will be a projection of the results of your initiation,' came a the response from a distinctly feminine energy.

'Who are you?'

'I am the energy you know as Guinevere. The information you recive from me will meld positively with your feminine side. The energy that you knew as Arthur will meld with your masculine side. It will not replace the person Vivian was but create a filter that will allow your reactions to have greater depth and insight.'

'Initiation into the ancient mysteries is not a status symbol or mystical badge of honour,' said Arthur. 'It meshes positively with what you were and allows you ro perceive the World Without to its very fullest. Past impressions of your subconscious mind will no longer control you in any way. You will immediately know them for what they are and be able take action accordingly.'

'Why do I feel as if I'm receiving something above and beyond what I am understanding from your thoughts communication?' asked Vivian.

'You are,' said Arthur and Guinevere in unison. 'When you eat a piece of bread you like the smell and taste but you never see what it does in your body. You will know that it is affecting it but not exactly where and how. Our thoughts are like that piece of bread and as the energy of Vivian absorbs the thoughts many triggers release and allow you to receive on levels that you will probably never be aware of.'

'What of Lancelot and Mordred, will I be taught by them too?'

'Yes and no, they are not separate energies but a part of the whole. Lancelot is the overly positive side and Mordred the overly negative side, which together affect masculine and feminine decisions.'

'What of Merlin and the Round Table?' Vivian asked.

'I am here!' replied a powerful thought form. 'I am your intuition, instinct and reality re-organizer. It is though me that you will learn the ultimate possibilities available to to you in the World Without…and how to use them! There are no limits to what a person can do in the World Without, for it is thought of, written about or spoken of…it can be done. You just have to have the courage and belief to do it. This is what you are receiving from me. The Round Table and the many knights represent the potential karmic interaction you could face in this lifetime in the World Without. Each knight represents a particular lesson or karmic situation you must face during your lifetime. The idea of each knight attached to a quest has its roots in the fact that a particular energy leaves this sanctuary to provide you with a quest. Each lesson or karmic confrontation is a quest. You have just read Miguel Cervantes' book, Don Quixote, and enjoyed it very much. Like you, Cervantes found his way to this sanctuary and afterwards tried to relate his experience in parable form in Don Quixote's adventures. The entire work is a description of an initiate's journey into the ancient mysteries and the confrontations that must be faced and overcome along the way. That is why the story resounds so powerfully even today, four hundred years later. The Grail will always be finding the right path in the lesson and completing it successfully.

'Each person who enters into the World Without has every tool within them to have joy, balance and beauty in their life every day. More people don't know how to accesss their tools but initiation shows you how to access them all. Intuition and instinct are the corridors to learning how to use your fullest potential and they are truly magic. To be able to use your intuition and instinct to the fullest would make you the greatest magician or enchanter ever. Self-belief is the magician's wand and keeping his knowledge to himself is his magic potions.'

Thrre was a long pause until Arthur said, 'Your three days are almost up. Do you have any last thoughts?'

Vivian thought for a moment. 'What about the Lady of the Lake, Arthur's death, Guinevere and Lancelot?'

'These are all a part of the whole and an intricate part of this initiation,' Guinevere answered. 'You have read too much about what initiation is in the World Without. As was said, true initiation into the

218

powers and mysteries of the ancients is from within, not from without to your subconscious and conscious minds. You have received much more into your spirit-soul than you now are aware. Now, it is time. Do you want to go back across the threshold to the world of Vivian or do you want to on to the other worlds beyond?'

Vivian didn't hesitate. 'Back to to my world, of course. I have a lost lamb to find!'

'What you have received here in the past three days, must be used in the World Without before your initiation is complete,' said Arthur. 'You have been communicated to on many levels and most of them are beyond the thoughts you have received from Guinevere, Merlin and me. Upon your return you, like Don Quixote, will find yourself on a quest. This quest will bring forward and put to use all that you have received here. Only then will your initiation be complete.'

'The seed has been planted. This place, known to you as Camelot, will grow and blossom within you during and after completion of your quest. Go, Vivian, and begin your new life,' prompted Guinevere.

There was silence and Vivian was only aware of her own thoughts as she moved through the brilliant light and began to reappear in the mouth of the woodland cave. Her first sight was the newborn lamb emerging from nearby bushes.

On returning to her village cottage a few hours later, Vivian saw a letter on the mat. She opened it to find that an application she had made to help set up a sheep-farming project in Patagonia had been successful. She had almost forgotten about it. It had been months since she sent off the paperwork and since then her mother had died and she and her brother Dafydd had had their hands full with family matters. Dafydd had said he would look after the sheep for the twelve months she would be away if the application came good. Wow, she was going to Chile, to Patagonia, the only other place on on the planet where Welsh was the first language! She was going on a quest!!

The esoteric record refers to the biblical story of Lazarus as an instance of an initiatory period that had run over time. It has parallels with Don Quixote's journey into the cave. Both accounts describe classic scenarios in which the initiate cannot be woken from the magical Temple Sleep into which they have been induced to enable them to travel the higher worlds for three days:

> Don Quixote said nothing in response, and when they had taken him completely out, they saw that his eyes were closed;

219

he was fast asleep. They stretched him out on the ground and untied him, yet with all this he didn't wake up. They then turned him from side to side and shook him for a good while until he came to, stretching as if he'd been woken out of a very deep and heavy slumber.

The Gospel of John narrates that Lazarus, the brother of Mary and Martha, is sick. The sisters send word to Jesus to come and heal their brother. Jesus tells his followers, 'This sickness will not end in death...'

Jesus does not come to Bethany immediately but stays where he is for two more days before beginning the journey; He knows that Lazarus is in coma while he undergoes his inner journey of initiation. The disciples are afraid of returning to Judea but Jesus says: 'Our friend Lazarus is asleep but I am going to awaken him.'

When Jesus arrives in Bethany, he is told that Lazarus is dead and has already been in his tomb for four days. Martha laments that Jesus did not arrive soon enough to heal her brother. In the presence of a crowd of Jewish mourners, Jesus comes to the tomb and asks for the stone of the tomb to be removed but Martha interjects that there will be a smell.

Jesus responds, 'Did I not tell you that if you believed, you would see the glory of God?'

Over the objections of Martha, Jesus has them roll the stone away from the entrance to the tomb and says a prayer. They take the stone away then Jesus looks up and says:

> Father, I thank you that you have heard me. I know that you always hear me, but I said this for the benefit of the people standing here, that they may believe that you sent me.

Jesus is the only person present who knows that Lazarus's spirit-soul is still roaming in the worlds beyond and needs to be brought back into his physical body so that he could emerge from Temple Sleep. Jesus calls Lazarus to come out ('Lazarus, come forth!'). Lazarus wakes and comes out from the tomb. Only Jesus at this time had the power to bring Lazarus "back to life".

'Welcome back, your grace, señor mío. We thought you were going to stay there for a generation.'

'How long ago did I go down?' asked Don Quixote.

'A little more than an hour ago,' responded Sancho.

'That cannot be,' replied Don Quixote, 'because night came upon me, then morning arrived, then night and morning came again three times. So by my count I've been in that remote area, hidden from our sight, for three days.'

Alice with Mock Turtle and Gryphon in Wonderland

Chapter 14

The Elf Kingdom of Laurin

One day, a Knight of the lineage of Dietrich de Berne was out riding in the Tyrol along the ancient Troj de Reses, the pathway of roses. He was trying vainly to find access to the fabled Kingdom of Laurin. Each time he believed he had attained this goal insurmountable walls would rise up in the mountains around him.

He then came upon a gorge and he passed through. Close by a stream he heard the marvellous singing of a multitude of birds. He stopped to listen. Then the Knight saw a shepherdess in a sunny meadow. He asked her if the birds always sang so. She replied that she had not heard them sing for a very long time, but that now that they were it was possible, she thought, to rediscover the windmill and again put it to work for the good of men.

'What sort of windmill is it?' asked the Knight.

'It is an enchanted windmill,' the shepherdess replied. 'In the past, it was dwarfs who worked it on behalf of King Laurin who owned it and milled flour for the poor. But there were those who had become greedy and one day one of the dwarfs had been tossed in the water because he had not given enough flour. Since then the mill wheel had stopped and no one knew where it was. It would be thus until the birds sang again. It is said that the windmill will be found at the bottom of a gorge. It is well concealed and even its wheel turns no longer. People call it the windmill of roses because it is covered in wild roses.'

The Knight finds it. The mill is covered in moss, its wooden sides are blackened with age and its wheel is stuck. The roses form a thicket around it such that a passer-by would not see the mill. The Knight tries to open the door but it will not budge. In the wall he sees a tiny window. The Knight climbs on his horse's back and peers through. Inside are seven dwarfs stretched out, sleeping. The Knight calls and taps on the window but there is no response. Defeated, the Knight returns to the meadow and sleeps for the night. The following day he climbs on a high point overlooking the gorge. Three rose bushes are in bloom before him. The Knight picks a rose from the first bush.

An elf cries out from the foliage, 'Bring me a rose from the good old days!'

Willingly,' replies the Knight, 'but how will I find it?'

The elf disappears in lament.

The Knight approaches the second bush and picks a flower. Again, an elf appears, asks the same question, gets the same answer and withdraws, lamenting. The Knight then picks a bloom from the third bush and another elf asks, 'Why do you knock at our door?'

'I wish to enter the garden of roses of King Laurin, for I seek the fiancé of the Month of May!'

'Only the child and the poet may enter the garden of roses. If you can sing a beautiful ballad then the way will be open to you.'

'I can do it.'

'Then come with me,' said the elf, who picks some wild roses and descends into the gorge followed by the Knight. They reach the windmill. Its door opens. The dwarfs sleep still. The elf brushes them with the roses, crying:

'Awaken, sleepers, the young roses are in flower!'

The dwarfs wake up, open their eyes and commence to mill. The elf shows the mill cellar to the Knight. From there runs a gallery deep into the mountain and finishes in a dazzling light. Before him is the garden paradise of King Laurin, with its multi-coloured flowerbeds, exquisite groves and resplendent roses. The Knight sees also a web of woven silk covering its entrance.

'Now, begin your song,' invites the elf.

The Knight then sings the song of Love and of the Month of May. The paradise of roses opens before him and the Knight penetrates into Eternity.

This tale, first recounted in my first book for AUP, on the subject of OttoRahn, is filled with powerful themes and images that are clues to the presence of Earth's companion worlds.

The Knight is of the lineage of Dietrich de Berne. "Dietrich" is a German word for "skeleton key". This is a classic symbol of initiation of someone pursuing a Quest, a thread of order, under the protection of ancient guardians.

In Pythagoras's School of Inner Learning in Crotona, there was an inner circle of students to whom the master philosopher taught more advanced metaphysical concepts. One of the most remarkable of these teachings was the revelation that by drawing on the secret powers of numbers one can journey in full consciousness to the worlds beyond and return safely. Pythagoras taught that one approaches this task by firstly understanding that the invisible energy centres of the human body, the chakras, are so arranged as to be capable of being visualised as a pyramid filled with smaller pyramids, each representing a corresponding number and colour. The student labours over many years to construct their personal pyramid and its powers to a point of initiatory mastery. At this stage, the student has developed a mental key that opens a doorway into their personal pyramid through which the spirit-soul can enter in full consciousness. The ultimate aim in Pythagoras' system was to use the power within one's pyramid to replicate the initiatory experience in the Great Pyramid's Kings Chamber. Having entered one's pyramid, one had the power to disentangle one's material body from the spiritual self, travel freely in the worlds beyond and experience initiation into the ancient mysteries.

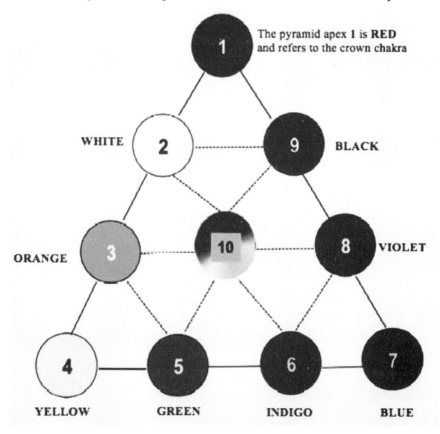

The pyramid apex 1 is **RED** and refers to the crown chakra

The Pythagorean personal pyramid, 10 is the "King's Chamber".

Troj de Reses is the Rose Trail, which symbolises the timeless power of Nature. The Knight picks a rose and is asked why he knocks at the elf's door; he must give the correct answer or password to gain admittance. We gain access into hidden realms by being at one with Nature's rhythms at the right place and at the right time.

The enchanted windmill returns us to Cervantes and the messages about the power of quest that he conveyed between the lines to those of his readers with the ears to hear and the sight to see.

When we think of seven dwarves, we think of Snow White (the Goddess) and her guardianship of Mother Earth and the Forces of Living Nature.

The web of woven silk alludes to the timeless thread of order that is ever-present in the midst of chaos. It is the magical thread between this world and the Otherworld, personified in mythology by Ariadne, Circe, Ceridwen and Hecate.

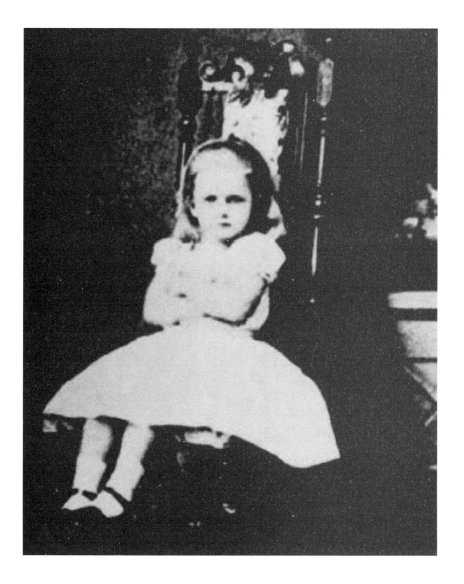

Mary Hilton Badcock: the probable inspiration for John
Tenniel's drawings of Alice

Christ Church Oxford

Chapter 15

High Strangeness

A Phantom Diner

In October 1974 Rick decided to leave the cold weather of New York, pack all his belongings in a U-Haul and head for the Southwest. Driving down I-40, Rick entered Texas and decided to take a break just east of Amarillo: 'I found a quaint looking diner on a spur of the old Route 66 just off I-40. When I pulled in, a plump older woman came out of the diner and asked if I needed gas. I had to chuckle at the set of old pumps and the image of the elderly woman pumping gas. I told her I didn't need any gas, but I sure could use something to eat.'

As Rick ate a delicious home-style meal of Texas cooking, the woman asked him where he was going. He told her that he was looking for a place to relocate, possibly in Texas, but he had no definite plans.

'The elderly woman, looking for all the world like a chubby cherub, started to speak to me in a kind, motherly way. She was very encouraging and really helped build up my confidence. She told me that I would do just fine in Amarillo and that I should drive into town and take some time to look around.'

Rick thanked her for the advice, and as he got up to leave she followed him out to his car. 'You'll do just fine in Amarillo,' she said again. 'You'll settle here for a good long while and you'll start a new life.'

Touched by her motherly concern and inspired by her confidence, Rick drove into Amarillo. On his second day in the city, he got a great job with Bell Helicopter Company and he rented a house. The company was located at the Amarillo Airport off I- 40 on the city's east side.

After several weeks on the job, Rick decided one day that he would drive out to the diner and see the nice old woman who had been so kind and who had offered him so much encouragement when he needed it most. He wanted to thank her for her inspiration and tell her how things had worked out so great, just as she had predicted.

Since he had lived in Amarillo for quite some time at this point,

Rick knew his way around the city. He drove east until he found the spur off old Route 66 where he knew the diner was located. At first, he thought he had somehow missed the quaint diner with its antiquated gas pumps, so he drove about 20 miles east then drove back again, looking for the place.

All that he could find was an old road that had once been part of Route 66, but there were no structures left on it. Discouraged, Rick drove home.

The next day at work, he asked a couple of friends who had grown up in Amarillo about the old diner east of town. Both of his friends agreed that there hadn't been any businesses open east of town since the early 1960s. He looked again and again, but he never found that diner and never got to thank that sweet old woman.

A Hotel in Oregon

In 1964 Cory took a vacation trip by car to visit his future in-laws in Kennewick, Washington. His fiancée was with him, but he left her with her parents after a few days to drive back to Burbank by himself. His car was a 1957 Corvette in excellent condition, and Cory was an experienced driver. The fall weather was dry and pleasant when he left the state of Washington. It would be a 12-hour trip down to the Los Angeles area. Cory left Washington around 11:30 p.m., and when he crossed the Oregon state line it was already dark. The weather had not changed.

He started to climb up into the mountains on a winding road going south. About four hours after he had left Washington, around 3:30 a.m., he was rounding a bend and with one fell swoop he found himself in a snowstorm! One moment it was a clear, dry, autumn night, the next, a raging snowstorm. It was unbelievable.

'I slowed down. I was frightened,' he explained, still shuddering at the experience now. 'The road was narrow, mountain on one side, a drop on the other.'

Cory got out of the car. He could drive no farther. It was ice cold and snowing. Then he saw in the distance what appeared to be a bright light, so he got back into the car and drove on. When he got to the "light" it turned out to be a road sign, reflecting light from somewhere. He was now on top of a hill, so he coasted downhill until the car came to a full stop. Cory looked out and discovered that he had rolled into some sort of village, for he saw houses. When he got out of the car he found he was standing in 6-8 inches of snow. He was on a bumpy street. It looked like he was in a Western town. Cory discovered that the car would not go any farther, anyway, and he was glad to be in this strange place. One building had the word "hotel" on it, and he walked toward it on wooden sidewalks. He noticed wagons parked outside the hotel, wagons that hitch onto horses.

Cory knocked at the door, which was open and entered the lobby. Everything was dark. He yelled fruitlessly for someone to come yet there was a potbellied stove with a fire in it. He moved near the stove to get warm. He noticed animal heads on the walls, old furniture of another era, and a calendar on the wall dating back to the early 1900s. Also, some notices on a board on the wall with dates in the late 1800s. The telephone had a sign reading 'CRANK BOX FOR OPERATOR.' There was a clock on the wall loudly ticking. There were kittens in one of the chairs.

To one side he noticed a barbershop chair. In the back he saw a desk and a big clock. He cranked the phone repeatedly. The noise he made worried him, so he took off his sweater and wrapped it around the box while cranking to keep the noise down. Nobody answered.

He went back to the stove, ready to go to sleep and maybe in the morning there would be somebody there to talk to. After all, they had got a fire going. There must be some life in the place. So, he lay down on a sofa, when he heard a rattling noise coming from what looked like a cardboard box in a corner. He figured it might be a snake and got real worried. The heat, however, was putting him to sleep.

'I was exhausted and so I just fell asleep,' he recounted to friends later. 'I woke up due to some sound upstairs, and I saw a smallish man coming down the steps, an old man of maybe seventy-five, wearing big boots, which made the noise. Was wearing old coveralls, like a farmer. Slowly he came down to where the stove was. He sat down in a rocking chair across from it, and then he went to the men's room, or something, and again sat down. He saw me, and we nodded to each other. Then he kept on rocking while I was trying to get up courage to ask him some questions.

The old man said, 'Nice day isn't it?' he said and put his hand on Cory's shoulder. Cory said later said it felt more like 'a chicken's foot.'

Finally, the old man said to Cory, 'You couldn't fall asleep…why don't you fall asleep?

'Well, that's all right,' Cory replied. 'I'm not really tired, you know.'

But he replied, 'No, you couldn't fall asleep, it's okay, it's okay.'

Presently, Cory did fall asleep. Once or twice he opened his eyes and saw the old man still sitting there. He slept till daybreak and when he woke up and opened his eyes, he saw eight or ten men walking around, talking, doing different things. He sat up, but no one paid attention to him, as if he wasn't there. But he got up and said hello to one of them, who said hello back.

There were a couple of men around the stove with their backs to Cory, talking, and then there was a man standing behind the barber chair shaving somebody who wasn't even there. It was very strange. The barber was shaving somebody, talking to him, moving his razor but there was no one in the chair. He held up the invisible chin and carefully wiped the razor into paper. It was frightening to watch this.

As for the other people they seemed normal enough except that Cory had the feeling they were in some way smaller. They all looked very old like the first man he saw coming down the stairs. One of the men was walking back and forth in the hotel lobby, talking to nobody, arguing, carrying on a conversation all by himself.

So, Cory got up finally and looked outside. His car was still there, and the snow had stopped. There was no sign of life outside.

He turned to the three men around the stove and asked, 'Is there a gas station around?'

Now he could understand they were speaking to him, but the words made no sense. One of the men grabbed his wrist as if to point out a direction. Then he heard someone yell out, 'Breakfast!'

Cory looked and noticed in the back of the lobby where the desk was. Two doors were open now, leading into a dining room. Again, the voice yelled, 'Breakfast. Come, breakfast,' and this time the old man, the one he had seen first coming down the stairs, came over and grabbed Cory's arm, saying, 'Come have breakfast.'

At this point Cory became so frightened that he backed off and for the first time raised his voice, saying, 'No, thank you.'

Everybody turned around and then they started to walk toward him, slowly, normally, not rushing. He said, 'Where am I? Where am I?' and the old man, who still held his arm, said, 'Don't worry. Don't worry.' But Cory turned and walked out and got into his car. He looked back at the old man whose eyes were streaming with tears.

Cory had forgotten about running out of gas but he was able to drive down the bumpy road. He saw the faces of the men looking out of the windows of the hotel behind him. He saw more people walking along the street. One of them was a woman. She wore a long dress like

232

the Salvation Army women.

As Cory drove past the people on the sidewalk he saw something like a cloud. He went through this fog for about thirty seconds. Next thing he knew, he came out into one of the brightest, shiniest days one could imagine. He drove another half a mile or so until he saw a gas station, just in time. He was back in today's life.

The Dimensional Traveller

Paranormal researcher Brad Steiger cites an interesting exchange with a man supposedly able to enter other levels of existence at will.[62] Missourian Al Kiessig wrote the author at length about his experiences with dimensional doorways or "points of access" into other realities. Kiessig informs Steiger that one of our "neighboring universes" is a soundless environment lacking wind or sun, although its sky is bright enough to suggest the existence of one, and that he himself entered into it while taking his dog for a walk in Arkansas in December 1965.

This silent world appeared to mimic our own countryside, down to the wood-frame houses Kiessig encountered along his walk, but the silence and lack of animals or humans was distressing. There appeared to be a considerable time difference between dimensions as well.

Steiger's correspondent went on to mention an unnamed region of the Ozarks in which he could clearly see into the other dimension and watch its inhabitants effortlessly coming into our own. Kiessig stated his belief that this parallel dimension was 'the Hell on Earth where Jesus went to preach for three days before he ascended to heaven.'

According to Kiessig, other dimensional doorways 'open into a land of no life. Some take you back into the past, and some take you into the future on this world.'

Was the correspondent a teller of tall tales having a laugh at Steiger's expense? A lunatic? Or was he truly gifted with the ability to enter and return from these dwipas? He was being truthful, according to the many thousands of South Americans who have expressed a belief in the theories set forth many decades ago by the late Prof. Guillermo Terrera, a man who appears to have lived his life in a middle realm between harsh reality and the possibility that other realms of existence coexist within our own. 'The enigma has been before us for a very long time,' writes Terrera in his book *El Valle de Los Espíritus*, 'and both hermetic science and metaphysics make reference to cosmic lights or

---

[62] *Strange Disappearances* (1972)

forces manipulated by the higher intelligences which have plowed Planet Earth's skies for millennia, or else find shelter in subterranean locations, or else moving about in dimensions completely unknown to the ancestral mind of the human species.'

Terra posited the existence of a number of interdimensional and/or subterranean realms having a physical "double" in our prime reality. Thus, Thule in the North would have a double in the Antarctic realm, although not necessarily in this dimension. The oft-mentioned Shamballah of Asian tradition would also have a physical counterpart in our world. Most important of all these cities is Erks, located within "the Lesser Triangle of Forces"; a triangle formed by the hills of Calaguala, the village of Serrezuela, and the Cerro Colorado, all of which are found in Argentina's Cordoba province. Basing himself upon the legends of tribes native to the area, the metaphysicist claims that the regents of Erks may allow certain individuals from our reality to find their way there, after achieving a higher intellectual capacity. The city of Erks, 'whose entrances no man has discovered,' according to Terrera, features three colossal mirrors constructed from a variety of materials. One of them is made of lapis lazuli, and the others of elements unknown to man. Terrera states that reports of a ghostly white light often reported in the hilltops of the region are produced by Erks and its mirrors.

The French Hotel
In October 1979, when Len and Cynthia Gisby and their friends, Geoff and Pauline Simpson, all of Dover, England, decided to take a trip, they certainly had no way of knowing precisely how far away they would be going. In fact, they were heading straight for one of the most baffling holidays of modern times.

Geoff Simpson, a railway worker, then 44, and his wife, then 45 and a cleaner at a social club, were quite excited when Len and Cynthia Gisby invited them to go along on their holiday trip. The plan was to take the ferry across the English Channel and drive through France to northern Spain for two weeks of late summer sunshine. Indeed, it all worked out perfectly. The weather was fine and the ride through the strange countryside was packed with interest.

On October 3, around 9:30 p.m., they were on the autoroute north of Montelimar, France, far to the south. It had been a pleasant day, but they were tired, and the arriving darkness led them to look for a place to stay. Ahead loomed a plush motel and after a short discussion they decided to stop there for the night. When Len went inside, he was confronted in the lobby by a man dressed in a rather strange plum-coloured uniform but he presumed this to be part of the local custom. The man informed Len that unfortunately there was no room at the motel. 'However,' Len was told, 'if you take the road off the autoroute there' – and he pointed south – 'then you will find a small hotel. They will have rooms.'

Len thanked the man and his party drove away. The last faint traces of daylight still painted the sky when they found the road indicated. As they drove on, Cynthia and Pauline commented on the old buildings lining the roadside. The posters plastered on them were promoting a circus. 'It was a very old-fashioned circus,' Pauline remarked. 'That's why we took so much interest.' The men were more interested in the road itself, cobbled and very narrow. When no other traffic passed by, they began to doubt the wisdom of this plan.

Suddenly, Cynthia spotted some lights and they pulled to a halt in front of a building by the roadside. It was long and low, with a row of brightly lit windows. There were some men standing in front of it. Cynthia got out but came back to the car saying, 'It's not a hotel. It's an inn.' So, they drove on, past a long border of trees that now lined the road.

Presently they reached two other buildings. One appeared to be a police station. The other had a sign saying "Hotel". Thankful that their journey was over, Len got out and went to ask for accommodation. He came back sighing with relief. 'They have rooms.' And so, the tired travelers unloaded their bags. It was about 10 p.m.; they estimated it had taken them about 10 minutes to reach the hotel from the autoroute motel.

The hotel itself was a curious ranch-style building. It had just two stories and looked quaint and old-fashioned. As they entered, two boys were just leaving. Because none of the four spoke French and the hotel manager apparently spoke no English, they made themselves known as best they could and were shown to their rooms. On the way they noticed that the building's interior was as strange as its exterior. Everything was old and made of heavy wood. There were no tablecloths on the tables in the dining room and some men in rough clothes sat drinking around one table near the bar. There seemed to be no telephones, elevators or other modern equipment anywhere. Upstairs in their rooms even odder delights awaited them. The beds were large but had no pillows, only bolsters. The sheets were heavy. The mattresses seemed to sag in the middle but felt comfortable enough to lie on. Besides, it was too late to go anywhere else. The doors had no locks, just wooden catches. And the two couples had to share a bathroom with old-fashioned plumbing and soap attached to a metal bar stuck in the wall. 'Look at this funny soap,' Geoff said, chuckling.

After unpacking they went down to the dining room for a meal. Although unable to understand the menu, they did recognize the word œuf (egg) and ordered four of that dish. After they had drunk lager from tankards supplied to them, their dinners arrived on huge heavy plates. Included with the eggs were steak and french-fried potatoes. Their meal finished, they drank more lager. The girl who served them could not understand English either, so they did not speak. Satisfied with their meal and facing another long journey the next day, they went straight to bed. It took no time at all for them to fall asleep.

Morning woke them early; sunlight filtered in through the windows, which had no glass in them, just wooden shutters. Pauline removed the chair she had wedged against the door because she was afraid to sleep without some way of holding the door shut. They dressed and went back down to the dining room for breakfast. This simple meal consisted of bread, jam and coffee. 'The coffee tasted black and horrible,' Geoff recalls with disgust. While they were eating, a woman came into the room and sat down opposite them. She wore a silk evening gown and carried a dog under her arm. 'It was strange,' Pauline says. 'It looked like she had just come in from a ball, but it was seven in the morning! I couldn't take my eyes off her.' Then two gendarmes arrived, wearing deep blue uniforms and capes and large peaked hats. 'They were nothing like the gendarmes we saw anywhere else in France,' Geoff says. 'Their uniforms seemed to be very old.'

As they finished breakfast they all decided they wanted some souvenir of this unusual hotel. They did not think of it as anything other than a charming rural place, which would be a delight to talk about when they got home. So, Geoff took his camera into the room and photographed Pauline standing by the shuttered windows. Len, while out packing his car, took a photograph of Cynthia inside the hotel silhouetted against the window. Then, to be certain of at least one good shot, he took another one. His camera was sophisticated and had an automatic wind-on.

Len and Geoff decided to ask the gendarmes, who were still there talking to the manager, the best way to take the autoroute to Avignon and the Spanish border. But the policemen shrugged at the word 'autoroute' and plainly did not know the term. Geoff presumed that Len's attempts at French dialect were just not successful.

Eventually the gendarmes understood that the travellers wished to go to Spain and directed them to the old Avignon road. From what little knowledge of the local geography they had, this seemed a long way round to the two Englishmen and they resolved to go back to the Montelimar autoroute by the way they had come.

With the car packed and all three companions ready to leave, Len went across to the manager and asked for the bill. The man scribbled a sum on a piece of paper and showed it to the rather astonished tourist. It read 19 francs (about $3.00). 'No, no.' Len motioned. 'For all four of us.' The manager simply nodded. When Len indicated that they had eaten a meal, the manager continued to nod. Len showed the piece of paper to the gendarmes who smiled and indicated that it was quite correct. Without further ado Len paid up in cash and they left. 'Come on,' Geoff remembers whispering. 'Let's get out of here before he changes his mind.'

The day was hot and sunny, and they travelled the tree-lined road back to the autoroute quite easily. Again, it was deserted of traffic until they joined the road toward Spain. Then, forgetting all about the hotel, they went on to pass a very happy two weeks in Spain.

On the drive back, naturally, the four decided to stop at the same hotel. Not many places offered such unique service at such phenomenal prices. The weather was miserable, with rain bucketing down, but they found the turnoff easily and drove down it. 'There are the circus signs,' Pauline called out. 'This is definitely the right road.' But there was no hotel.

They were concerned enough to return to the motel on the autoroute and ask directions. Not only did the man there know of no such hotel but he denied any knowledge of the man in the plum-coloured uniform who had directed them to it previously. Three times they drove up and down the road. But there was no hotel! It had vanished into thin air. By this time Cynthia was upset and crying. 'It has to be here! It can't just disappear like that,' she said. Somebody else suggested it had been knocked down. 'At those prices they probably went broke,' one person speculated. 'They couldn't do that in two weeks. Not without a trace,' Geoff concluded. They finally gave up the hunt. Shaking their heads, they drove on north to Lyon and a hotel there. Bed, breakfast and evening meal for four, with admittedly rather more modern facilities, cost them 247 francs.

The Gisbys and the Simpsons were mildly intrigued by their adventure, but it never crossed their minds to invest the story with a paranormal explanation until their holiday snapshots arrived back. Geoff had a 20-exposure Kodak film and had taken it to a local chain store. Len had a 36-exposure film that had been processed by the manufacturer.

The three photographs of the hotel (one by Geoff, two by Len) had all been taken in the middle of the respective films. But none of the hotel shots were returned. What's more, there were no spoiled negatives. Each film had its full quota of photographs. It was as if the pictures that they all clearly remember taking did not exist; they had disappeared into limbo just like the hotel. Utterly baffled and confused, the four resolved to tell only their families and friends. Geoff, raised in Rochdale, Lancashire, visited his home in January 1980 and told his family.

Research confirmed that gendarmes did wear the kind of uniform they saw in the inn but only prior to 1905. One or two persons suggested that they had experienced a 'time slip' and stayed at a hotel that existed around the turn of the century. Len and Cynthia thought this idea made sense. Geoff and Pauline preferred to forget the whole thing but unbeknown to them, one person they talked to actually worked for the local newspaper in Dover.

Three years after the events she published their tale and the cat was finally out of the bag. From then on, the publicity bandwagon began to roll. Looking back, in July 1985, Geoff was philosophical. 'We never wanted the publicity,' he said. 'We just wanted to forget it. But once it happened then we all wanted to go back and try again to find that hotel. This trip is the only thing we ever got out of it. A local TV station made a drama about it, but we never got paid. They jazzed it up, using actors like Gordon Jackson from Upstairs Downstairs. For instance, when it came to the photographs, they had us taking one picture of the group of us standing in front of the hotel. That never happened. Then, in the film, when the picture came back, we were in it, but the hotel wasn't. That's just eyewash. Why do they do things like that?'

In 1984 Yorkshire Television, filming the series Arthur C. Clarke's *World of Strange Powers*, flew the four of them to Lyon and then filmed reconstructed attempts to find the hotel. 'They set it all up by getting the police to pretend to call the tourist board. But we did go to the area and look. We even thought we had found the place. But it was not our hotel – just an old house – nothing like the hotel. At the place

238

where we were all sure the hotel had been there was nothing at all.'

The French tourist board in Lyon says there is no hotel like the one the Gisbys and Simpsons describe. Geoff and Pauline were adamant that, apart from this trip, they had never made any money out of their story. 'We don't want to,' they say. 'We just know it happened.'[63]

An Illinois town not on the map

Dominic Sondy, a salesman in the publishing business, was travelling for work one day and came to an Illinois town named National. He went to a diner for breakfast.

'Please pass the ketchup, brother,' asked the middle-aged man on the stool next to him.

Others came and went in and out of the diner. Almost everyone greeted each other with comments about the rain, the local high school football score and other small talk. Most of the people used the term "brother", just as the man with the grey moustache and long sideburns did when he thanked the traveller for the ketchup.

The Mercantile Hotel was across the street. Like so many midwestern small towns, the frame building with a wide veranda was a relic of a bygone era. Mostly, it served business folk coming from northern cities like Chicago, where Sondy's business was located.

During the Reconstruction period of the South, businesses sent salesmen to sell the people products. The visitor's particular product was lodge organizational advertising, which would appear in various magazines.

Sondy had two stops to make, and each would take about an hour. He could be well on his way north early in the afternoon, so he was not planning on staying overnight. After his toast and coffee, he walked a half block to his car. Across the street was the Merchants Bank of National. Sondy made a mental note of its location since he might have to cash an expense check before three o'clock when most banks closed for the day. Since all the towns he covered had a population of 5,000 or less, there wasn't much chance of having trouble finding the only bank in town.

At the barbershop, Sondy sat there reading a magazine waiting to get a trim. The man sitting next to me said, 'Brother, I don't ever

---

[63] *The Amazing Evidence of Time Warps, Space Rifts and Time Travel* (2001). FATE, January 1986.

remember seeing you here for a haircut before.' He explained that he was a salesman and that he was planning to see the secretary of a certain lodge in about an hour. The barber joined in the conversation and assured me him he would have no trouble finding her office as it was only a few blocks away.

It became obvious that almost everybody knew everyone else in this town. The visitor found this strange. People were helping him find his first contact of the day. Most people resented salesmen who came into their town and tried to sell them something and then take the money out of town.

After noon Sondy kept his first appointment. The lady was very polite but did not buy his advertising program. As he packed up his briefcase she asked him whom he was going to see next. She said he could use her telephone to call ahead and confirm my appointment. He started out the door when she said, 'Stop in next year when I am chairman of the lodge, brother.'

A short drive took Sondy to the outskirts of town and to a Georgian house. He left my car across the street and started walking to number 66. A girl of about eight or 10 years of age was singing rhymes and playing hopscotch. This was on the sidewalk next door to number 66. 'Dance with me, brother,' she said. She held out her arms as if she wanted him to swing her around by the hands. He thought it was a little strange that this girl was playing a game with the spaces marked out with chalk just like little girls did when he was her age.

The doorbell was the kind you twisted and sounded like a bicycle bell. Mrs. Jessup ushered Sondy into her Victorian living room. He quickly concluded their business and he snapped the locks on my briefcase.

A stunning young girl came down the staircase. She was wearing a blue cloth coat and a white knit hat. She was also carrying a white handbag. She appeared to be about 18 years of age. The young freshness of her blonde hair and fair skin was highlighted by the most perfect white teeth Sondy had ever seen. The mother introduced her to him. The girl told her mother that she was on her way downtown to do some shopping. Since it had stopped raining, she had decided to walk.

'Mr. Sondy is going that way,' the mother said. 'Maybe he wouldn't mind giving you a ride.'

As they rode the short distance back to Main Street, Sondy was tempted to keep sneaking peeks at those perfect white teeth. All too soon the ride was over. He dropped her off in front of the shop she pointed out. The question that came to Sondy's mind was: how could this mother trust a total stranger, whom she had never seen before, with her daughter? Mrs. Jessup's words kept coming back to him after we walked out the door. 'Don't forget to come back and see me when you come through here next year, brother.'

Sondy's curiosity about the people convinced him to stay overnight at the Mercantile. The room was on the second floor and faced the street. One tall, narrow window let in the late afternoon sunlight. The wallpaper was strangely familiar. Then he remembered: it was the same pattern in the living room of a house his father built in Detroit in 1927.

Sondy walked around the downtown section after dinner in the hotel dining room. As much as he was aware of the old-fashioned air about this town, the cars were still 1960 and before. They did have electricity and most modern conveniences. Many things were consistent with the times. Yet there were things strangely different; sort of outdated or out of the past, such as the 1930-style coat the girl wore, or the long sideburns and mutton chops on the barber. Most disturbing was the warm, trusting, friendly feeling that came from all the people he met. It was a sincere kind of brotherly love that was not put on for selfish reasons.

After leaving National, Sondy checked many old maps, atlases and zip code directories. He has searched again ans again but never has he found National on any Indiana map or listed in any kind of directory. He gets no answers, just more questions. He asks himself continuously, did the whole town and its people exist for the one fall day I made my visit? If so, why?[64]

Brigadoon

People who visit Scotland often ask where they can find the mysterious Highland village of Brigadoon, which, according to legend, appears every one hundred years for just one day. It is a place where the passing of the century seems to last no longer than the one night that it appears.

So the story goes, a long time ago the village fell under an evil magical curse. As part of an agreement made with God, the village must remain unchanged and invisible to the outside world except for one special day every hundred years when it can be seen and even visited by outsiders. That day is a moment of joy and celebration but the enchantment on the village of Brigadoon will only last as long as no

---

[64] Dominic P. Sondy FATE February 1991.

citizen leaves. If the enchantment is broken, the village will disappear forever into the Highland mists.

It is believed that the village of Brigadoon disappeared in 1754. Bob Curran writes in his book *Lost Lands, Forgotten Realms: Sunken Continents, Vanished Cities, and the Kingdoms that History Misplaced* that 'the spell that was cast over Brigadoon was put in place to protect it from advancing English Redcoats during the Jacobite Rebellion.'

Through Brigadoon is generally regarded as a fictional location, it is named after the (Lowland) Brig o' Doon, sometimes called the Auld Brig or Old Bridge of Doon. The word brig is Scots for "bridge", hence the "Bridge of Doon". It is a late medieval single arched bridge located south of Alloway in Ayrshire. It has a steeply humped span of 72-feet and a rise of 26-feet. The bridge has been repaired many times. The line of the cobbles in the roadway is cranked, due to the belief that this pattern will stop witches from crossing.

Brig o' Doon is used as the setting for the final verse of the Robert Burns's poem *Tam o' Shanter*. In this scene Tam is on horseback and is being chased by Nannie the witch. He is just able to escape her by crossing the bridge (over a running stream), narrowly avoiding her attack, as she is only able to grab the horse's tail, which comes away in her hands:

> The carlin caught her by the rump
> And left puir Meg wi' scarce a stump.

Those who have researched the Brigadoon myth have reason to think the legend does not originate from Scotland, but from Germany. There is an old German legend of a cursed village named Germelhausen. It was said that the village's bells were so loud that they could be heard ringing out across the Bavarian Mountains. The Brothers Grimm recorded these accounts in their collection of ghostly tales. Curran explains that those who followed the sound of the bells and entered the village were never seen again. They tried to return to the mortal world, but all their attempts were in vain. Germelhausen was allegedly inhabited by dark and evil forces that only desired to harm humanity. The evil village of Germelshausen, one to avoide at all costs, is said to still exist, hidden somewhere in the Bavarian Hills.

Today many people associate the name Brigadoon with a 1947 musical composed by Frederick Loewe and book and lyrics by Alan Jay Lerner. The musical is world-famous and its plot centres round the chaos that unfolds when a pair of travelling Americans stumbles upon the village prior to a wedding celebration. Tommy, one of the tourists, falls in love with Fiona, a young woman from Brigadoon. A 1954 film version starred Gene Kelly and Cyd Charisse.

The New York Times's theatre critic George Jean Nathan wrote that Lerner's book was based on a story about Germelhausen published in 1860 by Friedrich Gerstäcker, later translated by Charles Brandon Schaeffer. However, Lerner denied that he had based the book on an older story and stated that he did not learn of the existence of the Germelshausen story until after he had completed the first draft of Brigadoon. Lerner said that in his subsequent research, he found many other legends of disappearing towns in various countries' folklore, and he pronounced their similarities "unconscious coincidence".

'It's a great huge game of chess that's being played—all over the world— if this is the world at all, you know.' *Through the Looking Glass*

243

Photo of witch's head seen over Brig o' Doon, 2018 (courtesy Scott Wanstall)

Scene from 1954 film version of Lerner and Loewe's 1947 musical
Brigadoon. The film starred Gene Kelly and Cyd Charisse.

CELLULOID WORLDS

Eostte Saxon goddess of Spring accompanied as always by a rabbit

Chapter 16

Purgatory

In this section we explore three cinematic stories in which our physical world is emphatically not what it seems. We begin with *Purgatory*.

Purgatory is a 1999 American Western fantasy television film directed by Uli Edel. Its principal stars are Sam Shepard as Sheriff Forrest / "Wild Bill" Hickok, Eric Roberts as Jack "Blackjack" Britton, Randy Quaid as Doc Woods / "Doc" Holliday, Peter Stormare as Cavin Guthrie, Brad Rowe as Leon "Sonny" Miller, Donnie Wahlberg as Deputy Glen / Billy "The Kid," J.D. Souther as Brooks / Jesse James, and Native American Saginaw Grant as The Gatekeeper.

The film focuses on a gang of outlaws that finds its way to a hidden valley and a town called Refuge. The outcome is marked by its exploration of the interface between legend making, humanitarian values and one's spirit evolution. In my opinion, Purgatory is a terrific movie and well worth seeking out.

The gang, led by Blackjack Britton and Cavin Guthrie, robs a bank. During the subsequent gunfight, a prostitute named Dolly Sloan is shot and dies in the arms of Cavin's nephew, Sonny. The outlaws flee, pursued by a posse, and manage to escape through a dust storm by following a tunnel into an unusual green valley.

The town of Refuge welcomes them but the robbers are puzzled by the residents, who don't carry guns, won't drink the liquor in the saloon, don't cuss, and all go to church at the same time each day on the toll of the bell. A stagecoach arrives regularly and delivers new residents to the town.

The youngest gang member, Sonny, thinks he recognizes some of the townfolk from the dime novels he reads. He befriends a woman named Rose who deflects his questions and asks some pointed ones of her own, beginning with, 'How many men have you killed?'

The rest of the outlaws occupy the saloon and begin causing trouble. One of the gang members is struck by lightning when he prepares to throw his knife at the church door. His body is carried away by a Native American who guards the gates to a mist-filled property outside of town.

As Sonny investigates further, he realizes that the town appears to be occupied by former notorious gunfighters. These include Wild Bill Hickok, the town's Sheriff, Jesse James, Billy the Kid and Doc Holliday, although they deny their identities to Sonny. Later he talks to a gardener named Lamb whom he prompts to admit who he really is. Before Sonny can ask more questions, some of Blackjack's men tear up Lamb's garden. Enraged, Lamb beats one to death with his shovel and is led away by the mysterious Gatekeeper.

While talking to Doc, Sonny lets slip the true nature of the gang and the Sheriff asks them to saddle up and leave town. Blackjack orders all his men to assemble in the saloon except Sonny, who is ejected but steals back and overhears the gang planning to rob the town on their way out, while Cavin plans to rape Rose.

Sonny joins the townspeople in church, where he begs them to defend themselves. They finally admit to Sonny that Refuge is a form of Purgatory. The residents have to live ten years in peace while having the temptations of their former life all around them every moment. If they fail, they are taken by an old Indian to a mysterious mountain.

Those who succeed in maintaining peace, tranquillity and self-discipline in the ten-year period are given a white rose and taken by a mysterious stagecoach out of Refuge into the Light. They are therefore reluctant to face off against Blackjack's gang because it will cost them their well-earned transition to an eternal heaven world.

A frustrated Sonny leaves the church and is jumped by Blackjack and Cavin, who beat him unconscious. The next morning a battered Sonny straps on his guns and prepares to face Blackjack's gang alone. The townspeople are summoned by the church bells but while most of them comply, Hickok, Holliday, James, and Billy all join Sonny, inspired by his selfless bravery and his willingness to die to protect Rose.

A shootout erupts, during which Blackjack's gang are all slaughtered but Cavin manages to shoot Sonny before being killed by him in return. Sonny, despite being fatally wounded, does not feel pain and does not die. Hickok welcomes him to Refuge, realizing that Sonny has earned his second chance.

When Blackjack arrives and challenges Hickok, he loses. 'I guess I'm one of you now,' Blackjack jokes, realizing the truth of the situation. 'I wouldn't count on it,' Hickok replies before finally dispatching his opponent.

The Native American Gatekeeper arrives and carries the bodies of Cavin and Blackjack beyond the misty gates to the edge of a fiery pit into which they are thrown, screaming.

Hickok and the others grimly follow but the stagecoach arrives and the driver tells them that by their willingness to sacrifice their chance of a better future to protect the others, they have secured a place in Heaven. 'The Creator may be tough but He ain't blind,' he says.

Sonny asks to stay behind with Rose, and Hickok hands him the Sheriff's badge. Refuge still has validity in the mystical-metaphysical order of spirit-balance, and Sonny and Rose will henceforth serve as its guiding lights. The coach then leaves, riding upwards into the Light.

The concept that after death a person's spirit-soul could find itself in a parallel dimension that would give it a period of time to learn the lessons that were misused, opens up new avenues of metaphysical possibilities to consider for students of esoteric philosophy.

First, would be the concept that if the individual failed to adhere to the guidelines of their learning dimension, their soul is eliminated and purified by fire. This would mean that the life just led would never be placed in its "spirit library" (Akashic record) and their spirit would have to search for another place and period of time to bring a soul to life in a new body.

Second, is the realisation that there is no hell...just a place where our soul is eliminated after we were given a chance, one that is our choice to take or ignore, to relearn unlearned lessons.

SAM SHEPARD   ERIC ROBERTS

PURGATORY

For a band of outlaws,
the only thing worse than being bad
is spending eternity being good.

DVD
VIDEO

Chapter 17

The Ninth Gate

The Ninth Gate is not one of Roman Polanski's better-known movies (my personal favourite is *Un Pur Formalité*, starring Gerald Depardieu and Polanski, a superb work with a great twist) but I like it because of its ambiguity. Is the *Ninth Gate* a portal to hell, as the storyline appears to encourage the spectator to accept, or is it another kind of "supernatural" world that is beyond our human faculties to perceive but is nevertheless parallel to our own and accessible with the right key?

The Ninth Gate, a 1999 neo-noir horror thriller film, starring Johnny Depp, and directed, produced and co-written by Polanski, is loosely based upon Arturo Pérez-Reverte's 1993 novel *The Club Dumas* (original Spanish title *El Club Dumas*).

The Club Dumas book story follows the adventures of a middle-aged book dealer, Lucas Corso, a dealer with a reputation of doing anything—regardless of legality—for his privileged clientele. While in Madrid attempting to authenticate a previously unknown partial draft of *The Three Musketeers*, Corso is summoned to Toledo by Varo Borja, a notoriously eccentric and wealthy collector who hires Corso to authenticate a rare manuscript by Alexandre Dumas, père.

Corso's investigation leads him to seek out two copies of a fictional rare book known as *De Umbrarum Regni Novem Portis* (*Of the Nine Doors of the Kingdom of Shadows*), whose author was burned at the stake by the Inquisition. The book purportedly contains instructions for summoning the Devil. Only one copy of the book is supposed to have survived but Borja claims three exist, two of which are elaborate forgeries. Corso is hired to compare the three copies and obtain the legitimate one by any means necessary. Borja promises to pay handsomely and to cover all expenses.

Corso's travels will lead him down an increasingly dangerous path that causes him to flit around the world in search of a truth lost to humanity, specifically the gates to hell. On his travels, which take him to Madrid, Sintra, Paris and Toledo, he encounters devil worshippers, obsessed bibliophiles and a hypnotically enticing femme fatale.

While engaged in Borja's commission, Corso continues to research the partial Dumas draft. The widow of the draft's previous owner, Liana Taillefer, insists the draft is a fake but offers to buy it from Corso. After several encounters, she attempts to seduce Corso to obtain the draft. After they have sex, and he refuses to sell, Telfer attacks him and knocks him unconscious. Imagining herself as Dumas's femme fatale "Milady de Winter", Telfer employs a male associate (whom Corso nicknames "Rochefort") to follow Corso and attempt to retrieve the manuscript by force.

The day after Telfer attacks him, Corso goes to a bookseller with whom he had entrusted the book and finds him hanged in his store like an engraving in The Nine Gates. Corso retrieves the book and travels to Toledo, Spain, to speak to the Ceniza Brothers, book restorers who owned Balkan's copy before the Telfers. The two show him that, of the book's nine engravings, only six are signed "A.T."; the other three are signed "L.C.F." for Lucifer.

On his way to Lisbon to visit the owner of one of the copies, he encounters a beautiful blonde with striking green eyes. She identifies herself as "Irene Adler", (in *A Scandal in Bohemia* the only woman ever to foil Sherlock Holmes), and suggests that she is a fallen angel. They part company before he meets with Victor Fargas, a renowned collector who has been selling off his extensive library to maintain his ancestral mansion. Corso compares Fargas's copy of *The Nine Doors* to Borja's, and finds subtle differences in the illustration plates. Most bear the initials of the book's notorious author, but some of the plates bear the initials "L.F.".

Alexander Dumas' Milady de Winter and Conan Doyle's Irene Adler are synonyms for a particular kind of woman: one possessed of devastating intelligence, an unquenchable desire to achieve their goals no matter the collateral cost, and a preternatural ability to run rings around the male of the species.

As Corso returns to his hotel, "Irene" guards Corso against an attack by "Rochefort". Corso leaves her to arrange a robbery of Fargas's mansion to obtain his copy of the book. "Irene" informs him that Fargas has been murdered and his copy has been burned. She and Corso leave for Paris.

Corso confers with Replinger, an antiquarian and Dumas scholar, who authenticates the Dumas manuscript. As they talk, Corso spies Liana. He returns to his hotel and bribes the concierge to locate her hotel. "Irene" visits him, and they discuss theology; she implies that she is a witness to the events of the War in Heaven.

Corso visits Baroness Ungern, whose charitable institution possesses the largest occult collection in Europe, including the third copy of *The Nine Doors*. They discuss the book's author before Corso blackmails her with photo evidence of her Nazi sympathies so she will let him examine her copy. "Irene" calls to warn Corso that "Rochefort" is waiting outside. The Baroness translates the illustration captions while Corso compares Ungern's copy to Borja's.

Later, Corso realizes that while none of the three sets match each other the plates bearing the initials "L.F." form a complete set of nine without duplications, and that the nine illustrations form a list of instructions for the famed Satanic summoning ritual. "Rochefort" attacks again and once more is repelled by "Irene".

Using the concierge's information, Corso confronts Liana and her associate, but "Rochefort" renders him unconscious. When he revives, Borja's copy and the Dumas manuscript are gone. He learns that the Baroness has been killed in a fire at her library.

Corso returns to Spain to confront Borja. "Irene" insists that she is a fallen angel who has wandered the earth for millennia searching for him. Corso does not question this and finds himself even more strongly attracted to her. He accuses Borja of being responsible for both murders. Borja, intending to use the ritual described by the book's true nine plates to summon the Devil and gain ultimate knowledge, has destroyed his entire library to prevent others from following his lead.

Corso demands payment but Borja ignores him and begins the ritual. Corso leaves in disgust. As he leaves, he hears Borja's screams of deathly anguish as the ritual goes awry, remembering the Ceniza Brothers' discourse on false books and realizing one of the plates is a forgery. He joins "Irene" outside, and surmises that each of them will get the devil they deserve.

Roman Polanski's filmic take on Pérez-Reverte's work follows the basic elements of the novel, except for its open-ended conclusion and an overall looser stance in deepening the plot's convoluted mythos. Almost nothing is explained for clarity, as the film assumes that its religio-mythical metaphors speak for themselves. In the process, it posits a wild-goose-chase mystery that is heady and obtuse in its unravelling.

Corso is a man without a set moral compass, eager to take on investigations that promise profits, despite the risks involved. 'There's nothing more reliable than a man whose loyalty can be bought for hard cash,' says Corso's client (now named Boris Balkan, played by the excellent Frank Langella), when he hires the investigator to authenticate three copies of a rare book: Aristide Torchia's *The Nine Gates of the Kingdom of Shadows*, which contains a ritual for summoning the Devil, written in collaboration with Lucifer himself.

Only interested in hard facts and hard cash, Corso takes on the job of figuring out which copy is the real one, a quest that opens Pandora's box of conspiracies, shadowy secrets and hidden truths, which prove a bit too much for the antique book dealer to handle.

Apart from being followed by various parties, Corso is shadowed by a mysterious woman, no longer "Irene Adler" but "The Girl" (played by Polanski's real-world wife, Emmanuelle Seigner), who talks to Corso in cryptic ways, while nudging him in the right direction.

During his travels in search of the authentic copy of the book, Corso makes a startling discovery: all three copies look identical but differ in terms of the signatures of the artists beneath the engravings, which turn out to be significantly different on closer inspection. While some are signed A.T. (Torchia, the writer), others are signed L.C.F., which seems to be short for Lucifer, adding legitimacy to the claims that Torchia wrote it with the help of the Devil himself. This begs the question: Which copy is authentic? The answer is tricky, as there is no authentic copy at all because the ritual can only be completed when all nine L.C.F engravings are combined together for the purpose.When Balkan finally obtains all of the engravings he undertakes the ritual, confident of summoning the devil. However, the ritual goes awry and Corso looks on in horror as Balkan, having soaked himself in gasoline and striking a match to prove his newly won gift of immortality, is enmeshed in a fatal ball of fire. Corso puts him out of his misery.

Some time later as the two are travelling, "The Girl" explains to Corso that Balkan's ritual did not work because one of the engravings was forged. When they stop for gas she seemingly vanishes, but gives Corso a note sending him to the Ceniza brothers. At their shop, Corso finds they have mysteriously vanished and the shop is being cleaned out. As workmen remove a large bookcase, a dust-covered paper floats down from the top. This is the authentic engraving, which depicts a woman who resembles the "The Girl" riding atop a dragon-like beast in front of the burning castle. The last scene is up for interpretation, with Corso striding towards the gate depicted in the drawing, but does he complete the ritual?

The beauty of the film is that it is up to the viewer to decide if Corso's ultimate fate is to take the path of darkness or to open a gateway to an enchanting, sunny world imbued with mystical feminine power.

In Pythagoras's numerology system, of all the numbers, 9 (the Ennead), has the most potential for evolution and alludes to ultimate completion. This is the nature of Corso's destiny path as he undertakes his commission for the ill fated Balkan.

The nine's special energy transforms Corso, already one whose expertise and counsel is keenly sought by others, also a characteristic of the Ennead force, into a man who, on his quixotic journey, will stand apart from others.

During his quest Corso endures many mishaps and setbacks, a consequence of an inner link with the self-sacrificing attributes of the nine to grow and develop through trial and hardship. However, success will likely prevail. There is a special universal protection that is open to individuals caught up in the sweep and swirl of a "9" series of actions to help overcome difficulties.

However, gains made in service of the quest will be lost as quickly as they came if Corso does not have someone close by, in this case "The Girl", who can help him steer a path every step of the way. And so, ultimately, Polanski succeeds in encouraging the audience to consider that in many ways "The Girl" *is* the Ninth Gate. Her frenzied assault of Corso outside the burning castle, when she allows him entry into her sex-gate and rides him like an almighty leonine seductress, is what earns him entry into the world beyond the beckoning portal.

In this context "The Girl" can be likened to the Egyptian warrior cat goddess of the sun, pregnancy and childbirth, Bast or Bastet, daughter of Ra and Isis.

Bast was known as "She of the ointment jar" and images of her were often created from alabaster. The name of the material known as alabaster may, through Greek, come from her name. Much later, the Gospels would contain a passage (Luke 7:36-39), in which a sobbing, unnamed woman enters the home where Jesus is dining. She anoints his feet with her tears and with oil taken from an alabaster jar, wiping them with her hair.

One of the principal contenders in current research as to this person's identity is Mary Magdalene, described in the esoteric records as the High Priestess of the Temple of Ishtar, the Babylonian version of Isis, who, we note, was the mother of Bast.

In this imagery "The Girl" is symbolising the ancient tradition of the Sacred Prostitute, a priestess in the holy service of the Goddess Isis/Ishtar. She and the man in her presence know that the consummation of the love act is consecrated by the deity through which they are jointly renewed.

The ritual is transformative. "The Girl", no longer a maiden, is initiated into the fullness of womanhood, her true feminine nature awakened to life; the divine element of love resides deep within her.

Corso too is transformed. The qualities of the receptive feminine nature, so opposite to his own, are now embedded within his soul; the image of the sacred prostitute is viable within him.

His experience of the eternal mysteries of sex and religion opens the door to the potential of a new life beyond the physical. He is now equipped to pass through the Ninth Gate and enter the Temple of the Goddess. After all, Bast was also depicted as the goddess of protection against evil spirits. Why would she lure her priestess's lover into Hell? But enough of happy-ending speculation; in Polanski's world, the unsettling and often nightmarish environs of *Repulsion, Rosemary's Baby* and *Un Pur Formalité*, why the hell wouldn't she?

THE
NINTH
GATE

The Nine Doors book illustrations and the Ninth Gate castle

Chapter 18

Glastonbury Grove

In 1990 David Lynch (famed among his works for *Eraserhead, Blue Velvet, Wild at Heart* and *Lost Highway*) and Mark Frost (writer of *Hill Street Blues*) released their television drama *Twin Peaks*. Broadcast by ABC, it ran for two seasons until its cancellation in 1991. A year later saw the release of a prequel, the feature film *Twin Peaks: Fire Walk with Me*. *Twin Peaks* returned in 2017 on Showtime for a third season (*Twin Peaks: The Return*, alternatively: *Twin Peaks: A Limited Event Series*). *Twin Peaks* is regarded as one of the greatest television series of all time and has received universal acclaim from critics and audiences. *Twin Peaks* is impressive on many levels but in the context of the subject matter for this present work it is its otherworldly features that stand out.

The show's narrative draws on elements of detective fiction but its uncanny tone, supernatural elements and campy, melodramatic portrayal of eccentric characters also draws from American soap opera and horror tropes. Like much of Lynch's work, it is distinguished by surrealism, offbeat humour and distinctive cinematography. The haunting score was composed by the late Angelo Badalamenti in collaboration with Lynch.

The first two series follow an investigation, headed by FBI Special Agent Dale Cooper and local Sheriff Harry S. Truman, into the February 1989 murder of homecoming queen Laura Palmer in the fictional town of Twin Peaks, Washington. The third and final series is a *tour de force* roller coaster ride into a televisual multiverse of extraordinarily creative and downright freaky storytelling.

Season 1
The storyline in Season 1 begins with local logger Pete Martell discovering a naked corpse wrapped in plastic on the bank of a river outside of Twin Peaks. The body is identified as high school senior and homecoming queen Laura Palmer. A second girl, Ronette Pulaski, is

discovered badly injured and dissociative just across the state border. Laura's father, Leland, has a nervous breakdown when he hears the news of his daughter's murder.

FBI Special Agent Dale Cooper is called in to investigate. Cooper informs the community that Laura's death matches the signature of a killer who murdered another girl in southwestern Washington the previous year, and that evidence indicates the killer lives in Twin Peaks.

The authorities discover through Laura's diary that she had been living a double life. She was cheating on her boyfriend, football captain Bobby Briggs, with biker James Hurley, and prostituting herself with the help of truck driver Leo Johnson and drug dealer Jacques Renault. Laura was also addicted to cocaine, which she obtained by coercing Bobby into doing business with Jacques.

Cooper has a dream in which he is approached by a one-armed otherworldly being who calls himself MIKE. MIKE says that Laura's murderer is a similar entity, Killer BOB, a feral, denim-clad man with long grey hair.

Cooper finds himself, decades older, in a large red room. Laura is there also, together with a dwarf in a red business suit ("The Man from Another Place"), who engages in coded dialogue with Cooper. The next morning, Cooper tells Truman that if he can decipher the dream he will know who killed Laura.

The Red Room, also known as "the waiting room", was an anomalous extradimensional space connected to Glastonbury Grove in Twin Peaks' Ghostwood National Forest. Certain individuals could make use of this entrance at any time, including BOB, Leland Palmer, and Dale Cooper. As the seasons unfold we learn that the room was also connected to a dilapidated convenience store, which is a dimensional portal that allows malevolent energies to come and go into our world.

An ornate pictogram drawn on the wall of Owl Cave detailed how one might directly enter the Black Lodge itself. A gateway manifesting as a set of red curtains would open in Glastonbury Grove in the centre of a circle of twelve sycamore trees during the conjunction of Jupiter and Saturn. The curtains would stretch across the grove, the opening positioned above a pool containing a black, burnt-smelling oil. Those who stepped through would disappear and find themselves inside the red room.

Immediately beyond the Glastonbury Grove entrance to the red room is a short hallway, intermittently adorned with a statue of the

Venus de Milo. The statue and the adjoining rooms constantly shifted as one walked between them. A second statue was positioned at the opposite end of the hallway. The room was more accurately a set of seemingly infinite rooms and hallways; the only walls being the thick red velvet curtains that marked the division between different sections. The curtains' height and anchor was unclear. In one instance, the curtains lifted to reveal an endless black expanse, the patterned floor stretching out into nothingness. The floor was covered in a distinctive, alternating off-white and dark-brown chevron pattern. It was composed of a hard material, although in one of Dale Cooper's dreams it was instead a patterned carpet.

Although the Lodge inhabitants speak English, their voices are warped and strangely clipped and their movements are unnatural (this effect is accomplished by the actors performing in reverse and the footage then played backwards). Residents often speak in riddles and non-sequiturs.

First discovered as early as the 1800s, the red room was believed by many to be the Black Lodge, which place and its opposing counterpart, the White Lodge, originated in ancient legends passed down by the Nez Perce Native American tribes that once inhabited the Twin Peaks region. In the stories, the Black Lodge was the "shadow self" of the White, a place of pure evil through which all souls must pass on their journey to perfection. During this process, the pilgrim would confront the Dweller on the Threshold, their own shadow self or, as as described by mystical philosopher Manly P. Hall,[65] one's individual elemental force. If this challenge were not met with perfect courage, the lodge would utterly annihilate their soul.

While the White Lodge could supposedly be accessed with strong feelings of love, the Black would open to its opposite: fear. The settlers who followed the Nez Perce gradually became aware of a "darkness" or "presence" in the surrounding woods and formed a secret society, the Bookhouse Boys, dedicated to fighting against it. Dale Cooper hypothesized that this presence and the Black Lodge of lore were one and the same.

A "black lodge" of evil magicians figured in *Moonchild*, a 1923 novel by the notorious occultist Aleister Crowley. In the novel, the black lodge was one of two factions vying for an unborn child believed to be the Antichrist. Cooper speculated that BOB, the supposed

---

[65] ibid

demonic spirit who possessed Leland Palmer, had originally come from the Black Lodge. Generally speaking, earthly laws of physics did not necessarily apply within the red room, as its arrangement could change from moment to moment, making navigation or escape extremely difficult.

Cooper and the sheriff's department find the one-armed man from Cooper's dream, a travelling shoe salesman named Phillip Gerard. Gerard knows a Bob, the veterinarian who treats Renault's pet bird. Cooper interprets these events to mean that Renault is the murderer, and with Truman's help, tracks Renault to One-Eyed Jack's, a brothel across the border in Canada. He lures Renault back onto U.S. soil to arrest him but Renault is shot while trying to escape and is hospitalized.

Leland, learning that Renault has been arrested, sneaks into the hospital and murders him. Cooper returns to his room following Jacques's arrest and is shot by a masked gunman.

Season 2
Lying hurt in his hotel room, Cooper has a vision in which a giant appears and reveals three clues: 'there is a man in a smiling bag'; 'the owls are not what they seem'; and 'without chemicals, he points.' The giant takes a gold ring off Cooper's finger and explains that when Cooper understands the three premonitions, his ring will be returned. Subsequently, Cooper deduces that the "man in the smiling bag" is the corpse of Jacques Renault in a body bag.

MIKE reveals that he and BOB once collaborated in killing humans and that BOB similarly inhabits a man in the town. Cooper and the sheriff's department use MIKE, in control of Gerard's body, to help find BOB ('without chemicals, he points'). Cooper and the sheriff's department take possession of Laura's secret diary and learn that BOB, a friend of her father's, had been sexually abusing her since childhood and she used drugs to cope.

Cooper gathers all of his suspects in the belief that he will receive a sign to help him identify the killer. The Giant appears and confirms that Leland is BOB's host and (spoiler alert) Laura's killer, giving Cooper back his ring. Cooper and Truman take Leland into custody. In control of Leland's body, BOB admits to a string of murders, before forcing Leland to commit suicide. As Leland dies, he is freed from BOB's influence and begs for forgiveness. BOB's spirit disappears into the woods in the form of an owl and the lawmen wonder if he will reappear.

Glastonbury Grove, portal to the Black Lodge and the Red Room

Cooper is set to leave Twin Peaks when he is framed for drug trafficking by Jean Renault and is suspended from the FBI. Renault holds Cooper responsible for the death of his brothers, Jacques and Bernard. Jean Renault is killed in a shootout with police, and Cooper is cleared of all charges.

Windom Earle, Cooper's former mentor and FBI partner, escapes from a mental institution and comes to Twin Peaks. Earle described the Black Lodge as a source of world-altering power:

> For there is another place, [the White Lodge's] opposite, of almost unimaginable power, chock full of dark forces and vicious secrets. No prayers dare penetrate this frightful maw. Spirits there care not for good deeds and priestly invocations. They are as like to rip the muscle from our bones as greet you with a happy g'day. And, if harnessed, these spirits, this hidden land of unmuffled screams and broken hearts, will offer up a power so vast that its bearer might reorder the earth itself to his liking.

Cooper had previously been having an affair with Earle's wife, Caroline, while she was under his protection as a witness to a federal crime. Earle murdered Caroline and wounded Cooper. He now engages Cooper in a twisted game of chess during which Earle murders someone whenever a chess piece is captured.

Investigating BOB's origin and whereabouts with the help of Major Garland Briggs, who before his suspicious death was head of a top-secret U.S. "Blue Book" project. Cooper learns of the existence of the White Lodge and the Black Lodge, two dimensions whose entrances are somewhere in the woods surrounding Twin Peaks. We learn that when the U.S. Government shut down Project Blue Book, the FBI, in partnership with the U.S. military, established a top-secret programme, the "Blue Rose", to investigate the small number of UFO and paranormal phenomena, which had not been satisfactorily explained by Project Blue Book.

It was the opinion of Major Briggs and his colleagues in Gordon Cole's team that UFO and associated phenomena do not originate in outer space but in dimensions parallel to our planet, a topic that I explored in depth in *The Landing Lights of Magonia*.

Cooper falls in love with a new arrival in town, Annie Blackburn. When Annie wins the Miss Twin Peaks beauty contest, Earle kidnaps her and takes her to the entrance to the Black Lodge, whose power he seeks to use for himself.

Through a series of clues Cooper discovers the entrance to the Black Lodge, which turns out to be the strange, red-curtained room from his dream. He is greeted by the "Man From Another Place", the Giant and Laura Palmer, each of whom give Cooper cryptic messages.

Searching for Annie and Earle, Cooper encounters doppelgängers of various people, including Laura Palmer's cousin Maddy (the spitting image of Laura, also played by Sheryl Lee) and Leland Palmer.

Cooper finds Earle, who demands Cooper's soul in exchange for Annie's life. Cooper agrees but BOB appears and takes Earle's soul for himself. BOB then turns to Cooper, who is chased through the lodge by a doppelgänger of himself. Cooper and Annie reappear in the woods, both injured. Annie is taken to the hospital but Cooper recovers in his room at the Great Northern Hotel. It becomes clear that the "Cooper" who emerged from the Lodge is in fact his evil doppelgänger under BOB's control. Cooper smashes his head into a bathroom mirror and, possessed, laughs maniacally.

Season 3

Twin Peaks: The Return, in particular, is a multidimensional, metaphysical, neo-noir drama, a surrealist masterpiece interwoven with darkly comedic moments of absurdity. It is cleverly juxtaposed against the deceptively serene sentimentality of mid-century Americana and infused with esoteric and mystical symbolism.

In synopsis, twenty-five years after the cliffhanger ending of the previous season FBI Special Agent Dale Cooper (Kyle MacLachlan reprising his role) remains trapped in the Black Lodge and prepares his exit. Meanwhile, Cooper's doppelgänger—host to the evil spirit BOB and known as Mr. C in the series—lives in Cooper's place and works with the help of various associates to prevent his own imminent return to the Black Lodge.

A message from the psychic Log Lady (Catherine Coulson) leads the Twin Peaks Sheriff's Department to reopen investigations into the events surrounding the 1989 murder of Laura Palmer. The mysterious murder of a librarian in Buckhorn, South Dakota attracts the attention of FBI Deputy Director Gordon Cole (David Lynch) and his colleagues.

Season 3 delves deeper into the mystique of Twin Peaks and its characters, pushing the boundaries of conventional storytelling. Key themes and symbolism abound. One of its central themes is the exploration of duality within characters and the world they inhabit. Dale

Cooper's dual existence as both the virtuous FBI agent and the sinister Mr. C exemplifies this theme. It questions the very nature of good and evil, suggesting that these aspects coexist within all individuals. Characters in Twin Peaks frequently confront questions of identity and self-discovery. The enigmatic Dougie Jones, a seemingly blank slate, represents the idea of reinventing oneself, while Cooper's journey back to his true self underscores the quest for authenticity in a complex world.

"The Return" plays with the concept of time, often blurring the boundaries between past, present and future. This temporal ambiguity is exemplified by the frequently spoken cryptic question, 'Is it future or is it past?' It challenges our perception of time and reality, inviting viewers to ponder the nature of existence.

Season 3 is unique in the history of television. Before its release no one had ever seen anything remotely like it, and has certainly seen nothing like it since. It is pure Lynchian warp-speed, creative genius, so far outside of left field that the field has relocated to not just a different dimension of reality but to another universe.

The presence of other dimensions is a central and mind-bending element in the third season. Characters, particularly Dale Cooper, engage in interdimensional travel throughout the episodes. This involves crossing between the mundane world and the otherworldly realms, such as the Black Lodge, the White Lodge and various liminal spaces. This quantum-style travel highlights the permeable boundaries between dimensions and the idea that the characters' fates are intertwined with these alternate realities.

In New York, a mysterious glass box is used to observe an interdimensional rift. This plotline introduces the concept of portals and gateways, suggesting that different dimensions can intersect and that entities from other worlds can enter our reality.

The eyeless Naido is a representation of the mysterious and unexplained nature of these dimensions. The Fireman, an enigmatic figure, operates a theatre-like space from which he manipulates cosmic events and provides guidance. These locations underscore the idea that powerful beings exist in these alternate dimensions and influence the course of events.

In Lynch's intra-dimensional universe, the "Mauve Zone", resides a monstrous, nameless abomination from outside of reality, the entity referred to interchangeably in the episodes as the Mother, Judy ("Jowday" or "Joudy"), and the Experiment.

Judy, the Mother of all Evil, had always been known to humankind as some unspeakable entity from the earliest points in history; she is associated with ancient Sumerian and Native American mythologies. Judy is intentionally shrouded in mystery; her true nature is never fully revealed. This elusiveness adds to the intrigue and enigma of the character, keeping viewers in a state of uncertainty and curiosity. Her presence suggests that the struggles in Twin Peaks extend beyond the physical world, and characters must navigate the complexities of alternate dimensions to confront her. Members of the elite FBI Blue Rose Task Force are engaged in studying and tracking Judy's activities.

Although she supposedly remained passive for much of humanity's existence, Judy took an opportunity to manifest her influence into our world when on July 16, 1945, following the Trinity nuclear test at White Sands, New Mexico, Judy, floating in a dark void, expelled a stream of matter from her mouth, containing several speckled eggs. The stream also contained a large orb that bore an image of BOB's face.

An extreme negative force was subsequently birthed into the physical world when in 1956 an insectile creature, hatched from one of the eggs spewed forth by Judy, crawled into the mouth of a young New Mexico girl named "Sarah Judith Novack". Judy's energy merged with her being and remained largely inert within her host until decades later when it fed on the trauma caused by the death of Sarah's family.

In September 2016, the Experiment, white and female looking, with a gaping mouth and two small horns and its thumbs reversed, materialised in a black mist in the glass box in New York City. It violently shifted around for a few moments before breaking out and attacking Sam Colby and Tracey Barberato while they were having sex, hacking them to death.

Agent Tamara Preston later showed a still image of the figure, taken from a camera at the crime scene, to Agent Albert Rosenfield and FBI Deputy Director Gordon Cole, who were both visibly bewildered by the figure. The Fireman showed Twin Peaks Deputy Andy Brennan an image of the Experiment, seen before it broke out of the glass box.

The Secret History of Twin Peaks mentions the American occultist Jack Parsons. In 1947 British occultist Aleister Crowley gave colleague Gerald Gardner a charter to revive the Ordo Templis Orientis (O.T.O.) in Britain. In the summer of that year Gardner sailed for America to meet the American O.T.O heads, which included the enigmatic rocket propulsion researcher and occultist, Jack Parsons, one of Crowley's most ardent supporters.

After formally joining the O.T.O in 1941, Parsons, together with L. Ron Hubbard (founder of Scientology) and Parson's second wife Marjorie Cameron, participated at Devils Gate in Pasadena in what is probably the most famous and certainly one of the most bizarre magical rituals of the twentieth century, the Babalon Working.

This extraordinary ritual, commenced in 1946, was designed to fashion a Moonchild, a construct of etheric energies created by powerful thought-forms conjured by sex magick, as a means to raise the Antichrist. Parsons believed that by succeeding in this ritual the patriarchal power structure of the Piscean era would be supplanted by a resurgence of the Goddess energies, which had characterised and guided humankind in previous millennia.

The Babalon Working was an exhausting ritual designed to open an interdimensional doorway for the goddess Babalon, referred to in Twin Peaks Season 3 as Mother/Judy/The Experiment. It has since been widely rumoured that Parsons and his co-sorcerers succeeded in creating a rift in space-time, a doorway to the "other side". The culmination of these experiments is said by those who buy into these extraordinary accounts to have coincided with mass UFO sightings and the infamous Roswell incident, the latter occurring just prior to Crowley's death.

In 1952 Parsons was mortally wounded in his home in an explosion of fulminate of mercury, dying hours later. The incident was treated as accidental although considering Parson's scientific expertise the affair is regarded as highly suspicious. (Werner von Braun remarked that Parsons, and not he, should be regarded as the father of the American space programme.)

Many believe that Parsons and his cohorts' misguided occult efforts opened a gateway to terrible forces, much as Hitler was feared to have done years earlier in Europe.

Douglas Milford recounts President Richard Nixon showing him and actor Jackie Gleason a bizarre figure, similar in appearance to the Experiment, in an observation room at Homestead Air Base. When directly asked about a connection between the Experiment and the figure shown to Milford, co-author Mark Frost acknowledged the possibility without confirming or denying it. He reacted the same when asked if sex magic, in the same vein as Jack Parsons' rituals, was partly the cause of its appearance in Part 1.

In the White Lodge, the Fireman and his companion Senorita Dido are alerted to the monumental evil of BOB's existence. In response, they create a golden orb that contains the energy and image of Laura Palmer.

For 25 years, Cooper's doppelganger had been partnering with BOB, riding shotgun in an orgy of malignant behaviour. BOB possesses people; the doppelgangers reflect our worst selves. Both come to us in the faces of friends or loved ones. The Woodsmen, pitch-black vampiric bearded men brought into this world as a direct outcome of the Trinity nuclear test, hang around the outskirts of tragedy; when something criminal and ugly has happened to the innocent, they feed on the suffering like a silent Greek chorus.

However, Mr. C's time in the real world is rapidly coming to an end. At the 25-year mark, they would switch; Mr. C would return to the Black Lodge forever, while Cooper returns to the real world forever. To keep this from happening, Mr. C created tulpas: thought-form entities manufactured using small golden seed pearls.

The first tulpa was Diane, Cooper's former secretary. Tulpa-Diane worked with only limited understanding of her true nature and purpose and fed Mr. C information on the FBI. The real Diane was lost in another dimension, taking on the form of Naido who attempted to warn Cooper about the dangers of returning. The second tulpa was Dougie Jones.

Cooper travelled through multiple dimensions before returning to our world through a large electrical socket, as it is through electricity that the entities travel from the Lodges and our world. However, since Dougie Jones was wearing the ring, he was the one sent back instead of Mr. C. Cooper, meanwhile, was stuck in a kind of waking coma until an electrical charge blasted him back into coherence.

Cooper's experiences as Dougie recharged him. As Dougie, he experiences true frailty and total dependence on the kindness of others. When Cooper returned, he resembled the Dale Cooper from the first season: full of the same vigour and self-assurance he had prior to being shot. It allowed him to regain his optimism and faith in people.

Iconography plays a significant role in the third season of Twin Peaks, Director David Lynch and co-creator Mark Frost utilize a range of recurring symbols and imagery to deepen the show's themes and create a visually rich narrative.

The Owl Cave Ring is a mysterious and recurring symbol. It's associated with the Black Lodge and is often linked to malevolent forces. The ring's circular design and the owl motif are laden with meaning, hinting at the interconnectedness of the show's mysteries and the dangers that lurk in the shadows.

Camelot—in Las Vegas where Cooper makes his dimensional transfer from the Mauve Zone we see repeated references to the Arthurian theme. The tulpa Dougie Jones lives in Lancelot Court. Dougie's wife, Janey-E (Naomi Watts), arranges a meeting with hoodlums on the corner of Merlin and Guinevere. In another episode Cooper is riding in a limousine and for a short moment a big sign bearing the word Excalibur catches his eyes. It does not mock the limits of credibility to suggest that the whole of Season 3 resembles an initiate's journey through the twists and turns of a dimensional Camelot.

Numerology—numbers hold great significance in Twin Peaks. They are used to create an aura of mystery and to emphasize the supernatural aspects of the narrative. The numbers 3 and 8, in particular, appear frequently. For instance, room 315 at the Great Northern Hotel and the coordinates 48°30'08.0' N, 117°15'08.3' W play pivotal roles. The Giant told Dale Cooper to remember the number 430. That turned out to be a reference point for Cooper to drive 430 miles into Texas. At that exact spot was a dimensional gateway that he would use to attempt to find Judy. The number 253 was repeatedly mentioned. It represented the window in which Cooper could leave the Black Lodge: at 2:53 p.m., no later. 253 was also the yards east Bobby Briggs and other officers of the Twin Peaks sheriff's department had to travel from Jack Rabbit's Palace in the Twin Peaks forest region to find Naido. 6 is the number on several electric poles, most importantly the one outside of Carrie Page's house. Another electrical pole was marked 324810. It was repeated throughout the franchise. Agent Chester Desmond, Carl and Andy have all glared at or otherwise passed the pole around the town. There's the electrical outlet in the Purple Room that had the numbers 15 and 3 on it. 315 was Cooper's room at the Great Northern, and the 15th episode of The Return is where Cooper finally becomes Cooper again

The image of a white horse appears periodically throughout the series, often in unsettling contexts. In the third season, this symbol resurfaces, evoking a sense of foreboding and otherworldly presence. The white horse is associated with death, dreams, and the mystical, reflecting the show's themes of duality and transcendence.

Trees are recurring symbols in Twin Peaks. The sycamore tree outside the sheriff's station is particularly significant, as it conceals an entrance to the Black Lodge. Trees are emblematic of both life and death, serving as gateways between realms and symbolizing the interconnectedness of all things.

Fire and electricity are elemental forces that feature prominently in Twin Peaks. The mysterious fire at the Packard Mill, flickering electrical currents, and the use of fire symbolism in the Red Room all contribute to a sense of danger and transformation. These elements represent the volatile and unpredictable nature of the show's supernatural occurrences.

Laura Palmer's image in her high school prom queen portrait is an enduring symbol of innocence and tragedy. It serves as a reminder of the show's central mystery—her murder—and her impact on the town's residents. The portrait becomes a touchstone for characters grappling with their own dark secrets.

The ethereal Fireman and Senorita Dido are introduced in the third season and possess a mystical quality. Their appearances are marked by surreal and vivid imagery, including the floating golden orb. They embody the enigmatic nature of Twin Peaks' supernatural elements.

These symbols and iconographic elements contribute to the layered and complex narrative of *Twin Peaks: The Return*, inviting viewers to explore deeper themes of duality, dreams and the interplay between the ordinary and the extraordinary. Lynch and Frost's meticulous use of symbolism enhances the show's enigmatic and captivating atmosphere, making it a visual and intellectual feast for fans and scholars alike.

Twin Peaks: The Return is a masterclass in the use of symbolism and thematic depth to create a compelling narrative that challenges viewers to delve into the mysteries of existence, inter-dimensional realities, morality and the human psyche. Through its enigmatic storytelling and rich symbolism, the series continues to captivate and provoke thought long after its initial release.

Will there be a fourth season of Twin Peaks? Lynch and Frost are keeping tightlipped but Lynch has remarked that from time to time he hears Carrie Page, Laura Palmer's alter ego in a parallel Earth, calling to him.

.

271

The Fireman (courtesy Common Licence deviantart.com)

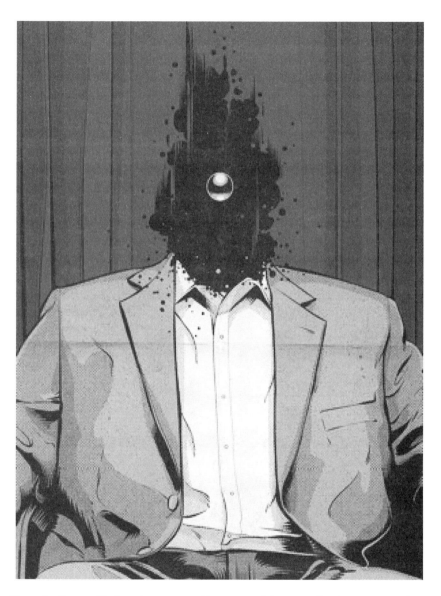

Dougie Jones Tulpa (courtesy Common Licence deviantart.com)

Laura Palmer "Goddess of Light" (courtesy Common Licence
deviantart.com)

ALICE'S WORLDS

Lewis Carroll

Chapter 19

Carroll

My life is so strangely free from all trial and trouble that I cannot doubt my own happiness is one of the talents entrusted to me to 'occupy' with, till the Master shall return, by doing something to make other lives happy.

—Lewis Carroll diary entry

This book is neither a biography of Lewis Carroll nor of his "Wonderland" muse, Alice Liddell. Nevertheless, it would be incomplete in the absence of sufficient personal material by which to achieve a degree of familiarisation with the two protagonists, writer and heroine, of the most famous, most loved, and most re-read children's story in literary history. The effort involved is especially rewarded when one comes to peel back both certain features of Carroll's personality of an esoteric nature, and also elements of Alice Liddell's family's life connected with nineteenth century Wales. Taken together, these facets are vital elements in our quest to identify the location of Alice's Wonderland and its companion world, the Looking-glass house and gardens.

Charles Dodgson was not all that he seemed. He was a member of the Society for Psychical Research (together with Arthur Conan Doyle) and a member of the Ghost Society. He was interested in telepathy ("thought-reading"). Dodgson's library contained many occult works. He was a sincere believer in the existence of fairy folk. He also believed that in trance-state we could migrate to other realms and meet with nature spirits. He said that miracles helped us believe in the power of God and in things that are normally invisible. In Carroll's personal cosmos, Wonderland and the Looking-glass house were as real and substantial as the physical world in which he taught mathematics to Christ Church undergraduates. But let us begin at the beginning. Charles Lutwidge Dodgson, the author of *Alice in Wonderland*, *Through the Looking-glass* and many other works on diverse topics, was born 27 January 1832 in the parsonage of Daresbury, a Cheshire hamlet about ten miles south-west of the town of Warrington. Today, Daresbury is a very peculiar place indeed.

In 1972 Manchester citizen, Peter Taylor, was driving home from work one night. As on the two previous nights, at 7:30 p.m. Taylor reached Daresbury. On this third night, the lights of Taylor's brand new Ford car faltered at precisely the same spot as before. However, events then unfolded in a very dramatic fashion. To his utter dismay, Taylor found that he was on an unfamiliar road and completely lost. Astonishingly, he discovered that he was forty miles north of Daresbury near the town of Preston in Lancashire. He phoned his wife Sandra from a roadside call box and learned that he had gained two hours in as many seconds.

Daresbury, centred round the Ring o' Bells Inn, is at the epicentre of a zone of high strangeness where witnesses have repeatedly claimed the occurrence of all manner of bizarre goings-on. The hamlet and its neighbouring villages of Moore, Helsby Hill and Runcorn encompass a triangular UFO hotspot area and is a magnet for many other instances of unexplained phenomena and supernatural goings-on that date back more than fifty years.

Because of Daresbury's connection with the Dodgson family the area has been dubbed by researchers "Wonderland". In recent times there have been repeated reports of car engines cutting out, the appearance of bright lights, a golden ball hovering above Sankey Way, a huge cigar-shaped object the size of an aeroplane that travelled beside a car near Preston Brook, and even the claim of an abduction to another planet! UFO expert Jenny Randles, a former resident of Warrington, told a local newspaper,

> There are locations around the world where there are more than the average number of paranormal occurrences. They have been described as being like doorways to another dimension. The evidence in these areas is often part of a track record dating back centuries, and linked with legends... Hotspots such as "Wonderland" are known as as "window" areas. There are 50 or 60 around the world, and a few in Britain. Wonderland is among the strangest places in the world. We need to figure out why it is happening.

Charles was the Dodgsons' third child. His mother would go on to bear eleven children, most of whom, including Charles, were inveterate stammerers. His father, also Charles, curate of the parish, had married his first cousin, Frances Jane Lutwidge, in 1827. The older north country Dodgsons were county families, gentry and nobility but immediate antecedents were mostly upper middle class men of the cloth, an army captain and a lawyer. While privileged, they were not exceptional: no knaves, nor geniuses; that is, until Charles junior came along.

Money was a constant concern but the family never let the issue dull religious fervour, devotion to social good, pursuit of learning and dedication to improving the human condition.

The living at Daresbury was obscure, a minor tributary of a larger parish. The hamlet was so quiet that even the passing of a cart was a matter of great interest. The Reverend Mr. Charles Dodgson had been granted the curacy from his university college, Christ Church Oxford, six years after being awarded a double first in classics and mathematics. Evidently, he was a very intelligent man, a trait inherited by his son. Dodgson senior was high-church, inclining toward Anglo-Catholicism, an admirer of John Henry Newman and the Tractarian movement, and did his best to instil these views in his children. However, his son developed an ambivalent relationship with father's values and, subsequently, with the Church of England as a whole

Charles spent his first eleven years in the tiny village, a period that sewed many creative seeds as attested by his scribblings, sketches and early efforts at verse. At the parsonage Charles invented many strange diversions to keep him occupied. He numbered certain snails and toads among his closest friends, and even tried to encourage civilised warfare among earthworms. He lived mentally, in fact, in a charming Wonderland of his own devising. It is not hard to deduce that the many creatures in Wonderland and the Looking-glass worlds—the White Rabbit, the animals in the Caucus–Race, the Caterpillar, the garden of live flowers and much more, owe their origins to the fields, farmyards and gardens of Daresbury. S.D. Collingwood, Dodgson's nephew-biographer, described his uncle's eleven years in Daresbury as 'years of complete seclusion from the world.'

Life in the Dodgson household was busy and followed a strict routine. Hours were allocated for games and light activities but by far the most important responsibilities, requiring strict adherance, were matters of religious observance. The family assembled for prayers morning and night. Bible reading was a staple activity. Both work and play were forbidden on Sunday, and the family ate cold meals to ensure that the servants were not required to work on the Lord's day.

For sixteen years Reverend Dodgson struggled in obscurity at Daresbury but in 1843, occasioned by successful lobbying of the Prime Minister, Robert Peel, by the curate's old friend, Charles Longley, the Bishop of Ripon, and by other notables, Dodgson was awarded the curacy of Croft-on-Tees in the far away North Riding of Yorkshire, four miles south of Darlington and twenty-five miles north of the cathedral town of Ripon.

Young Charles would never forget Daresbury. Sadly, his childhood parsonage was burned to the ground in 1884. The church in Daresbury where he was baptised contains a stained glass window depicting characters from the Alice books.

The Croft-on-Tees rectory was a large, three-storied Georgian pile across the road from an ancient heavy stone Gothic Church. The Dodgson's new residence was sourrounded by spacious gardens accommodating flowers, bushes and trees in bloom. As for Croft, the village dwarfed the Daresbury hamlet. It boasted its own town hall and a posting inn for coaches plying the London-Edinburgh route. Its sulphurous spa waters were acclaimed for their healing properties.

Young Charles was bewitched by his new surroundings. Echoing scenes from his future Alice stories, he constructed a miniature replica in the rectory garden of a primitive train made out of a wheelbarrow, a barrel and a small truck that conveyed his passengers from one station to another. All passengers were required to buy tickets in advance and each station on Charles' imaginary line had a refreshment room. He devised a timetable and a set of rules for travelling. 'Station master can put anyone who behaves badly to prison,' and passengers 'may not get in or put out of the train when moving...'

In Croft Rectory the boy grew into a youth and his innate creative talents emerged. It was evident that Charles was adept in mechanical matters and the creative arts. With a carpenter's help, he designed and built a marionette theatre, composed plays and learned to manipulate the puppets for presentations. Drawings, verses and short stories came into being quickly. Dodgson biographer Morton Cohen[66] remarks that 'so mature does he appear so early that one wonders whether he moved from childhood directly into adulthood, somehow skipping boyhood.'

Charles was the driving force behind the family's industrious productions of domestic magazines and scrapbooks, which were filled

---

[66] Cohen, M., *Lewis Carroll: a Biography*, Alfred A. Knopf, Inc., New York, 1995.

with cuttings, photos, pressed leaves, dried flowers and all manner of Dodgson clan memorabilia. Charles was the only significant contributor to them. In one issue of the magazine, *Useful and Instructive Poetry*, thirteen-year-old Charles came up with a limerick that would not have been out of place in Edward Lear's first book of nonsense poems, published in 1846:

> His sister named Lucy O'Finner
> Grew constantly thinner and thinner,
> The reason was plain,
> She slept out in the rain,
> And was never allowed any dinner.

The booklet shows a sophisticated turn of wit in one so young, and is packed with impressive literary allusions and influences, including Shakespeare, Blake, the Romantic poets, Izaak Walton and Tennyson. In it we see the genesis of much loved Wonderland imagery—the "Mouse's Tail", the cook and her stew, and some of the words that Humpty Dumpty will utter. It also contains a poem, "My Fairy", a composition that should invite serious contemplation when we learn in later pages that the true source of inspiration for Carroll's Alice stories may lie in a land imagined but very rarely seen. Its first verse reads:

> I have a fairy by my side
>   Which says I must not sleep,
> When once in pain I loudly cried,
>   It said "you must not weep".

For sixteen months, Charles was a boarding pupil at Richmond School. Here he excelled, especially in mathematics. The headmaster reported to his parents that their son possessed 'a very uncommon share of genius... that he is capable of acquirements and knowledge far beyond his years.'

On his fourteenth birthday, Charles left Richmond to attend Rugby School, an establishment that was enjoying a reputation as England's best public school, the result of the fourteen-year tenure, 1828-1842, of Dr. Thomas Arnold. He rid Rugby School of its reputation of being a breeding ground for vice and re-shaped it into a training ground for Christian gentlemen.

Despite Arnold's labours, by the time of Charles' arrival the school of five-hundred pupils was still characterised by its zeal in enacting excesses of fagging[67] and bullying. Initiating ceremonies were sometimes brutal, especially the practice of "lamb-singing". New boys were conducted to one of the smaller dormitories. The head of the house and the captain of the school football team sat on a bed as a bench of judges. Then on another bed the new "lamb" was made to stand up, a fag on each side lighting his face with a candle set in a tin candlestick. The lamb must now sing a song. If it passed muster with the judges, all to the good; if it didn't, the bench started singing "Rule Britannia", which was taken up by all present, and the unsuccessful songster was made to drink a dreadful concoction of tooth-powder, salt, mustard and other unsavoury ingredients mixed with water.

Charles did very well in his studies and won prizes, leaving Rugby School in 1849. He wrote in his diary in 1855, 'I made some friends there [Rugby]… but I cannot say that I look back upon my life at Public School with any sensations of pleasure, or that any earthly considerations would induce me to go through my three years again.'

One shudders to think what miserable ordeals he was made to endure there. In what may be a reference to sexual abuse, Charles wrote in his diary in 1857, 'From my own experience of school life at Rugby I can say that if I could have been… secure from annoyance at night, the hardships of the daily life would have been comparative trifles to bear.'

The young adult Charles Dodgson was about 6 feet tall and slender; he had curly brown hair and blue or grey eyes (depending on the account). He was described in later life as somewhat asymmetrical and carried himself rather stiffly and awkwardly, although this might be on account of a knee injury sustained in middle age. As a very young child, he suffered a fever that left him deaf in one ear. At the age of 17, he suffered a severe bout of whooping cough, which was probably responsible for his chronically weak chest in later life. In early childhood, he acquired the Dodgson line's genetic stammer, which he referred to as his "hesitation"; it remained throughout his life.

Charles returned to Croft to spend almost a year preparing for Oxford. A year before his son left Rugby, Charles' father wrote to his old friend and very distinguished cleric, Dr. E.B. Pusey, Regius Professor of Hebrew at the University of Oxford, to ask if he would nominate young Charles to a studentship at Christ Church. Charles'

---

[67] The former practice in public schools and other boarding establishments in which younger pupils were required to act as personal servants to the eldest boys.

Rugby record and his early command of the classics and mathematics assured his admission and on 23 May, 1850 he journeyed to Oxford to present himself to Osborne Gordon, Censor of Christ Church, for enrollment into the university.

Perhaps Charles' first view of Christ Church, in common with most freshers, was from Magdalen Bridge. From here one could look across the college cricket ground to the meadows beyond Cherwell for an uninterrupted view of every gleaming tower in Oxford, the noblest of cities, which accommodates a fairy land of spires and pinnacles that rise from a foreground of trees and nature landscapes.

Eight months later, 24 January 1851, Dodgson returned to Oxford to become a fully-fledged member of Christ Church. Tragically, two days later Charles had to return to Croft because his mother had suddenly died at the age of 47 of 'inflammation of the brain,' perhaps meningitis or a stroke. For a time the son was inconsolable with grief.

Charles soon settled however into university life and exercised his intellectual powers to impressive effect. In December 1852, Dr. Pusey recommended him for a Studentship, an appointment that crowned Charles's university achievements thus far. He could henceforth remain a Student for the rest of his life with lodgings, an honoured place in the acedemic community of the finest college in the oldest university in the land, and a secure income of thirty pounds annually.

He added to this modest emolument through his appointment as Sub-Librarian (where his office was close to the Deanery, Alice's home) which brought in an extra £35, from his award of one of the 'Bostock' Scholarships worth £20 a year, and by lecture fees.

Six years later, as a result of the 1858 Ordinance which created a Christ Church Salaries Board, Charles's tenure was upgraded to that of Senior Student earning £200 per annum. This appointment came with strings attached. He was obliged to proceed to holy orders and must not marry; failure to comply would cost him his Studentship. However, he was not required to teach if he so desired, nor was he expected to publish academic papers or to achieve any other distinction. If he wished he could put his feet up and do nothing for the rest of his life. But indolence was not Charles's style; he took quite the opposite course.

He threw himself into his studies for the remainder of his undergraduate years, working 13-hour days, with the result that in quick succession in the autumn of 1854 he made first-class honours in the Final Mathematical School and, days later, received his Bachelor of

Arts. Charles was now a fully paid up don.

In June 1855, Dean of Christ Church, Thomas Gaisford, died. Four months later Charles learned that he had been appointed as Christ Church's Mathematical Lecturer, and so ended the year as a Master with an income of more than £300 a year. He was not yet twenty-four.

Gaisford was replaced in 1856 by the aristocratic Henry George Liddell, nephew of Baron Ravensworth, first cousin of the earl of Strathmore and Kinghorne, headmaster of prestigious Westminster School, and Chaplain to Prince Albert. The Christ Church Deanery had served as King Charles's palace during the English Civil War.

Liddell was father to Alice, who would subsequently achieve worldwide fame as the muse for Carroll's Wonderland stories. Not only did the Dean run Christ Church college and manage its great wealth and substantial property portfolio but, by virtue of the post, he became the most important ecclesiastical figure in Oxford.

Undaunted by his increasing workload in Christ Church, in January 1856 Dodgson asked his Uncle Skeffington 'to get me a photographic apparatus, as I want some other occupation here than mere reading and writing.' And so began Charles' preoccupation with the nascent art of photography, a diversion in which he became eminently skilled.

In March 1856, he published his first piece of fictional work under the name that would make him famous. A romantic poem called "Solitude" appeared in *The Train* under the authorship of Lewis Carroll. This pseudonym was a play on his real name: Lewis was the anglicised form of Ludovicus, which was the Latin for Lutwidge, and Carroll an Irish surname similar to the Latin name Carolus, from which comes the name Charles. The transition went as follows: "Charles Lutwidge" translated into Latin as "Carolus Ludovicus". This was then translated back into English as "Carroll Lewis" and then reversed to make "Lewis Carroll". This pseudonym was chosen by editor Edmund Yates from a list of four submitted by Dodgson, the others being Edgar Cuthwellis, Edgar U. C. Westhill, and Louis Carrol. We will now refer to him solely as Carroll.

After Carroll returned to Christ Church from the Easter vacation he encountered Alice Liddell for the first time. It was a Friday, April 25th. On this day Carroll, accompanied by his friend and fellow photography enthusiast Reginald Southey, took his camera equipment to the Deanery to try to take photographs of the cathedral but 'both attempts proved failures.' He added in his diary that 'the three little girls [Lorina ("Ina"), 7; Alice, 4; and Edith, 2] were in the garden most of the time, and we became excellent friends: we tried to group them in the foreground of the picture, but they were not patient sitters.' He added auspiciously, 'I mark this day with a white stone.'

Carroll and Southey returned to the Deanery on three successive occasions the following week and took pictures of some of the children. From then on Carroll became a regular visitor to the Liddells' home. Although lower in social standing than the Liddells, Carroll was clearly well thought of because by May the family were inviting him to dinner.

Carroll's increasing skills in photography were also instrumental in fast-tracking him into the Liddells' inner circle of influential figures, such as Henry Acland, the Dean's personal physician, Fellow of All Souls and soon to be Regius Professor of Medicine.

The years passed, Carroll spending the greater part of his time on his Christ Church duties but also producing acclaimed mathematical works. By 1861 he had written three impressive books: *A Syllabus of Plane Algebraical Geometry*, *Two Books of Euclid*, and *The Formulae of Plane Trigonometry*. Also during this year, after several years of preparation, Carroll was ordained as a deacon in the Church of England by Samuel Wilberforce, Bishop of Oxford.

At the same time, Carroll continued to enjoy cordial relations with the Liddells. He visisted the Deanery frequently and took the children on long walks and on river expeditions. Carroll walked with an upright carriage, almost leaning backwards as if, in the words of contemporaries, he had swallowed a poker. His white flannel trousers flapped comically over black boots.

The young ones visited his rooms so often they virtually dominate his diary. There they would have observed that Mr Dodgson shared his quarters with music boxes, dolls, wind-up animals (including a walking bear), an American "orguinette" (a kind of musical instrument), "Bob the Bat", a microscope, field glasses, telescope, pocket sundial, magic lantern, aneroid barometer, human skull, printing press, typewriter, "Nyetograph" (for taking notes in the dark), humane mousetrap, magic pens, dumb-bells and mechanical exercisers.

Carroll's friendship with the girls became deeply rooted, and it it is equally clear that they were enormously fond of him, often proferring their own invitations, seeking him out, wanting his company and companionship. Had Mrs Liddell encountered Dodgson for the first time a decade later, a man adept at at meeting little girls in trains and on beaches, carrying a black bag of wire puzzles and safety pins to pin up the trailing skirts of paddling girls, or seen his diary entry for 25 March

1863, listing the names, with dates of birth, of 107 girls 'photographed or to be photographed,' she may very well have decided that her children should have no contact with him at all.

Alice Liddell later wrote her recollection of the boat trips and outings period, one that provides fascinating insights into Carroll's creative imagination:

> We used to go to his rooms... escorted by our nurse. When we got there, we used to sit on the big sofa on each side of him, while he told us stories, illustrating them by pencil or ink drawings as he went along. When we were thoroughly happy and amused at his stories, he used to pose us, and expose the plates before the right mood had passed. He seemed to have an endless store of these fantastical tales, which he made up as he told them, drawing busily on a large sheet of paper all the time. They were not always entirely new. Sometimes they were new versions of old stories: sometimes they started on the old basis, but grew into new tales owing to the frequent interruptions which opened up fresh and undreamed of possibilities. In this way the stories, slowly enunciated in his quiet voice with its curious stutter, were perfected...

> Being photographed was a joy to us and not a penance as it is to most children. We looked forward to the happy hours in the mathematical tutor's rooms. He used sometimes to come to the Deanery on the afternoon when we had a half-holiday... On the other hand, when we went on the river for the afternoon with Mr. Dodgson, which happened at most four or five times every summer term, he always brought out with him a large basket full of cakes, and a kettle, which we used to boil under a haycock, if we could find one.

> On rarer occcasions we went out for the whole day with him, and then we took a larger basket with luncheon—cold chicken and salad and all sorts of good things. One of our favourite whole-day excursions was to row down to Nuneham and picnic in the woods there, in one of the huts specially provided by Mr. Harcourt for picnickers... To us the hut might have been a Fairy King's palace, and the picnic a banquet in our honour. Sometimes we were told stories after luncheon that transported us into Fairyland... On these occasions we did not get home until about seven o'clock.

Alice wins her crown and becomes Queen

Nuneham was one of the Liddells' cherished destinations for outings. With a landscaped park and deep, green woods, it provided the freedom and mystery to whet young appetites and imaginations; it also stimulated Carroll's storytelling gifts. The location lay five miles downstream from Christ Church, an ideal distance and in the right direction for the children to take turns rowing.

The children were stowed away in the stern of the boat, while Carroll, assisted by a companion, sometimes Harcourt or Robinson Duckworth, Fellow of Trinity College and later Chaplain to the Queen and Canon of Westminster, took the stroke oar. Alice remarked later that 'it was a good day when we could "feather our oars" properly.' The scene is captured in the first verse of *Alice in Wonderland's* prefatory poem:

> All in the golden afternoon[68]
> Full leisurely we glide;
> For both our oars, with little skill,
> By little arms are plied,
> While little hands make vain pretence
> Our wanderings to guide.

Another route for expeditions was upriver to Godstow. Carroll's diary entry records one such occasion for July 4, 1862. It reads:

> Duckworth and I made an expedition *up* the river to Godstow with the 3 Liddells: we had tea on the bank there, and did not reach Christ Church again till ½ past 8, when we took them on to my rooms to see my collection of micro-photographs,[69] and restored them to the Deanery, just before 9.
>
> [On February 10, 1863, Carroll added a note on the blank page opposite the July '62 note:] On which occasion I told them [the "cruel Three", as he described the sisters[70]] the fairy-tale of *Alice's Adventures Under Ground*, which I undertook to write out for Alice, and which is now finished.

The boat trip began at Salter's boatyard (still present) by Folly Bridge in Oxford and ended five miles away at Port Meadow near

---

[68] Actually, the weather on that day was reported as 'cool and rather wet.'

[69] Ingenious miniature versions of photographs that Carroll then set in tiny ivory telescope viewers which, when held up the eye, revealed the image.

[70] Carroll nicknamed the sisters. Lorina was the flashing "Prima"; Alice, the hoping "Secunda"; and Edith, the interrupting "Tertia."

Godstow.

Until the late 17th century Folly Bridge was known as South Bridge and formed part of a long causeway, Grandpont, which stretched along most of the line of Abingdon Road. In the 13th century, the noted alchemist Roger Bacon lived and worked at "Friar Bacon's Study", which stood across the north end of the bridge until 1779 when it was removed to widen the road. It is believed that Folly Bridge may be derived from the name of a one-time tenant in Bacon's study.

Before long, the boat and its occupants arrived on a peaceful stretch of the Isis where trees overhang the banks. The Isis is the historical name for the stretch of the Thames beginning from its source in the Cotswolds to the place where it joins with the River Thame at Dorchester, two miles southwest of Clifton Hampden.[71] Leaving Oxford behind, the boat party shortly passed through Osney Lock.

At some point Carroll began telling the girls a story that featured a bored little girl named Alice who goes looking for an adventure. As Carroll wrote years later, he had begun by sending his 'heroine straight down a rabbit-hole without the least idea what was to happen afterwards.'

Presently, the party arrived at Port Meadow, a vast open space used for grazing, graced today by geese, ducks and the occasional blue heron. Nearby lay the hamlet of Godstow. A picnic was laid out and Carroll went on with his story. Only through the prodding and interruption of the children did it move forward to a conclusion. The girls loved it. Alice Liddell, especially taken by the story, pressed Carroll to write it down for her. Carroll began writing the manuscript the next day, although that earliest version is lost to history. Carroll and the girls took another boat trip a month later when he elaborated the plot of the story of Alice. In November, Carroll began working on the manuscript in earnest.

The relationship between the Liddells and Dodgson began to break down in late 1862, a falling out of grace that Carroll's diary notes had taken place ever since the 'Lord Newry business.' This "business" was a disagreement about lifting the college curfew for Lord Newry's ball, which Dodgson was opposed to, while Mrs. Liddell was in favour. She

---

[71] For readers interested in ley lines and earth energies, see my AUP book *Gods in the Fields*, regarding Clifton Hampden's unique "Golden Mean" position along England's famed "Michael and Mary" line.

rather hoped that one of her daughters could marry the aristocratic Francis Charles Needham, 3rd Earl of Kilmorey (1842-1915), styled Viscount Newry, who was a student of Carroll's.

Relations eventually became cordial again for a while but there occurred a sudden break in June 1863. There was no record of why the rift occurred, since the Liddells never openly spoke of it and the single page in Carroll's diary recording 27–29 June 1863 (which seems to cover the period in which it began) was missing.

It has been speculated by biographers such as Morton N. Cohen that Carroll may have wanted to marry the 11-year-old Alice Liddell, expressed his desire openly, and that this was the cause of the unexplained break with the family. Alice Liddell's biographer, Anne Clark, writes that Alice's descendants were under the impression that Carroll wanted to marry her but that Alice's parents expected a much better match for her. Clark argues that in Victorian England such arrangements were not as improbable as they might seem. John Ruskin, for example, fell in love with a 12-year-old girl, while Carroll's younger brother sought to marry a 14-year-old, but postponed the wedding for six years.

One fact alone may serve to indicate that Carroll had little or no romantic love for Alice. On Boxing Day, 1862, Alice's new pony fell while she was riding along the Abingdon road. Alice broke her thigh and was subsequently laid up in bed for six weeks. Seventy-years later, an aggrieved Alice Hargreaves was still remarking that 'during all these weeks Mr. Dodgson never came ro see me.'

In 1996, Karoline Leach found the cut pages in Carroll's diary, in which was a note allegedly written by Carroll's niece, Violet Dodgson, summarising the missing page from 27–29 June 1863. It reads:

> L.C. learns from Mrs. Liddell that he is supposed to be using the children as a means of paying court to the governess [Mary Prickett, "Pricks" to the children]—he is also supposed by some to be courting Ina.

This might imply that the break between Carroll and the Liddell family was caused by concern over alleged gossip linking Carroll to the family governess or to Ina. In her biography, *The Mystery of Lewis Carroll*, Jenny Woolf suggests that the problem was caused by Lorina becoming too attached to Dodgson and not the other way around. That this latter explanation is more likely is indicated by Carroll's opinion expressed in Easter 1863 that Ina had reached, for him, a dangerous age: 'so tall as to look odd without an escort.'

After this incident, Dodgson avoided the Liddell home for six months but eventually returned for a visit in December 1863. All was well for a while but five months later, possibly because Carroll was in opposition to Dean Liddell over college politics, Mrs Liddell put her daughters out of his reach by refusing them any more outings with him on the river, an act that Carroll described in his diary as 'rather superfluous caution.' Carroll saw little of the Liddell children thereafter. He lamented his separation from Alice in the sad preface to Alice Through the Looking-Glass:

> I have not seen thy sunny face,
> Nor heard thy silver laughter;
>   No thought of me shall find a place
> In thy young life's hereafter.

So far, so good but we need to see all sides of the man. Carroll is presented in Alice Liddell's and other contemporary remembrances as an endearing young man who loves children's company and tells them extemporized stories to keep them amused. But how does one square this innocent persona with the Mr. Hyde character who wrote to eleven-year-old Isa Bowman, saying:

> If only I could fly to Fulham with a handy little stick, ten inches by four inches is my favourite size, how I would rap your wicked little knuckles. The Fulham policeman will fit you with a nice pair of handcuffs, lock you in a nice cosy dark cell and feed you on nice dry bread and delicious cold water.

And what was running through Dodgson's mind when he sent a penknife to young Kathleen Tidy for her birthday, adding in his letter:

> Whenever you wish to punish your brothers do so by running the knife into their hands and faces, particularly at the end of the nose.

Making presents of knives to juveniles was an obsession of Dodgson's. He sent one to poet Alfred Tennyson's elder son Hallam and in a follow-up letter suggested how he might use it on his brother:

> If Lionel ever wants his fingers cut, be kind to him and cut him as much as he likes.

Ostensibly, these were the actions of a man who hated children, girls especially, and wanted to hurt them. This darker description of Carroll's character is not lightened when we learn that the Christ Church don was fascinated by surgical operations, including observing amputations at London hospitals, and that he owned skeletal remains.

It is evident that Carroll was plagued by sexual contradictions throughout his life. At the age of sixty-two he wrote *Pillow Problems Worked Out During Wakeful Hours,* a book consisting of 72 problems with solutions that he worked out in his head at night while waiting to fall asleep, in which he referred to 'unholy thoughts, which torture with thir hateful presence the fancy that would be fain.'

And what of his photography? After taking it up in 1856 Carroll was soon excelling at the art and became a wellknown gentleman-photographer. He even seemed to have to have toyed with the idea of making a living out of it in his very early years.

A study by Roger Taylor and Edward Wakeling[72] exhaustively lists every surviving print, and Taylor calculates that just over half of Carroll's surviving work depicts young girls. Thirty surviving photographs depict nude or semi-nude children. About 60% of Carroll's original photographic portfolio was deliberately destroyed.

In 2015 the BBC broadcast a documentary, *The Secret World of Lewis Carroll,* which explored whether Lewis Carroll was a "repressed paedophile". The show detailed a photograph recently discovered in a French museum of a naked girl. It had an inscribed attribution on the frame saying it was by Lewis Carroll. The documentary did not provide comprehensive proof that the photo, believed to show Alice's elder sister, Lorina, entirely nude, had been taken by Carroll.

So dark did Carroll's character traits seem to one American child psychologist that his 1996 work *Jack the Ripper: Your Light-Hearted Friend,* a follow-up to *The Agony of Lewis Carroll* in which he portrays the writer as an anguished homosexual pederast, Richard Wallace built his case against Carroll and his friend Thomas Vere Bayne as the 1888 Whitechapel murderers. He analysed anagrams he had identified in Carroll's works and in the many so-called Jack the Ripper letters of confession. In these Wallace professed to find connecting threads, which led in the author's opinion to one inescapable conclusion.

Wallace's theories were ridiculed but they highlight the starkly

---

[72] Taylor, R; Wakeling, E. *Lewis Carroll, Photographer.* Princeton University Press. 2002.

ambivalent attitudes that divide opinion concerning Carroll and the true nature of his personality. In my 2015 novel *The Looking Glass Ripper*, I created a 270-letter text in verse form to demonstrate how relatively simple it is to present a case for the prosecution:

Mrs Risco's Milk Chocolate Ghost

The legless leopard and the haughty mole
Were rapt in discourse beneath the moon.
One savoured huss and the other sole.
And both slid through the ladling spoon.

Nine fair alabaster maidens,
All named Saucy but for twelve,
Sipped chilled whisky through a chimney
And spoke of wicks and wayward elves.

Which, when the letter containing the verse addressed to Alice (Hargreaves) years after the Wonderland years was inadvertently pressed with a steam iron, produced this damning first-level anagram:

I, C.L.Dodgson, betake the cross and don my father's holy works. Forlorn, I am down on whores and I'll s-s-stab their c...s [letters hidden here for decency but in full form part of the anagram] *and cut them up raw. Bane and I, avowed homos and arse fags, paint the V white roses red. Suck large puss, glee! Kelly, Nichols and Chapman guild the lily. Others slice up Mary to hide the motive, tee hee hee! Hail Baal. Oh, God, help us.*

Then, subsequently, in the story when the reverse side of the letter was accidentally doused with a mixture of water and bircarbonate of soda, it revealed a second-level anagram, which pointed in my fictional narrative to the involvement of the Vatican in the Whitechapel affair:

I, Charles Lutwidge Dodgson, hold a glass high to the many worlds, past and present and future.
Oh, Alice, Holy Mother Isis, conceal threshold and keep womb safe.
The key is to believe. Church slays millions for Grail.
Pius serves the Magdalene.
Unknown to any, Red Hat and Thule band behind Ripper deaths.
Worse comes, vow maketh a Holocaust.

It took me months to find a short poem that could be anagramized in two different ways, using the same 270 letters that the title and the eight lines are composed from. I'm quite proud of the end result but, like Wallace's theory on Carroll's culpability, it's all nonsense (except for the part about the Vatican; see my book for AUP: *Jack the Ripper's New Testament* for my argument concerning the Church's participation in the murders).

Are we tempted though to cut Carroll some slack? Carroll had his quirks and evidently identified with the precepts of the Victorian Cult of the Child, which perceived child nudity as a natural expression of innocence. The practice of taking photos of children *déshabillés* was mainstream activity in Britain during the nineteenth century. Surprisingly, the movement's adherents were not drawn solely from male society. Carroll's friend, professional photographer Julia Margaret Cameron, was an enthusiastic snapper of young children in various shades of undress. Perhaps Carroll's lifelong penchant for children's company should be seen in the context of his time, an era in which so many seemed to crave the secrets of eternal youth and sought them vicariously through the worship of unclothed, artless innocents.

But what of Carroll's mystical side? It is already noted that he believed in the existence of multiple worlds that one can visit provided one has the right key, a *dietrich*, which, as in the case of the Knight of Berne, will admit one to Wonderland, the Looking-glass House and Fairyland.

What of Carroll's philosophical and metaphysical leanings? In Carroll's teens, the spiritualist movement was born. I wrote in *Jack the Ripper's New Testament*:

In an existential sense the world went mad on 31 March 1848, the date that spiritualism was "invented".

What is spiritualism? It is the belief in the continued existence of the human personality after death in a spirit form with which, through mediumistic channels, the living may communicate. Adherents of the movement believe that the next world is one in which spirits evolve into higher forms, hence bestowing upon them the power to inform, guide and educate humans on moral and ethical issues...

Occultism, on the other hand, is based on the belief that phenomena are a consequence of working with unknown natural forces (the Elementals).

Even before that momentous early spring day in New

294

York State's Wayne County the carriage of reason, once a fine coach with shiny brass and all the trappings, had become increasingly rickety. The mysterious events in the tiny hamlet of Hydesville finally delivered its deathblow, bowling all four wheels into the brush. The Hydesville phenomena occurred in the period when Europe and America were experiencing an overwhelming reaction against the excesses of logic generated by the eighteenth-century Age of Reason. As man began to achieve greater mastery of his physical environment consequent to the Industrial Revolution and parallel increases in scientific development, his hold upon his relationship with the intangibles in the universe became more precarious. Rapid change of this nature has the tendency both to confuse and to frighten. After 1789 the threat of social revolution terrified large swathes of Europe. In the short but significant European "Revolutions of 1848," which began five weeks before Hydesville more than fifty violent but largely uncoordinated attempts were made to bring down governments, remove old monarchical structures and create independent national states.

One cannot attribute the demise of cool reason and the birth of spooky spiritualism solely to the Fox sisters and the rappings of "Mr Splitfoot" in their country cottage. To observers, the beginnings of spiritualism would have appeared inevitable when considered alongside the increasing episodes of esoteric phenomena that occurred during the preceding 75 years.

Spiritualism became a fashionable form of entertainment for those, especially in the middle classes, who loved the frisson of encountering the unknown and, of course, the prospect of holding hands in a darkened séance room without fear of censure. Others were not so glib about the burgeoning phenomenon and welcomed it as the cutting edge of the natural sciences and a new expression of religious belief in a world where many had pronounced the death of God.

In 1862 fellows in Cambridge University, under the leadership of Edward White Benson (later Archbishop of Canterbury), founded the Cambridge Ghost Society or "Ghostly Guild", 'for the investigation of ghosts and all supernatural appearances and effects, being all disposed to believe that such things really exist, and ought to be discriminated from hoaxes and mere subjective delusions.' Its early membership included Charles Dickens and Sir Arthur Conan Doyle. Outsiders called it the "Cock and Bull Club".

The creation of the Ghost Club was not based on new thinking but was a reboot of a short-lived campus society, The Cambridge Association for Spiritual Inquiry, formed in the early 1850s by Benson and fellow clerics Brooke Foss Westcott, Fenton John Anthony Hort and other colleagues. The Ghost Club was a precursor to the Society for Psychical Research (SPR), which was founded in February 1882. William Gladstone, British Prime Minister 1865-1874 and a friend of Henry Liddell, called psychical research, 'the most important work which is being done in the world, by far the most important work.'

Lewis Carroll was excited by the advent of Spiritualism and its many esoteric tributaries. It is not known if Carroll allied himself officially with any of its initial smovements but it is more likely than not considering his early membership of the SPR, and his little known connection with England's mystical Christian alliances from the mid-1850s.

In this latter period Carroll had begun to move in the pre-Raphaelite social circle. He first met John Ruskin in 1857 and became friendly with him. Around 1863, he developed a close relationship with Dante Gabriel Rossetti and his family. Carroll would often take pictures of the family in the garden of the Rossetti house in Chelsea. He also knew William Holman Hunt, John Everett Millais and Arthur Hughes, among other artists. He knew fairy-tale author George MacDonald well; it was the enthusiastic reception of Alice by the young MacDonald children that persuaded Carroll to submit the work for publication.

It was during Carroll's relationship with the pre-Raphaelite clan that he revealed his interest in the esoteric and spiritualist movements of the day. In 1862, Arthur Hughes painted a stylised portrait of a woman, as a working study for the younger figure featured in a subsequent work, Silver and Gold. Hughes titled the 1862 oil on panel work, The Lady with the Lilacs. It measures 17½ x 9 inches and was cut to its final arched shape after the wood was primed and painted. In The Lady with the Lilacs the redheaded subject is standing beneath a lilac tree. Around her neck is a five-point "Star of Isis" pendant suspended from a double chain. Pendant and chain appear to be fashioned from gold. Widely accepted opinion has it that Hughes's wife, Tryphena, modelled the subject just as it is believed that she similarly posed for her husband's April Love and Home from the Sea works.

Hughes expert, Canadian Leonard Roberts, compiler in 1997 of the catalogue raisonné: *Arthur Hughes: his Life and Works*, for the Antique

Collector Club Ltd., told me in correspondence in 2002 that Lewis Carroll saw the work while visiting the painter on 31 July 1863 and was immediately captivated. So much so, that Carroll asked Hughes to re-work it for his own collection, a task which he completed 8 October. Carroll's diary records that he took formal possession of the painting on the 12th.

Carroll is believed to have first become aware of Hughes's work in July 1862 when he saw and admired the illustrations the artist produced for George MacDonald's *The Light Princess*. Twelve months later Carroll accompanied pre-Raphaelite sculptor Alexander Munro to the Hughes household seeing, as noted in his diary, 'some lovely pictures, and his four little children… He also is to come with his children to be photographed.' "Uncle" Lewis Carroll, as the Hughes children dubbed him, conducted the sitting with the family 12 October 1863.

The story that Carroll became enamoured with The Lady with the Lilacs after seeing it in partly finished format while making his first visit to Hughes's studio is challenged by a remark in Leonard's catalogue raisonné, which describes the provenance as 'Commissioned in 1863 by Lewis Carroll.' The Cambridge Dictionary defines "commission" in this context as 'to formally choose someone to do a special piece of work, or to formally ask for a special piece of work from someone.' The use of the term therefore implies that the commissioner is the sole personality motivating the undertaking of an original artistic project to fulfill that person's unique requirements or specifications.

That Carroll saw a picture out of the blue, liked what he saw and asked the artist to finish it off does not meet the usual criteria of a commission. It does suggest, however, that Carroll had a special interest in the subject and instigated the sitter's representation in oils as The Lady with the Lilacs. The theory might seem a touch over-imaginative were it not for the consideration that, by all accounts, The Lady with the Lilacs was the only painting that Carroll ever owned.

Recent years have seen the emergence of a body of opinion that the subject in the The Lady with the Lilacs is a very mysterious woman named Mary Heath. Interestingly, in Roberts' response to my letter of 2001 in which I made the case for Heath as The Lady with the Lilacs, he first set out the popularly understood facts that support Tryphena Hughes as being the model before concluding, 'Having said all this, I remain open-minded about the identity of the model…' In a subsequent email exchange, Roberts also noted Hughes' "odd" inclusion of the Star of Isis in The Lady with the Lilacs, as it had not been used in the artist's previous pictures. It was clear that Roberts was also beginning to entertain doubts about the sitter's identity.

Had Carroll, a man who populated his library with books on occult and spirit phenomena, known of Mary Heath and desired to immortalise her in a work of art in a specially commissioned portrait that provided clues to a secret life in Victorian England? Just who was the enigmatic Mary Heath?

By means of ground research and psychic research, British investigator Andrew Collins and his colleagues have presented a fascinating account of her life. Mary is believed to have been born in France around 1840, the illegitimate daughter of wealthy and eminent printer and designer, Thomas de la Rue. She first came to London around 1855, possibly under the guardianship of the Dalziel brothers: engravers for Lewis Carroll's illustrator, John Tenniel, and illustrators for Madame Michelet's nature works. In this period Mary Heath was introduced to a number of individuals in pre-Raphaelite circles.

Collins speculates that Carroll was among those that were smitten by the fifteen-year old French girl. Such an encounter would have taken place around seven years before the "golden afternoon" when Carroll told a story to the Liddell sisters of a little girl's adventures underground.

Any mystery of how Carroll might have made up, on the spot, the complete story of Alice's adventures could be explained, at least in part, if he was narrating a work in which he had invested time and energy beforehand. If, as some believe, the source of creative and esoteric inspiration for the tales was Mary Heath, a Christian mystic with a magical, spirited personality that sought adventure, then the question of timing and pre-preparedness may be addressed.

Collins states that Mary returned to France. A few years later, prompted by the death of her mother, Mary's father revealed that the family was part of a clandestine mystical fraternity that linked their bloodline to the Guise-Lorraine family, which had championed Mary Queen of Scots. The Guise-Lorraine family is also a scion of the Merovingian line of kings, which, as many will know from numerous books and films on the subject, is reputed to have originated from a child born to Jesus and Mary Magdalene, mother and child brought to safety from Judea on a rudderless boat to the South of France after the crucifixion. It is believed that Julia Cameron (1815-1879), the leading photographer of her day, depicted Heath as Mary Magdalene in her

Angel at the Sepulchre. Mary's family furnished her with the names of contacts and societies in England that shared similar beliefs and allegiances. The de la Rue family asked Mary to meet with them and establish, through their support, a new group of like-minded mystical Christians who accepted that the wisdom of Moses and King Solomon originated in ancient Egypt. This group became known as the Fire Phoenix.

Mary established the order at a ceremony held in the grounds of Biddulph Grange in Staffordshire, a few miles distant from a magical location known as the "Place of the Double Setting Sun". The area was also associated with a mysterious Gypsy tribe ("the golden red-haired folk") known as the "Azarkre", which, Collin's research indicates, was brought to Britain by the Knights Templar from the Holy Land.

In 1869, Biddulph Grange was sold by its owner, James Bateman, to Robert Heath, the wealthy owner of a number of coal mines, ironstone pits, blast furnaces and rolling mills. It appears that Mary lived at the Grange posing as Robert's sister or close relative, taking the surname as part of her cover.

Collins suggests that the Hermetic knowledge underpinning the Fire Phoenix was brought to Britain by a colony of Egyptians from the time of Pharaoh Akhenaten. These exiles, Mary's group understood, were the progenitors of the Celtic civilisation and the Druids.

Akhenaten, born Amenhotep IV, is known in history as the Pharaoh who, uniquely, introduced into Egypt the worship of the one god, Aten the Sun-god. After a brief period (ruling seventeen years, circa 1352 to 1335 BC) Akhenaten, ousted by an all-powerful priesthood that yearned for the re-introduction of the traditional Egyptian pantheon, was forced into exile with his followers.

Historians (notably Ahmed Osman) have argued that the Old Testament story of Moses and the Israelites' miraculous crossing of the Red Sea is an account of Akhenaten's enforced departure from Egypt. Mystical Christian groups go further, claiming that the exiles brought to Britain the hermetic teachings of Thoth, the Egyptian god of writing, knowledge and philosophy, which eventually became the basis of alchemic learning.

Additionally, the Collins' group claims that the Moses-Akhenaten followers also brought to Britain an emerald-green stone which four hundred years later came to be worn as a symbol of magical authority by a Celtic priestess named Gwevaraugh. In the Middle Ages it became known as the Philosopher's Stone and in Mary Queen of Scots' time as the Meonia Stone. In common with other nineteenth-century esoteric groups, Mary's Fire Phoenix believed that the world would shortly be challenged by great changes which, once confronted and overcome, would open the way for a new golden age. Believing that Britain was the epicentre of metaphysical progression in the Western world, the group anticipated that the revitalising energy of the new millennium would ripple outwards from these Isles into the rest of Europe to bring universal harmony.

Mary took into her confidence artist friend Arthur Hughes who, according to Collins' research, incorporated her image into a painting initially known as A Mother's Grave. It depicts a small boy who, tired after his long journey to visit his mother's resting place, is sleeping beneath a tree. In 1863, seven years after beginning the work, Hughes added the figure of a petite young woman clad in a dark shawl and dress sitting on the grass with her hands clasped. Art scholars commonly accept that the figure is that of Hughes' wife, Tryphena. Collins disagrees, arguing that the sitter was actually twenty-three year old Mary Heath whom Hughes added soon after her arrival from France. Hughes then gave the painting the alternative title, Home from the Sea.

Hughes also reportedly inserted in the section of the picture that depicts a wild tree rose festooned with spiders' webs a clue about a mysterious ceremony called the "Form of the Lamb", which the seven members of the inner order of the Fire Phoenix had carried out at a secret location called the "Heart of the Rose". The objective of the ritual was to open the gates to the coming golden age.

The arch adversary of the Fire Phoenix was the "Wheel", a European occult group established after the fall of the Templars in the early fourteenth century. The British arm of the Wheel was led by John Newton Langley who ran a school for boys in Wolverhampton. Langley is described as a tall man who wore a top hat, thick floor-length cape and white kid gloves. In his black magic rituals Langley used a large polished black stone referred to as the Running Stone.

Collins' investigations indicated that the Wheel's operations in England were funded and controlled by an organisation known as the People of Hexe, a name derived from the Germanic form of Hecate. The group comprised occult adepts of European origin whose mission was to take control of Britain's invisible energy matrix. To this end, the People of Hexe conducted ceremonies at power sites such as stone circles, long-barrows, holy hills and former pagan sites reconstituted as

300

Christian shrines. The adepts regarded Britain as a giant labyrinth of all-powerful earth energies and invoked in their rituals the archetypes and symbols of the Cretan Minotaur and the spider-goddess Arachne.

At the time of Mary Heath's move to England one of her closest friends in France was Nina Chevret who was considerably older than Mary and married to artist, lithographer and occultist Édouard Chevret. In the early 1840s Nina was asked by her husband to infiltrate Eugène Vintras's L'Ouevre de la Miséricorde. Édouard had learned that Vintras and his movement were under the control of the "Saviours of Louis XVII", a political organisation dedicated to restoring the monarchy (the Bourbon Restoration) under Louis-Charles, Dauphin of France (son of the executed King Louis XVI and Queen Marie Antoinette).

In the course of her intelligence activities, Nina also discovered connections between L'Ouevre de la Miséricorde and the Johannite Church of Primitive Christians founded by Templar revivalist Bernard-Raymond Fabré-Palaprat, which was an arm of the Wheel. Nina learned that in promoting these occult alliances Vintras made contact with Langley and appointed him British head of the Wheel in 1863.

Collin's research indicates that Mary Heath died of natural causes in the mid-1890s. Some of her followers in the Fire Phoenix developed connections with the Hermetic Order of the Golden Dawn while others continued with Mary's work. The group survived in England until the outbreak of the Great War and then moved to Port Hueneme in California where its members fell in with Harvey Spencer Lewis, former member of de Guaïta and Péladan's Ordre Kabballistique de la Rose Croix and founder in 1915 of the Ancient and Mystical Order Rosae Crucis (AMORC).

Wheels within wheels within wheels—the story of Mary Heath, a visionary with precocious intellect and an impassioned sense of adventure, is a fantastical account of occult intrigue and spooky shenanigans in mid- to late-nineteenth century Victorian Britain. It is also a story which connects seemingly straightlaced cleric, Reverend Charles Lutwidge Dodgson, to the underground activities of England's mystical Christian enterprise.

In a wider sense, despite its singularly eccentric British character, the tale of Mary Heath is dominated by many of the principle features of Europe's occult scene: ancient Egyptian mysteries, a shadowy German magical sect, French occultists, Hermetic and Templar influences, Christian mysticism, and the all-pervasive invisible presence of the mysterious Orphic Society.

Present day research undertaken by "Dark Journalist" Daniel Liszt and his cohorts indicates that the Orphic Society's practice was to identify young girls aged around ten with mediumistic potential and to bring them into the cult's inner circle for an approximate five-year period. During this time the girls would be encouraged to develop their skills as trance-mediums so that on "graduation" as fully-fledged seers they could be of life-long service to the ultra-secret Society.

Liszt claims that by use of their finely honed esoteric faculties, the teenage mediums would be used to infiltrate powerful groups of high standing in areas such as politics, science, philosophy, the Church, spiritualism, Theosophy and the occult. Once in place they were expected to tap into and report back on matters concerning state secrets, cutting edge thinking on the nature of reality, other dimensions and planes of existence, closely guarded secrets of ancient mystical fraternities and other like areas of vital interest to the furtherance of the Society's occult objectives.

Liszt further makes the sensational claim that around 1862 Alice Liddell, then aged 10, was brought into the Orphic Society for mediumistic development through psychic enthusiast Carroll. Later, when Alice as the widowed Mrs Hargreaves visited America in the 1932 (having lost her husband Reginald in 1926), she is said to have made veiled allusions about this period. No proof supporting these frankly absurd claims exists.

Personally, I reckon there are aspects of the Mary Heath topic that could be argued support an inspirational link with Carroll's storytelling; however, it does not satisfactorily provide a complete solution to the whys and wherefores of how Wonderland emerged from his imagination. I believe we will find the missing pieces of this puzzle in mysterious Wales, a quest we will undertake in upcoming pages.

Lewis Carroll was a man with a Janus profile, one side revealing a kindly soul who loved his mathematical life at Christ Church, his photography, his theatre visits, and, owing to his master-servant relationship with Dean Liddell, the many opportunities to be enjoyed with children and to keep them amused with fantastical tales that he seemingly conjured from thin air. The darker Janus face revealed a man who wrestled to stay afloat in a darker stream of subconscious conflict, one characterised by deeper, more ambivalent attitudes towards children, and also by lifelong spiritual battles that remained largely unalleviated despite his ostensible faith in God and the Chistian Church.

But let us not forget; Carroll was the genius who created Wonderland and the Looking-glass world. Perhaps that genius would not have flourished had it not been seeded with some elements of a darker substance. After all, it has been said that eccentrics provide the condiment for an otherwise bland stew of humanity.

Carroll with George McIntosh's family; Christ Church

The Lady with the Lilacs by Arthur Hughes

Chapter 20

"Secunda"

Then fill up the glasses as quick as you can,
And sprinkle the table with buttons and bran:
Put cats in the coffee, and mice in the tea—
And welcome Queen Alice with thirty-times-three!

Then fill up the glasses with treacle and ink,
Or anything else that is pleasant to drink:
Mix sand with the cider, and wool with the wine
And welcome Queen Alice with ninety-times-nine!

Alice Hargreaves lived with her immortality, gifted to her through her intimate association with a literary masterpiece penned by another's hand, for more than seventy years up to her death on a chill November day in July 1934. Her vicarious fame achieved through Lewis Carroll's books made it hard for the world to visualise Alice as having an independent life outside Wonderland, or even to realise that she did not *really* fall down a hole in pursuit of a talking White Rabbit. People struggled to distinguish between Alice and "Alice".

To the public she was always the longhaired little girl whom John Tenniel drew, an ironic state of affairs because Alice Liddell, who had dark hair cut short with straight bangs across her forehead, was not the model for the original woodcut drawings for Alice in Wonderland. If there was a human model it was probably Mary Hilton Badcock. Carroll sent Tenniel a photo of his childhood friend Mary, recommending that he use her for a model but whether Tenniel accepted that advice is a matter of dispute. That he did not is strongly suggested by these rather petulant lines from a letter Carroll wrote sometime after both of the Alice books had been published:

Mr. Tenniel is the only artist, who has drawn for me, who has resolutely refused to use a model, and declared he no more need one than I should need a multiplication table to work a mathematical problem! I venture to think that he was mistaken and that for want of a model, he drew several pictures of

'Alice' entirely out of proportion — head decidedly too large and feet decidedly too small.

Alice Liddell was the daughter of a distinguished family. The Liddell line can be traced in *Burke's Peerage* under "Ravensworth", the name of the family castle in County Durham, acquired in 1607 in the reign of James I. Staunch royalists in this period, their loyalty was rewarded when Charles I created the first baronetcy of Ravensworth in honour of the family's doughty defence of Newcastle against the Scots during the Civil War.

By the nineteenth century what money might have once enriched the family coffers had long gone, and so Alice's father had to rely on his wits and formidable intelligence to put food on the family table. He proved his mettle by attaining the Vice-Chancellorship of Oxford University and Domestic Chaplaincy to the Prince Consort.

Henry married Lorina Reeve in July 1846. Among their children they would number a Justice of the Peace, Fellow of All Souls College and Counsel to the Speaker of the House of Commons, and a Consul at Lyons and Copenhagen.

The famous three sisters, Ina, Alice and Edith, were born in London where their father was headmaster of Westminster School (1846–1855). The Liddell's first born, 1847, was a boy, Edward Henry, who became "Harry" to everyone (and whom Carroll described as 'certainly the handsomest boy I ever saw,' a comment strangely at odds with a remark he once made that 'boys are not my line; I think they are a mistake').

The Liddell's first daughter was Lorina, born May 1849. A second boy, James Arthur, was born at the end of 1850. Alice came along on 4 May, 1852. A grief-stricken pall descended over the family in November 1853 when James Arthur died after contracting scarlet fever. Lorina Liddell must have been pregnant at the time because a third daughter, Edith, was born in early 1854. The family departed for Oxford in June 1855, Henry having been appointed successor to the recently deceased Dean of Christ Church, Thomas Gaisford.

We noted in the previous chapter that Lewis Carroll met Alice and her sisters for the first time at Easter 1856, the beginning of a friendship with the children that persisted until the spring of 1864 when Mrs Liddell forbade any further social interactions, especially river outings. By then, of course, Carroll had no artistic need for the company of the Liddell girls from which to draw inspiration to write the Wonderland story; he had already written it. And there were plenty of memories left over to fuel the next instalment in Carroll's "Alice" canon. The Looking-glass tale was published Christmas 1871, but post-dated 1872 on the title page

What is not widely known is that the inspiration for the Wonderland tale may well pre-date the River Isis boating period. According to the recollections of time witnesses, its origin lies nearly two-hundred miles north-west of Oxford in the Welsh seaside town of Llandudno and its surrounding Celtic countryside.

In 1859, on the advice of family friends William Gladstone and Sir Henry Acland, Regius Professor of Medicine at Oxford University and Henry's medical adviser, the Liddells travelled to Llandudno by train via Crewe and Chester and then onwards ten miles west to the village of Penmaenmawr to holiday at "Pendyffryn", the family home of Manchester solicitor Samuel Derbishire. Alice was then 7 years old.

This was not the Liddells' first visit to the principality. Henry and Lorina honeymooned in north Wales in 1846. Thirteen years later, Mrs Liddell, having arrived in North Devon to spend a holiday in a property lent by Acland took such a dislike to the region that at her insistence the family, accompanied by Acland and his family, decamped to Wales.

"Pendyffryn" was a fine property built in 1790 in ample parkland. Beside its ornamental lake ran the Chester-Holyhead railway line. "Pendyffryn" boasted its own railway halt on the line. From Penmaenmawr the family could see the Great Orme limestone headland that towers above the delightful seaside town of Llandudno. From Great Orme's 679ft summit one is treated to breathtaking views of Snowdonia, Anglesey and, further, the Isle of Man, Blackpool and the Lake District. The Liddells repeated the trip to "Pendyffryn" in 1860.

The town of Llandudno developed from Stone Age, Bronze Age and Iron Age settlements over many hundreds of years on the slopes of the Great Orme, known to landsmen as the Creuddyn peninsular. Its origins in recorded history begin with the Manor of Gogarth conveyed by King Edward I to Annan, Bishop of Bangor in 1284. The manor comprised three townships: Y Gogarth in the southwest, Y Cyngreawdr in the north and Yn Wyddfid in the southeast.

Large-scale human activity on the Great Orme began around 4,000 years ago during the Bronze Age with the opening of several copper mines. The copper ore malachite was mined using stones and bone tools. The mine was most productive in the period between 1700 BCE and 1400 BCE.

White Rabbit Memorial, West Shore, Llandudno, Wales

A steam engine was introduced into the Great Orme copper mines in 1832 and ten years later an 822-metre-long tunnel was mined at sea level to drain the deeper mine workings. Commercial-scale mining on the Great Orme ended in 1850, although small-scale mining continued until the mines were finally abandoned in 1881. Today, the Great Orme is noted for its Iron Age fort, scattered Stone Age, its sixth century church of St Tudno, and its populatons of wild Kashmir goats (which annoy Llandudno folk by coming down the mountain, running into people's gardens and eating the plants!) and rare Silver Studded Blue Butterflies.

Henry Liddell was impressed with Llandudno and decided to make it the venue for the family's 1861 Easter holiday. The Liddell party (including a footman, a lady's maid, a nurse, a Swiss nursery maid, and 28-year-old governess Mary Prickett) quartered themselves at Tudno Villa, a lodging house owned by Liberal activist Thomas Jones, situated near the northern end of the town's promenade.

According to the 1861 census held that Easter, Llandudno's population, including guests visiting the town, was 1,338. The town was continuing its steady rate of expansion. In the 1840s Llandudno had been principally a mining town with a little agriculture and some fishing. By 1849 leasehold building plots were being auctioned for development. Rapidly, the town grew into a boom resort, attracting middle and upper classes. The Empire Hotel commissioned in 1854 the building of a chemist and a grocer / Italian warehouse. Prior to this there had been a small tin shack, "Pritchards", which supplied grocery needs to local residents. Also in 1854 St George's Hotel was built. 1856 saw the establishment of the town's first omnibus service. Christ Church English Congregational Church was built in 1858, the same year as the town's first pier and the completion of the railway link from Llandudno Junction. One year later disaster struck the town.

On the morning of 25 October 1859 a strengthening northeasterly wind rapidly increased to gale force and hurled huge waves into Llandudno Bay. Accounts describe waves like mountains roaring into the bay and smashing on the site of the present promenade. White foam, like a mist, covered the bay as a hurricane force wind drove the huge breakers ashore. There was unanimous agreement, even amongst experienced seamen, that such waves had never before been witnessed in Llandudno Bay.

In those days a row of thatched cottages stood near the site of the present Washington Hotel. They were overwhelmed by the waves and their inhabitants forced to flee inland. One witness describes watching a kitchen table being carried out to sea with its legs pointing upwards. The new pier was battered mercilessly. Most of the large timbers were torn out, smashed to matchwood and strewn over a wide area of the beach. The report mentions the tollbooth being carried on the crest of a large wave and deposited at the eastern end of the beach. The damage was a fatal blow, not only to the pier, but also to the hopes of establishing a new port at Llandudno. Any chance the town had to challenge Holyhead as the Irish Port disappeared with the demolition of the pier. From now on, Llandudno's future was to be a seaside resort, not a seaport.

The town's main thoroughfare was Mostyn Street, its premises originally built as hotels and only later turned into retail outlets. Upper Mostyn Street was lined with boarding houses. The photographic studio of Thomas Edge was at 12 Gloddaeth Street on the corner of Bodhyfryd Road. Opposite Edge's studio at the corner of Mostyn Street and Gloddaeth Street was George Lowe's jewellery store.

In April 1861 the Liddells commissioned the building of a large house at Penmorfa on Llandudno's west shore, which overlooked Conwy Estuary and the Menai Straits with the mountains of Snowdonia beyond. Penmorfa means "end of the sea marsh". On their way to worship at the Anglican church of St George, Henry Liddell saw in the window of John Copley's architect's practice, at what is now 5 Church Walk, a drawing for a proposed house in pseudo-Gothic style. Liking what he saw, Liddell spent much of the Easter break searching for a suitable site before leasing from Mostyn Estate office a building plot, eventually to be named "Penmorfa" in honour of its location. Church Walk was then the only road linking the two shores of Llandudno. At the same time, Liddell commissioned the building works.

The Liddells next returned to Llandudno for their summer holiday of 1861, this time staying at St. George's Hotel, to enable the Dean to oversee some arrangements for building the house. They were back at Llandudno at Easter 1862 for a further reconnaissance trip, the family staying once again at St. George's from where on Easter Monday Henry Liddell wrote a letter to Gladstone. During this visit Liddell was very unhappy with the slow progress of building work. He started legal proceedings against Copley for overcharging of professional fees and paid off the contractor. Work was transferred to Robert R. Williams & Sons of Bank Quay, Caernarfon who put his son Richard and 40 men on the job.

In her letters describing the Easter 1862 trip, Alice referred to her 'rambles over the Great Orme,' which were reached via Cust's Path, a hazardous footway cut into the cliffs operated by Mostyn Estate for a toll of a penny (1d). Gladstone was once very embarrassed to have to ask for assistance when he became frightened while traversing the steep paths on the Orme with the Liddells. He had to shut his eyes while being led to safety.

During the lengthy slog up to the Orme's chalky grasslands, the Liddell party was rewarded by dramatic scenes of red-legged choughs wheeling round newly made cliff-face nests. Miss Prickett admonished the children not to stray out of sight and to keep away from old mine workings.

One of their favourite destinations on the Orme was the pretty church of St Tudno's. According to local tradition, St Tudno was one of the seven sons of the sixth century Welsh King, Seithenyn, whose legendary kingdom of Cantref y Gwaelod in Cardigan Bay was submerged by tidal activity. The legend relates how Tudno enrolled for study at St. Dunawd's College in the monastery of Bangor Iscoed in recompense for the drunken incompetence of his father, which had led to the loss of the kingdom under the waves. Penance completed and seeking a place to live out the religious life, Tudno travelled to the Great Orme to bring the message of Christianity to its people. He lived firstly as a hermit in a small, nigh inaccessible cave known as Ogof Llech, which provided protection from the elements and fresh water from Fynnon Llech spring. While quartered in this primitive hermitage Tudno constructed a church. Nothing remains of his original building and it was its twelfth century successor church that drew the Liddells to explore. Overlooking the sea, St Tudno's is situated two hundred yards from the cliff edge on the Orme's northeast flank. Together with its extensive cemetery and chapel to the west, it occupies a roughly shaped reactangular area with sides of around three hundred yards. In Alice's day the church was not in good repair. In 1839 the roof had been damaged by a severe storm and the church authorities deemed it a waste of funds to make the necessary repairs. Instead, they built in the following year a new church dedicated to St Tudno in Church Walk when Llandudno was little more than a village. The church's interior has few ancient features except for its twelfth century font, some early sepulchral stones, a rood beam bearing a carved serpent in the chancel and one remarkable medieval survival: a carved wooden roof boss high above the chancel step depicting the "stigmata" or five wounds of Christ.

Also during the Easter break the family visited Alice's cousin, Lady Florentia Hughes, at "Kinmel", a mansion near the small town of Abergele, fourteen miles from Llandudno. The house was built in splendid parkland behind the estate of St George. At the time, the Hughes were occupying only a part of the house, the rest of it having been destroyed by fire in 1841. Alice and Florentia were great-granddaughters of Sir Henry George Liddell, the 5th baronet (coat of arms depicting a red trellis on a field of silver, surmounted by the gold faces of 3 lions on a red field).

Alice also befriended Marianne Rigby, nicknamed Polly, and her younger sister, Susie. Polly was a few months older than Alice. The sisters had been orphaned in 1860 on the death of their father Dr Edward Rigby, their mother Marianne (née Derbishire) having died in 1853. Consequently, grandparents Samuel and Mary Derbishire brought up the girls at "Pendyffryn". In 1875 Marianne Rigby married John Greaves, the son of the founder of Llechwedd Slate Mines at Blaenau Ffestiniog. Today Llechwedd offers a wealth of Wonderland background scenery: multiple holes and caverns, a dramatic underground "Pool of Tears" used a set for two Hollywood film productions, a Victorian "sheep shop", unusual trains, a perfect mock Tudor Disraeli/Gladstone house, and an open air "tea party" table.

On the day that the Liddell family took possession of their new holiday home, 16 August 1862, the grateful Dean provided a formal celebration supper of roast, beef, plum pudding and beer, presided over by builder Robert Williams. Dean Liddell briefly addressed the men, who responded by endorsing the chairman's toast: 'The health of the Very Reverend Dean and his family, and long life and happiness to them.' A few days later the children and their governess were photographed on the steps of the house, for which the Dean decided to preserve the name of "Penmorfa".

Did Lewis Carroll visit Llandudno in this period? The members of the Llandudno and Colwyn Bay History Society believe so. The Society claims[73] that the man striking an artistic pose in the photo overleaf of "Penmorfa" is almost certainly Carroll. There appear to be three other people present, one of which may well be 10-year-old Alice.

---

[73] https://historypoints.org/index.php?page=site-of-alice-liddell-s-holiday-home-west-shore

"Penmorfa"—the man in foreground is believed to be
Lewis Carroll, and the child to his right Alice Liddell

The photo was in an album that Carroll presented to Alice. Also in the album was a photo from the zigzag path behind the property. The question as to the identity of the photographer is undetermined. Some researchers claim that in late 1862 Carroll acquired photographs taken by Thomas Edge of the newly built "Penmorfa" and gave them to Alice Liddell in a presentation album that Christmas. Those that support this theory suggest that Carroll knew of the photos because his friend, Viscountess Newry, mother of Francis, Earl of Kilmorey, lodged above Lowe's jewellers during August and September 1862. It has been suggested that Carroll visited Newry

Other investigators believe that it was Carroll who took the photo. He would have posed Alice, her family and himself and then instructed an assistant, perhaps Edge, to remove the lens cap for the 30-second exposure.

The debate surrounding Carroll's putative presence in Llandudno during the Liddell's visits has been a hot topic since 1933 when the White Rabbit memorial in celebration of Carroll's centenary was unveiled on the West Shore by former Prime Minister David Lloyd George. Local stonemason Frederick Forrester chiselled an inscription: 'On this very shore, during happy rambles with Alice Liddell, LEWIS CARROLL was inspired to write the literary treasure Alice in Wonderland,' words presumably expressing the sentiments of the memorial's commissioners, most likely the town council.

Also in this year, Mrs Hargreaves was asked if Carroll had visited "Penmorfa". The elderly Alice confirmed in the affirmative when she replied, 'It could not have been before 1862, as we were not there then,' from which circuitous remark one deduces an Easter visit.

In his book Chris Draper[74] quotes from a booklet published by the Llandudno Memorial Committee at the time of the unveiling in 1933. Its sources are unknown but the booklet claimed that 'Lewis Carroll was a frequent visitor to Llandudno as a guest of Dean Liddell at "Penmorfa," and it was Carroll's rambles on the West Shore with Dean Liddell's little girl, Alice, that inspired him to write the book, and it is known that Carroll would read his manuscript to the family at the fireside in the evening at "Penmorfa".'

Moreover, if one stands in front of the Penmorfa location, one can see below the cliffs two rocks reaching up from the shoreline. Their close resemblance to Tenniel's subsequent illustrations of the Walrus

---

[74] Draper C., *Walks from Llandudno*, Llygad Gwalch Cyf, 2010.

and the Carpenter suggests that Carroll saw them in situ prior to his first telling of the Alice in Wonderland story, sketched or photographed them quite possibly during the Easter trip that year, and made the reproductions subsequently available to Tenniel.

Additionally, in a conversation in 1907 between Sir James Crichton Browne and Sir William Richmond, the latter said he saw Carroll at "Penmorfa" writing part of the Alice story. The case seems fairly and squarely proven.

The Liddells spent nine summers in Llandudno until the spread of the town finally encroached too much on the peace and quiet of Penmorfa for the Liddells to bear. In April 1872 the Liddells severed links with Penmorfa. A Mr Taylor offered what was then the huge sum of £2000 for the house. The offer was considered at length and, finally and regretfully, accepted.

We arrive at a bewitching conclusion. Based on a balance of probability, there is sufficient weight of evidence in the Liddells's Llandudno presence to indicate strongly that the seeds for the Wonderland story were sewn not in the hallowed college halls and riverside haunts of Oxford but in the Celtic heartland of Wales.

Above all else, *Alice in Wonderland* and its follow-up *Through the Looking-glass* are fairy tales, and Wales is blessed with a rich trove of myths and legends concerning the wee folk (in Welsh the Tylwyth Teg—the Fair Family). So expansive is the tradition and so highly populated is the Celts' invisible race that long ago the Welsh decided to divide its fairy brethren into five distinct classes: the Ellyllon that haunt the groves and valleys, and correspond with the English elves; the Coblynau, or mine fairies; the Bwbachod, or household fairies; the Gwragedd Annwn, or fairies of the lakes and streams; and the Gwyllion, or mountain fairies. The Ellyllon are the tiny elves. The English word "elf" is probably derived from the Welsh el, a spirit, and elf, an element. It would be remarkable if Carroll had not been acquainted with these aspects of Welsh fairy lore.

Moreover, through conversations with locals Carroll may have known of a truly bizarre incident that occurred a few years before the Liddells' bought "Penmorfa", and whose supernatural elements would surely have provided a budding children's storyteller with enticing material for a gripping tale of enchantment. One night David Williams, a servant living at Penrhyndeudraeth thirty or so miles southwest of Llandudno, was walking some distance behind his mistress, carrying home a flitch (a side) of bacon. He arrived back three hours later insisting he had been gone for only three minutes. He told of how he had seen a meteor overhead and a hoop of fire. In the hoop were standing a handsomely dressed man and woman of small size. With one arm they embraced each other and with the other they held on to the hoop, their feet resting on its concave surface. When the hoop reached the earth the pair jumped out and immediately inscribed a circle on the ground. Out of the circle emerged a large number of Little People, men and women, who straightaway danced around to the sound of sweet music. A subdued light lit up the ground. After a while the meteor and hoop returned. The pair boarded and went off and the fairies vanished from the circle.

This true-life account describes human forms descending to earth and making a circle from which emerge fairy folk dancing to music. From these elements it is a small leap for a fertile mind such as Carroll's to visualise a little girl's time-bending passage down a rabbit hole, and the subsequent appearance of a deep pool of tears and its host of talking, singing and dancing animals with which an enchanted youngster runs a Caucus race.

Being a well read savant, it is likely too that Carroll was familiar with The Mabinogion, a collection of early medieval Welsh stories that connects to ancient Celtic mythology and provides the first literary mentions of King Arthur and Guinevere. The Mabinogion is steeped in magic and traces of fairy-lore and fairy-glamour, the use of concealment, deception and transformation, abound in its pages.

Of the several features that explicitly demonstrate the fairy presence in The Mabinogion, one is reminded of Alice's adventures in *Through the Looking-glass*. Characters in the Mabinogion tales can travel with a telltale gliding motion, most notably Rhiannon in the story of Pwyll; and she cannot be pursued either slowly or quickly but always mysteriously moves ahead of those following her. This gait is distinctively fairy-like and echoes Alice's experience in the company of the Red Queen:

> Just at this moment, somehow or other, they began to run. Alice never could quite make out, in thinking it over afterwards, how it was that they began: all she remembers is, that they were running hand in hand, and the Queen went so fast that it was all she could do to keep up with her: and still the Queen kept crying 'Faster! Faster!' but Alice felt she could not go faster, though she had not breath left to say so.

316

The most curious part of the thing was, that the trees and the other things round them never changed their places at all: however fast they went, they never seemed to pass anything. 'I wonder if all the things move along with us?' thought poor puzzled Alice. And the Queen seemed to guess her thoughts, for she cried, 'Faster! Don't try to talk!'

Not that Alice had any idea of doing that. She felt as if she would never be able to talk again, she was getting so much out of breath: and still the Queen cried 'Faster! Faster!' and dragged her along. 'Are we nearly there?' Alice managed to pant out at last.

'Nearly there!' the Queen repeated. 'Why, we passed it ten minutes ago! Faster!'

'Now! Now!' cried the Queen. 'Faster! Faster!' And they went so fast that at last they seemed to skim through the air, hardly touching the ground with their feet, till suddenly, just as Alice was getting quite exhausted, they stopped, and she found herself sitting on the ground, breathless and giddy.

The Queen propped her up against a tree, and said kindly, 'You may rest a little now.'

Alice looked round her in great surprise. 'Why, I do believe we've been under this tree the whole time! Everything's just as it was!'

'Of course it is,' said the Queen, 'what would you have it?'

Well, in our country,' said Alice, still panting a little, 'you'd generally get to somewhere else—if you ran very fast for a long time, as we've been doing.'

'A slow sort of country!' said the Queen. 'Now, here, you see, it takes all the running you can do, to keep in the same place. If you want to get somewhere else, you must run at least twice as fast as that!'

Wales is a Celtic nation with a profoundly important mythic heritage. At the same time, Wales is also a nation component of the British Isles, a northern land described by ancient historians as the source of a powerful spiritual force that is vital for our planet's continual wellbeing.

An understanding of Britain's unique role as a provider of spiritual nourishment brings us closer to finding the door to Wonderland, an enchanted realm that we shall shortly discover is paved with philosophers' stones.

Queen Alice between sleeping White Queen and Red Queen;
Alice, Ina and Edith Liddell

Long-necked Alice!

Barry Lawton's beautiful limited edition model of "Penmorfa" (mine here is No. 3 of 500). Alice Liddell's room is the top right in the picture.

Chapter 21

Avalon

Alice could not help her lips curling up into a smile as she began:
'Do you know, I always thought Unicorns were fabulous monsters,
too? I never saw one alive before!' 'Well, now that we have seen
each other,' said the Unicorn, 'if you'll believe in me, I'll believe in
you. Is that a bargain?'

—Through the Looking-glass

We noted in earlier pages that in ancient historical writings one finds
references to certain realms that are not physically present in our world
but which nevertheless exert a powerful grip on the human imagination.
Two such enchanted regions were Thule and Hyperborea, mythic lands
draped in perpetual sunshine where its peoples enjoy utopian existence.

Although many chroniclers were content to describe these realms
as purely make-believe, others insisted that they had tangible physical
form. Historians in the latter camp such as Pytheas of Massalia and
Pliny the Elder claimed that Thule lies six-days travel north of Britain,
while Hecataeus of Abdera, for example, said that Britain itself was the
location of Hyperborea. Drawing on unnamed sources, Hecataeus said
that Britain possessed a sacred precinct of Apollo and a notable temple,
spherical in shape. Some scholars identified the temple with
Stonehenge, others with Avebury, or the megaliths of Callanish on the
Isle of Lewis in Scotland.

In Gaelic and Brittonic myth the Otherworld is not merely a
distant, fantastical realm; it is an integral part of Celtic cosmology. The
Gaulish druids believed that the soul went to an Otherworld before
being reincarnated. Byzantine scholar Procopius of Caesarea described
the ancient Gauls' belief that the land of the dead from which souls
reincarnate anew lies west of Britain.

The myths describe how once the souls of the dead had left their
bodies, they travelled to the northwest coast of Gaul and took a boat
toward Britain. When they crossed the Channel, the souls went to the
homes of the fishermen and knocked desperately at their doors. The
fishermen then went out of their houses and led the souls to their

destination in ghostly ships. There are still remains of those beliefs in the folklore of Brittany, where the name Bag an Noz is used to denote those ships who carry the dead to their destination.

Celts in ancient Britain saw in the sun's passage through the heavens a symbolic representation of an individual's mystical passage through life. At dawn the sun appeared to rise from Annwen, the underworld. In the daylight hours, it traversed Abred, the physical plane, the world of trial, test and experiment, the university of the physical curriculum from which man must continually strive to evolve. At night it sank into Gwynvyd, the sphere of the conscious and wholly developed spirit in perfect man. Britain's esoteric tradition makes it clear that the goal of man was to attain a passage into Gwynvyd by an initiatory process to find the Cauldron of Inspiration and to drink from its magical waters.

Similarly, many eminent authorities have argued that Shambhala is based in Britain, or even corresponds geographically to the whole of the British Isles. This amazing notion is supported by Geoffrey Ashe:[75]

> … a belief among the lamas that about 543 BCE, towards the end of Buddha's life… a European came to him to be taught the wisdom of Shambhala. This man, the lamas suspected, was a Celt. They believed that the Shambhalic "presence"… was transplanted to Britain… Nothing shows in what sense Shambhala was established in Britain, or whether it ever ceased to be there, and if so, how and why it disappeared… In terms of history I suppose the notion would have to be that initiates of some kind carried Shambhalic lore westwards, and planted it in a British centre. This would still have been important at the time when Britain was the headquarters of Druid teaching… The impression is that the lamas thought the British Shambhala (whatever it was) ceased to function a long time ago. This might only mean that, from their point of view, it did not count any more after the advent of Christianity. The 'island' Shambhala might be Celtic Britain itself or, of course, it might be the Isle of Avalon.

Buddhist historian Stephen Jenkins[76] reaffirms the notion:

---

[75] Ashe, G., *The Ancient Wisdom*, Macmillan, 1977.
[76] Jenkins, S., *The Undiscovered Country: Adventures in Ufology, Tibetan Buddhism, and Other Dimensions of Reality*, New Saucerian Press, 2017.

I was considerably taken aback when I began my instruction in the secret doctrines of the realm of Shambhala to be told by high-ranking Mongolian lamas... that it had had a literal existence on the surface of the earth, and that it had lain far to the west. In the last 100 years discussion of the problem among them had narrowed down the possibilities, and opinion was now unanimous. The Kingdom of Shambhala had once been, they said, in the Island of Britain, the Celtic Britain of the last centuries before Christ.

Lewis Spence, a great authority on magic, mysticism and Celtic folklore, wrote:[77]

> To the peoples of antiquity the isle of Britain was the very home and environment of mystery, a sacred territory, to enter which was to encroach upon a region of enchantment, the dwelling of gods, the shrine and habitation of a cult of peculiar sanctity and mystical power. Britain was the insula sacra of the West, an island veiled and esoteric, the Egypt of the Occident... in the early centuries... Britain was regarded as specifically sacred, *an enclosure of the gods.*

Christine Hartley, a pupil of British magician and celebrated occultist Dion Fortune,[78] offers more food for thought, including a fascinating morsel that describes Orme's Head as one of Britain's holy places:

> Merrie does not mean gay; it is from an old German word which means Fairy. Merrie England was Fairyland or - later - Maryland. It was the Holy Land of the West... At one time the whole Island of Britain was called Insula Pomorum, or Isle of Apples, and though subsequently this title was confined to Glastonbury, it shows how in the early days that set-apartness of our land was recognised. All through Britain may be greater and lesser mounds - the holier places in a holy land - and where there are traces of serpent worship and a mound, there will have been a seat of Druid culture and pre-Druid worship. Arthur's Seat in Edinburgh, the town of Eden in Westmorland, Cader Idris (Arthur's Chair) in Snowdonia,

---

[77] Spence L. *The Mysteries of Britain*, Rider, London, 1928.
[78] Hartley, C., *The Western Mystery Tradition*, Aquarian Press, 1968.

the Tor at Avalon, the old ruin on Great Orme's Head called Gogarth, which must surely be a corruption of God's Garth or Orchard - all these are holy places in this holy land.

Hartley stressed the importance of Brtain's Druid priesthood, pointing out that Roman philosophers regarded its members as examples of wisdom and models for imitation on account of their pre-eminent merit. After all, remarked Clement of Alexandria, the Druids owed nothing to Pythagoras as so often claimed. Indeed, Pythagoras visited the Druids, whom he believed were descended from the Atlantean priesthood, to be instructed in their theology and mysteries, aware that there was considerable resemblance between some of the Druid beliefs and symbols and those of the Brahmans.

Why should the apparently insignificant small land of the Britons have been afforded by the ancients the prestige of being the location of the magical realm of Hyperborea, Shambhala and the Celtic Otherworld? Remarkably, it appears that in the metaphysical sense this little island was, and continues to be, a uniquely special place in the context of its pan-global influence upon humankind and its spiritual evolution.

I have written elsewhere[79] of the late Grace Cooke, an acclaimed British medium who conveyed her esoteric teachings through a spirit energy known as White Eagle. Cooke's guide described Hyperborea as an ancient paradise realm whose inhabitants were the "God-Men" from the great Sun Brotherhood, 'the perfect sons of God who came as guardians of a young race on a young planet.'[80]

White Eagle stated that these god-men impregnated the very stones with the light of their being from the upper worlds. He added that Britain's isles were a part of Hyperborea and, later, Atlantis. Because of the tremendous power released into Britain by the Sun Brotherhood, many ancient people journeyed to these Isles after the Biblical Flood and established mystery centres of great light and wisdom. Such, said White Eagle, were the beginnings of the noble and learned Celtic races.

Long, long ago, the spirit-guide explained, humans descended from their original "god-man" form in accordance with a divine plan. Gradually, man underwent a process of descent in order to inhabit a physical vehicle, which, in its turn, had evolved from a lower state of life, stage by stage, until the brain had developed to such a degree that it

---

[79] Graddon, N., *The Gods in the Fields*, AUP, 2020.
[80] Cooke, G., *The Light in Britain*, White Eagle Publishing Trust, 1971.

could begin to comprehend the power and beauty of the God-force within. This process entailed not just a development of the physical body but also the development of the subtler bodies that clothe the spirit of man. This was the divine plan and process of man's fall (the Adam and Eve story), brought into play in order that in time there would be awakened in man his self-conscious, which would lead in time to God consciousness and realisation.

The "evil"—the serpent—was man's love of power, a mental craving that asserts itself in man's lower aspect. At the same time, the fall ("evil") also caused development and growth of man's individual soul and mind. Therefore, in accordance with the principle of reciprocity, "evil" produced individualisation, a necessary part of man's evolutionary growth, without which there would be no stimulus or desire to grow to become a more complete, perfected "Son of God".

Expanding on this teaching, White Eagle explained that there is a world composed of finer ethers just within our own "solid" world. Long ago the ancient masters taught that the heaven world is not beyond the stars but is a plane that is here, around us all the time, interpenetrating all physical life. White Eagle reiterated this teaching, clarifying that this world of "finer ethers" is not the spirit world after death but a realm or dimension closer to Earth. Here the ancient Brethren of the Sun live and worship in the Sun temples and Sun cities.

The Brethren of the Sun, the "Sun-Men", arrived in this world after the fall, coming to a land submerged by the waters so very long ago, long before Atlantis. They came to this planet in the form of an indescribably beautiful light, the spiritual Sun. White Eagle explained that the Sun-Men were messengers from the Brotherhood of the Cross of Light within the Circle of Light: the Great White Brotherhood, which since the beginning of life on Earth has had mankind in its care.

Their purpose was to bring wisdom to a humanity in its infancy so that it might learn the Law of God and to eventually break the bondage of physical matter and return to full spiritual awareness and consciousness with the Godforce. In the distant past White Eagle had been an initiate of this Brotherhood.

White Eagle spoke many times on the role of Britain in the continual battles between the forces of Light and Darkness.

> Throughout the ages the light of the sun brothers has been centred within... this mystic isle, a sacred domain, thousands and thousands years since. They travelled all over the earth but this isle was their home. They had great knowledge... of

physics, of the proportions of matter. This knowledge and influence still lingers, hidden; we [Britons] are the inheritors of an ancient wisdom, a great light.

He said that in the Atlantean period there was a tremendous battle on the etheric plane between these forces. The dark priests of Atlantis gained knowledge of a destructive power that would have destroyed the earth. A great battle took place at Dragon Hill in Britain (situated immediately below the Uffington White Horse in Oxfordshire), which manifested right through to the physical plane. The forces of darkness were defeated. Subsequently, the Dragon Hill area became a principal centre for the enactment of powerful ceremonies in which the forces of nature played a vital part.

Cooke's spirit sight observed one such occasion in which was gathered in the amphitheatre below Dragon Hill a great assembly for a mighty ceremony of sun worship. Twelve high priests standing on the top of the hill summoned the great angels of the White Light. Among the celestial beings present were representatives of the four orders of the Elemental nature spirits. An ever-rising spiral of golden light filled the amphitheatre, its radiation appearing as a fountain of light that cascaded brilliantly over the earth. A great being, a cosmic Christ-form, appeared in the light. Then appeared another figure, a king wearing a crown of gold and robed in light, the points of his crown emitting rays of great brilliance. This great "knight of the spirit" is symbolised as King Ar-Thor, the ancient King of Hyperborea who had come to bring blessings for a ceremony convened to show people how to overcome man's material self (the "slaying of the dragon"), and, later, as St. George.

White Eagle taught that centres of the ancient brotherhood have been established in many countries but he declared that Britain, which he described as the Grail Chalice of the planet, was the first home of the white brothers of the Hyperborea regions. These centres cannot be discerned with the naked eye because they occupy a higher dimension. The brotherhood is engaged in slowing down the vibration of the etheric plane in which it exists until its members can once again come amongst humanity to impart their knowledge to those willing to listen and to understand. He added:

> The age of Earth's humanity is beyond man's calculation; many, many civilisations and continents now submerged of which we know nothing. The human race is not highly evolved

but will be when the secret ancient spiritual power in Britain is released and the whole vibration of the earth is raised accordingly. Dragon Hill is one area where the god-men left their blessings for future races of men.

The Sun-priests were almost worshipped as gods in acknowledgement of their supernatural control over the elements and because of the light they had brought from the celestial spheres to Britain, long before the young earth had fully solidified. The God-men travelled here on rays from the higher spheres and dimensions, all rays converging on the Isle of Britain. Avebury and Stonehenge mark the place where the cosmic rays meet. By breath alone the Sun-priests could raise giant weights or raze buildings to the ground.

White Eagle said that these circles and at other points all over Britain are located the chakras of this mystic isle. They played a vital role in the enactment of rituals to bring about the physical manifestation of life from the etheric world. The Avebury Temple was a great creative centre on this planet, the heart of ancient and powerful ceremonies. The communities in the surrounding hills, peopled by a race that White Eagle said originated in the Greek part of the world, came to the temple to witness and participate in extraordinary marvels.

Avebury was associated with the moon and with obeisance to the moon goddess. The goddess was enthroned upon Silbury Hill. The ancient mother-ritual, which eventually brought about the creation of life in physical form, came from Mu, the Motherland. The rituals invoked the invisible power of the gods and then concentrated upon the movement of the cells and the building up of form. The stones came into physical manifestation from the etheric forms created by ritual, all the stone temples in Britain being created in this manner. All things created in the Avebury Temple were steeped in music and harmony (the "Music of the Spheres") and reflected the harmony of the Cosmos, the whole interacting with higher intelligences and the Universal Powers.

Avebury and Stonehenge, entrances into the inner worlds, served also as temples of magic. Fairies, elementals and all other constituents of etheric life united with the Sun-priests to perform inconceivable acts of power. In these rituals the bluestones brought from the fairy-ruled mountains of Prescelly in Wales played a vital role. These stones had the power to draw forth the fairies and the souls of the stones.

Lewis Carroll's stories similarly possess a tremendous hidden power, a timeless magical force that reveals its subtle presence to those who are pulled again and again to re-visit and share in Alice's adventures. During a discourse on nature spirits White Eagle revealed the true source of inspiration for Carroll's Wonderland stories:

Did we tell you of the ability of... elemental creatures to grow to a great size if necessary, or to diminish their size? This is one of their attributes. That remarkable book 'Alice in Wonderland' deals with this happening. Do you think that book came only from the mind of its writer? Do you not see that such a story originated from the sylphs [the elemental air spirits of the air] trying to teach humans great mystical truths? If you want to learn mysticism... read your fairy stories again. You will learn some beautiful truths if you ponder on what they have to tell you.

The power of ancient Hyperborea endures. White Eagle taught that what is happening in our day is the bringing into manifestation from the very soil of Britain the true light of global spiritual brotherhood. This is a truly sublime magical-mystical process felt in the hearts of those who are open to its divine energies.

Through Grace Cooke, White Eagle said that Britain is the omphalos for this global renewal of divine power in which Ar-thor, the Once and Future King, aided by the Sun-Men and the forces of Living Nature, will re-emerge to do final battle with the forces of darkness.

Lewis Carroll, who, we shall see, was a true mystic, illuminated his Alice tales with the magical sunlight of a Hyperborean "golden afternoon", and, for good measure, paved its pathways with philosophers' stones.

Do not let it be forgotten that there is a native Mystery Tradition of our race which has its mature aspect in the sun-worship of the Druids and the beautiful fairy-lore of the Celts, its philosophical aspect in the traditions of alchemy, and its spiritual aspect in the Hidden Church of the Holy Grail, the Church behind the Church, not made with hands, eternal in the heavens. All these have their holy places, mounds and pools of initiation, which are part of our spiritual inheritance. Let those who follow the Inner Way study our native tradition, and re-discover and re-sanctify its holy places. Let them keep vigil in the high places when the cosmic tides are flowing, and the Powers of the Unseen are changing guard and the rituals of the Invisible Church are being worked near the earth.

—Dion Fortune, *Avalon of the Heart*

'Proserpine', Dante Gabriel Rossetti, 1874

Chapter 22

Alice and the Rosy Cross

... a few times in my life, I've seen things. Things I can't explain. And I've come to believe it's not so much what you believe. It's how hard you believe it.

—*Indiana Jones and the Dial of Doom*

In the Preface to *Sylvia and Bruno Concluded*, Carroll wrote of our capabilities in attaining various degrees of psychic states. He set out his ideas in the context of Human/Fairy interaction. He said:

> ... supposing that Fairies really existed; and that they were sometimes visible to us, and we to them; and that they were sometimes able to assume human form: and supposing, also, that human beings might sometimes become conscious of what goes on in the Fairy-world—by actual transference of their immaterial essence, such as we meet with in "Esoteric Buddhism". I have supposed a Human being to be capable of various psychical states, with varying degrees of consciousness, as follows:
>
> > (a) the ordinary state, with no consciousness of the presence of Fairies;
> > (b) the "eerie" state, in which, while conscious of actual surroundings, he is also conscious of the presence of Fairies;
> > (c) a form of trance, in which, while unconscious of actual surroundings, and apparently asleep, he (i.e. his immaterial essence) migrates to other scenes, in the actual world, or in Fairyland, and is conscious of the presence of Fairies.
>
> I have also supposed a Fairy to be capable of migrating from Fairyland into the actual world, and of assuming... a Human form; and also to be capable of various psychical states, viz.

(a) the ordinary state, with no consciousness of the presence of Human beings;

(b) a sort of eerie state, in which he is conscious, if in the actual world, of the presence of actual Human beings; if in Fairyland, of the presence of the immaterial essences of Human beings.

In Madame Blavatsky's introduction to her *Secret Doctrine*, we recognize the source of Carroll's philosophical belief system:

Since the appearance of Theosophical literature in England, it has become customary to call its teachings "Esoteric Buddhism".

David Day[81] explains that Carroll's interest in theosophy long preceded Madame Blavatsky's Theosophical Society. As Carroll was aware—and as his Oxford colleague Max Müller explained in his *Theosophy, or Psychological Religion*—the term theosophy was coined by the Alexandrian mystics and Neoplatonists of the fourth century AD. It was derived from the Greek theosophia, meaning "god-wisdom" or "knowledge of the divine". It entered the English language in the seventeenth century and came to mean "wisdom about God and nature obtained through mystical study".

Day suggests that Carroll's writing was profoundly influenced by Rosicrucian teachings, and that Alice's descent down a rabbit-hole into Wonderland has an historic precedent in the publication of *Cabala, Mirror of Art and Nature: in Alchemy*. Published in 1615 by Steffan Michelspacher, the work was dedicated 'to the Brotherhood of the Rosy Cross; than which in this matter let no fuller statement be desired.'

Rosicrucianiam is a worldwide brotherhood claiming to possess esoteric wisdom handed down from ancient times. The movement arose in Bohemia in the early seventeenth century, and rapidly spread throughout Europe. Pointedly, in Britain it was particularly influential in Oxford. Its name derives from the order's symbol, a rose on a cross, which is similar to Martin Luther's family coat of arms. It is also theorized that the term derives from "Ros" and "Crux"—alchemical terms connected with dew as a solvent of gold, and crux as the equivalent of Light.

---

[81] Day, D., *Alice's Adventures in Wonderland Decoded*, Doubleday Canada, Random House, 2015.

Rosicrucian Mountain of Alchemy topped by a rose garden

Rosicrucian teachings are a combination of occultism and other religious beliefs and practices, including Hermeticism, Jewish mysticism and Christian Gnosticism. The central feature of Rosicrucianism is the belief that its members possess secret wisdom handed down from generation to generation. Its sacred mission was to advance and inspire the arts and sciences through the study of symbolic and spiritual alchemy. Initiates were instructed to undergo certain rites of passage that resulted in the attainment of ancient esoteric knowledge.

The origins and teachings of the Rosicrucians are described in three anonymously published books that have been attributed to Johann Valentin Andreae (1568–1654), a Lutheran theologian and teacher who wrote the utopian treatise *Christianopolis* (1619). *The Fama Fraternitatis of the Meritorious Order of the Rosy Cross* (1614) and *The Confession of the Rosicrucian Fraternity* (1615), which two together constitute the Rosicrucian Manifestos, and also *The Chymical Marriage of Christian Rosenkreuz* (1616), which recounts the travels of Father C.R.C. or Christian Rosenkreuz, the putative founder of the group.

According to the books, Rosenkreuz was born in 1378 and lived for 106 years. After visiting the Middle East and North Africa in search of secret wisdom, he returned to Germany and organized the Rosicrucian order (1403). He erected a sanctuary (1409), where he was entombed after his death in 1484. The alleged discovery of the tomb 120 years later became the occasion for the public announcement of the order's existence.

The secretive nature of the early brotherhood would have made contact with it difficult. The combination of alchemy and mysticism associated with it, however, became quite influential. Rosicrucianism was attractive to many thinkers throughout Europe, including Goethe and the English philosopher and scientist Francis Bacon.

The overall theme of the *Fama* is the discovery or, rather, the re-discovery of an ancient philosophy, primarily alchemical and related to the healing arts but also concerned with number and geometry, all ingredients underlining the importance of the document as a pathway to illumination of a religious and spiritual nature. The story emphasises the importance of the miraculous discovery in 1604 of the vault housing the body of Brother Rosenkreutz.

The allegory of the vault and its everlasting light is a central feature of the Roscicrucian legend. The sun never shines in the vault, which is eternally lit by an inner sun. Geometrical figures adorn the walls.

Treasures lie all around, including the works of Paracelsus, magical bells, lamps and "artificial songs".

In his *Secret Teachings of All Ages*, Manly P. Hall describes four distinct theories regarding the Rosicrucian enigma. The first proposes that the Order existed historically in accordance with the description of its foundation and subsequent activities published in the *Fama Fraternitatis*. To assist in bringing about the reformation to counter past egotism and greed, a poor person called "The Highly Illuminated Father C.R.C.", a German noble by birth, instituted the Secret Society of the Rosy Cross. At the age of five, C.R.C. was placed in a cloister, much later associating himself with a brother of Holy Orders who died while they were travelling in Cyprus. After studying in Damascus, Damcar (a place that has never been identified) and in Fez, C.R.C. journeyed to Spain where he was ridiculed by the intelligentsia. Not discouraged, C.R.C. returned to Germany for five years of contemplative study before renewing his struggle for a reformation in the arts and sciences of his day. He went to the cloister where his early training had been received and called to him three brethren whom he bound by an inviolable oath to preserve the secrets he would impart.

Hall's second theory explores the belief held in some quarters that the Fraternity originated in medieval Europe as an outgrowth of alchemical philosophy. This theory proposes that Johann Valentin Andreae was the true founder of Rosicrucianism, reforming and amplifying a society that had been previously founded by German Renaissance polymath, physician and occultist Sir Henry Cornelius Agrippa. Some believed that Rosicrucianism represented the first invasion into Europe of Buddhist and Brahmic culture. Still others held that the society was founded in Egypt and that it also perpetuated the mysteries of ancient Chaldea and Persia. Whatever its origins the Order, incredibly, was able to retain absolute secrecy for many centuries.

Thirdly, Hall submits the theory that there never was a Rosicrucian Order, which was no more than a satire to ridicule the gullibility of Europe's intelligentsia. Nevertheless, the mystery has resulted in endless controversies and has occupied some of the finest minds in the history of Europe mysticism: scholars such as Michael Maier, Eugenius Philalethes (Thomas Vaughan) and Robert Fludd.

The final proposal, Hall explains, has a transcendental premise, asserting that the Rosicrucians actually did possess all the supernatural powers with which they were credited; that they were literally citizens of two worlds (much like Agent Cooper), being able to function fully consciously in both a physical and an etheric body, the latter not subject to the laws of time and space. These adepts were conversant with the very highest mysteries that concerned the quest to regenerate through a process of transmutation the "base elements" of man's lower nature into the "gold" of intellectual and spiritual realisation.

Rosicrucian initiates taught that spiritual nature was attached to the physical form at certain points, symbolised by the three nails of the crucifixion. By three alchemical processes they were able to draw these nails and permit the divine nature of Man to come down from its cross. They concealed the processes by which this was accomplished under three alchemical metaphorical expressions: "The Casting of the Molten Sea", "The Making of the Rose Diamond", and "The Achieving of the Philosopher's Stone". The mystic believes that the true Brethren of the Rosy Cross exist in the inner planes of Nature and may only be reached by those who can transcend the limitations of the material world. To substantiate this view the mystic quotes the Confessio Fraternitatis: '…wherefore now no longer are we beheld by human eyes, unless they have received strength borrowed from the eagle.'

John Heydon, prominent Rosicrucian thinker, wrote in The Rosie Cross Uncovered that the mysterious brethren possessed polymorphous powers, appearing in any desired form at will and had the gift of appearing in more than one place at the same time. Thomas Vaughan corroborated Heydon's claims of the brethren's powers of invisibility, saying that they 'can move in this white mist. Whosoever would communicate with us must be able to see in this light…'

Brethren were buried in a womb, a glass casket, sometimes called the Philosophical Egg (strong echoes of Humpty Dumpty), out of which they would occasionally emerge to function before returning to their shell of glass.

Dr. Franz Hartmann, in his *Secret Symbols of the Rosicrucians*, believed that the brethren were able to command the elementals and the fairy folk, and knew the secret of the Philosopher's Stone,

David Day draws attention to the feature in Michelspacher's *Cabala* that explores the meaning of the acronym "V.I.T.R.I.O.L.", which stands for the phrase, "Visita interiora terrae rectificandoque invenies occultum lapidem verum medicinalem". This is an instruction to the Rosicrucian initiate to 'visit the interior of the earth and by rectifying discover the true medicinal stone'—the Philosopher's Stone. Through text and illustrations, the initiate is encouraged to 'visit the interior of the earth' and to 'ferret out' the rabbit. In this context it is significant that the White Rabbit of Wonderland is fearful that he will be hunted down, 'as sure as ferrets are ferrets!'

The Rosicrucian notion of a secret repository for universal knowledge was an inspiration for the establishment of Oxford's Ashmolean Institute and Museum, opened in 1683, of which Carroll was in his day an active member. The Institute possessed one of the world's foremost Rosicrucian alchemical libraries. Day suggests that among the many hermetic books, the *Cabala* was one that would have been of supreme interest to the young Christ Church sub-librarian Charles Dodgson.

As the hermetic scholar Joscelyn Godwin[82] has observed, there probably was no such thing as 'a card-carrying member of the Brotherhood,' but there were a multitude over the next three centuries that shared the ideals set forth in its manifestos, Carroll included.

The Rosicrucian neophyte discovers a secret underground hall for the testing of initiates. It is under a mountain and, like Wonderland's hall, is fitted with many doors and contains many symbolic objects: magic looking glasses, telescopes, sacred books and keys.

The step-pyramid that forms the foundation of the Rosicrucian hall is labelled with the seven steps of the alchemical process. However, these are in the wrong sequence. It is up to the initiate by trial and error to "rectify" and eventually understand the alchemical process, then to put them in the proper order. Similarly, in Wonderland's underground hall, Alice is tested to learn the proper order of actions so that she may use her golden key and enter the garden.

Within the engravings in the *Cabala* engraving, one sees on the pinnacle of the Mountain of Alchemy the true goal of the initiate: a miniature rose garden, a paradisiacal place of living nature that echoes the King and Queen of Hearts' garden of 'bright flowers and those cool fountains' that is Alice's goal in Wonderland. The great European Rosicrucian master, Michael Maier, wrote about this secret rose garden and the golden key to its gate, saying in his *Atalanta Fugiens* (1617): 'He who tries to enter the Rose-garden of Philosophers without the key is like a man wanting to walk without feet.' Alice, too, was denied entry into the Wonderland garden until she worked out how to take

---

[82] Godwin, J., *Rosicrucian Trilogy: Modern Translations of the Three Founding Documents, Fama Fraternitatis, 1644; Confessio Fraternitatis, 1615; The Chemical Wedding of Christian Rosenkreutz, 1616*, Weiser Books, 2016.

337

possession of the golden key.

On the mythological level, the counterpart to the Wonderland hall is the great hall in the Temple of Demeter-Persephone at Eleusis where all pilgrims gathered to seek admittance for initiation into the higher mysteries.

In the Bronze Age era, the great goddesses of the day were given names. In Sumeria, Egypt and Anatolia, for example, their principal goddesses were Innana (or Ishtar as she was called in northern Sumeria), Isis and Cybele respectively. All three reflect the image of the Great Mother who presided over the earliest civilisations that arose between Europe and the Indian subcontinent.

This was a period when nature was still experienced as numinous: a divine force that is both sacred and alive. It was seen in the sun's rays, in the river's rise and fall, in the twinkling stars of heaven, in the violence of floodwaters, in the green shoots of cereals crops, and in the grapes of the vine. Similarly, its mysterious energies were perceived in the attraction of male and female, in health and disease, and in life and death. These phenomena revealed to humanity not so much that the divine is every*where* but that the divine is every*thing*.

In Sumerian cosmology the Mother Goddess, Ki-Ninhursag, was the mother of all living, of the gods and of humanity, mother of the earth itself, the soil and the rocky ground, and all the plants and crops it brought forth. She was the Holy Shepherdess, Queen of Stall and Fold. Later she was personified by Inanna, Great Mother, Virgin Queen of Heaven and Earth, Holy Shepherdess, Light of the World, Moon Goddess and Morning and Evening Star. Inanna said, 'I step onto the heavens, and the rain rains down; I step onto the earth, and grass and herbs sprout up.' Inanna was clothed with the heavens and crowned with the stars, her lapis crystal jewels reflecting the blue of the sky and the blue of the waters of space that the Sumerians named "The Deep". She wore the rainbow as her necklace and the zodiac as her girdle. Innana was truly Mother Nature in all her power and glory. She was also known as "The Green One, she of the springing verdure", after the green corn that the earth wears as her mantle in spring.

The myth of Ishtar and Tammuz, esoteric god of the sun and one of the guardians of the gates of the underworld, is one of the earliest examples of the dying-God allegory. According to the myth, Tammuz was killed every year by a wild boar but was rescued from the nether world by Ishtar, who descended into the underworld in search for the sacred elixir, which alone could restore Tammuz to life.

Manly P. Hall relates the story of Ishtar's mission to rescue her lover.[83] With outspread wings, Ishtar, the daughter of Sin (the Moon), sweeps downward to the gates of death. The house of darkness—the dwelling of the god Irkalla—is described as "the place of no return". It is without light; the nourishment of those who dwell therein is dust, and their food is mud. Over the bolts on the door of the house of Irkalla is scattered dust, and the keepers of the house are covered with feathers like birds. Ishtar demands that the keepers open the gates, otherwise she will shatter the doorposts, strike the hinges and raise up dead devourers of the living. The guardians of the gates beg her to be patient while they go to the queen of Hades from whom they secure permission to admit Ishtar, but only in the same manner as all others came to this dreary house.

Ishtar thereupon descends through the seven gates, which lead downward into the depths of the underworld. At the first gate the great crown is removed from her head, at the second gate the earrings from her ears, at the third the necklace from her neck, at the fourth the ornaments from her breast, at the fifth the girdle from her waist, at the sixth the bracelets from her hands and feet, and, at the seventh gate, the covering cloak of her body. Ishtar remonstrates as each successive article of apparel is taken from her but the guardian tells her that this is the experience of all who enter the sombre domain of death. Enraged upon beholding Ishtar, the Mistress of Hades inflicts upon her all manner of disease and imprisons her in the underworld. As Ishtar represents the spirit of fertility, her loss prevents the ripening of the crops and the maturing of all life upon the earth. In this respect the story parallels the Greek legend of Persephone.

The gods, realizing that the loss of Ishtar is disorganizing all Nature, send a messenger to the underworld and demand her release. The Mistress of Hades is forced to comply, and the water of life is poured over Ishtar. Cured of the infirmities inflicted on her, Ishtar retraces her way upward through the seven gates, at each of which she is reinvested with the article of apparel that the guardians had removed.

The myth of Ishtar symbolizes the descent of the human spirit through the seven worlds, or spheres, of the sacred planets until, finally deprived of its spiritual adornments, it incarnates in the physical body—Hades—where the mistress of that body heaps every form of sorrow and misery upon the imprisoned consciousness. The waters of life cure

---

[83] ibid

the diseases of ignorance; and the spirit, re-ascending to its divine source, regains its God-given adornments as it passes upward through the rings of the planets.

Lewis Carroll's fairy tale about a young girl's descent underground is also based on the story of the Mesopotamian goddess Ishtar/Inanna's descent into the underworld realm of the dead. The story is best known as the Greek myth of Persephone. In the Temple of Demeter-Persephone at Eleusis pilgrims were tested on their knowledge of the procedures of the Mysteries before entering a labyrinth of chambers where they witnessed miraculous tableaux or epiphanies relating to the myth of Persephone and her experiences in the depths of the underworld.

In classical times, pilgrims at Eleusis dressed in white and wore wreaths of flowers during their initiation into the Mysteries of the Goddess. Carroll refers to this ancient practice alludes to this ancient pilgrimage in the final lines of Alice in Wonderland's prelude poem:

> Like pilgrim's wither'd wreath of flowers
> Pluck'd in a far-off land.

In the nine days required for the enactment of the Greater Eleusinian Rites in ancient Greece, those to be initiated were questioned about their qualifications; took part in a procession to the sea for the submerging of the presiding goddess; participated in the sacrifice of a mullet; witnessed a mystic basket containing sacred symbols brought to Eleusis; ran a torch race; took part in an athletics contest; and, finally, witnessed the exhibition of a sacred urn or jar, an item of supreme importance in the ritual with which to celebrate the deepest truths of the mysteries.

In Alice's adventures we read of her being tested on her arithmetic; swimming with mythical creatures in the pool of tears; listening to the decidedly Innana flavoured story ["seven maids with seven mops"] of the Walrus and the Carpenter tricking and eating baby oysters; running a bizarre Caucus Race; and running the Red Queen's race ["Now, here, you see, it takes all the running you can do, to keep in the same place. If you want to get somewhere else, you must run at least twice as fast as that!"]. Carroll's stories are also littered with references to bottles and jars—there is plenty of food for thought in Carroll's bottles and jars.

David Day compares the circumstances of Alice's discovery of Wonderland with the Persephone initiation ritual. Persephone begins in an idyllic meadow with her older sister, the earth goddess Demeter who, shockingly, is also her mother. Persephone is daydreaming and picking flowers when she falls down an infinitely deep fissure into a subterranean world. She experiences many adventures and trials, but at last escapes and returns to her sister Demeter's arms. In Alice's case, she is sitting in a lovely meadow with her older sister, Lorina, (described by Day as 'rather motherly'). She is daydreaming and vaguely considering if it's worth the bother to make a daisychain. She then drifts into a dream state wherein she tumbles down a seemingly endless rabbit-hole before landing unscathed in Wonderland where, like Persephone, she experiences many adventures and trials, but finally escapes from the underground world.

In Alice's adventures, the White Rabbit symbolizes the psychopomp, the guide of souls that in the Mysteries escorts newly deceased souls (and occasionally the souls of those occupying deep dream states) to the underworld, where they are to be judged by its rulers. In a few cases, such as that of Persephone, these souls are allowed to return to the world of the living. Alice's is such a soul. In the end, Alice returns to her dreaming body by her sister's side and to her everyday normal life. But she is not the same Alice; she is now an older soul that retains the memory of her Wonderland dreamworld and her extraordinary adventures within it. Are we now able to locate the doorway to Wonderland?

Occasionally, a writer tells a story so memorable, so enticing and, above all, so inviting—*Don Quixote*, *The Chronicles of Narnia*, *The Lord of the Rings* and *The Secret Garden* spring readily to mind—that one wonders if its very pages are sprinkled with a pinch of fairy glamour, just a pinch but enough to cast a powerful spell of enchantment over the reader. Once enchanted, always enchanted.

No matter how many times the reader, young or old, returns to the text the effect is not just the same, it grows over time. In my personal experience, this is especially true of Carroll's Alice tales. Why? Because the sylphs of our companion world, the secret world of the Forces of Living Nature, spoke directly to Carroll to remind us that we are not alone. Moreover, in staging his story underground Carroll reveals that the pathways to these worlds of enchantment exist deep within us. Shakespeare, who knew a thing or two, described this gift from the gods in his famous line: 'We are such stuff that dreams are made of…'

It is in Nature that we find the entrances to Alice's Wonderland on the "other side of things". It may take a lifetime...or even more. But time is not an obstacle; we have more of it than we will ever need. The key is belief, an unlimited and unquenchable belief in impossible possibilities.

The trigger to discovery of our personal rabbit hole may be a humble daisy or a mighty oak, a cool stream or a tumbling waterfall, a green hill or a snowy peak, a lowly sparrow or a soaring eagle, a suckling bee or a flutter-by butterfly, a fresh breeze, lightly falling snow or a raging storm.

All it takes is for a person to *so* love what draws their glance in those seemingly endless moments that a magical doorway swings open and a winding pathway is revealed. Then, take a deep breath, put one foot in front of the other and go talk with lillies, daisies, unicorns, walruses and caterpillars. Who knows what they may teach us!

And remember, no matter what pitfalls might stand in the way of one's private and personal Wonderland journey, they are there for a reason. Because, as the Blue Smoke wise woman fondly reminds us;

'Everything is beautiful in its own way.'

—Dolly Parton

Lewis Carroll's original illustration for Alice's Adventures Underground

quite dull and stupid for things to
go on in the common way.

So she set to work, and very
soon finished off the cake.

*   *   *   *   *

"Curiouser and curiouser!" cried
Alice, (she was so surprised that she
quite forgot how to speak good English,)
"now I'm opening out like the largest
telescope that ever was! Goodbye,
feet!" (for when she looked down
at her feet, they seemed almost
out of sight, they were getting so
far off,) "oh, my poor little feet, I
wonder who will put on your shoes
and stockings for you now, dears?
I'm sure I ca'nt! I shall be a great
deal too far off to bother myself about
you: you must manage the best
way you can — but I must be kind
to them", thought Alice, "or perhaps
they won't walk the way I want
to go! Let me see: I'll give them
a new pair of boots every Christmas."
And she went on planning
to herself how she would manage it:

Lewis Carroll's original illustration for Alice's Adventures Underground

Bibliography

Angelucci, O., *The Secrets of the Saucers*, Amherst Press, 1955.

Ashe, G., *The Ancient Wisdom*, Macmillan, 1977.

Bergier, J. *Visa Pour Une Autre Terre*, Albin Michel, 1974.

Bergier , J., and Pauwels, L., Le Matin des Magiciens, Éditions Gallimard, 1960.

Blavatsky, H., *Isis Unveiled: A Master-Key to the Mysteries of Ancient and Modern Science and Theology*, Theosophical Publishing Company, 1877.

—, *The Secret Doctrine*, Theosophical Publishing Company, 1889.

Bohm, D., *Wholeness and the Implicate Order*, Great Britain. Routledge, 1980.

Bond, F., *The Gate of Remembrance*, Oxford, Blackwell, 1919.

—, The Company of Avalon, Oxford, Blackwell, 1924.

Bronder, D., *Bevor Hitler Kam*, H. Pfeiffer, Hannover, 1964.

Brown, M., *Hyperborea and Polar Exploration in the 19th Century*, Arctic Studies Journal, vol. 33, no. 4, 2007, pp. 412-428.

Buechner, H; Bernhart, W., *Adolf Hitler and the Secrets of the Holy Lance*, Thunderbird Press, 1988.

—, *Emerald Cup-Ark of Gold: the Quest of Lt. Col. Otto Rahn*, Thunderbird Press, 1991.

Bulwer-Lytton, E., *The Coming Race*, ptivately published, 1871.

van Burren, E., *Refuge of the Apocalypse: Doorway into Other Dimensions*, C. W. Daniel Co. Ltd., 1986.

Campbell, J., *The Gaelic Otherworld*, Glasgow. James Maclehose and Sons, 1900.

Carroll, L., *Alice's Adventures in Wonderland*, Macmillan, London, 1865.

—, *Through the Looking Glass*, Macmillan, London, 1872.

—, *Sylvie and Bruno*, Macmillan, London, 1889.

—, *Sylvia and Bruno Concluded,* Macmillan, London, 1893.

Cathie, B., *The Energy Grid,* Adventures Unlimited Press, Illinois,

1990.

Chanel, C; Deveney, J; Godwin, J., *The Hermetic Brotherhood of Luxor. Initiatic and Historical Documents of an Order of Practical Occultism.* York Beach: Weister, 1995.

Cohen, M., *Lewis Carroll: A Biography*, Alfred A. Knopf, 1995.

Cooke, G., *Sun-Men of the Americas*, Liss, Hampshire. The White Eagle Trust, 1983.

—, and Cooke, I., *The Light in Britain*, Liss. The White Eagle Publishing Trust, 1971.

Cutcliffe-Hyne, C., *Beneath Your Very Boots*, 1889.

Day, D., *Alice's Adventures in Wonderland Decoded*, Doubleday Canada, Random House, 2015.

Devereaux, P., *Spirit Roads*, Collins & Brown, London, 2003.

Draper C., *Walks from Llandudno*, Llygad Gwalch Cyf, 2010.

Emmerson, W., *The Smoky God: A Voyage to the Inner World*, 1908.

Evans-Wentz, W., *The Fairy-Faith in Celtic Countries*. London: Oxford University Press, 1911.

Faivre, A., *Theosophy, Imagination, Tradition: Studies in Western Esotericism*, State University of New York Press, 2000.

—, *The Golden Fleece and Alchemy*, State University of New York Press, 2000.

Gardner, L.E., *Fairies: A Book of Real Fairies*, The Theosophical Publishing House, London, 1945.

Gardner, M., *The Annotated Alice: The Definitive Edition*, W. W. Norton & Company, 2000.

Godwin, J., *Atlantis and the Cycles of Time*, Raoulster, Vermont. Inner Traditions, 2011.

—, Godwin, J., *Rosicrucian Trilogy: Modern Translations of the Three Founding Documents, Fama Fraternitatis, 1644; Confessio Fraternitatis, 1615; The Chemical Wedding of Christian Rosenkreutz, 1616*, Weiser Books, 2016.

Godwin, J; McLean, A., *The Chemical Wedding of Christian Rosenkreutz*, Phanes Press, 1991.

Goodrick-Clarke, Nicholas, *The Occult Roots of Nazism*, N.Y. University Press, 1985.

Graddon, N., *Otto Rahn and the Quest for the Grail*, Kempton, Illinois, Adventures Unlimited Press, 2008.

—, *The Landing Lights of Magonia: UFOs, Aliens and the Fairy Kingdom*, Adventures Unlimited Press, 2018.

—, *The Gods in the Field*s, Adventures Unlimited Press, 2020.

—, *Pythagoras of Samos: First Philosopher and Magician of Numbers*, Adventures Unlimited Press, 2021.

Gray, D., *Lewis Carroll's Mirrors and Tesseracts*, The Carrollian, no. 15, 2005, pp. 3-14.

Guénon, R., *Le Roi du Monde*, Paris, Ch. Bosse, 1927.

Hall, M., *Orders of the Quest*, Philosophical Research Society, 1949.

—, *The Secret Teachings of All Ages*, Philosophical Research Society, Inc., Los Angeles, 1928.

—, *Unseen Forces*, Los Angeles. Philosophical Research Society, Inc., 1978.

Hartley, C., *The Western Mystery Tradition*, Aquarian Press, 1968.

Hartmann, F., *Secret Symbols of the Rosicrucians*, Boston Occult Publishing Co., 1888.

Herodotus. 'Histories.' Translated by Tom Holland. Penguin Classics, 2013.

Hesiod. 'Works and Days.' Translated by M. L. West. Oxford University Press, 1997.

Howe, L.M., *Glimpses of Other Realities, Volume II: High Strangeness*, New Orleans. Paper Chase Press, 1998.

Jeans, J., *The Mysterious Universe*, New York. E.P. Dutton, 1932.

Jennings, H., *The Rosicrucians, their Rites and Mysteries*, Volumes 1 and 2, 3rd edition, John C. Nimmo, London, 1887.

Jenkins, S., *The Undiscovered Country: Adventures in Ufology, Tibetan Buddhism, and Other Dimensions of Reality*, New Saucerian Press, 2017.

Jung, C., *Flying Saucers: A Modern Myth of Things Seen in the Sky*, London. Ark Paperbacks edition, 1987.

Keel, J., *Operation Trojan Horse*, San Antonio. Anomalist Books, 1970.

—, *Haunted Planet*, West Virginia. New Saucerian Books, 2014.

—, *The Endles Procession*, Pursuit Magazine, Third Quarter, 1982.

Layne, M., *The Coming of the Guardians*, San Diego. Inner Circle Press, 2009.

— *MAT and DEMAT: Etheric Aspects of the UFO*, Flying Saucer Review, Vol. 1, No. 4, 1955.

LePage, V., *Shambhala: The Fascinating Truth Behind the Myth of Shangri-La*, Quest Books, Illinois, 1996.

LeShan, L., *The Medium, The Mystic and the Physicist*, Viking Press, NY, 1974.

Lewis, C., *The Magician's Nephew*, Bodley Head, 1955.

Maclellan, A., *The Lost World of Agarthi*, Souvenir Press, 1982.

Matthews, C., *Celtic Spirituality*, Paulist Press, 1996.

McIntosh, C., *The Rosicrucians: The History, Mythology, and Rituals of an Esoteric Order*, Red Wheel Weiser, 1998.

Michell, J., *The Flying Saucer Vision*, London. Abacus, 1974.

—, *The New View Over Atlantis*, London. Thames and Hudson, 1983.

Nicholson, E., *Myth and the Human Sciences: Hans Blumenberg's Theory of Myth*, Routledge, 2016.

Olcott, H. *Old Diary Leaves: The True Story of the Theosophical Society*, G.P. Putnam's Sons, 1895.

Ossendowski, F., *Beasts, Men and Gods*, Dutton, New York, 1922

Pennick, N., *Celtic Sacred Landscapes*, Thames & Hudson, 1996.

O'Sullivan, T., Legends of Hy-Brasil, Gill & Macmillan, 1999.

Pindar. 'Pythian Odes.' Translated by Diane Arnson Svarlien. University of California Press, 1990.

Plato. 'The Republic.' Translated by Allan Bloom. Basic Books, 1968.

Raftery, B., *Pagan Celtic Ireland: The Enigma of the Irish Iron Age*. Thames and Hudson, 1981.

Randles, J; Warrington, P., *UFOs-A British Viewpoint*, Robert Hale Limited, London, 1979.

Reiser, O., *This Holyest Erthe: The Glastonbury Zodiac and King Arthur's Camelot*, Perennial Books, London, 1974.

Roerich, N., *Shambhala*, Frederick A. Stoke, 1930.

Ross, A., *Pagan Celtic Britain*, Academy Chicago Publishers, 1996.

Piggott, S., *The Druids*, Thames & Hudson, 1968.

Plotinus. 'Enneads.' Translated by A. H. Armstrong. Harvard University Press, 1966.

Saint Yves d'Alveydre, A., *Mission de l'Inde en Europe*, Lahur, 1886.

Sinclair, A., *Sword and the Grail: The Story of the Grail, the Templars and the Discovery of America*, Crown, 1992 .

Smith, J., *Hyperborea: Mythical Land or Ancient Reality?, Journal of Mythological Studies*, vol. 45, no. 2, 2009, pp. 87-104.

Smith, R., *Myth and Modernity: Hyperborea in 21st-Century Literature*, Modern Literary Criticism, vol. 62, no. 1, 2020, pp. 134-152.

Snelling, R., *The Planetary Matrix*, Spiritual Genesis Books 2013.

—, *The Atlantis Line*, 2017.

Spence, L., *The Mysteries of Britain*. London. Senate, 1994.

Srinivasan, R., *Dimensions and Topology in Lewis Carroll's 'Through the Looking-Glass.' Victorian Literature and Culture*, vol. 35, no. 2, 2007, pp. 661-675.

Talbot, M*., Mysticism and the New Physics*, London. Arkana, 1993.

—, *The Holographic Universe*, London. Harper Collins Publishers, 1996.

Taylor, R; Wakeling, E. *Lewis Carroll, Photographer*. Princeton University Press. 2002.

The Mabinogion, translated by Lady Charlotte Guest, Dover Publications, 1997.

Vallée, J., *Passport to Magonia*, Brisbane. Daily Grail Publishing, 2014.

—, *UFOs: The Psychic Solution*, St. Albans. Panther Books Ltd, 1977.

Vallée, J; Hynek, J., *The Edge of Reality: A Progress Report on Unidentified Flying Objects*. Regnery, 1975

Waite, A., *The Real History of the Rosicrucians*, London, 1887.

Walker, B., *Hindu World: An Encyclopedic Survey of Hinduism*, George Allen and Unwin, London, 1968

White Eagle Publishing Trust, *White Eagle on Divine Mother: the*

Feminine & the Mysteries, 2004.

White, S., *Hyperborea Reimagined: Ethical Considerations in Contemporary Adaptations*, Cultural Critique, vol. 74, no. 3, 2019, pp. 72-89.

Woolf, J., *The Mystery of Lewis Carroll: Understanding the Author of Alice in Wonderland*, London: Haus Books, 2010.

Yates, F., *The Rosicrucian Enlightenment*, Routledge and Kegan Paul, London and Boston, 1972.

David Williams of Penrhyndeudraeth in the Fairy Ring of Fire

Get these fascinating books from your nearest bookstore or directly from:
Adventures Unlimited Press
www.adventuresunlimitedpress.com

COVERT WARS AND BREAKAWAY CIVILIZATIONS
By Joseph P. Farrell

Farrell delves into the creation of breakaway civilizations by the Nazis in South America and other parts of the world. He discusses the advanced technology that they took with them at the end of the war and the psychological war that they waged for decades on America and NATO. He investigates the secret space programs currently sponsored by the breakaway civilizations and the current militaries in control of planet Earth. Plenty of astounding accounts, documents and speculation on the incredible alternative history of hidden conflicts and secret space programs that began when World War II officially "ended."

292 Pages. 6x9 Paperback. Illustrated. $19.95. Code: BCCW

THE ENIGMA OF CRANIAL DEFORMATION
Elongated Skulls of the Ancients
By David Hatcher Childress and Brien Foerster

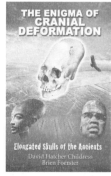

In a book filled with over a hundred astonishing photos and a color photo section, Childress and Foerster take us to Peru, Bolivia, Egypt, Malta, China, Mexico and other places in search of strange elongated skulls and other cranial deformation. The puzzle of why diverse ancient people—even on remote Pacific Islands—would use head-binding to create elongated heads is mystifying. Where did they even get this idea? Did some people naturally look this way—with long narrow heads? Were they some alien race? Were they an elite race that roamed the entire planet? Why do anthropologists rarely talk about cranial deformation and know so little about it? Color Section.

250 Pages. 6x9 Paperback. Illustrated. $19.95. Code: ECD

ARK OF GOD
The Incredible Power of the Ark of the Covenant
By David Hatcher Childress

Childress takes us on an incredible journey in search of the truth about (and science behind) the fantastic biblical artifact known as the Ark of the Covenant. This object made by Moses at Mount Sinai—part wooden-metal box and part golden statue—had the power to create "lightning" to kill people, and also to fly and lead people through the wilderness. The Ark of the Covenant suddenly disappears from the Bible record and what happened to it is not mentioned. Was it hidden in the underground passages of King Solomon's temple and later discovered by the Knights Templar? Was it taken through Egypt to Ethiopia as many Coptic Christians believe? Childress looks into hidden history, astonishing ancient technology, and a 3,000-year-old mystery that continues to fascinate millions of people today. Color section.

420 Pages. 6x9 Paperback. Illustrated. $22.00 Code: AOG

JACK THE RIPPER'S NEW TESTAMENT
Occultism and Bible Mania in 1888
By Nigel Graddon
This book offers evidence, for the first time, that those responsible for the Whitechapel murders were members of a hit team associated with a centuries-old European occult confederacy dedicated to human sacrifice. This was corroborated in the private papers of a Monsignor who carried out intelligence work for Pope Pius X in the run-up to the outbreak of global conflict in 1914. The priest told of the existence of a Vatican-based cabal of assassins formed by the infamous Borgias that is in alliance with a Teuton occult group formed in the 9th century. It was from within this unholy alliance that assassins travelled to London to carry out the Ripper murders to "solve a sticky problem for the British Royal Family"
302 Pages. 6x9 Paperback. Illustrated. $19.95. Code: JRNT

SECRETS OF THE HOLY LANCE
The Spear of Destiny in History & Legend
by Jerry E. Smith
Secrets of the Holy Lance traces the Spear from its possession by Constantine, Rome's first Christian Caesar, to Charlemagne's claim that with it he ruled the Holy Roman Empire by Divine Right, and on through two thousand years of kings and emperors, until it came within Hitler's grasp—and beyond! Did it rest for a while in Antarctic ice? Is it now hidden in Europe, awaiting the next person to claim its awesome power? Neither debunking nor worshiping, *Secrets of the Holy Lance* seeks to pierce the veil of myth and mystery around the Spear.
312 PAGES. 6x9 PAPERBACK. ILLUSTRATED. $16.95. CODE: SOHL

THE CRYSTAL SKULLS
Astonishing Portals to Man's Past
by David Hatcher Childress and Stephen S. Mehler
Childress introduces the technology and lore of crystals, and then plunges into the turbulent times of the Mexican Revolution form the backdrop for the rollicking adventures of Ambrose Bierce, the renowned journalist who went missing in the jungles in 1913, and F.A. Mitchell-Hedges, the notorious adventurer who emerged from the jungles with the most famous of the crystal skulls. Mehler shares his extensive knowledge of and experience with crystal skulls. Having been involved in the field since the 1980s, he has personally examined many of the most influential skulls, and has worked with the leaders in crystal skull research. Color section.
294 pages. 6x9 Paperback. Illustrated. $18.95. Code: CRSK

THE LAND OF OSIRIS
An Introduction to Khemitology
by Stephen S. Mehler
Was there an advanced prehistoric civilization in ancient Egypt? Were they the people who built the great pyramids and carved the Great Sphinx? Did the pyramids serve as energy devices and not as tombs for kings? Chapters include: Egyptology and Its Paradigms; Khemitology—New Paradigms; Asgat Nefer— The Harmony of Water; Khemit and the Myth of Atlantis; The Extraterrestrial Question; more. Color section.
272 PAGES. 6x9 PAPERBACK. ILLUSTRATED . $18.95. CODE: LOOS

VIMANA:
Flying Machines of the Ancients
by David Hatcher Childress
According to early Sanskrit texts the ancients had several types of airships called vimanas. Like aircraft of today, vimanas were used to fly through the air from city to city; to conduct aerial surveys of uncharted lands; and as delivery vehicles for awesome weapons. David Hatcher Childress, popular *Lost Cities* author, takes us on an astounding investigation into tales of ancient flying machines. In his new book, packed with photos and diagrams, he consults ancient texts and modern stories and presents astonishing evidence that aircraft, similar to the ones we use today, were used thousands of years ago in India, Sumeria, China and other countries. Includes a 24-page color section.
408 Pages. 6x9 Paperback. Illustrated. $22.95. Code: VMA

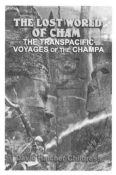

THE LOST WORLD OF CHAM
The Trans-Pacific Voyages of the Champa
By David Hatcher Childress

The mysterious Cham, or Champa, peoples of Southeast Asia formed a megalith-building, seagoing empire that extended into Indonesia, Tonga, and beyond—a transoceanic power that reached Mexico and South America. The Champa maintained many ports in what is today Vietnam, Cambodia, and Indonesia and their ships plied the Indian Ocean and the Pacific, bringing Chinese, African and Indian traders to far off lands, including Olmec ports on the Pacific Coast of Central America. opics include: Cham and Khem: Egyptian Influence on Cham; The Search for Metals; The Basalt City of Nan Madol; Elephants and Buddhists in North America; The Olmecs; The Cham in Colombia; tons more. 24-page color section.
328 Pages. 6x9 Paperback. Illustrated. $22.00 Code: LPWC

OTTO RAHN & THE QUEST FOR THE HOLY GRAIL
The Amazing Life of the Real "Indiana Jones"
By Nigel Graddon

Otto Rahn, a Hessian language scholar, is said to have found runic Grail tablets in the Pyrenean grottoes, unearthed as a result of his work in decoding the hidden messages within the Grail masterwork *Parsifal*. The fabulous artifacts identified by Rahn were believed by Himmler to include the Grail Cup, the Spear of Destiny, the Tablets of Moses, the Ark of the Covenant, the Sword and Harp of David, the Sacred Candelabra and the Golden Urn of Manna. Some believe that Rahn was a Nazi guru who wielded immense influence within the Hitler regime, persuading them that the Grail was the Sacred Book of the Aryans, which, once obtained, would justify their extreme political theories.
450 pages. 6x9 Paperback. Illustrated. Index. $18.95. Code: ORQG

THE LANDING LIGHTS OF MAGONIA
UFOs, Aliens and the Fairy Kingdom
By Nigel Graddon

British UFO researcher Graddon takes us to that magical land of Magonia—the land of the Fairies—a place from which some people return while others go and never come back. Graddon on fairies, the wee folk, elves, fairy pathways, Welsh folklore, the Tuatha de Dannan, UFO occupants, the Little Blue Man of Studham, the implications of Mars, psychic connections with UFOs and fairies. He also recounts many of the strange tales of fairies, UFOs and Magonia. Chapters include: The Little Blue Man of Studham; The Wee Folk; UFOlk; What the Folk; Grimm Tales; The Welsh Triangle; The Implicate Order; Mars—an Atlantean Outpost; Psi-Fi; High Spirits; "Once Upon a Time…"; more.
270 Pages. 6x9 Paperback. Illustrated. $19.95. Code: LLOM

ADVENTURES OF A HASHISH SMUGGLER
by Henri de Monfreid

The son of a French artist who knew Paul Gaugin as a child, de Monfreid sought his fortune by becoming a collector and merchant of the fabled Persian Gulf pearls. He was then drawn into the shadowy world of arms trading, slavery, smuggling and drugs. Infamous as well as famous, his name is inextricably linked to the Red Sea and the raffish ports between Suez and Aden in the early years of the twentieth century. De Monfreid (1879 to 1974) had a long life of many adventures around the Horn of Africa where he dodged pirates as well as the authorities.
284 Pages. 6x9 Paperback. $16.95. Illustrated. Code AHS

TECHNOLOGY OF THE GODS
The Incredible Sciences of the Ancients
by David Hatcher Childress

Childress looks at the technology that was allegedly used in Atlantis and the theory that the Great Pyramid of Egypt was originally a gigantic power station. He examines tales of ancient flight and the technology that it involved; how the ancients used electricity; megalithic building techniques; the use of crystal lenses and the fire from the gods; evidence of various high tech weapons in the past, including atomic weapons; ancient metallurgy and heavy machinery; the role of modern inventors such as Nikola Tesla in bringing ancient technology back into modern use; impossible artifacts; and more.

356 pages. 6x9 Paperback. Illustrated. $16.95. code: TGOD

THE ANTI-GRAVITY HANDBOOK
edited by David Hatcher Childress

The new expanded compilation of material on Anti-Gravity, Free Energy, Flying Saucer Propulsion, UFOs, Suppressed Technology, NASA Cover-ups and more. Highly illustrated with patents, technical illustrations and photos. This revised and expanded edition has more material, including photos of Area 51, Nevada, the government's secret testing facility. This classic on weird science is back in a new format!

230 pages. 7x10 paperback. Illustrated. $16.95. code: AGH

ANTI-GRAVITY & THE WORLD GRID

Is the earth surrounded by an intricate electromagnetic grid network offering free energy? This compilation of material on ley lines and world power points contains chapters on the geography, mathematics, and light harmonics of the earth grid. Learn the purpose of ley lines and ancient megalithic structures located on the grid. Discover how the grid made the Philadelphia Experiment possible. Explore the Coral Castle and many other mysteries, including acoustic levitation, Tesla Shields and scalar wave weaponry. Browse through the section on anti-gravity patents, and research resources.

274 pages. 7x10 paperback. Illustrated. $14.95. code: AGW

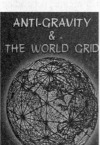

ANTI-GRAVITY & THE UNIFIED FIELD
edited by David Hatcher Childress

Is Einstein's Unified Field Theory the answer to all of our energy problems? Explored in this compilation of material is how gravity, electricity and magnetism manifest from a unified field around us. Why artificial gravity is possible; secrets of UFO propulsion; free energy; Nikola Tesla and anti-gravity airships of the 20s and 30s; flying saucers as superconducting whirls of plasma; anti-mass generators; vortex propulsion; suppressed technology; government cover-ups; gravitational pulse drive; spacecraft & more.

240 pages. 7x10 Paperback. Illustrated. $14.95. Code: AGU

THE TIME TRAVEL HANDBOOK
A Manual of Practical Teleportation & Time Travel
edited by David Hatcher Childress

The Time Travel Handbook takes the reader beyond the government experiments and deep into the uncharted territory of early time travellers such as Nikola Tesla and Guglielmo Marconi and their alleged time travel experiments, as well as the Wilson Brothers of EMI and their connection to the Philadelphia Experiment—the U.S. Navy's forays into invisibility, time travel, and teleportation. Childress looks into the claims of time travelling individuals, and investigates the unusual claim that the pyramids on Mars were built in the future and sent back in time. A highly visual, large format book, with patents, photos and schematics. Be the first on your block to build your own time travel device!

316 pages. 7x10 Paperback. Illustrated. $16.95. code: TTH

ANCIENT ALIENS ON THE MOON
By Mike Bara
What did NASA find in their explorations of the solar system that they may have kept from the general public? How ancient really are these ruins on the Moon? Using official NASA and Russian photos of the Moon, Bara looks at vast cityscapes and domes in the Sinus Medii region as well as glass domes in the Crisium region. Bara also takes a detailed look at the mission of Apollo 17 and the case that this was a salvage mission, primarily concerned with investigating an opening into a massive hexagonal ruin near the landing site. Chapters include: The History of Lunar Anomalies; The Early 20th Century; Sinus Medii; To the Moon Alice!; Mare Crisium; Yes, Virginia, We Really Went to the Moon; Apollo 17; more. Tons of photos of the Moon examined for possible structures and other anomalies.
248 Pages. 6x9 Paperback. Illustrated.. $19.95. Code: AAOM

ANCIENT ALIENS ON MARS
By Mike Bara
Bara brings us this lavishly illustrated volume on alien structures on Mars. Was there once a vast, technologically advanced civilization on Mars, and did it leave evidence of its existence behind for humans to find eons later? Did these advanced extraterrestrial visitors vanish in a solar system wide cataclysm of their own making, only to make their way to Earth and start anew? Was Mars once as lush and green as the Earth, and teeming with life? Chapters include: War of the Worlds; The Mars Tidal Model; The Death of Mars; Cydonia and the Face on Mars; The Monuments of Mars; The Search for Life on Mars; The True Colors of Mars and The Pathfinder Sphinx; more. Color section.
252 Pages. 6x9 Paperback. Illustrated. $19.95. Code: AMAR

ANCIENT ALIENS ON MARS II
By Mike Bara
Using data acquired from sophisticated new scientific instruments like the Mars Odyssey THEMIS infrared imager, Bara shows that the region of Cydonia overlays a vast underground city full of enormous structures and devices that may still be operating. He peels back the layers of mystery to show images of tunnel systems, temples and ruins, and exposes the sophisticated NASA conspiracy designed to hide them. Bara also tackles the enigma of Mars' hollowed out moon Phobos, and exposes evidence that it is artificial. Long-held myths about Mars, including claims that it is protected by a sophisticated UFO defense system, are examined. Data from the Mars rovers Spirit, Opportunity and Curiosity are examined; everything from fossilized plants to mechanical debris is exposed in images taken directly from NASA's own archives.
294 Pages. 6x9 Paperback. Illustrated. $19.95. Code: AAM2

ANCIENT TECHNOLOGY IN PERU & BOLIVIA
By David Hatcher Childress
Childress speculates on the existence of a sunken city in Lake Titicaca and reveals new evidence that the Sumerians may have arrived in South America 4,000 years ago. He demonstrates that the use of "keystone cuts" with metal clamps poured into them to secure megalithic construction was an advanced technology used all over the world, from the Andes to Egypt, Greece and Southeast Asia. He maintains that only power tools could have made the intricate articulation and drill holes found in extremely hard granite and basalt blocks in Bolivia and Peru, and that the megalith builders had to have had advanced methods for moving and stacking gigantic blocks of stone, some weighing over 100 tons.
340 Pages. 6x9 Paperback. Illustrated.. $19.95 Code: ATP

HESS AND THE PENGUINS
The Holocaust, Antarctica and the Strange Case of Rudolf Hess
By Joseph P. Farrell

Farrell looks at Hess' mission to make peace with Britain and get rid of Hitler—even a plot to fly Hitler to Britain for capture! How much did Göring and Hitler know of Rudolf Hess' subversive plot, and what happened to Hess? Why was a doppleganger put in Spandau Prison and then "suicided"? Did the British use an early form of mind control on Hess' double? John Foster Dulles of the OSS and CIA suspected as much. Farrell also uncovers the strange death of Admiral Richard Byrd's son in 1988, about the same time of the death of Hess.

288 Pages. 6x9 Paperback. Illustrated. $19.95. Code: HAPG

HIDDEN FINANCE, ROGUE NETWORKS & SECRET SORCERY
The Fascist International, 9/11, & Penetrated Operations
By Joseph P. Farrell

Farrell investigates the theory that there were not *two* levels to the 9/11 event, but *three*. He says that the twin towers were downed by the force of an exotic energy weapon, one similar to the Tesla energy weapon suggested by Dr. Judy Wood, and ties together the tangled web of missing money, secret technology and involvement of portions of the Saudi royal family. Farrell unravels the many layers behind the 9-11 attack, layers that include the Deutschebank, the Bush family, the German industrialist Carl Duisberg, Saudi Arabian princes and the energy weapons developed by Tesla before WWII.

296 Pages. 6x9 Paperback. Illustrated. $19.95. Code: HFRN

THRICE GREAT HERMETICA & THE JANUS AGE
By Joseph P. Farrell

What do the Fourth Crusade, the exploration of the New World, secret excavations of the Holy Land, and the pontificate of Innocent the Third all have in common? Answer: Venice and the Templars. What do they have in common with Jesus, Gottfried Leibniz, Sir Isaac Newton, Rene Descartes, and the Earl of Oxford? Answer: Egypt and a body of doctrine known as Hermeticism. The hidden role of Venice and Hermeticism reached far and wide, into the plays of Shakespeare (a.k.a. Edward DeVere, Earl of Oxford), into the quest of the three great mathematicians of the Early Enlightenment for a lost form of analysis, and back into the end of the classical era, to little known Egyptian influences at work during the time of Jesus.

354 Pages. 6x9 Paperback. Illustrated. $19.95. Code: TGHJ

ROBOT ZOMBIES
Transhumanism and the Robot Revolution
By Xaviant Haze and Estrella Eguino,

Technology is growing exponentially and the moment when it merges with the human mind, called "The Singularity," is visible in our imminent future. Science and technology are pushing forward, transforming life as we know it—perhaps even giving humans a shot at immortality. Who will benefit from this? This book examines the history and future of robotics, artificial intelligence, zombies and a Transhumanist utopia/dystopia integrating man with machine. Chapters include: Love, Sex and Compassion—Android Style; Humans Aren't Working Like They Used To; Skynet Rises; Blueprints for Transhumans; Kurzweil's Quest; Nanotech Dreams; Zombies Among Us; Cyborgs (Cylons) in Space; Awakening the Human; more. Color Section.

180 Pages. 6x9 Paperback. Illustrated. $16.95. Code: RBTZ

THE GODS IN THE FIELDS
Michael, Mary and Alice-Guardians of Enchanted Britain
By Nigel Graddon

We learn of Britain's special place in the origins of ancient wisdom and of the "Sun-Men" who taught it to a humanity in its infancy. Aspects of these teachings are found all along the St. Michael ley: at Glastonbury, the location of Merlin and Arthur's Avalon; in the design and layout of the extraordinary Somerset Zodiac of which Glastonbury is a major part; in the amazing stone circles and serpentine avenues at Avebury and nearby Silbury Hill: portals to unimaginable worlds of mystery and enchantment; Chapters include: Michael, Mary and Merlin; England's West Country; The Glastonbury Zodiac; Wiltshire; The Gods in the Fields; Michael, Mary and Alice; East of the Line; Table of Michael and Mary Locations; more.

280 Pages. 6x9 Paperback. Illustrated. $19.95. Code: GIF

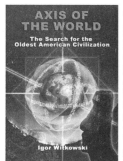

AXIS OF THE WORLD
The Search for the Oldest American Civilization
by Igor Witkowski

Polish author Witkowski's research reveals remnants of a high civilization that was able to exert its influence on almost the entire planet, and did so with full consciousness. Sites around South America show that this was not just one of the places influenced by this culture, but a place where they built their crowning achievements. Easter Island, in the southeastern Pacific, constitutes one of them. The Rongo-Rongo language that developed there points westward to the Indus Valley. Taken together, the facts presented by Witkowski provide a fresh, new proof that an antediluvian, great civilization flourished several millennia ago.

220 pages. 6x9 Paperback. Illustrated. $18.95. Code: AXOW

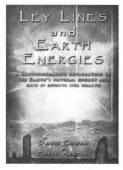

LEY LINE & EARTH ENERGIES
An Extraordinary Journey into the Earth's Natural Energy System
by David Cowan & Chris Arnold

The mysterious standing stones, burial grounds and stone circles that lace Europe, the British Isles and other areas have intrigued scientists, writers, artists and travellers through the centuries. How do ley lines work? How did our ancestors use Earth energy to map their sacred sites and burial grounds? How do ghosts and poltergeists interact with Earth energy? How can Earth spirals and black spots affect our health? This exploration shows how natural forces affect our behavior, how they can be used to enhance our health and well being.

368 pages. 6x9 Paperback. Illustrated. $18.95. Code: LLEE

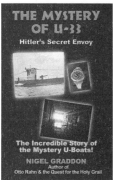

THE MYSTERY OF U-33
By Nigel Graddon

The incredible story of the mystery U-Boats of WWII! Graddon first chronicles the story of the mysterious U-33 that landed in Scotland in 1940 and involved the top-secret Enigma device. He then looks at U-Boat special missions during and after WWII, including U-Boat trips to Antarctica; U-Boats with the curious cargos of liquid mercury; the journey of the Spear of Destiny via U-Boat; the "Black Subs" and more. Chapters and topics include: U-33: The Official Story; The First Questions; Survivors and Deceased; August 1985—the Story Breaks; The Carradale U-boat; The Tale of the Bank Event; In the Wake of U-33; Wrecks; The Greenock Lairs; The Mystery Men; "Brass Bounders at the Admiralty"; Captain's Log; Max Schiller through the Lens; Rudolf Hess; Otto Rahn; U-Boat Special Missions; Neu-Schwabenland; more.

351 Pages. 6x9 Paperback. Illustrated. $19.95. Code: MU33

ANCIENT ALIENS AND JFK
The Race to the Moon & the Kennedy Assassination
By Mike Bara
Relying on never-before-seen documents culled from the recent Kennedy assassination papers document dump, Bara shows the secret connections between key assassination figures like Oswald, LBJ, and highly placed figures inside NASA who had reasons to want Kennedy dead. Bara also looks into the bizarre billion-dollar Treasury bonds that Japanese businessmen attempted to deposit in a Swiss bank that had photos of Kennedy and the Moon on them. Is the wealth of the Moon being used as collateral by the USA? The book will dig deeply into Kennedy's silent war with shadowy Deep State figures who were desperate to shut down his Disclosure agenda. Also: the Apollo mission; "Apollo 20," and more. Includes 8-page color section.
248 Pages. 6x9 Paperback. Illustrated. $19.95. Code: AAJK

HIDDEN AGENDA
NASA and the Secret Space Program
By Mike Bara
Bara delves into secret bases on the Moon, and exploring the many other rumors surrounding the military's secret projects in space. On June 8, 1959, a group at the ABMA produced for the US Department of the Army a report entitled Project Horizon, a "Study for the Establishment of a Lunar Military Outpost." The permanent outpost was predicted to cost $6 billion and was to become operational in December 1966 with twelve soldiers stationed at the Moon base. Does hacker Gary Mackinnon's discovery of defense department documents identifying "non-terrestrial officers" serving in space? Includes an 8-page color section.
346 Pages. 6x9 Paperback. Illustrated. $19.95. Code: HDAG

THE ANTI-GRAVITY FILES
A Compilation of Patents and Reports
Edited by David Hatcher Childress
In the tradition of *The Anti-Gravity Handbook* and *the Time-Travel Handbook* comes this compilation of material on anti-gravity, free energy, flying saucers and Tesla technology. With plenty of technical drawings and explanations, this book reveals suppressed technology that will change the world in ways we can only dream of. Chapters include: A Brief History of Anti-Gravity Patents; The Motionless Electromagnet Generator Patent; Mercury Anti-Gravity Gyros; The Tesla Pyramid Engine; Anti-Gravity Propulsion Dynamics; The Machines in Flight; More Anti-Gravity Patents; Death Rays Anyone?; The Unified Field Theory of Gravity; and tons more. Heavily illustrated. 4-page color section.
216 pages. 8x10 Paperback. Illustrated. $22.00. Code: AGF

SECRET MARS: The Alien Connection
By M. J. Craig
While scientists spend billions of dollars confirming that microbes live in the Martian soil, people sitting at home on their computers studying the Mars images are making far more astounding discoveries... they have found the possible archaeological remains of an extraterrestrial civilization. Hard to believe? Well, this challenging book invites you to take a look at the astounding pictures yourself and make up your own mind. *Secret Mars* presents over 160 incredible images taken by American and European spacecraft that reveal possible evidence of a civilization that once lived, and may still live, on the planet Mars... powerful evidence that scientists are ignoring! A visual and fascinating book!
352 Pages. 6x9 Paperback. Illustrated. $19.95. Code: SMAR

PROJECT RAINBOW AND THE PHILADELPHIA EXPERIMENT
By David Hatcher Childress
The story of the "Philadelphia Experiment" originated in late 1955 when Carl M. Allen sent an anonymous package marked "Happy Easter" containing a copy of Morris K. Jessup's book *The Case for the UFO: Unidentified Flying Objects* to the US Office of Naval Research. The book was filled with handwritten notes in its margins, written with three different shades of blue ink, appearing to detail a debate among three individuals. Jessup was then discovered with a hose wired to his exhaust pipe to bring the toxic fumes into his car. It was ruled a suicide. Was Jessup murdered as many people believe? Was he part of Project Rainbow—an effort to teleport a battleship through time and space? Did the Defense Industrial Security Command (DISC), commanded by Wernher von Braun, have something to do with his death?
232 Pages. 6x9 Paperback. Illustrated. $22.00. Code: PRPE

CRYSTALS, MOTHER EARTH AND THE FORCES OF LIVING NATURE
By Nigel Graddon
Graddon presents a three-part narrative through the medium of crystal, "solidified light," according to the ancients. Part 1, Physical Crystal, describes the origins of the Universe and our Earth, and the gradual evolution of the mineral kingdom in its diverse forms, which find their highest vibrational power in the mysterious world of crystal. Part 2, Amazing Crystal, examines mind-blowing uses of crystal in the past and present.. Among its highlights are: in the past, the Great Pyramid's original crystal tip, the legend of the Rose Queen Goddess of Languedoc, Dr. Dee's scrying mirror and amethyst pendant, and the Black Stone and the Goddess; and exotic future applications such as Time Crystals and Quasicrystals. This is followed by an analysis of Mother Earth's living forces, including the legendary Crystal Skulls of Mesoamerica.
336 Pages. 6x9 Paperback. Illustrated. $19.95. Code: CMEF

THE ENCYCLOPEDIA OF MOON MYSTERIES
By Constance Victoria Briggs
Our moon is an enigma. The ancients viewed it as a light to guide them in the darkness, and a god to be worshipped. Did you know that: Aristotle and Plato wrote about a time when there was no Moon? Several of the NASA astronauts reported seeing UFOs while traveling to the Moon?; the Moon might be hollow?; Apollo 10 astronauts heard strange "space music" when traveling on the far side of the Moon?; strange and unexplained lights have been seen on the Moon for centuries?; there are said to be ruins of structures on the Moon?; there is an ancient tale that suggests that the first human was created on the Moon?; Tons more. Tons of illustrations with A to Z sections for easy reference and reading.
152 Pages. 7x10 Paperback. Illustrated. $19.95. Code: EOMM

OBELISKS: TOWERS OF POWER
The Mysterious Purpose of Obelisks
By David Hatcher Childress
Some obelisks weigh over 500 tons and are massive blocks of polished granite that would be extremely difficult to quarry and erect even with modern equipment. Why did ancient civilizations in Egypt, Ethiopia and elsewhere undertake the massive enterprise it would have been to erect a single obelisk, much less dozens of them? Were they energy towers that could receive or transmit energy? With discussions on Tesla's wireless power, and the use of obelisks as gigantic acupuncture needles for earth, Chapters include: The Crystal Towers of Egypt; The Obelisks of Ethiopia; Obelisks in Europe and Asia; The Terrible Crystal Towers of Atlantis; Tesla's Wireless Power Distribution System; Obelisks on the Moon; more. 8-page color section.
336 Pages. 6x9 Paperback. Illustrated. $22.00 Code: OBK

ORDER FORM

**10% Discount
When You Order
3 or More Items!**

One Adventure Place
P.O. Box 74
Kempton, Illinois 60946
United States of America
Tel.: 815-253-6390 • Fax: 815-253-6300
Email: auphq@frontiernet.net
http://www.adventuresunlimitedpress.com

ORDERING INSTRUCTIONS

✓ Remit by USD$ Check, Money Order or Credit Card

✓ Visa, Master Card, Discover & AmEx Accepted

✓ Paypal Payments Can Be Made To:
  info@wexclub.com

✓ Prices May Change Without Notice

✓ 10% Discount for 3 or More Items

SHIPPING CHARGES

United States

✓ POSTAL BOOK RATE

✓ Postal Book Rate { $5.00 First Item
                     50¢ Each Additional Item

✓ Priority Mail { $8.50 First Item
                  $2.00 Each Additional Item

✓ UPS { $9.00 First Item (Minimum 5 Books)
        $1.50 Each Additional Item

  NOTE: UPS Delivery Available to Mainland USA Only

Canada

✓ Postal Air Mail { $19.00 First Item
                    $3.00 Each Additional Item

✓ Personal Checks or Bank Drafts MUST BE
  US$ and Drawn on a US Bank

✓ Canadian Postal Money Orders OK

✓ Payment MUST BE US$

All Other Countries

✓ Sorry, No Surface Delivery!

✓ Postal Air Mail { $29.00 First Item
                    $7.00 Each Additional Item

✓ Checks and Money Orders MUST BE US$
  and Drawn on a US Bank or branch.

✓ Paypal Payments Can Be Made in US$ To:
  info@wexclub.com

SPECIAL NOTES

✓ RETAILERS: Standard Discounts Available

✓ BACKORDERS: We Backorder all Out-of-
  Stock Items Unless Otherwise Requested

✓ PRO FORMA INVOICES: Available on Request

✓ DVD Return Policy: Replace defective DVDs only

ORDER ONLINE AT: www.adventuresunlimitedpress.com

**10% Discount When You Order
3 or More Items!**

Please check: ✓

☐ This is my first order   ☐ I have ordered before

Name			
Address			
City			
State/Province		Postal Code	
Country			
Phone: Day		Evening	
Fax		Email	

Item Code	Item Description	Qty	Total

Please check: ✓

	Subtotal ▶	
	Less Discount-10% for 3 or more items ▶	
☐ Postal-Surface	Balance ▶	
☐ Postal-Air Mail (Priority in USA)	Illinois Residents 6.25% Sales Tax ▶	
	Previous Credit ▶	
☐ UPS	Shipping ▶	
(Mainland USA only)	Total (check/MO in USD$ only) ▶	

☐ Visa/MasterCard/Discover/American Express

Card Number:

Expiration Date: Security Code:

✓ SEND A CATALOG TO A FRIEND: